BRIEF
MICROSOFT® OFFICE 2000 PROFESSIONAL

BRIEF MICROSOFT® OFFICE 2000 PROFESSIONAL

Robert T. Grauer / Maryann Barber

University of Miami

Prentice Hall, Upper Saddle River, New Jersey 07458

Executive Editor: Alex von Rosenberg
Managing Editor: Susan Rifkin
Editorial Assistant: Jennifer Surich
Director of Strategic Marketing: Nancy Evans
Production Manager: Gail Steier
Production Editor: Greg Hubit
Project Manager: Lynne Breitfeller
Senior Manufacturing Supervisor: Paul Smolenski
Manufacturing Coordinator: Dawn-Marie Reisner
Manufacturing Manager: Vincent Scelta
Design Manager: Patricia Smythe
Cover Design: Marjory Dressler
Composition: GTS Graphics

Copyright © 1999 by Prentice-Hall, Inc.
Pearson Education
Upper Saddle River, New Jersey 07458

All rights reserved. No part of this book may be reproduced, in any form or by any means, without written permission from the Publisher.

ISBN 0-13-083582-X

Prentice-Hall International (UK) Limited, London
Prentice-Hall of Australia Pty. Limited, Sydney
Prentice-Hall Canada Inc., Toronto
Prentice-Hall Hispanoamericana, S.A., Mexico
Prentice-Hall of India Private Limited, New Delhi
Prentice-Hall of Japan, Inc., Tokyo
Editora Prentice-Hall do Brasil, Ltda., Rio de Janeiro

Printed in the United States of America

10 9 8 7 6 5 4

To Marion—my wife, my lover, and my best friend
—Robert Grauer

To my Mother and Father—for all their love and support these many years
—Maryann Barber

CONTENTS

PREFACE   XI

EXPLORING MICROSOFT® WORD 2000

1

MICROSOFT® WORD 2000: WHAT WILL WORD PROCESSING DO FOR ME?   1

CHAPTER OBJECTIVES   1
OVERVIEW   1
The Basics of Word Processing   2
    The Insertion Point   2   Word Wrap   2
    Toggle Switches   3   Insertion versus
    Overtype   4   Deleting Text   5
Introduction to Microsoft Word   5
The File Menu   8
Learning by Doing   9
HANDS-ON EXERCISE 1: MY FIRST DOCUMENT   10
Troubleshooting   17
HANDS-ON EXERCISE 2: MODIFYING AN EXISTING DOCUMENT   19
The Spell Check   25
    AutoCorrect and AutoText   27
Thesaurus   28
Grammar Check   29
Save Command   31
    Backup Options   31

HANDS-ON EXERCISE 3: THE SPELL CHECK   33
Summary   40
Key Words and Concepts   40
Multiple Choice   41
Practice with Microsoft Word   43
Case Studies   48

2

GAINING PROFICIENCY: EDITING AND FORMATTING   51

CHAPTER OBJECTIVES   51
OVERVIEW   51
Select-Then-Do   52
Moving and Copying Text   53
Undo and Redo Commands   53
Find, Replace, and Go To Commands   54
Scrolling   55
View Menu   58
HANDS-ON EXERCISE 1: EDITING A DOCUMENT   59
Typography   67
    Typeface   67   Type Size   69
    Format Font Command   69

Page Setup Command 71
    Page Breaks 73
An Exercise in Design 73
HANDS-ON EXERCISE 2: CHARACTER FORMATTING 74
Paragraph Formatting 80
    Alignment 81   Indents 81   Tabs 84
    Hyphenation 85   Line Spacing 85
Format Paragraph Command 85
    Borders and Shading 87
Column Formatting 88
HANDS-ON EXERCISE 3: PARAGRAPH FORMATTING 89
Summary 98
Key Words and Concepts 98
Multiple Choice 99
Practice with Microsoft Word 101
Case Studies 106

A Compound Document 110
    Microsoft Clip Gallery 111   Insert Symbol Command 112   Microsoft WordArt 113
The Drawing Toolbar 114
HANDS-ON EXERCISE 1: CREATING A COMPOUND DOCUMENT 115
Word 2000 and the Internet 123
    Copyright Protection 124
    Footnotes and Endnotes 125
HANDS-ON EXERCISE 2: WORD 2000 AND THE WEB 126
Wizards and Templates 134
HANDS-ON EXERCISE 3: WIZARDS AND TEMPLATES 137
Summary 142
Key Words and Concepts 143
Multiple Choice 143
Practice with Microsoft Word 145
Case Studies 153

3

ENHANCING A DOCUMENT: THE WEB AND OTHER RESOURCES 109

CHAPTER OBJECTIVES 109
OVERVIEW 109

EXPLORING MICROSOFT® EXCEL 2000

1

INTRODUCTION TO MICROSOFT® EXCEL: WHAT IS A SPREADSHEET? 1

CHAPTER OBJECTIVES 1
OVERVIEW 1

Introduction to Spreadsheets 2
    The Professor's Grade Book 3   Row and Column Headings 4   Formulas and Constants 5

Introduction to Microsoft Excel 6
    Toolbars 7
The File Menu 9
HANDS-ON EXERCISE 1: INTRODUCTION TO MICROSOFT EXCEL 11
Modifying the Worksheet 19
The Page Setup Command 21
HANDS-ON EXERCISE 2: MODIFYING A WORKSHEET 23
Summary 33
Key Words and Concepts 33
Multiple Choice 33
Practice with Excel 2000 36
Case Studies 39

2
GAINING PROFICIENCY: COPYING, FORMATTING, AND ISOLATING ASSUMPTIONS 41

CHAPTER OBJECTIVES 41
OVERVIEW 41
A Better Grade Book 42
Cell Ranges 43
Copy Command 43
Move Operation 45
Learning by Doing 46
HANDS-ON EXERCISE 1: CREATING A WORKBOOK 47
Formatting 53
    Column Widths 54   Row Heights 54
Format Cells Command 54
    Numeric Formats 54   Alignment 56
    Fonts 56   Borders, Patterns, and Shading 58
HANDS-ON EXERCISE 2: FORMATTING A WORKSHEET 59
Excel 2000 and the Internet 68
HANDS-ON EXERCISE 3: EXCEL 2000 AND THE INTERNET 70
Summary 75
Key Words and Concepts 75
Multiple Choice 76
Practice with Excel 2000 78
Case Studies 84

3
GRAPHS AND CHARTS: DELIVERING A MESSAGE 85

CHAPTER OBJECTIVES 85
OVERVIEW 85
Chart Types 86
    Pie Charts 87   Column and Bar Charts 89
Creating a Chart 92
    The Chart Wizard 94   Modifying a Chart 96
HANDS-ON EXERCISE 1: THE CHART WIZARD 97
Multiple Data Series 106
    Rows versus Columns 108
HANDS-ON EXERCISE 2: MULTIPLE DATA SERIES 110
Object Linking and Embedding 116
HANDS-ON EXERCISE 3: OBJECT LINKING AND EMBEDDING 118
Additional Chart Types 126
    Line Chart 128   Combination Chart 128
Use and Abuse of Charts 128
    Improper (Omitted) Labels 128   Adding Dissimilar Quantities 129
Summary 131
Key Words and Concepts 131
Multiple Choice 132
Practice with Excel 2000 134
Case Studies 137

EXPLORING MICROSOFT® ACCESS 2000

1
INTRODUCTION TO MICROSOFT® ACCESS: WHAT IS A DATABASE? 1

CHAPTER OBJECTIVES 1
OVERVIEW 1
Case Study: The College Bookstore 2
Introduction to Microsoft Access 3
    The Database Window 3   Tables 4
HANDS-ON EXERCISE 1: INTRODUCTION TO MICROSOFT ACCESS 6
Maintaining the Database 13
    Find and Replace Commands 13   Data Validation 14
Forms, Queries, and Reports 14
HANDS-ON EXERCISE 2: MAINTAINING THE DATABASE 17
Filters and Sorting 25
HANDS-ON EXERCISE 3: FILTERS AND SORTING 27

Looking Ahead: A Relational Database   32
HANDS-ON EXERCISE 4: A LOOK AHEAD   34
Summary   41
Key Words and Concepts   41

Multiple Choice   42
Practice with Access 2000   44
Case Studies   48

EXPLORING MICROSOFT® POWERPOINT 2000

1

INTRODUCTION TO POWERPOINT: PRESENTATIONS MADE EASY   1

CHAPTER OBJECTIVES   1
OVERVIEW   1
A PowerPoint Presentation   2
Introduction to PowerPoint   4
    Six Different Views   5   The File Menu   7

HANDS-ON EXERCISE 1: INTRODUCTION TO POWERPOINT   9
Creating a Presentation   18
    Slide Layouts   20
Templates   21
HANDS-ON EXERCISE 2: CREATING A PRESENTATION   22
Creating a Slide Show   30
    Delivering the Presentation   30
HANDS-ON EXERCISE 3: ANIMATING THE PRESENTATION   32
Summary   38
Key Words and Concepts   38
Multiple Choice   39
Practice with PowerPoint 2000   41
Case Studies   47

INDEX

PREFACE

We are proud to announce the fourth edition of the *Exploring Windows* series in conjunction with Microsoft® Office 2000. The series has expanded in two important ways—recognition by the **Microsoft Office User Specialist (MOUS)** program, and a significantly expanded Web site at *www.prenhall.com/grauer*. The Web site provides password-protected solutions for instructors and online study guides (Companion Web sites) for students. Practice files and PowerPoint lectures are available for both student and instructor. The site also contains information about Microsoft Certification, CD-based tutorials for use with the series, and SkillCheck® assessment software.

The organization of the series is essentially unchanged. There are separate titles for each application—*Word 2000, Excel 2000, Access 2000,* and *PowerPoint 2000,* a book on *Windows® 98,* and eventually, *Windows® 2000.* There are also four combined texts—*Exploring Microsoft Office Professional, Volumes I* and *II, Exploring Microsoft Office Proficient Certification Edition,* and *Brief Office. Volume I* is a unique combination of applications and concepts for the introductory computer course. It covers all four Office applications and includes supporting material on Windows 95/98, Internet Explorer, and Essential Computing Concepts. The modules for Word and Excel satisfy the requirements for proficient certification. The *Proficient Certification Edition* extends the coverage of Access and PowerPoint from *Volume I* to meet the certification requirements, but (because of length) deletes the units on Internet Explorer and Essential Computing Concepts that are found in *Volume I. Volume II* includes the advanced features in all four applications and extends certification to the expert level. *Brief Office* is intended to get the reader "up and running," without concern for certification requirements.

The Internet and World Wide Web are integrated throughout the series. Students learn Office applications as before, and in addition are sent to the Web as appropriate for supplementary exercises. The sections on Object Linking and Embedding, for example, not only draw on resources within Microsoft Office, but on the Web as well. Students are directed to search the Web for information, and then download resources for inclusion in Office documents. The icon at the left of this paragraph appears throughout the text whenever there is a Web reference.

The *Exploring Windows* series is part of the Prentice Hall custom-binding (*Right PHit*) program, enabling instructors to create their own texts by selecting modules from *Volume I, Volume II,* the *Proficient Certification Edition,* and/or *Brief Office* to suit the needs of a specific course. An instructor could, for example, create a custom text consisting of the proficient modules in Word and Excel, coupled with the brief modules for Access and PowerPoint. Instructors can also take advantage of our *ValuePack program* to shrink-wrap multiple books together at a substantial saving for the student. A ValuePack is ideal in courses that require complete coverage of multiple applications.

Instructors will want to obtain the *Instructor's Resource CD* from their Prentice Hall representative. The CD contains the student data disks, solutions to all exercises in machine-readable format, PowerPoint lectures, and the Instructor Manuals themselves in Word format. The CD also has a Windows-based test generator. Please visit us on the Web at *www.prenhall.com/grauer* for additional information.

FEATURES AND BENEFITS

Our text is written for the novice and assumes no previous knowledge of application software. The introductory chapter for each application presents basic concepts, then quickly gets the student up and running.

A total of 24 in-depth tutorials (hands-on exercises) guide the reader at the computer. This exercise from Chapter 3 in Word describes how to download a photograph from the Web for subsequent inclusion in a Word document.

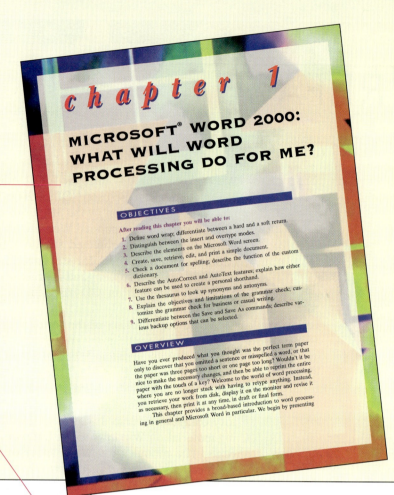

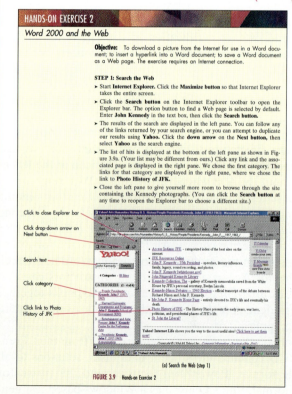

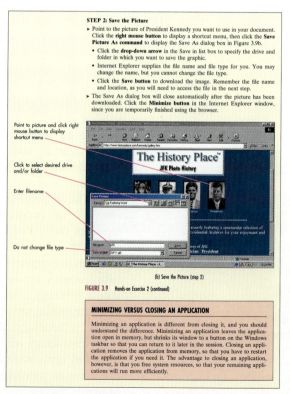

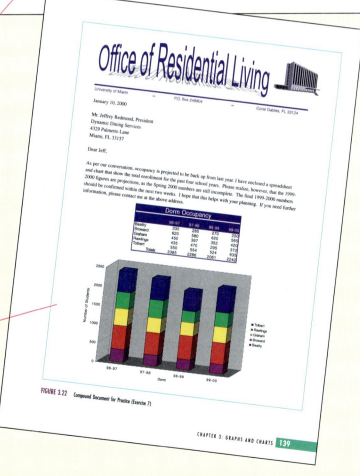

Every chapter contains a variety of assignments to avoid repetition from one semester to the next. The exercises vary in scope and difficulty and encourage the student to create a large number of different documents. These examples are from Chapter 1 in Excel.

Object Linking and Embedding is stressed throughout the text, as the reader is encouraged to create documents that draw on multiple applications. This figure is from Chapter 3 in Excel and links an Excel spreadsheet and chart to a Word document.

LOOKING AHEAD: A RELATIONAL DATABASE

The Bookstore and Employee databases are both examples of simple databases in that they each contained only a single table. The real power of Access, however, is derived from multiple tables and the relationships between those tables. This type of database is known as a *relational database* and is illustrated in Figure 1.9. This figure expands the original Employee database by adding two tables, for locations and titles, respectively.

The Employees table in Figure 1.9a is the same table we used at the beginning of the previous exercise, except for the substitution of a LocationID and TitleID for the location and title, respectively. The Locations table in turn has all of the fields that pertain to each location: LocationID, Location, Address, State, Zipcode, and Office Phone. One field, the LocationID, appears in both Employees and Locations tables and links the two tables to one another. In similar fashion, the Titles table has the information for each title: the TitleID, Title, Description, Education Required, and Minimum and Maximum Salary. The TitleID appears in both the Employees and Titles tables to link those tables to one another.

It sounds complicated, but it is really quite simple and very elegant. More importantly, it enables you to obtain detailed information about any employee, location, or title. To show how it works, we will ask a series of questions that require you to look in one or more tables for the answer. Consider:

Query: At which location does Pamela Milgrom work? What is the phone number of her office?
Answer: Pamela works in the Boston office, at 3 Commons Blvd., Boston, MA, 02190. The phone number is (617) 123-4444.

Did you answer the question correctly? You had to search the Employees table for Pamela Milgrom to obtain the LocationID (L02 in this example) corresponding to her office. You then searched the Locations table for this LocationID to obtain the address and phone number for that location. The process required you to use both the Locations and Employees tables, which are linked to one another through a *one-to-many relationship*. One location can have many employees, but a specific employee can work at only one location. Let's try another question:

Query: Which employees are managers?
Answer: There are four managers: Pamela Milgrom, Tracey Coulter, Billy Marlin, and David Adamson

The answer to this question is based on the one-to-many relationship that exists between titles and employees. One title can have many employees, but a given employee has only one title. To answer the query, you search the Titles table for "manager" to determine its TitleID (T02). You then go to the Employees table and select those records that have this value in the TitleID field.

The design of a relational database enables us to extract information from multiple tables in a single query. Equally important, it simplifies the way data is changed in that modifications are made in only one place. Consider:

Query: Which employees work in the Boston office? What is their phone number? How many changes would be necessary if the Boston office were to get a new phone number?
Answer: There are four employees in Boston: Pamela Milgrom, Ann Manin, Patricia Rubin, and Kenneth Charles, each with the same number (617) 123-4444). Only one change (in the Locations table) would be necessary if the phone number changed.

Once again, we draw on the one-to-many relationship between locations and employees. Thus, we begin in the Locations table where we search for "Boston" to determine its LocationID (L02) and phone number (617 123-4444). Then we go to the Employees table to select those records with this value in the LocationID field. Realize, however, that the phone number is stored in the Locations table. Thus, the new phone number is entered in the Boston record, where it is reflected automatically for each employee with a LocationID of L02 (corresponding to the Boston office).

(a) The Employees Table

SSN	LastName	FirstName	LocationID	TitleID	Salary	Gender	Performance
000-01-0000	Milgrom	Pamela	L02	T02	$57,500	F	Average
000-02-2222	Adams	Jennifer	L01	T03	$19,500	F	Average
111-12-1111	Johnson	James	L03	T01	$47,500	M	Good
123-45-6789	Coulter	Tracey	L01	T02	$100,000	F	Good
222-23-2222	Marlin	Billy	L04	T02	$125,000	M	Good
222-52-5555	Smith	Mary	L03	T01	$42,500	F	Average
333-34-3333	Manin	Ann	L02	T01	$49,500	F	Average
333-43-4444	Smith	Frank	L01	T01	$65,000	M	Good
333-66-1234	Brown	Marietta	L01	T03	$18,500	F	Poor
444-45-4444	Frank	Vernon	L04	T01	$75,000	M	Good
555-22-3333	Rubin	Patricia	L02	T01	$45,000	F	Average
555-56-5555	Charles	Kenneth	L02	T01	$40,000	M	Poor
776-67-6666	Adamson	David	L03	T02	$52,000	M	Poor
777-78-7777	Marder	Kelly	L03	T01	$38,500	F	Average

(b) The Locations Table

LocationID	Location	Address	State	Zipcode	OfficePhone
L01	Atlanta	450 Peachtree Road	GA	30316	(404) 333-5555
L02	Boston	3 Commons Blvd	MA	02190	(617) 123-4444
L03	Chicago	500 Loop Highway	IL	60620	(312) 444-6666
L04	Miami	210 Biscayne Blvd	FL	33103	(305) 787-9999

(c) The Titles Table

TitleID	Title	Description	EducationRequired	MinimumSalary	MaximumSalary
T01	Account Rep	A marketing …	Four year degree	$25,000	$75,000
T02	Manager	A supervisory …	Four year degree	$50,000	$150,000
T03	Trainee	An entry-level …	Two year degree	$18,000	$25,000

FIGURE 1.9 A Relational Database

The *Exploring Windows* series is known for its conceptual approach that supplements the hands-on exercises. Students not only learn the commands within an application but are also taught the underlying theory for a much broader understanding. This example is from Chapter 1 in Access and uses color to explain a relational database.

Every chapter ends with a number of less-structured case studies to challenge the student. The Web icon appears whenever the reader is directed to the Web as a source of additional information.

CASE STUDIES

Companion Web Sites

A Companion Web site (or online study guide) accompanies each book in the Exploring Microsoft Office 2000 series. Go to the Exploring Windows home page at www.prenhall.com/grauer, click the book to Office 2000, and click the Companion Web site tab at the top of the screen. Choose the appropriate text (Exploring Word 2000) and the chapter within the text (e.g., Chapter 1).

Each chapter contains a series of short-answer exercises (multiple-choice, true/false, and matching) to review the material in the chapter. You can take practice quizzes by yourself and/or e-mail the results to your instructor. You can try the essay questions for additional practice and engage in online chat sessions. We hope you will find the online guide to be a valuable resource.

It's a Mess

Newcomers to word processing quickly learn the concept of word wrap and the distinction between hard and soft returns. This lesson was lost, however, on your friend who created the *Please Help Me* document on the data disk. The first several sentences were entered without any hard returns at all, whereas the opposite problem exists toward the end of the document. This is a good friend, and her paper is due in one hour. Please help.

Planning for Disaster

Do you have a backup strategy? Do you even know what a backup strategy is? You should learn, because sooner or later you will wish you had one. You will erase a file, be unable to read from a floppy disk, or worse yet suffer a hardware failure in which you are unable to access the hard drive. The problem always seems to occur the night before an assignment is due. The ultimate disaster is the disappearance of your computer, by theft or natural disaster (e.g., Hurricane Andrew). Describe in 250 words or less the backup strategy you plan to implement in conjunction with your work in this class.

A Letter Home

You really like this course and want very much to have your own computer, but you're strapped for cash and have decided to ask your parents for help. Write a one-page letter describing the advantages of having your own system and how it will help you in school. Tell your parents what the system will cost, and that you can save money by buying through the mail. Describe the configuration you intend to buy (don't forget to include the price of software) and then provide prices from at least three different companies. Cut out the advertisements and include them in your letter. Bring your material to class and compare your research with that of your classmates.

Computer Magazines

A subscription to a computer magazine should be given serious consideration if you intend to stay abreast in a rapidly changing field. The reviews on new products are especially helpful and you will appreciate the advertisements should you

Our one chapter in PowerPoint contains everything the reader needs in order to create an effective presentation, quickly and easily. The student is led through the basic steps, from developing the content, to applying a template, to creating a slide show.

All material is presented in conceptual form prior to its inclusion in a hands-on exercise. Students are provided with the rationale for what they are doing and are able to extend the information to additional learning on their own.

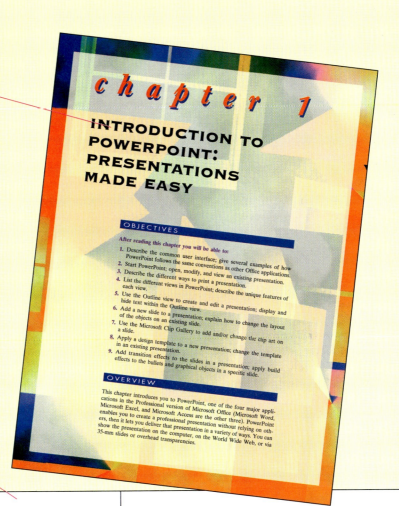

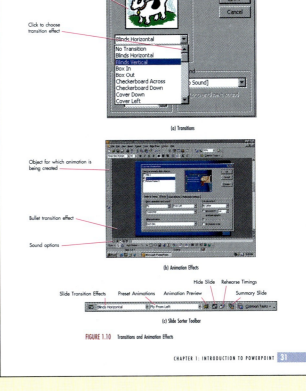

Acknowledgments

We want to thank the many individuals who have helped to bring this project to fruition. We are especially grateful to Nancy Evans and PJ Boardman, who continue to offer inspiration and guidance. Alex von Rosenberg, executive editor at Prentice Hall, has provided new leadership in extending the series to Office 2000. Nancy Welcher did an absolutely incredible job on our Web site. Susan Rifkin coordinated the myriad details of production and the certification process. Greg Christofferson was instrumental in the acquisition of supporting software. Lynne Breitfeller was the project manager. Paul Smolenski was senior manufacturing supervisor. Greg Hubit has been masterful as the external production editor for every book in the series. Cecil Yarbrough did an outstanding job in checking the manuscript for technical accuracy. Jennifer Surich was the editorial assistant. Leanne Nieglos was the supplements editor. Cindy Stevens, Karen Vignare, and Michael Olmstead wrote the Instructor Manuals. Patricia Smythe developed the innovative and attractive design. We also want to acknowledge our reviewers who, through their comments and constructive criticism, greatly improved the series.

Lynne Band, Middlesex Community College
Don Belle, Central Piedmont Community College
Stuart P. Brian, Holy Family College
Carl M. Briggs, Indiana University School of Business
Kimberly Chambers, Scottsdale Community College
Alok Charturvedi, Purdue University
Jerry Chin, Southwest Missouri State University
Dean Combellick, Scottsdale Community College
Cody Copeland, Johnson County Community College
Larry S. Corman, Fort Lewis College
Janis Cox, Tri-County Technical College
Martin Crossland, Southwest Missouri State University
Paul E. Daurelle, Western Piedmont Community College
David Douglas, University of Arkansas
Carlotta Eaton, Radford University
Judith M. Fitspatrick, Gulf Coast Community College
Raymond Frost, Central Connecticut State University
Midge Gerber, Southwestern Oklahoma State University
James Gips, Boston College
Vernon Griffin, Austin Community College
Michael Hassett, Fort Hays State University
Wanda D. Heller, Seminole Community College
Bonnie Homan, San Francisco State University
Ernie Ivey, Polk Community College
Mike Kelly, Community College of Rhode Island
Jane King, Everett Community College
Rose M. Laird, Northern Virginia Community College
John Lesson, University of Central Florida
David B. Meinert, Southwest Missouri State University
Bill Morse, DeVry Institute of Technology
Alan Moltz, Naugatuck Valley Technical Community College
Kim Montney, Kellogg Community College
Kevin Pauli, University of Nebraska
Mary McKenry Percival, University of Miami
Delores Pusins, Hillsborough Community College
Gale E. Rand, College Misericordia
Judith Rice, Santa Fe Community College
David Rinehard, Lansing Community College
Marilyn Salas, Scottsdale Community College
John Shepherd, Duquesne University
Barbara Sherman, Buffalo State College
Robert Spear, Prince George's Community College
Michael Stewardson, San Jacinto College—North
Helen Stoloff, Hudson Valley Community College
Margaret Thomas, Ohio University
Mike Thomas, Indiana University School of Business
Suzanne Tomlinson, Iowa State University
Karen Tracey, Central Connecticut State University
Sally Visci, Lorain County Community College
David Weiner, University of San Francisco
Connie Wells, Georgia State University
Wallace John Whistance-Smith, Ryerson Polytechnic University
Jack Zeller, Kirkwood Community College

A final word of thanks to the unnamed students at the University of Miami, who make it all worthwhile. Most of all, thanks to you, our readers, for choosing this book. Please feel free to contact us with any comments and suggestions.

Robert T. Grauer
rgrauer@sba.miami.edu
www.bus.miami.edu/~rgrauer
www.prenhall.com/grauer

Maryann Barber
mbarber@sba.miami.edu
www.bus.miami.edu/~mbarber

chapter 1

MICROSOFT® WORD 2000: WHAT WILL WORD PROCESSING DO FOR ME?

OBJECTIVES

After reading this chapter you will be able to:

1. Define word wrap; differentiate between a hard and a soft return.
2. Distinguish between the insert and overtype modes.
3. Describe the elements on the Microsoft Word screen.
4. Create, save, retrieve, edit, and print a simple document.
5. Check a document for spelling; describe the function of the custom dictionary.
6. Describe the AutoCorrect and AutoText features; explain how either feature can be used to create a personal shorthand.
7. Use the thesaurus to look up synonyms and antonyms.
8. Explain the objectives and limitations of the grammar check; customize the grammar check for business or casual writing.
9. Differentiate between the Save and Save As commands; describe various backup options that can be selected.

OVERVIEW

Have you ever produced what you thought was the perfect term paper only to discover that you omitted a sentence or misspelled a word, or that the paper was three pages too short or one page too long? Wouldn't it be nice to make the necessary changes, and then be able to reprint the entire paper with the touch of a key? Welcome to the world of word processing, where you are no longer stuck with having to retype anything. Instead, you retrieve your work from disk, display it on the monitor and revise it as necessary, then print it at any time, in draft or final form.

This chapter provides a broad-based introduction to word processing in general and Microsoft Word in particular. We begin by presenting (or perhaps reviewing) the essential concepts of a word processor, then show you how these concepts are implemented in Word. We show you how to create a document, how to save it on disk, then retrieve the document you just created. We introduce you to the spell check and thesaurus, two essential tools in any word processor. We also present the grammar check as a convenient way of finding a variety of errors but remind you there is no substitute for carefully proofreading the final document.

THE BASICS OF WORD PROCESSING

All word processors adhere to certain basic concepts that must be understood if you are to use the programs effectively. The next several pages introduce ideas that are applicable to any word processor (and which you may already know). We follow the conceptual material with a hands-on exercise that enables you to apply what you have learned.

The Insertion Point

The *insertion point* is a flashing vertical line that marks the place where text will be entered. The insertion point is always at the beginning of a new document, but it can be moved anywhere within an existing document. If, for example, you wanted to add text to the end of a document, you would move the insertion point to the end of the document, then begin typing.

Word Wrap

A newcomer to word processing has one major transition to make from a typewriter, and it is an absolutely critical adjustment. Whereas a typist returns the carriage at the end of every line, just the opposite is true of a word processor. One types continually *without* pressing the enter key at the end of a line because the word processor automatically wraps text from one line to the next. This concept is known as *word wrap* and is illustrated in Figure 1.1.

The word *primitive* does not fit on the current line in Figure 1.1a, and is automatically shifted to the next line, *without* the user having to press the enter key. The user continues to enter the document, with additional words being wrapped to subsequent lines as necessary. The only time you use the enter key is at the end of a paragraph, or when you want the insertion point to move to the next line and the end of the current line doesn't reach the right margin.

Word wrap is closely associated with another concept, that of hard and soft returns. A *hard return* is created by the user when he or she presses the enter key at the end of a paragraph; a *soft return* is created by the word processor as it wraps text from one line to the next. The locations of the soft returns change automatically as a document is edited (e.g., as text is inserted or deleted, or as margins or fonts are changed). The locations of the hard returns can be changed only by the user, who must intentionally insert or delete each hard return.

There are two hard returns in Figure 1.1b, one at the end of each paragraph. There are also six soft returns in the first paragraph (one at the end of every line except the last) and three soft returns in the second paragraph. Now suppose the margins in the document are made smaller (that is, the line is made longer) as shown in Figure 1.1c. The number of soft returns drops to four and two (in the first and second paragraphs, respectively) as more text fits on a line and fewer lines are needed. The revised document still contains the two original hard returns, one at the end of each paragraph.

The original IBM PC was extremely pr

primitive cannot fit on current line

The original IBM PC was extremely primitive

primitive is automatically moved to the next line

(a) Entering the Document

The original IBM PC was extremely primitive (not to mention expensive) by current standards. The basic machine came equipped with only 16Kb RAM and was sold without a monitor or disk (a TV and tape cassette were suggested instead). The price of this powerhouse was $1565. ¶
You could, however, purchase an expanded business system with 256Kb RAM, two 160Kb floppy drives, monochrome monitor, and 80-cps printer for $4425. ¶

Hard returns are created by pressing the enter key at the end of a paragraph.

(b) Completed Document

The original IBM PC was extremely primitive (not to mention expensive) by current standards. The basic machine came equipped with only 16Kb RAM and was sold without a monitor or disk (a TV and tape cassette were suggested instead). The price of this powerhouse was $1565. ¶
You could, however, purchase an expanded business system with 256Kb RAM, two 160Kb floppy drives, monochrome monitor, and 80-cps printer for $4425. ¶

Revised document still contains two hard returns, one at the end of each paragraph.

(c) Completed Document

FIGURE 1.1 Word Wrap

Toggle Switches

Suppose you sat down at the keyboard and typed an entire sentence without pressing the Shift key; the sentence would be in all lowercase letters. Then you pressed the Caps Lock key and retyped the sentence, again without pressing the Shift key. This time the sentence would be in all uppercase letters. You could repeat the process as often as you like. Each time you pressed the Caps Lock key, the sentence would switch from lowercase to uppercase and vice versa.

The point of this exercise is to introduce the concept of a ***toggle switch,*** a device that causes the computer to alternate between two states. The Caps Lock key is an example of a toggle switch. Each time you press it, newly typed text will change from uppercase to lowercase and back again. We will see several other examples of toggle switches as we proceed in our discussion of word processing.

Insert versus Overtype

Microsoft Word is always in one of two modes, **insert** or **overtype**, and uses a toggle switch (the Ins key) to alternate between the two. Press the Ins key once and you switch from insert to overtype. Press the Ins key a second time and you go from overtype back to insert. Text that is entered into a document during the insert mode moves existing text to the right to accommodate the characters being added. Text entered from the overtype mode replaces (overtypes) existing text. Regardless of which mode you are in, text is always entered or replaced immediately to the right of the insertion point.

The insert mode is best when you enter text for the first time, but either mode can be used to make corrections. The insert mode is the better choice when the correction requires you to add new text; the overtype mode is easier when you are substituting one or more character(s) for another. The difference is illustrated in Figure 1.2.

Figure 1.2a displays the text as it was originally entered, with two misspellings. The letters *se* have been omitted from the word *insert,* and an *x* has been erroneously typed instead of an *r* in the word *overtype*. The insert mode is used in Figure 1.2b to add the missing letters, which in turn moves the rest of the line to the right. The overtype mode is used in Figure 1.2c to replace the *x* with an *r*.

Misspelled words

The inrt mode is better when adding text that has been omitted; the ovextype mode is easier when you are substituting one (or more) characters for another.

(a) Text to Be Corrected

se has been inserted and existing text moved to the right

The insert mode is better when adding text that has been omitted; the ovextype mode is easier when you are substituting one (or more) characters for another.

(b) Insert Mode

r replaces the *x*

The insert mode is better when adding text that has been omitted; the overtype mode is easier when you are substituting one (or more) characters for another.

(c) Overtype Mode

FIGURE 1.2 Insert and Overtype Modes

Deleting Text

The backspace and Del keys delete one character immediately to the left or right of the insertion point, respectively. The choice between them depends on when you need to erase a character(s). The backspace key is easier if you want to delete a character immediately after typing it. The Del key is preferable during subsequent editing.

You can delete several characters at one time by selecting (dragging the mouse over) the characters to be deleted, then pressing the Del key. And finally, you can delete and replace text in one operation by selecting the text to be replaced and then typing the new text in its place.

LEARN TO TYPE

The ultimate limitation of any word processor is the speed at which you enter data; hence the ability to type quickly is invaluable. Learning how to type is easy, especially with the availability of computer-based typing programs. As little as a half hour a day for a couple of weeks will have you up to speed, and if you do any significant amount of writing at all, the investment will pay off many times.

INTRODUCTION TO MICROSOFT WORD

We used Microsoft Word to write this book, as can be inferred from the screen in Figure 1.3. Your screen will be different from ours in many ways. You will not have the same document nor is it likely that you will customize Word in exactly the same way. You should, however, be able to recognize the basic elements that are found in the Microsoft Word window that is open on the desktop.

There are actually two open windows in Figure 1.3—an application window for Microsoft Word and a document window for the specific document on which you are working. The application window has its own Minimize, Maximize (or Restore) and Close buttons. The document window has only a Close button. There is, however, only one title bar that appears at the top of the application window and it reflects the application (Microsoft Word) as well as the document name (Word Chapter 1). A menu bar appears immediately below the title bar. Vertical and horizontal scroll bars appear at the right and bottom of the document window. The Windows taskbar appears at the bottom of the screen and shows the open applications.

Microsoft Word is also part of the Microsoft Office suite of applications, and thus shares additional features with Excel, Access, and PowerPoint, that are also part of the Office suite. ***Toolbars*** provide immediate access to common commands and appear immediately below the menu bar. The toolbars can be displayed or hidden using the Toolbars command in the View menu.

The ***Standard toolbar*** contains buttons corresponding to the most basic commands in Word—for example, opening a file or printing a document. The icon on the button is intended to be indicative of its function (e.g., a printer to indicate the Print command). You can also point to the button to display a ***ScreenTip*** showing the name of the button. The ***Formatting toolbar*** appears under the Standard toolbar and provides access to common formatting operations such as boldface, italics, or underlining.

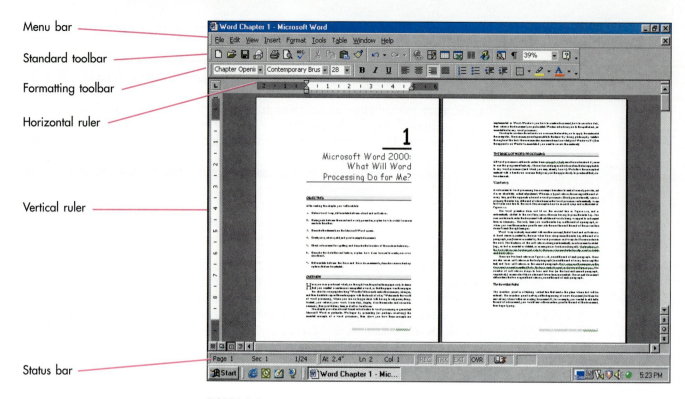

FIGURE 1.3 Microsoft Word

The toolbars may appear overwhelming at first, but there is absolutely no need to memorize what the individual buttons do. That will come with time. We suggest, however, that you will have a better appreciation for the various buttons if you consider them in groups, according to their general function, as shown in Figure 1.4a. Note, too, that many of the commands in the pull-down menus are displayed with an image that corresponds to a button on a toolbar.

The ***horizontal ruler*** is displayed underneath the toolbars and enables you to change margins, tabs, and/or indents for all or part of a document. A ***vertical ruler*** shows the vertical position of text on the page and can be used to change the top or bottom margins.

The ***status bar*** at the bottom of the document window displays the location of the insertion point (or information about the command being executed.) The status bar also shows the status (settings) of various indicators—for example, OVR to show that Word is in the overtype, as opposed to the insert, mode.

CHANGES IN OFFICE 2000

Office 2000 implements one very significant change over previous versions in that it displays a series of short menus that contain only basic commands. The bottom of each menu has a double arrow that you can click to display the additional commands. Each time you execute a command it is added to the menu, and conversely, Word will remove commands from a menu if they are not used after a period of time. You can, however, display the full menus through the Customize command in the Tools menu by clearing the check boxes associated with personalized menus and toolbars.

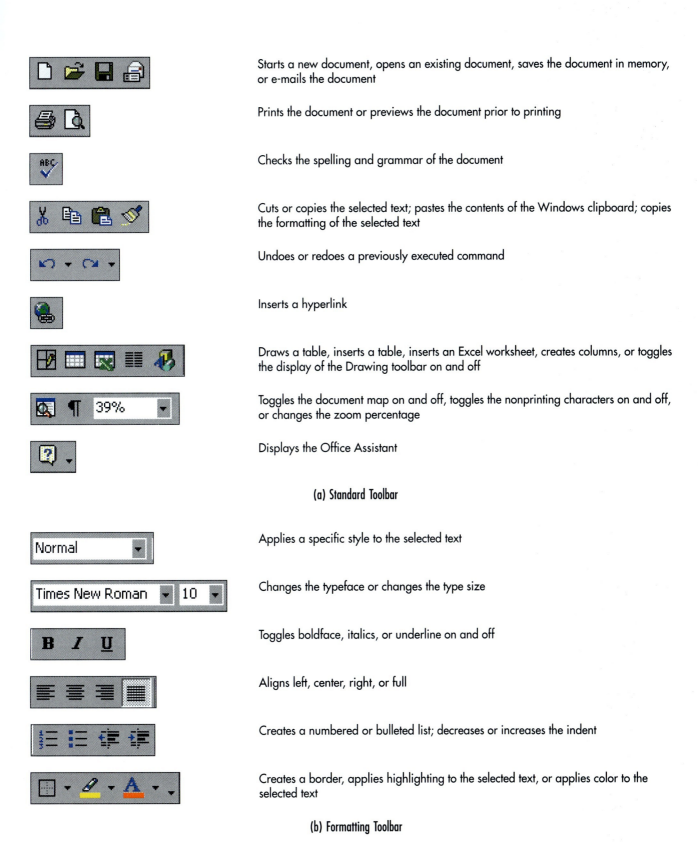

FIGURE 1.4   Toolbars

THE FILE MENU

The *File Menu* is a critically important menu in virtually every Windows application. It contains the Save and Open commands to save a document on disk, then subsequently retrieve (open) that document at a later time. The File Menu also contains the *Print command* to print a document, the *Close command* to close the current document but continue working in the application, and the *Exit command* to quit the application altogether.

The *Save command* copies the document that you are working on (i.e., the document that is currently in memory) to disk. The command functions differently the first time it is executed for a new document, in that it displays the Save As dialog box as shown in Figure 1.5a. The dialog box requires you to specify the name of the document, the drive (and an optional folder) in which the document is stored, and its file type. All subsequent executions of the command will save the document under the assigned name, each time replacing the previously saved version with the new version.

The *file name* (e.g., My First Document) can contain up to 255 characters including spaces, commas, and/or periods. (Periods are discouraged, however, since they are too easily confused with DOS extensions.) The Save In list box is used to select the drive (which is not visible in Figure 1.5a) and the optional folder (e.g., Exploring Word). The *Places Bar* provides a shortcut to any of its folders without having to search through the Save In list box. Click the Desktop icon, for example, and the file is saved automatically on the Windows desktop. The *file type* defaults to a Word 2000 document. You can, however, choose a different format such as Word 95 to maintain compatibility with earlier versions of Microsoft Word. You can also save any Word document as a Web page (or HTML document).

The *Open command* is the opposite of the Save command as it brings a copy of an existing document into memory, enabling you to work with that document. The Open command displays the Open dialog box in which you specify the file name, the drive (and optionally the folder) that contains the file, and the file type. Microsoft Word will then list all files of that type on the designated drive (and folder), enabling you to open the file you want. The Save and Open commands work in conjunction with one another. The Save As dialog box in Figure 1.5a, for example, saves the file My First Document in the Exploring Word folder. The Open dialog box in Figure 1.5b loads that file into memory so that you can work with the file, after which you can save the revised file for use at a later time.

The toolbars in the Save As and Open dialog boxes have several buttons in common that facilitate the execution of either command. The Views button lets you display the files in either dialog box in one of four different views. The Details view (in Figure 1.5a) shows the file size as well as the date and time a file was last modified. The Preview view (in Figure 1.5b) shows the beginning of a document, without having to open the document. The List view displays only the file names, and thus lets you see more files at one time. The Properties view shows information about the document including the date of creation and number of revisions.

SORT BY NAME, DATE, OR FILE SIZE

The files in the Save As and Open dialog boxes can be displayed in ascending or descending sequence by name, date modified, or size. Change to the Details view, then click the heading of the desired column; e.g., click the Modified column to list the files according to the date they were last changed. Click the column heading a second time to reverse the sequence.

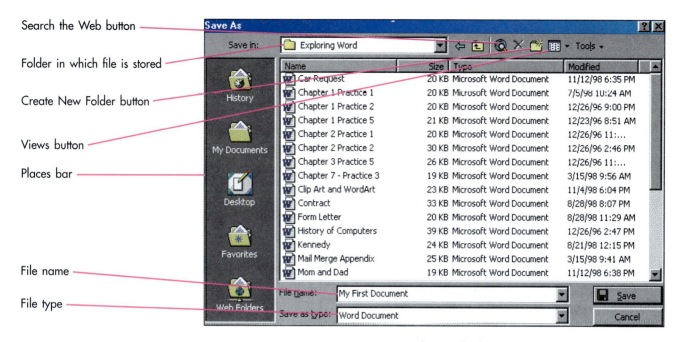

(a) Save As Dialog Box (details view)

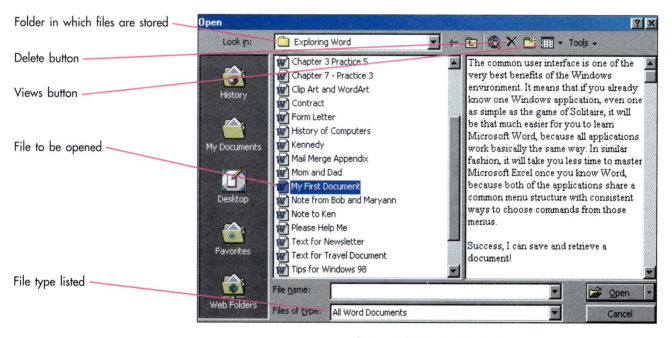

(b) Open Dialog Box (preview view)

FIGURE 1.5 The Save and Open Commands

LEARNING BY DOING

Every chapter contains a series of hands-on exercises that enable you to apply what you learn at the computer. The exercises in this chapter are linked to one another in that you create a simple document in exercise one, then open and edit that document in exercise two. The ability to save and open a document is critical, and you do not want to spend an inordinate amount of time entering text unless you are confident in your ability to retrieve it later.

HANDS-ON EXERCISE 1

My First Document

Objective: To start Microsoft Word in order to create, save, and print a simple document; to execute commands via the toolbar or from pull-down menus. Use Figure 1.6 as a guide in doing the exercise.

STEP 1: The Windows Desktop

➤ Turn on the computer and all of its peripherals. The floppy drive should be empty prior to starting your machine. This ensures that the system starts from the hard disk, which contains the Windows files, as opposed to a floppy disk, which does not.

➤ Your system will take a minute or so to get started, after which you should see the Windows desktop in Figure 1.6a. Do not be concerned if the appearance of your desktop is different from ours.

➤ You may see additional objects on the desktop in Windows 95 and/or the active desktop content in Windows 98. It doesn't matter which operating system you are using because Office 2000 runs equally well under both Windows 95 and Windows 98 (as well as Windows NT).

➤ You may see a Welcome to Windows 95/Windows 98 dialog box with command buttons to take a tour of the operating system. If so, click the appropriate button(s) or close the dialog box.

Start button

(a) The Windows Desktop (step 1)

FIGURE 1.6 Hands-on Exercise 1

STEP 2: Obtain the Practice Files

➤ We have created a series of practice files (also called a "data disk") for you to use throughout the text. Your instructor will make these files available to you in a variety of ways:

- The files may be on a network drive, in which case you use Windows Explorer to copy the files from the network to a floppy disk.
- There may be an actual "data disk" that you are to check out from the lab in order to use the Copy Disk command to duplicate the disk.

➤ You can also download the files from our Web site provided you have an Internet connection. Start Internet Explorer, then go to the Exploring Windows home page at **www.prenhall.com/grauer**.

- Click the book for **Office 2000,** which takes you to the Office 2000 home page. Click the **Student Resources tab** (at the top of the window) to go to the Student Resources page as shown in Figure 1.6b.
- Click the link to **Student Data Disk** (in the left frame), then scroll down the page until you can select Word 2000. Click the link to download the student data disk.
- You will see the File Download dialog box asking what you want to do. The option button to save this program to disk is selected. Click **OK.** The Save As dialog box appears.
- Click the down arrow in the Save In list box to enter the drive and folder where you want to save the file. It's best to save the file to the Windows desktop or to a temporary folder on drive C.
- Double click the file after it has been downloaded to your PC, then follow the onscreen instructions.

➤ Check with your instructor for additional information.

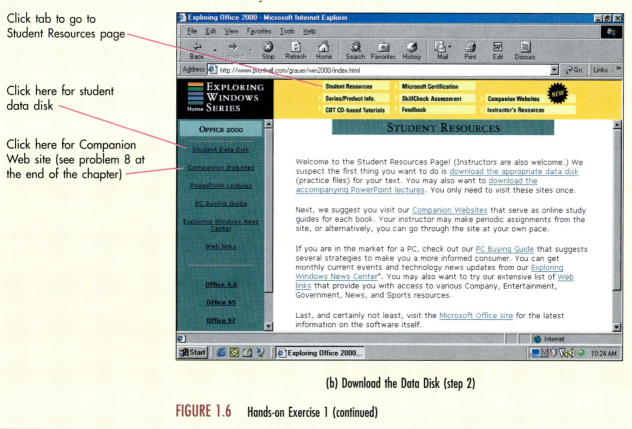

(b) Download the Data Disk (step 2)

FIGURE 1.6 Hands-on Exercise 1 (continued)

STEP 3: Start Microsoft Word

➤ Click the **Start button** to display the Start menu. Click (or point to) the **Programs menu,** then click **Microsoft Word 2000** to start the program.

➤ Click and drag the Office Assistant out of the way. (The Office Assistant is illustrated in step 6 of this exercise.)

➤ If necessary, click the **Maximize button** in the application window so that Word takes the entire desktop as shown in Figure 1.6c.

➤ Do not be concerned if your screen is different from ours as we include a troubleshooting section immediately following this exercise.

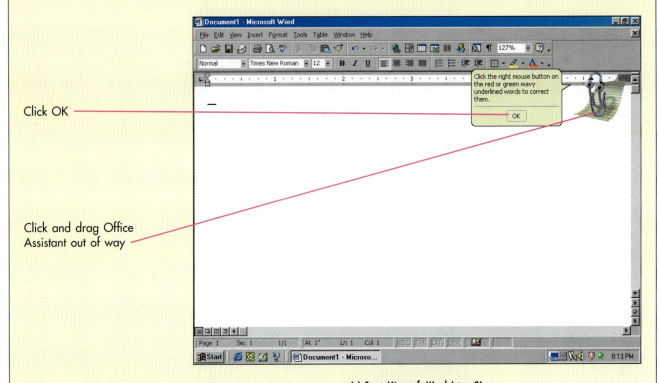

Click OK

Click and drag Office Assistant out of way

(c) Start Microsoft Word (step 3)

FIGURE 1.6   Hands-on Exercise 1 (continued)

ABOUT THE ASSISTANT

The Assistant is very powerful and hence you want to experiment with various ways to use it. To ask a question, click the Assistant's icon to toggle its balloon on or off. To change the way in which the Assistant works, click the Options tab within this balloon and experiment with the various check boxes to see their effects. If you find the Assistant distracting, click and drag the character out of the way or hide it altogether by pulling down the Help menu and clicking the Hide Office Assistant command. Pull down the Help menu and click the Show Office Assistant command to return the Assistant to the desktop.

STEP 4: Create the Document

➤ Create the document in Figure 1.6d. Type just as you would on a typewriter with one exception; do *not* press the enter key at the end of a line because Word will automatically wrap text from one line to the next.

➤ Press the **enter key** at the end of the paragraph.

➤ You may see a red or green wavy line to indicate spelling or grammatical errors respectively. Both features are discussed later in the chapter.

➤ Point to the red wavy line (if any), click the **right mouse button** to display a list of suggested corrections, then click (select) the appropriate substitution.

➤ Ignore the green wavy line (if any).

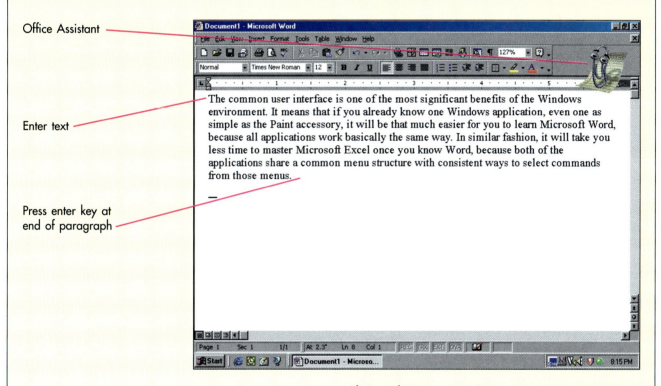

(d) Create the Document (step 4)

SEPARATE THE TOOLBARS

Office 2000 displays the Standard and Formatting toolbars on the same row to save space within the application window. The result is that only a limited number of buttons are visible on each toolbar, and hence you may need to click the double arrow (More Buttons) tool at the end of the toolbar to view additional buttons. You can, however, separate the toolbars. Pull down the Tools menu, click the Customize command, click the Options tab, then clear the check box that has the toolbars share one row.

STEP 5: Save the Document

➤ Pull down the **File menu** and click **Save** (or click the **Save button** on the Standard toolbar). You should see the Save As dialog box in Figure 1.6e.

➤ If necessary, click the **drop-down arrow** on the View button and select the **Details View,** so that the display on your monitor matches our figure.

➤ To save the file:
  • Click the **drop-down arrow** on the Save In list box.
  • Click the appropriate drive, e.g., drive C or drive A, depending on whether or not you installed the data disk on your hard drive.
  • Double click the **Exploring Word folder,** to make it the active folder (the folder in which you will save the document).
  • Click and drag over the default entry in the File name text box. Type **My First Document** as the name of your document. (A DOC extension will be added automatically when the file is saved to indicate that this is a Word document.)
  • Click **Save** or press the **enter key.** The title bar changes to reflect the document name.

➤ Add your name at the end of the document, then click the **Save button** on the Standard toolbar to save the document with the revision. This time the Save As dialog box does not appear, since Word already knows the name of the document.

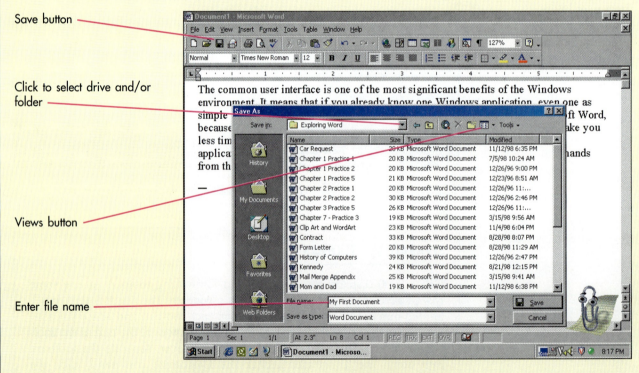

(e) Save the Document (step 5)

FIGURE 1.6   Hands-on Exercise 1 (continued)

STEP 6: The Office Assistant

➤ If necessary, pull down the **Help menu** and click the command to **Show the Office Assistant.** You may see a different character than the one we have selected.

➤ Click the Assistant, enter the question, **How do I print?** as shown in Figure 1.6f, then click the **Search button** to look for the answer. The size of the Assistant's balloon expands as the Assistant suggests several topics that may be appropriate.

➤ Click the topic, **Print a document** which in turn displays a Help window that contains links to various topics, each with detailed information. Click the Office Assistant to hide the balloon (or drag the Assistant out of the way).

➤ Click any of the links in the Help window to read the information. You can print the contents of any topic by clicking the **Print button** in the Help window. Close the Help window when you are finished.

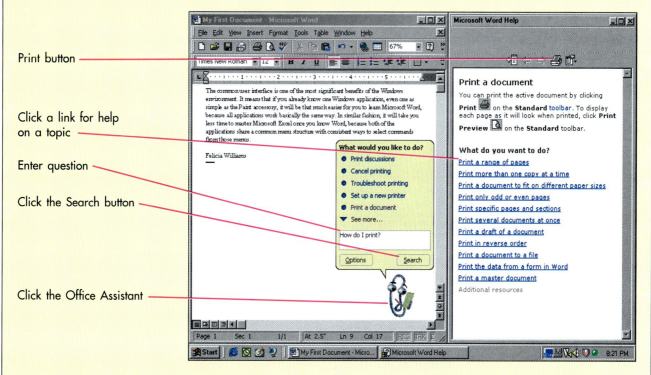

(f) The Office Assistant (step 6)

FIGURE 1.6 Hands-on Exercise 1 (continued)

TIP OF THE DAY

You can set the Office Assistant to greet you with a "tip of the day" each time you start Word. Click the Microsoft Word Help button (or press the F1 key) to display the Assistant, then click the Options button to display the Office Assistant dialog box. Click the Options tab, then check the Show the Tip of the Day at Startup box and click OK. The next time you start Microsoft Word, you will be greeted by the Assistant, who will offer you the tip of the day.

STEP 7: Print the Document

➤ You can print the document in one of two ways:

- Pull down the **File menu.** Click **Print** to display the dialog box of Figure 1.6g. Click the **OK command button** to print the document.
- Click the **Print button** on the Standard toolbar to print the document immediately without displaying the Print dialog box.

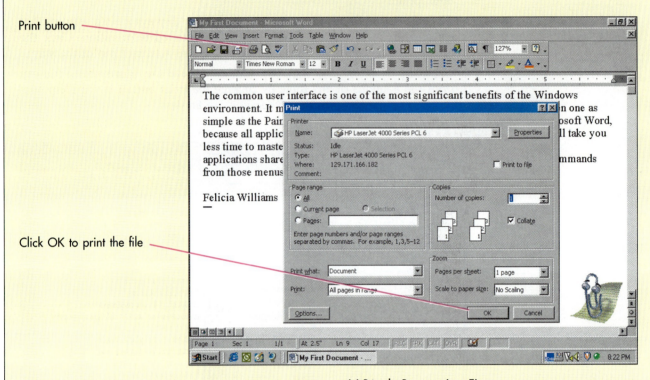

(g) Print the Document (step 7)

FIGURE 1.6   Hands-on Exercise 1 (continued)

ABOUT MICROSOFT WORD

Pull down the Help menu and click About Microsoft Word to display the specific release number and other licensing information, including the product ID. This help screen also contains two very useful command buttons, System Information and Technical Support. The first button displays information about the hardware installed on your system, including the amount of memory and available space on the hard drive. The Technical Support button provides telephone numbers for technical assistance.

STEP 8: Close the Document

➤ Pull down the **File menu.** Click **Close** to close this document but remain in Word. If you don't see the Close command, click the double arrow at the bottom of the menu. Click **Yes** if prompted to save the document.

➤ Pull down the **File menu** a second time. Click **Exit** to close Word if you do not want to continue with the next exercise at this time.

TROUBLESHOOTING

We trust that you completed the hands-on exercise without difficulty, and that you were able to create, save, and print the document in the exercise. There is, however, considerable flexibility in the way you do the exercise in that you can display different toolbars and menus, and/or execute commands in a variety of ways. This section describes various ways in which you can customize Microsoft Word, and in so doing, will help you to troubleshoot future exercises.

Figure 1.7 displays two different views of the same document. Your screen may not match either figure, and indeed, there is no requirement that it should. You should, however, be aware of different options so that you can develop preferences of your own. Consider:

- Figure 1.7a uses the default settings of short menus (note the double arrow at the bottom of the menu to display additional commands) and a shared row for the Standard and Formatting toolbars. Figure 1.7b displays the full menu and displays the toolbars on separate rows. We prefer the latter settings, which are set through the Customize command in the Tools menu.

- Figure 1.7a shows the Office Assistant (but drags it out of the way) whereas Figure 1.7b hides it. We find the Assistant distracting, and display it only when necessary by pressing the F1 key. You can also use the appropriate option in the Help menu to hide or show the Assistant and/or you can right click the Assistant to hide it.

- Figure 1.7a displays the document in the ***Normal view*** whereas Figure 1.7b uses the ***Print Layout view.*** The Normal view is simpler, but the Print Layout view more closely resembles the printed page as it displays top and bottom margins, headers and footers, graphic elements in their exact position, a vertical ruler, and other elements not seen in the Normal view. We alternate between the two. Note, too, that you can change the magnification in either view to make the text larger or smaller.

- Figure 1.7a displays the ¶ and other nonprinting symbols whereas they are hidden in Figure 1.7b. We prefer the cleaner screen without the symbols, but on occasion display the symbols if there is a problem in formatting a document. The ***Show/Hide ¶ button*** toggles the symbols on or off.

- Figure 1.7b displays an additional toolbar, the Drawing toolbar, at the bottom of the screen. Microsoft Word has more than 20 toolbars that are suppressed or displayed through the Toolbars command in the View menu. Note, too, that you can change the position of any visible toolbar by dragging its move handle (the parallel lines) at the left of the toolbar.

THE MOUSE VERSUS THE KEYBOARD

Almost every command in Office can be executed in different ways, using either the mouse or the keyboard. Most people start with the mouse and add keyboard shortcuts as they become more proficient. There is no right or wrong technique, just different techniques, and the one you choose depends entirely on personal preference in a specific situation. If, for example, your hands are already on the keyboard, it is faster to use the keyboard equivalent. Other times, your hand will be on the mouse and that will be the fastest way.

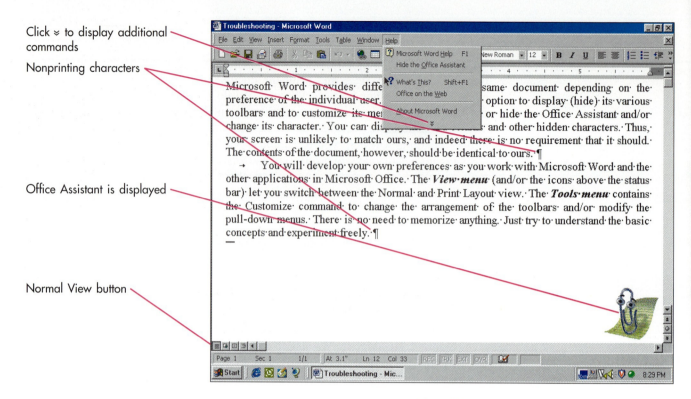

(a) Normal View

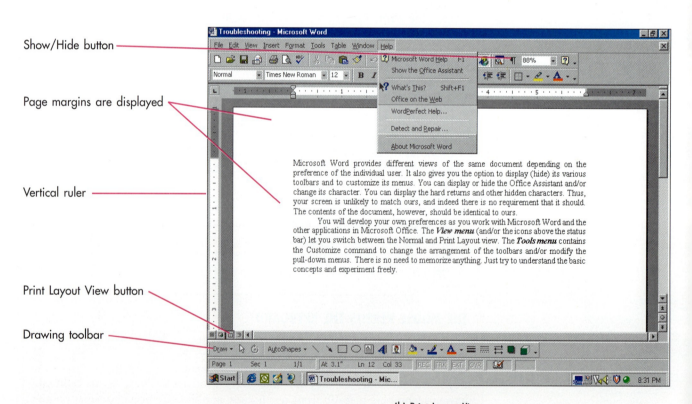

(b) Print Layout View

FIGURE 1.7 Troubleshooting

HANDS-ON EXERCISE 2

Modifying an Existing Document

Objective: To open an existing document, revise it, and save the revision; to use the Undo and Help commands. Use Figure 1.8 as a guide in doing the exercise.

STEP 1: Open an Existing Document

➤ Start Microsoft Word. Click and drag the Assistant out of the way if it appears.

➤ Pull down the **File menu** and click **Open** (or click the **Open button** on the Standard toolbar). You should see a dialog box similar to the one in Figure 1.8a.

➤ To open a file:
- If necessary, click the **drop-down arrow** on the View button and change to the **Details view.** Click and drag the vertical border between columns to increase (or decrease) the size of a column.
- Click the drop-down arrow on the Look In list box.
- Click the appropriate drive; for example, drive C or drive A.
- Double click the **Exploring Word folder** to make it the active folder (the folder from which you will open the document).
- Click the **down arrow** on the vertical scroll bar in the Name list box, then scroll until you can select the **My First Document** from the first exercise. Click the **Open command button** to open the file.

➤ Your document should appear on the screen.

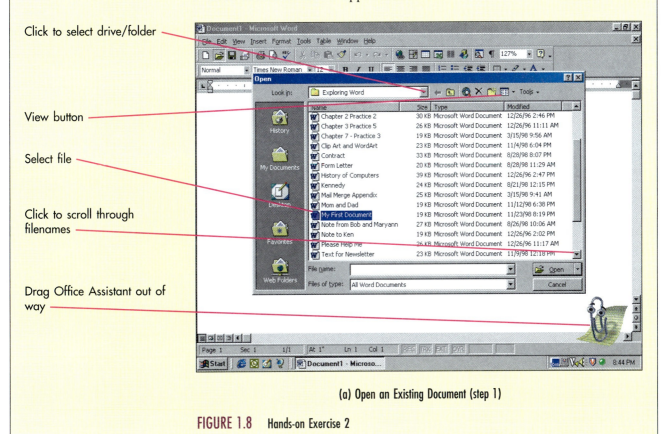

(a) Open an Existing Document (step 1)

FIGURE 1.8 Hands-on Exercise 2

CHAPTER 1: MICROSOFT WORD 2000   19

STEP 2: Troubleshooting

➤ Modify the settings within Word so that the document on your screen matches Figure 1.8b.

- To separate the Standard and Formatting toolbars, pull down the **Tools menu,** click **Customize,** click the **Options tab,** then clear the check box that indicates the Standard and Formatting toolbars should share the same row.

- To display the complete menus, pull down the **Tools menu,** click **Customize,** click the **Options tab,** then clear the **Menus show recently used commands** check box.

- To change to the Normal view, pull down the **View menu** and click **Normal** (or click the **Normal View** button at the bottom of the window).

- To change the amount of text that is visible on the screen, click the drop-down arrow on the **Zoom box** on the Standard toolbar and select **Page Width.**

- To display (hide) the ruler, pull down the **View menu** and toggle the **Ruler command** on or off. End with the ruler on. (If you don't see the Ruler command, click the double arrow at the bottom of the menu, or use the Options command in the Tools menu to display the complete menus.)

➤ Click the **Show/Hide ¶ button** to display or hide the hard returns as you see fit. The button functions as a toggle switch.

➤ There may still be subtle differences between your screen and ours, depending on the resolution of your monitor. These variations, if any, need not concern you as long as you are able to complete the exercise.

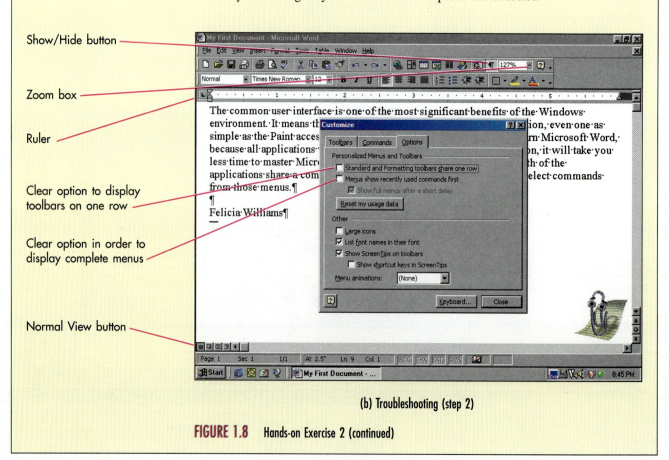

(b) Troubleshooting (step 2)

FIGURE 1.8 Hands-on Exercise 2 (continued)

STEP 3: Modify the Document

➤ Press **Ctrl+End** to move to the end of the document. Press the **up arrow key** once or twice until the insertion point is on a blank line above your name. If necessary, press the **enter key** once (or twice) to add additional blank line(s).

➤ Add the sentence, **Success, I can save and retrieve a document!,** as shown in Figure 1.8c.

➤ Make the following additional modifications to practice editing:
- Change the phrase *most significant* to **very best.**
- Change *Paint accessory* to **game of Solitaire.**
- Change the word *select* to **choose.**

➤ Use the **Ins key** to switch between insert and overtype modes as necessary. (You can also double click the **OVR indicator** on the status bar to toggle between the insert and overtype modes.)

➤ Pull down the **File menu** and click **Save,** or click the **Save button.**

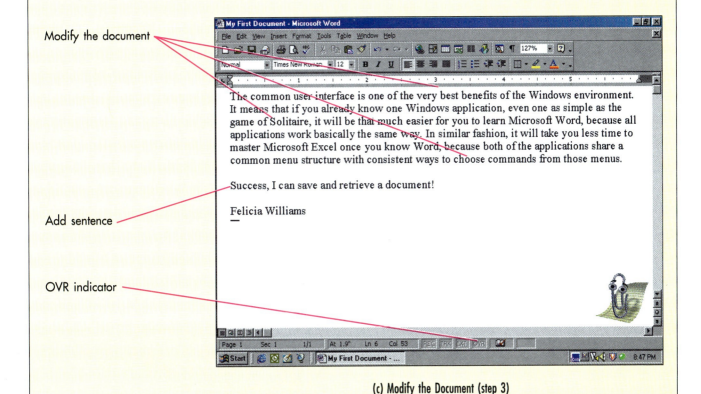

(c) Modify the Document (step 3)

FIGURE 1.8 Hands-on Exercise 2 (continued)

MOVING WITHIN A DOCUMENT

Press Ctrl+Home and Ctrl+End to move to the beginning and end of a document, respectively. You can also press the Home or End key to move to the beginning or end of a line. These shortcuts work not just in Word, but in any Office application, and are worth remembering as they allow your hands to remain on the keyboard as you type.

STEP 4: Deleting Text

➤ Press and hold the left mouse button as you drag the mouse over the phrase, **even one as simple as the game of Solitaire,** as shown in Figure 1.8d.

➤ Press the **Del** key to delete the selected text from the document. Pull down the **Edit menu** and click the **Undo command** (or click the **Undo button** on the Standard toolbar) to reverse (undo) the last command. The deleted text should be returned to your document.

➤ Pull down the **Edit menu** a second time and click the **Redo command** (or click the **Redo button**) to repeat the Delete command.

➤ Click the **Save button** on the Standard toolbar to save the revised document a final time.

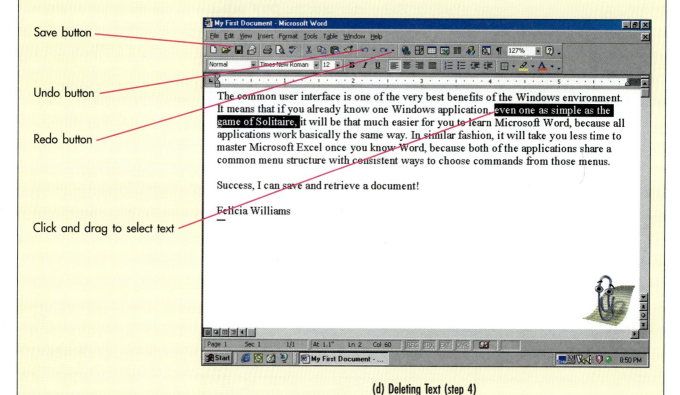

(d) Deleting Text (step 4)

FIGURE 1.8 Hands-on Exercise 2 (continued)

THE UNDO AND REDO COMMANDS

Click the drop-down arrow next to the Undo button to display a list of your previous actions, then click the action you want to undo which also undoes all of the preceding commands. Undoing the fifth command in the list, for example, will also undo the preceding four commands. The Redo command works in reverse and cancels the last Undo command.

STEP 5: The Office Assistant

➤ Click the **Office Assistant** to display the balloon. Enter a question such as **How do I get help,** then click the **Search button.** The Assistant returns a list of topics that it considers potential answers. Click any topic you think is appropriate (we chose **How to get started with Word 2000**) to open the Help window as shown in Figure 1.8e.

➤ Click the link to **printed and online resources that are available.** Read the information, then click the **Print button** in the Help window to print this topic.

➤ Use the **Contents, Answer Wizard,** and/or **Index tabs** to search through the available help. Close the Help window when you have finished.

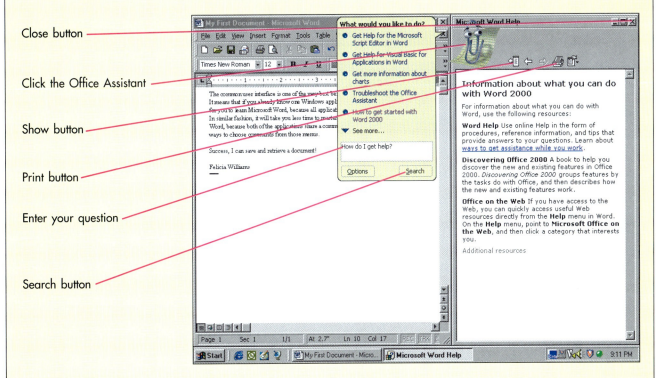

(e) The Office Assistant (step 5)

FIGURE 1.8 Hands-on Exercise 2 (continued)

CHOOSE YOUR OWN ASSISTANT

You can choose your own personal assistant from one of several available candidates. If necessary, press the F1 key to display the Assistant, click the Options button to display the Office Assistant dialog box, then click the Gallery tab where you choose your character. (The Office 2000 CD is required in order to select some of the other characters.) Some assistants are more animated (distracting) than others. The Office logo is the most passive, while Rocky is quite animated. Experiment with the various check boxes on the Options tab to see the effects on the Assistant.

STEP 6: E-mail Your Document

➤ You should check with your professor before attempting this step.

➤ Click the **E-mail button** on the Standard toolbar to display a screen similar to Figure 1.8f. The text of your document is entered automatically into the body of the e-mail message.

➤ Enter your professor's e-mail address in the To text box. The document title is automatically entered in the Subject line. Press the **Tab key** to move to the body of the message. Type a short note above the inserted document to your professor, then click the **Send a Copy button** to mail the message.

➤ The e-mail window closes and you are back in Microsoft Word. The introductory text has been added to the document. Pull down the **File menu.** Click **Close** to close the document (there is no need to save the document).

➤ Pull down the **File menu.** Click **Exit** if you do not want to continue with the next exercise at this time.

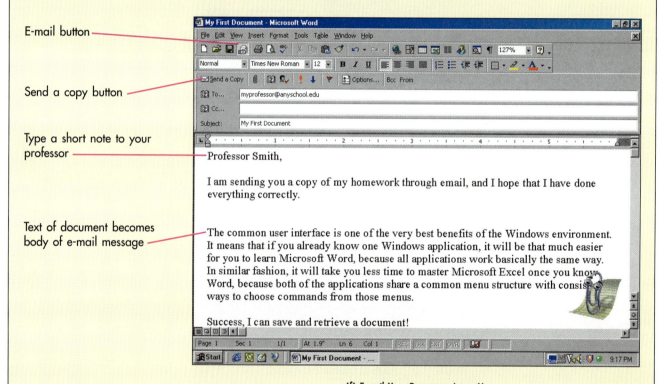

(f) E-mail Your Document (step 6)

FIGURE 1.8 Hands-on Exercise 2 (continued)

DOCUMENT PROPERTIES

Prove to your instructor how hard you've worked by printing various statistics about your document including the number of revisions and the total editing time. Pull down the File menu, click the Print command to display the Print dialog box, click the drop-down arrow in the Print What list box, select Document properties, then click OK. You can view the information (without printing) by pulling down the File menu, clicking the Properties command, then selecting the Statistics tab.

THE SPELL CHECK

There is simply no excuse to misspell a word, since the **spell check** is an integral part of Microsoft Word. (The spell check is also available for every other application in the Microsoft Office.) Spelling errors make your work look sloppy and discourage the reader before he or she has read what you had to say. They can cost you a job, a grade, a lucrative contract, or an award you deserve.

The spell check can be set to automatically check a document as text is entered, or it can be called explicitly by clicking the Spelling and Grammar button on the Standard toolbar. The spell check compares each word in a document to the entries in a built-in dictionary, then flags any word that is in the document, but not in the built-in dictionary, as an error.

The dictionary included with Microsoft Office is limited to standard English and does not include many proper names, acronyms, abbreviations, or specialized terms, and hence, the use of any such item is considered a misspelling. You can, however, add such words to a **custom dictionary** so that they will not be flagged in the future. The spell check will inform you of repeated words and irregular capitalization. It cannot, however, flag properly spelled words that are used improperly, and thus cannot tell you that *Two bee or knot too be* is not the answer.

The capabilities of the spell check are illustrated in conjunction with Figure 1.9a. Microsoft Word will indicate the errors as you type by underlining them in red. Alternatively, you can click the Spelling and Grammar button on the Standard toolbar at any time to move through the entire document. The spell check will then go through the document and return the errors one at a time, offering several options for each mistake. You can change the misspelled word to one of the alternatives suggested by Word, leave the word as is, or add the word to a custom dictionary.

The first error is the word *embarassing*, with Word's suggestion(s) for correction displayed in the list box in Figure 1.9b. To accept the highlighted suggestion, click the Change command button and the substitution will be made automatically in the document. To accept an alternative suggestion, click the desired word, then click the Change command button. Alternatively, you can click the AutoCorrect button to correct the mistake in the current document, and, in addition, automatically correct the same mistake in any future document.

The spell check detects both irregular capitalization and duplicated words, as shown in Figures 1.9c and 1.9d, respectively. The last error, *Grauer*, is not a misspelling per se, but a proper noun not found in the standard dictionary. No correction is required and the appropriate action is to ignore the word (taking no further action)—or better yet, add it to the custom dictionary so that it will not be flagged in future sessions.

A spell check will catch embarassing mistakes, iRregular capitalization, and duplicate words words. It will also flag proper nouns, for example Robert Grauer, but you can add these terms to a custom dictionary. It will not notice properly spelled words that are used incorrectly; for example, too bee or knot to be are not the answer.

(a) The Text

FIGURE 1.9   The Spell Check

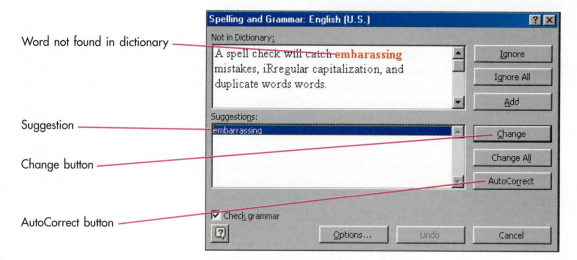

(b) Ordinary Misspelling

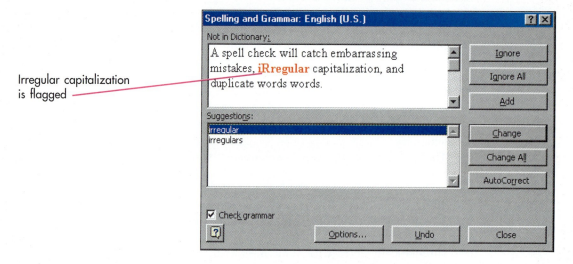

(c) Irregular Capitalization

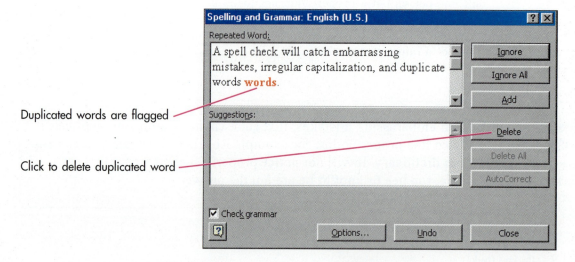

(d) Duplicated Word

FIGURE 1.9 The Spell Check (continued)

AutoCorrect and AutoText

The ***AutoCorrect*** feature corrects mistakes as they are made without any effort on your part. It makes you a better typist. If, for example, you typed *teh* instead of *the*, Word would change the spelling without even telling you. Word will also change *adn* to *and, i* to *I,* and occu*r*ence to occu*rr*ence. All of this is accomplished through a predefined table of common mistakes that Word uses to make substitutions whenever it encounters an entry in the table. You can add additional items to the table to include the frequent errors you make. You can also use the feature to define your own shorthand—for example, cis for Computer Information Systems as shown in Figure 1.10a.

The AutoCorrect feature will also correct mistakes in capitalization; for example, it will capitalize the first letter in a sentence, recognize that MIami should be Miami, and capitalize the days of the week. It's even smart enough to correct the accidental use of the Caps Lock key, and it will toggle the key off!

The ***AutoText*** feature is similar in concept to AutoCorrect in that both substitute a predefined item for a specific character string. The difference is that the substitution occurs automatically with the AutoCorrect entry, whereas you have to take deliberate action for the AutoText substitution to take place. AutoText entries can also include significantly more text, formatting, and even clip art.

Microsoft Word includes a host of predefined AutoText entries. And as with the AutoCorrect feature, you can define additional entries of your own. (You may, however, not be able to do this in a computer lab environment.) The entry in Figure 1.10b is named "signature" and once created, it is available to all Word documents. To insert an AutoText entry into a new document, just type the first several letters in the AutoText name (signature in our example), then press the enter key when Word displays a ScreenTip containing the text of the entry.

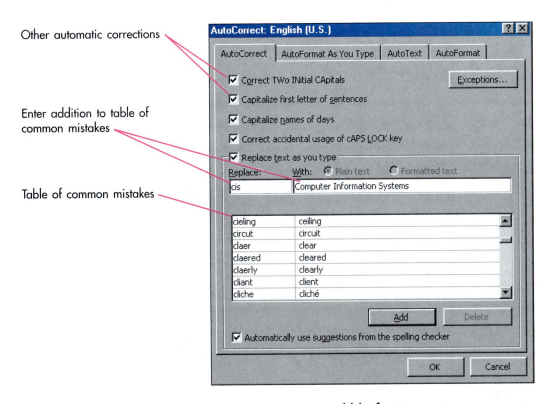

(a) AutoCorrect

FIGURE 1.10 AutoCorrect and AutoText

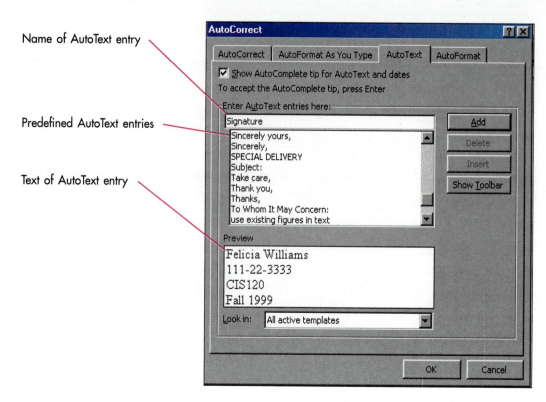

(b) AutoText

FIGURE 1.10 AutoCorrect and AutoText (continued)

THESAURUS

The *thesaurus* helps you to avoid repetition and polish your writing. The thesaurus is called from the Language command in the Tools menu. You position the cursor at the appropriate word within the document, then invoke the thesaurus and follow your instincts. The thesaurus recognizes multiple meanings and forms of a word (for example, adjective, noun, and verb) as in Figure 1.11a. Click a meaning, then double click a synonym to produce additional choices as in Figure 1.11b. You can explore further alternatives by selecting a synonym or antonym and clicking the Look Up button. We show antonyms in Figure 1.11c.

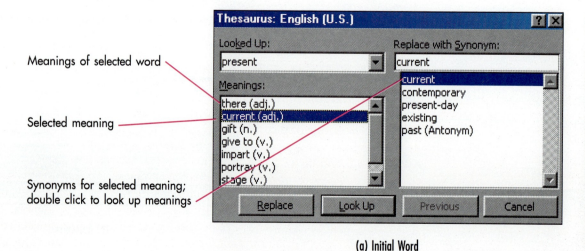

(a) Initial Word

FIGURE 1.11 The Thesaurus

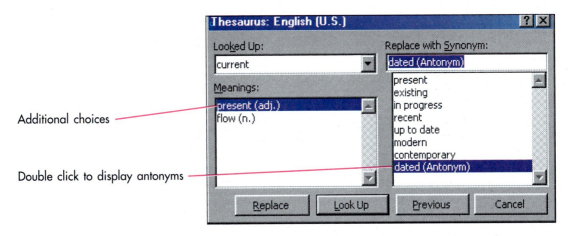

(b) Additional Choices

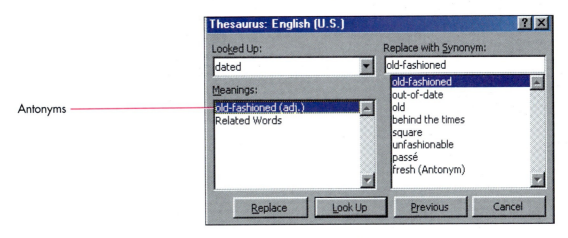

(c) Antonyms

FIGURE 1.11 The Thesaurus (continued)

GRAMMAR CHECK

The *grammar check* attempts to catch mistakes in punctuation, writing style, and word usage by comparing strings of text within a document to a series of predefined rules. As with the spell check, errors are brought to the screen where you can accept the suggested correction and make the replacement automatically, or more often, edit the selected text and make your own changes.

You can also ask the grammar check to explain the rule it is attempting to enforce. Unlike the spell check, the grammar check is subjective, and what seems appropriate to you may be objectionable to someone else. Indeed, the grammar check is quite flexible, and can be set to check for different writing styles; that is, you can implement one set of rules to check a business letter and a different set of rules for casual writing. Many times, however, you will find that the English language is just too complex for the grammar check to detect every error, although it will find many errors.

The grammar check caught the inconsistency between subject and verb in Figure 1.12a and suggested the appropriate correction (am instead of are). In Figure 1.12b, it suggested the elimination of the superfluous comma. These examples show the grammar check at its best, but it is often more subjective and less capable. It detected the error in Figure 1.12c, for example, but suggested an inappropriate correction, "to complicate" as opposed to "too complicated". Suffice it to say, that there is no substitute for carefully proofreading every document.

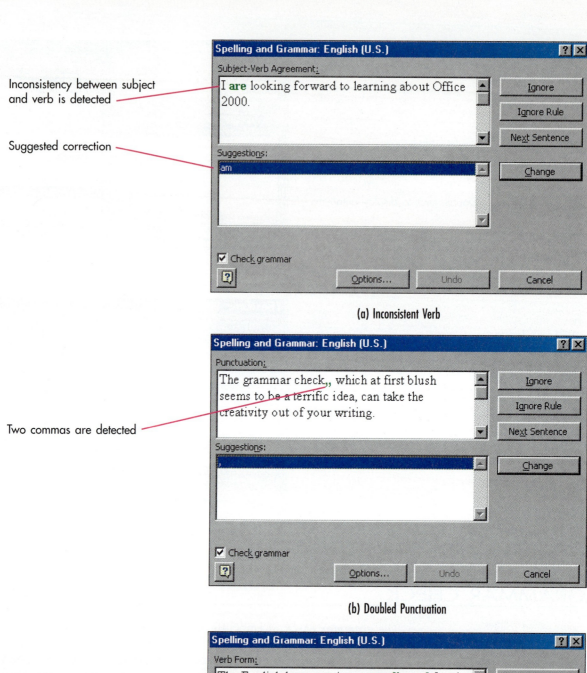

(a) Inconsistent Verb

(b) Doubled Punctuation

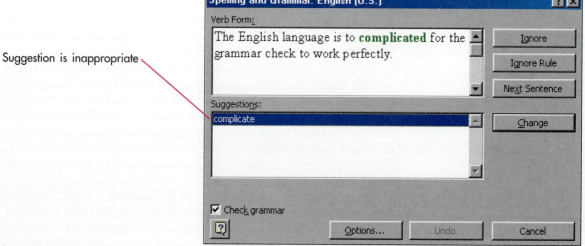

(c) Limitation

FIGURE 1.12 The Grammar Check

SAVE COMMAND

The Save command was used in the first two exercises. The Save As command will be introduced in the next exercise as a very useful alternative. We also introduce you to different backup options. We believe that now, when you are first starting to learn about word processing, is the time to develop good working habits.

You already know that the Save command copies the document currently being edited (the document in memory) to disk. The initial execution of the command requires you to assign a file name and to specify the drive and folder in which the file is to be stored. All subsequent executions of the Save command save the document under the original name, replacing the previously saved version with the new one.

The **Save As command** saves another copy of a document under a different name (and/or a different file type), and is useful when you want to retain a copy of the original document. The Save As command provides you with two copies of a document. The original document is kept on disk under its original name. A copy of the document is saved on disk under a new name and remains in memory. All subsequent editing is done on the new document.

We cannot overemphasize the importance of periodically saving a document, so that if something does go wrong, you won't lose all of your work. Nothing is more frustrating than to lose two hours of effort, due to an unexpected program crash or to a temporary loss of power. Save your work frequently, at least once every 15 minutes. Pull down the File menu and click Save, or click the Save button on the Standard toolbar. Do it!

> **QUIT WITHOUT SAVING**
>
> There will be times when you do not want to save the changes to a document, such as when you have edited it beyond recognition and wish you had never started. Pull down the File menu and click the Close command, then click No in response to the message asking whether you want to save the changes to the document. Pull down the File menu and reopen the file (it should be the first file in the list of most recently edited documents), then start over from the beginning.

Backup Options

Microsoft Word offers several different **backup** options. We believe the two most important options are to create a backup copy in conjunction with every save command, and to periodically (and automatically) save a document. Both options are implemented in step 3 in the next hands-on exercise.

Figure 1.13 illustrates the option to create a backup copy of the document every time a Save command is executed. Assume, for example, that you have created the simple document, *The fox jumped over the fence* and saved it under the name "Fox". Assume further that you edit the document to read, *The quick brown fox jumped over the fence,* and that you saved it a second time. The second save command changes the name of the original document from "Fox" to "Backup of Fox", then saves the current contents of memory as "Fox". In other words, the disk now contains two versions of the document: the current version "Fox" and the most recent previous version "Backup of Fox".

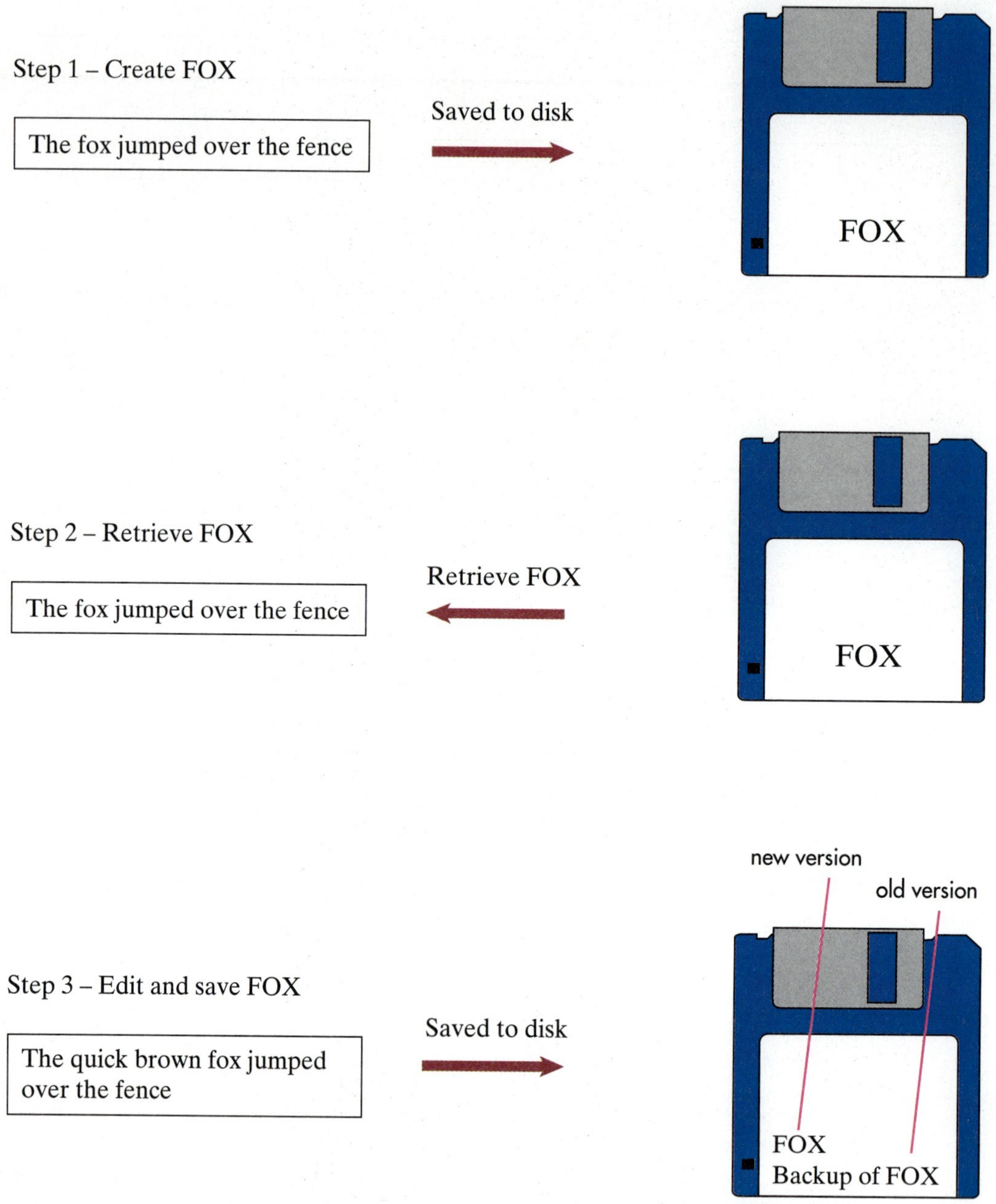

Step 1 – Create FOX

| The fox jumped over the fence |

Saved to disk →

FOX

Step 2 – Retrieve FOX

| The fox jumped over the fence |

← Retrieve FOX

FOX

Step 3 – Edit and save FOX

| The quick brown fox jumped over the fence |

Saved to disk →

new version
old version

FOX
Backup of FOX

FIGURE 1.13 Backup Procedures

The cycle goes on indefinitely, with "Fox" always containing the current version, and "Backup of Fox" the most recent previous version. Thus if you revise and save the document a third time, "Fox" will contain the latest revision while "Backup of Fox" would contain the previous version alluding to the quick brown fox. The original (first) version of the document disappears entirely since only two versions are kept.

The contents of "Fox" and "Backup of Fox" are different, but the existence of the latter enables you to retrieve the previous version if you inadvertently edit beyond repair or accidentally erase the current "Fox" version. Should this occur (and it will), you can always retrieve its predecessor and at least salvage your work prior to the last save operation.

HANDS-ON EXERCISE 3

The Spell Check

Objective: To open an existing document, check it for spelling, then use the Save As command to save the document under a different file name. Use Figure 1.14 as a guide in the exercise.

STEP 1: Preview a Document

➤ Start Microsoft Word. Pull down the **Help menu.** Click the command to **Hide the Office Assistant.**

➤ Pull down the **File menu** and click **Open** (or click the **Open button** on the Standard toolbar). You should see a dialog box similar to the one in Figure 1.14a.

➤ Select the appropriate drive, drive C or drive A, depending on the location of your data. Double click the **Exploring Word folder** to make it the active folder (the folder from which you will open the document).

➤ Scroll in the Name list box until you can select (click) the **Try the Spell Check** document. Click the **drop-down arrow** on the **Views button** and click **Preview** to preview the document as shown in Figure 1.14a.

➤ Click the **Open command button** to open the file. Your document should appear on the screen.

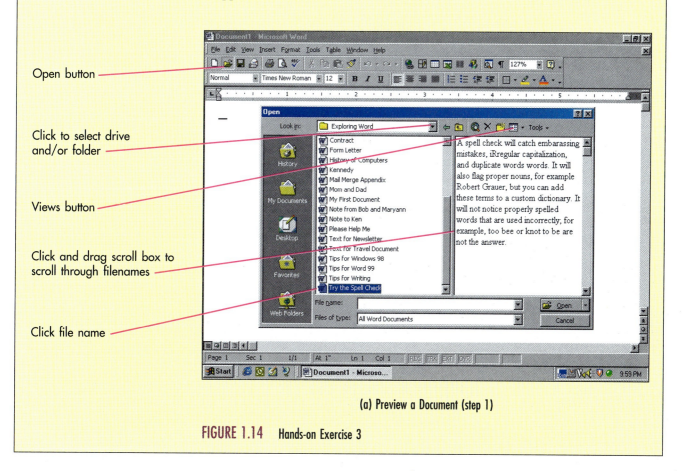

(a) Preview a Document (step 1)

FIGURE 1.14 Hands-on Exercise 3

STEP 2: The Save As Command

➤ Pull down the **File menu.** Click **Save As** to produce the dialog box in Figure 1.14b.

➤ Enter **Modified Spell Check** as the name of the new document. (A file name may contain up to 255 characters, and blanks are permitted.) Click the **Save command button.**

➤ There are now two identical copies of the file on disk: Try the Spell Check, which we supplied, and Modified Spell Check, which you just created. The title bar shows the latter name as it is the document in memory.

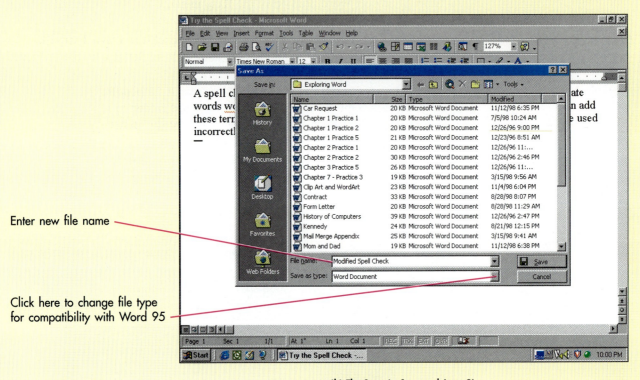

Enter new file name

Click here to change file type for compatibility with Word 95

(b) The Save As Command (step 2)

FIGURE 1.14 Hands-on Exercise 3 (continued)

DIFFERENT FILE TYPES

The file format for Word 2000 is compatible with Word 97, but incompatible with earlier versions such as Word 95. The newer releases can open a document that was created using the older program (Word 95), but the reverse is not true; that is, you cannot open a document that was created in Word 2000 in Word 95 unless you change the file type. Pull down the File menu, click the Save As command, then specify the earlier (Word 6.0/Word 95) file type. You will be able to read the file in Word 95, but will lose any formatting that is unique to the newer release.

STEP 3: Create a Backup Copy

➤ Pull down the **Tools menu.** Click **Options.** Click the **Save tab** to display the dialog box of Figure 1.14c.

➤ Click the first check box to choose **Always create backup copy.**

➤ Set the other options as you see fit; for example, you can specify that the document be saved automatically every 10–15 minutes. Click **OK.**

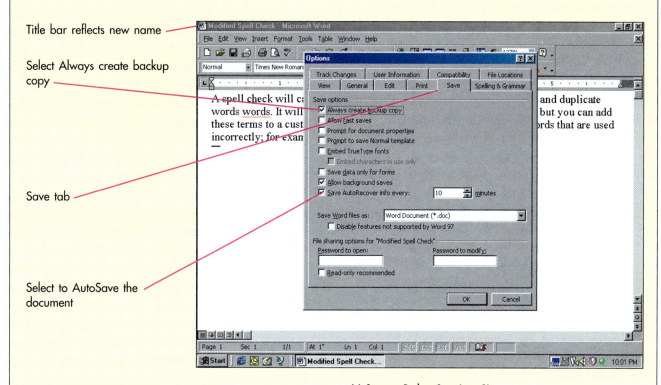

(c) Create a Backup Copy (step 3)

FIGURE 1.14 Hands-on Exercise 3 (continued)

STEP 4: The Spell Check

➤ If necessary, press **Ctrl+Home** to move to the beginning of the document. Click the **Spelling and Grammar button** on the Standard toolbar to check the document.

➤ "Embarassing" is flagged as the first misspelling as shown in Figure 1.14d. Click the **Change button** to accept the suggested spelling.

➤ "iRregular" is flagged as an example of irregular capitalization. Click the **Change button** to accept the suggested correction.

➤ Continue checking the document, which displays misspellings and other irregularities one at a time. Click the appropriate command button as each mistake is found.

- Click the **Delete button** to remove the duplicated word.
- Click the **Ignore button** to accept Grauer (or click the **Add button** to add Grauer to the custom dictionary).

➤ The last sentence is flagged because of a grammatical error and is discussed in the next step.

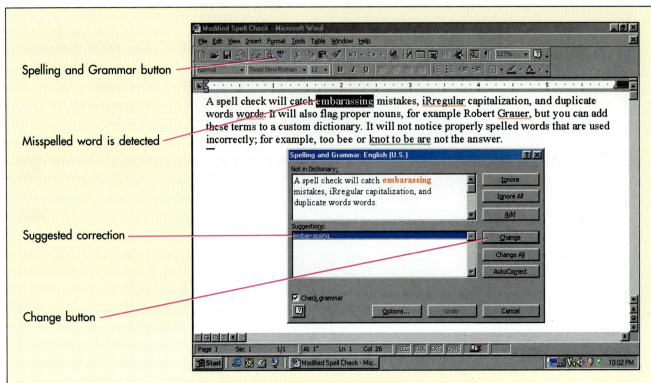

(d) The Spell Check (step 4)

FIGURE 1.14   Hands-on Exercise 3 (continued)

AUTOMATIC SPELLING AND GRAMMAR CHECKING

Red and green wavy lines may appear throughout a document to indicate spelling and grammatical errors, respectively. Point to any underlined word, then click the right mouse button to display a context-sensitive help menu with suggested corrections. To enable (disable) these options, pull down the Tools menu, click the Options command, click the Spelling and Grammar tab, and check (clear) the options to check spelling (or grammar) as you type.

STEP 5: The Grammar Check

➢ The last sentence, "Two bee or knot to be is not the answer", should be flagged as an error, as shown in Figure 1.14e. If this is not the case:

- Pull down the **Tools menu,** click **Options,** then click the **Spelling and Grammar tab.**
- Check the box to **Check Grammar with Spelling,** then click the button to **Recheck document.** Click **Yes** when told that the spelling and grammar check will be reset, then click **OK** to close the Options dialog box.
- Press **Ctrl+Home** to return to the beginning of the document, then click the **Spelling and Grammar button** to recheck the document.

➢ Click the **Office Assistant button** in the Spelling and Grammar dialog box.

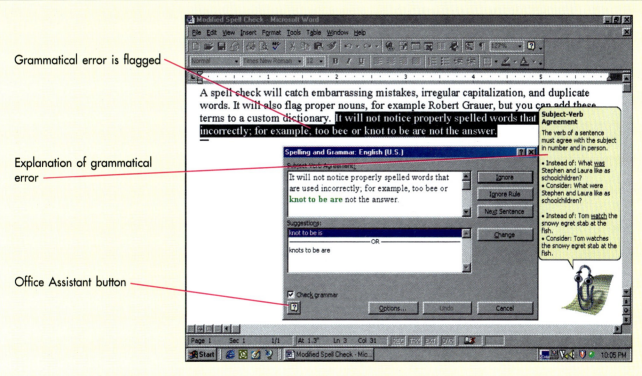

(e) The Grammar Check (step 5)

FIGURE 1.14 Hands-on Exercise 3 (continued)

➤ The Office Assistant will appear, indicating that there needs to be number agreement between subject and verb. Hide the Office Assistant after you have read the explanation.

➤ Click **Ignore** to reject the suggestion. Click **OK** when you see the dialog box, indicating the spelling and grammar check is complete.

CHECK SPELLING ONLY

The grammar check is invoked by default in conjunction with the spell check. You can, however, check the spelling of a document without checking its grammar. Pull down the Tools menu, click Options to display the Options dialog box, then click the Spelling and Grammar tab. Clear the box to check grammar with spelling, then click OK to accept the change and close the dialog box.

STEP 6: The Thesaurus

➤ Select (click) the word *incorrectly,* which appears on the last line of your document as shown in Figure 1.14f.

➤ Pull down the **Tools menu,** click **Language,** then click **Thesaurus** to display synonyms for the word you selected.

➤ Select (click) *inaccurately,* the synonym you will use in place of the original word. Click the **Replace button** to make the change automatically.

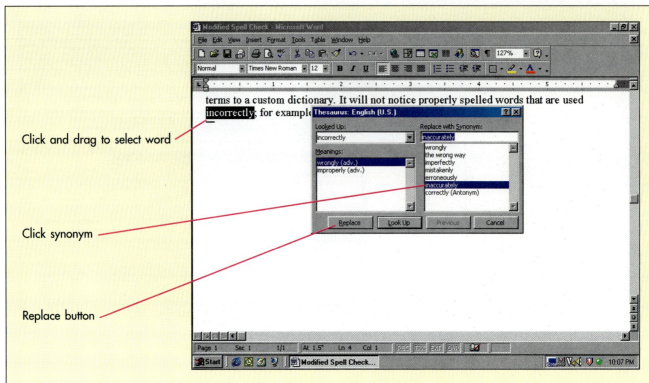

(f) The Thesaurus (step 6)

FIGURE 1.14 Hands-on Exercise 3 (continued)

STEP 7: AutoCorrect

➤ Press **Ctrl+Home** to move to the beginning of the document.

➤ Type the *misspelled* phrase **Teh Spell Check was used to check this document.** Try to look at the monitor as you type to see the AutoCorrect feature in action; Word will correct the misspelling and change *Teh* to *The*.

➤ If you did not see the correction being made, click the arrow next to the Undo command on the Standard toolbar and undo the last several actions. Click the arrow next to the Redo command and redo the corrections.

➤ Pull down the **Tools menu** and click the **AutoCorrect command** to display the AutoCorrect dialog box. If necessary, click the AutoCorrect tab to view the list of predefined corrections.

➤ The first several entries in the list pertain to symbols. Type (c), for example, and you see the © symbol. Type :) or :(and you see a happy and sad face, respectively. Click **Cancel** to close the dialog box.

CREATE YOUR OWN SHORTHAND

Use AutoCorrect to expand abbreviations such as "usa" for United States of America. Pull down the Tools menu, click AutoCorrect, type the abbreviation in the Replace text box and the expanded entry in the With text box. Click the Add command button, then click OK to exit the dialog box and return to the document. The next time you type usa in a document, it will automatically be expanded to United States of America.

STEP 8: Create an AutoText Entry

➤ Press **Ctrl+End** to move to the end of the document. Press the **enter key** twice. Enter your name, social security number, and class.

➤ Click and drag to select the information you just entered. Pull down the **Insert menu,** select the **AutoText command,** then select **AutoText** to display the AutoCorrect dialog box in Figure 1.14g.

➤ Your name (Felicia Williams in our example) is suggested automatically as the name of the AutoText entry. Click the **Add button.**

➤ To test the entry, you can delete your name and other information, then use the AutoText feature. Your name and other information should still be highlighted. Press the **Del key** to delete the information.

➤ Type the first few letters of your name and watch the screen as you do. You should see a ScreenTip containing your name and other information. Press the **enter key** or the **F3 key** when you see the ScreenTip.

➤ Save the document. Print the document for your instructor. Exit Word.

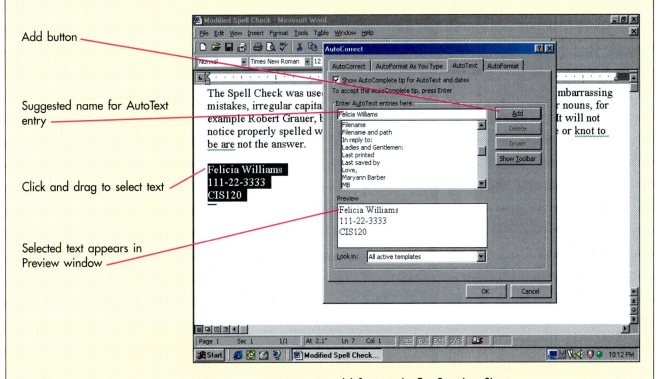

(g) Create an AutoText Entry (step 8)

FIGURE 1.14 Hands-on Exercise 3 (continued)

THE AUTOTEXT TOOLBAR

Point to any visible toolbar, click the right mouse button to display a context-sensitive menu, then click AutoText to display the AutoText toolbar. The AutoText toolbar groups the various AutoText entries into categories, making it easier to select the proper entry. Click the down arrow on the All Entries button to display the various categories, click a category, then select the entry you want to insert into the document.

SUMMARY

The chapter provided a broad-based introduction to word processing in general and to Microsoft Word in particular. Help is available from many sources. You can use the Help menu or the Office Assistant as you can in any Office application. You can also go to the Microsoft Web site to obtain more recent, and often more detailed, information.

Microsoft Word is always in one of two modes, insert or overtype; the choice between the two depends on the desired editing. The insertion point marks the place within a document where text is added or replaced.

The enter key is pressed at the end of a paragraph, but not at the end of a line because Word automatically wraps text from one line to the next. A hard return is created by the user when he or she presses the enter key; a soft return is created by Word as it wraps text and begins a new line.

The Save and Open commands work in conjunction with one another. The Save command copies the document in memory to disk under its existing name. The Open command retrieves a previously saved document. The Save As command saves the document under a different name and is useful when you want to retain a copy of the current document prior to all changes.

A spell check compares the words in a document to those in a standard and/or custom dictionary and offers suggestions to correct the mistakes it finds. It will detect misspellings, duplicated phrases, and/or irregular capitalization, but will not flag properly spelled words that are used incorrectly.

The AutoCorrect feature corrects predefined spelling errors and/or mistakes in capitalization, automatically, as the words are entered. The AutoText feature is similar in concept except that it can contain longer entries that include formatting and clip art. Either feature can be used to create a personal shorthand to expand abbreviations as they are typed.

The thesaurus suggests synonyms and/or antonyms. It can also recognize multiple forms of a word (noun, verb, and adjective) and offer suggestions for each. The grammar check searches for mistakes in punctuation, writing style, and word usage by comparing strings of text within a document to a series of predefined rules.

KEY WORDS AND CONCEPTS

AutoCorrect	Insert mode	Soft return
AutoText	Insertion point	Spell check
Backup	Normal view	Standard toolbar
Close command	Office Assistant	Status bar
Custom dictionary	Open command	Text box
Exit command	Overtype mode	Thesaurus
File menu	Places Bar	Toggle switch
File name	Print command	Toolbar
File type	Print Layout view	Undo command
Formatting toolbar	Save As command	Vertical ruler
Grammar check	Save command	View menu
Hard return	ScreenTip	Word wrap
Horizontal ruler	Show/Hide ¶ button	

MULTIPLE CHOICE

1. When entering text within a document, the enter key is normally pressed at the end of every:
   (a) Line
   (b) Sentence
   (c) Paragraph
   (d) All of the above

2. Which menu contains the commands to save the current document, or to open a previously saved document?
   (a) The Tools menu
   (b) The File menu
   (c) The View menu
   (d) The Edit menu

3. How do you execute the Print command?
   (a) Click the Print button on the standard toolbar
   (b) Pull down the File menu, then click the Print command
   (c) Use the appropriate keyboard shortcut
   (d) All of the above

4. The Open command:
   (a) Brings a document from disk into memory
   (b) Brings a document from disk into memory, then erases the document on disk
   (c) Stores the document in memory on disk
   (d) Stores the document in memory on disk, then erases the document from memory

5. The Save command:
   (a) Brings a document from disk into memory
   (b) Brings a document from disk into memory, then erases the document on disk
   (c) Stores the document in memory on disk
   (d) Stores the document in memory on disk, then erases the document from memory

6. What is the easiest way to change the phrase, *revenues, profits, gross margin*, to read *revenues, profits, and gross margin*?
   (a) Use the insert mode, position the cursor before the *g* in *gross*, then type the word *and* followed by a space
   (b) Use the insert mode, position the cursor after the *g* in *gross*, then type the word *and* followed by a space
   (c) Use the overtype mode, position the cursor before the *g* in *gross*, then type the word *and* followed by a space
   (d) Use the overtype mode, position the cursor after the *g* in *gross*, then type the word *and* followed by a space

7. A document has been entered into Word with a given set of margins, which are subsequently changed. What can you say about the number of hard and soft returns before and after the change in margins?
   (a) The number of hard returns is the same, but the number and/or position of the soft returns is different
   (b) The number of soft returns is the same, but the number and/or position of the hard returns is different
   (c) The number and position of both hard and soft returns is unchanged
   (d) The number and position of both hard and soft returns is different

8. Which of the following will be detected by the spell check?
   (a) Duplicate words
   (b) Irregular capitalization
   (c) Both (a) and (b)
   (d) Neither (a) nor (b)

9. Which of the following is likely to be found in a custom dictionary?
   (a) Proper names
   (b) Words related to the user's particular application
   (c) Acronyms created by the user for his or her application
   (d) All of the above

10. Ted and Sally both use Word but on different computers. Both have written a letter to Dr. Joel Stutz and have run a spell check on their respective documents. Ted's program flags *Stutz* as a misspelling, whereas Sally's accepts it as written. Why?
    (a) The situation is impossible; that is, if they use identical word processing programs they should get identical results
    (b) Ted has added *Stutz* to his custom dictionary
    (c) Sally has added *Stutz* to her custom dictionary
    (d) All of the above reasons are equally likely as a cause of the problem

11. The spell check will do all of the following *except:*
    (a) Flag properly spelled words used incorrectly
    (b) Identify misspelled words
    (c) Accept (as correctly spelled) words found in the custom dictionary
    (d) Suggest alternatives to misspellings it identifies

12. The AutoCorrect feature will:
    (a) Correct errors in capitalization as they occur during typing
    (b) Expand user-defined abbreviations as the entries are typed
    (c) Both (a) and (b)
    (d) Neither (a) nor (b)

13. When does the Save As dialog box appear?
    (a) The first time a file is saved using either the Save or Save As commands
    (b) Every time a file is saved by clicking the Save button on the Standard toolbar
    (c) Both (a) and (b)
    (d) Neither (a) nor (b)

14. Which of the following is true about the thesaurus?
    (a) It recognizes different forms of a word; for example, a noun and a verb
    (b) It provides antonyms as well as synonyms
    (c) Both (a) and (b)
    (d) Neither (a) nor (b)

15. The grammar check:
    (a) Implements different rules for casual and business writing
    (b) Will detect all subtleties in the English language
    (c) Is always run in conjunction with a spell check
    (d) All of the above

ANSWERS

1. c	**6.** a	**11.** a
2. b	**7.** a	**12.** c
3. d	**8.** c	**13.** a
4. a	**9.** d	**14.** c
5. c	**10.** c	**15.** a

PRACTICE WITH MICROSOFT WORD

1. Retrieve the *Chapter1 Practice 1* document shown in Figure 1.15 from the Exploring Word folder, then make the following changes:
   a. Select the text *Your name* and replace it with your name.
   b. Replace *May 31, 1999* with the current date.
   c. Insert the phrase *one or* in line 2 so that the text reads *... one or more characters than currently exist.*
   d. Delete the word *And* from sentence four in line 5, then change the w in *when* to a capital letter to begin the sentence.
   e. Change the phrase *most efficient* to *best*.
   f. Place the insertion point at the end of sentence 2, make sure you are in the insert mode, then add the following sentence: *The insert mode adds characters at the insertion point while moving existing text to the right in order to make room for the new text.*
   g. Place the insertion point at the end of the last sentence, press the enter key twice in a row, then enter the following text: *There are several keys that function as toggle switches of which you should be aware. The Caps Lock key toggles between upper- and lowercase letters, and the Num Lock key alternates between typing numbers and using the arrow keys.*
   h. Save the revised document, then print it and submit it to your instructor.

2. Select-Then-Do: Formatting is not covered until Chapter 2, but we think you are ready to try your hand at basic formatting now. Most formatting operations are done in the context of select-then-do as described in the document in Figure 1.16. You select the text you want to format, then you execute the appropriate formatting command, most easily by clicking the appropriate button on the Formatting toolbar. The function of each button should be apparent from its icon, but you can simply point to a button to display a ScreenTip that is indicative of the button's function.

> To: Your name
>
> From: Robert Grauer and Maryann Barber
>
> Subject: Microsoft® Word 2000
>
> Date: May 31, 1999
>
> This is just a short note to help you get acquainted with the insertion and replacement modes in Word for Windows. When the editing to be done results in more characters than currently exist, you want to be in the insertion mode when making the change. On the other hand, when the editing to be done contains the same or fewer characters, the replacement mode is best. And when replacing characters, it is most efficient to use the mouse to select the characters to be deleted and then just type the new characters; the selected characters are automatically deleted and the new characters typed take their place.

FIGURE 1.15   Editing Text (Exercise 1)

An unformatted version of the document in Figure 1.16 exists on the data disk as *Chapter1 Practice 2*. Open the document, then format it to match the completed version in Figure 1.16. Just select the text to format, then click the appropriate button. We changed type size in the original document to 24 points for the title and 12 points for text in the document itself. Be sure to add your name and date as shown in the figure, then submit the completed document to your instructor.

3. **Your Background:** Write a short description of your computer background similar to the document in Figure 1.17. The document should be in the form of a note from student to instructor that describes your background and should mention any previous knowledge of computers you have, prior computer courses you have taken, your objectives for this course, and so on. Indicate whether you own a PC, whether you have access to one at work, and/or whether you are considering purchase. Include any other information about yourself and/or your computer-related background.

   Place your name somewhere in the document in boldface italics. We would also like you to use boldface and italics to emphasize the components of any computer system you describe. Use any font or point size you like.

   Note, too, the last paragraph, which asks you to print the summary statistics for the document when you submit the assignment to your instructor. (Use the tip on Document Properties on page 25 to print the total editing time and other information about your document.)

4. **The Cover Page:** Create a cover page that you can use for your assignments this semester. Your cover page should be similar to the one in Figure 1.18 with respect to content and should include the title of the assignment, your name, course information, and date. The formatting is up to you. Print the completed cover page and submit it to your instructor for inclusion in a class contest to judge the most innovative design.

Select-Then-Do

Many operations in Word are executed as select-then-do operations. You first select a block of text, and then you issue a command that will affect the selected text. You may select the text in many different ways, the most basic of which is to click and drag over the desired characters. You may also take one of many shortcuts, which include double clicking on a word, pressing Ctrl as you click a sentence, and triple clicking on a paragraph.

Once text is selected, you may then delete it, **boldface** or *italicize* it, or even change its color. You may move it or copy it to another location in the same or a different document. You can highlight it, underline, or even check its spelling. Then, depending on whether or not you like what you have done, you may undo it, redo it, and/or repeat it on subsequently selected text.

Jessica Kinzer
March 1, 1999

FIGURE 1.16   Select-Then-Do (Exercise 2)

The Computer and Me

My name is Jessica Kinzer and I am a complete novice when it comes to computers. I did not take a computer course in high school and this is my first semester at the University of Miami. My family does not own a computer, nor have I had the opportunity to use one at work. So when it comes to beginners, I am a beginner's beginner. I am looking forward to taking this course, as I have heard that it will truly make me computer literate. I know that I desperately need computer skills not only when I enter the job market, to but to survive my four years here as well. I am looking forward to learning Word, Excel, and PowerPoint and I hope that I can pick up some Internet skills as well.

I did not buy a computer before I came to school as I wanted to see what type of system I would be using for my classes. After my first few weeks in class, I think that I would like to buy a 400 **MZ Pentium II** machine with **64MB RAM** and a **10 GB hard drive**. I would like a **DVD CD-ROM** and a **sound card** (with **speakers**, of course). I also would like to get a high-speed **modem** and a **laser printer**. Now, if only I had the money.

This document did not take long at all to create as you can see by the summary statistics that are printed on the next page. I think that I will really enjoy this class.

Jessica Kinzer
March 2, 1999

FIGURE 1.17   Your Computer Background (Exercise 3)

Exploring Word Assignment

Jessica Kinzer
CIS 120
March 2, 1999

FIGURE 1.18 The Cover Page (Exercise 4)

5. Proofing a Document: Figure 1.19 contains the draft version of the *Chapter 1 Practice 5* document contained on the data disk.
   a. Proofread the document and circle any mistakes in spelling, grammar, capitalization, or punctuation.
   b. Open the document in Word and run the spell check. Did Word catch any mistakes you missed? Did you find any errors that were missed by the program?
   c. Use the thesaurus to come up with alternative words for *document,* which appears entirely too often within the paragraph.
   d. Run the grammar check on the revised document. Did the program catch any grammatical errors you missed? Did you find any mistakes that were missed by the program?
   e. Add a short paragraph with your opinion of the spelling and grammar check.
   f. Add your name to the revised document, save it, print it, and submit the completed document to your instructor.

6. Webster Online: Figure 1.20 shows our favorite online dictionary. We have erased the address, however, or else the problem would be too easy. Thus, you have to search the Web to look for our dictionary or its equivalent. Once you locate a dictionary, enter the word you want to look up (*oxymoron,* for example), then press the Look Up Word button to display the definition in Figure 1.21. This is truly an interactive dictionary because most words in it are created as hyperlinks, which in turn will lead you to other definitions. Use the dictionary to look up the meaning of the word *palindrome.* How many examples of oxymorons and palindromes can you think of?

The Grammar Check

All documents should be thoroughly proofed before they be printed and distributed. This means that documents, at a minimum should be spell cheked, grammar cheked,, and proof read by the author. A documents that has spelling errors and/or grammatical errors makes the Author look unprofessional and illiterate and their is nothing worse than allowing a first impression too be won that makes you appear slopy and disinterested, and a document full or of misteakes will do exactly that. Alot of people do not realize how damaging a bad first impression could be, and documents full of misteakes has cost people opportunities that they trained and prepared many years for.

Microsoft Word includes an automated grammar check that will detect many, but certainly not all, errors as the previous paragraph demonstrates. Unlike the spell check, the grammar check is subjective, and what seems appropriate to you may be objectionable to someone else. The English language is just to complicated for the grammar check to detect every error, or even most errors. Hence, there is no substitute for carefully proof reading a document your self. Hence there is no substitute for carefully proof reading a document your self.

FIGURE 1.19   Proofing a Document (Exercise 5)

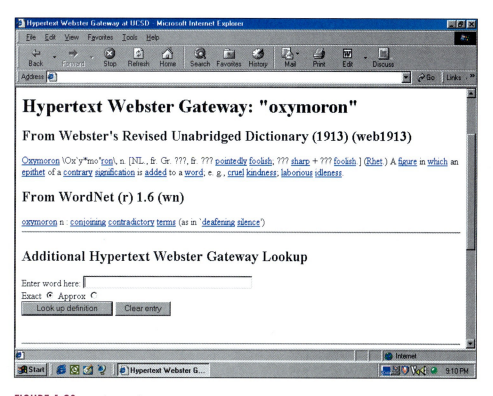

FIGURE 1.20   Webster Online (Exercise 6)

CASE STUDIES

Companion Web Sites

A Companion Web site (or online study guide) accompanies each book in the *Exploring Microsoft Office 2000* series. Go to the Exploring Windows home page at www.prenhall.com/grauer, click the book to Office 2000, and click the Companion Web site tab at the top of the screen. Choose the appropriate text (Exploring Word 2000) and the chapter within the text (e.g., Chapter 1).

Each chapter contains a series of short-answer exercises (multiple-choice, true/false, and matching) to review the material in the chapter. You can take practice quizzes by yourself and/or e-mail the results to your instructor. You can try the essay questions for additional practice and engage in online chat sessions. We hope you will find the online guide to be a valuable resource.

It's a Mess

Newcomers to word processing quickly learn the concept of word wrap and the distinction between hard and soft returns. This lesson was lost, however, on your friend who created the *Please Help Me* document on the data disk. The first several sentences were entered without any hard returns at all, whereas the opposite problem exists toward the end of the document. This is a good friend, and her paper is due in one hour. Please help.

Planning for Disaster

Do you have a backup strategy? Do you even know what a backup strategy is? You should learn, because sooner or later you will wish you had one. You will erase a file, be unable to read from a floppy disk, or worse yet suffer a hardware failure in which you are unable to access the hard drive. The problem always seems to occur the night before an assignment is due. The ultimate disaster is the disappearance of your computer, by theft or natural disaster (e.g., Hurricane Andrew). Describe in 250 words or less the backup strategy you plan to implement in conjunction with your work in this class.

A Letter Home

You really like this course and want very much to have your own computer, but you're strapped for cash and have decided to ask your parents for help. Write a one-page letter describing the advantages of having your own system and how it will help you in school. Tell your parents what the system will cost, and that you can save money by buying through the mail. Describe the configuration you intend to buy (don't forget to include the price of software) and then provide prices from at least three different companies. Cut out the advertisements and include them in your letter. Bring your material to class and compare your research with that of your classmates.

Computer Magazines

A subscription to a computer magazine should be given serious consideration if you intend to stay abreast in a rapidly changing field. The reviews on new products are especially helpful and you will appreciate the advertisements should you need to buy. Go to the library or a newsstand and obtain a magazine that appeals to you, then write a brief review of the magazine for class. Devote at least one paragraph to an article or other item you found useful.

A Junior Year Abroad

How lucky can you get? You are spending the second half of your junior year in Paris. The problem is you will have to submit your work in French, and the English version of Microsoft Word won't do. Is there a foreign-language version available? What about the dictionary and thesaurus? How do you enter the accented characters, which occur so frequently? You are leaving in two months, so you'd better get busy. What are your options? *Bon voyage!*

The Writer's Reference

The chapter discussed the use of a spell check, thesaurus, and grammar check, but many other resources are available. The Web contains a host of sites with additional resources that are invaluable to the writer. You can find Shakespeare online, as well as Bartlett's quotations. You can also find Webster's dictionary as well as a dictionary of acronyms. One way to find these resources is to click the Search button in Internet Explorer, then scroll down the page to the Writer's Reference section. You can also go to the address directly (home.microsoft.com/access.allinone.asp). Explore one or more of these resources, then write a short note to your instructor to summarize your findings.

Microsoft Online

Help for Microsoft Word is available from a variety of sources. You can consult the Office Assistant, or you can pull down the Help menu to display the Help Contents and Index. Both techniques were illustrated in the chapter. In addition, you can go to the Microsoft Web site to obtain more recent, and often more detailed, information. You will find the answers to the most frequently asked questions and you can access the same knowledge base used by Microsoft support engineers. Experiment with various sources of help, then submit a summary of your findings to your instructor. Try to differentiate among the various techniques and suggest the most appropriate use for each.

Changing Menus and Toolbars

Office 2000 implements one very significant change over previous versions of Office in that it displays a series of short menus that contain only basic commands. The additional commands are made visible by clicking the double arrow that appears at the bottom of the menu. New commands are added to the menu as they are used, and conversely, other commands are removed if they are not used. A similar strategy is followed for the Standard and Formatting toolbars that are displayed on a single row, and thus do not show all of the buttons at one time. The intent is to simplify Office 2000 for the new user by limiting the number of commands that are visible. The consequence, however, is that the individual is not exposed to new commands, and hence may not use Office to its full potential. Which set of menus do you prefer? How do you switch from one set to the other?

chapter 2

GAINING PROFICIENCY: EDITING AND FORMATTING

OBJECTIVES

After reading this chapter you will be able to:

1. Define the select-then-do methodology; describe several shortcuts with the mouse and/or the keyboard to select text.
2. Move and copy text within a document; distinguish between the Windows clipboard and the Office clipboard.
3. Use the Find, Replace, and Go To commands to substitute one character string for another.
4. Define scrolling; scroll to the beginning and end of a document.
5. Distinguish between the Normal and Print Layout views; state how to change the view and/or magnification of a document.
6. Define typography; distinguish between a serif and a sans serif typeface; use the Format Font command to change the font and/or type size.
7. Use the Format Paragraph command to change line spacing, alignment, tabs, and indents, and to control pagination.
8. Use the Borders and Shading command to box and shade text.
9. Describe the Undo and Redo commands and how they are related to one another.
10. Use the Page Setup command to change the margins and/or orientation; differentiate between a soft and a hard page break.
11. Enter and edit text in columns; change the column structure of a document through section formatting.

OVERVIEW

The previous chapter taught you the basics of Microsoft Word and enabled you to create and print a simple document. The present chapter significantly extends your capabilities, by presenting a variety of commands to change the contents and appearance of a document. These operations are known as editing and formatting, respectively.

You will learn how to move and copy text within a document and how to find and replace one character string with another. You will also learn the basics of typography and be able to switch between the different fonts included within Windows. You will be able to change alignment, indentation, line spacing, margins, and page orientation. All of these commands are used in three hands-on exercises, which require your participation at the computer, and which are the very essence of the chapter.

As you read the chapter, realize that there are many different ways to accomplish the same task and that it would be impossible to cover them all. Our approach is to present the overall concepts and suggest the ways we think are most appropriate at the time we introduce the material. We also offer numerous shortcuts in the form of boxed tips that appear throughout the chapter and urge you to explore further on your own. It is not necessary for you to memorize anything as online help is always available. Be flexible and willing to experiment.

WRITE NOW, EDIT LATER

You write a sentence, then change it, and change it again, and one hour later you've produced a single paragraph. It happens to every writer—you stare at a blank screen and flashing cursor and are unable to write. The best solution is to brainstorm and write down anything that pops into your head, and to keep on writing. Don't worry about typos or spelling errors because you can fix them later. Above all, resist the temptation to continually edit the few words you've written because overediting will drain the life out of what you are writing. The important thing is to get your ideas on paper.

SELECT-THEN-DO

Many operations in Word take place within the context of a **select-then-do** methodology; that is, you select a block of text, then you execute the command to operate on that text. The most basic way to select text is by dragging the mouse; that is, click at the beginning of the selection, press and hold the left mouse button as you move to the end of the selection, then release the mouse.

There are, however, a variety of shortcuts to facilitate the process; for example, double click anywhere within a word to select the word, or press the Ctrl key and click the mouse anywhere within a sentence to select the sentence. Additional shortcuts are presented in each of the hands-on exercises, at which point you will have many opportunities to practice selecting text.

Selected text is affected by any subsequent operation; for example, clicking the Bold or Italic button changes the selected text to boldface or italics, respectively. You can also drag the selected text to a new location, press the Del key to erase the selected text, or execute any other editing or formatting command. The text continues to be selected until you click elsewhere in the document.

INSERT THE DATE AND TIME

Most documents include the date and time they were created. Pull down the Insert menu, select the Date and Time command to display the Date and Time dialog box, then choose a format. Check the box to update the date automatically if you want your document to reflect the date on which it is opened or clear the box to retain the date on which the document was created. See exercise seven at the end of the chapter.

MOVING AND COPYING TEXT

The ability to move and/or copy text is essential in order to develop any degree of proficiency in editing. A move operation removes the text from its current location and places it elsewhere in the same (or even a different) document; a copy operation retains the text in its present location and places a duplicate elsewhere. Either operation can be accomplished using the Windows clipboard and a combination of the **Cut, Copy,** and **Paste commands.**

The **Windows clipboard** is a temporary storage area available to any Windows application. Selected text is cut or copied from a document and placed onto the clipboard from where it can be pasted to a new location(s). A move requires that you select the text and execute a Cut command to remove the text from the document and place it on the clipboard. You then move the insertion point to the new location and paste the text from the clipboard into that location. A copy operation necessitates the same steps except that a Copy command is executed rather than a cut, leaving the selected text in its original location as well as placing a copy on the clipboard.

The Cut, Copy, and Paste commands are found in the Edit menu, or alternatively, can be executed by clicking the appropriate buttons on the Standard toolbar. The contents of the Windows clipboard are replaced by each subsequent Cut or Copy command, but are unaffected by the Paste command. The contents of the clipboard can be pasted into multiple locations in the same or different documents.

Office 2000 introduces its own clipboard that enables you to collect and paste multiple items. The **Office clipboard** differs from the Windows clipboard in that the contents of each successive Copy command are added to the clipboard. Thus, you could copy the first paragraph of a document to the Office clipboard, then copy (add) a bulleted list in the middle of the document to the Office clipboard, and finally copy (add) the last paragraph (three items in all) to the Office clipboard. You could then go to another place in the document or to a different document altogether, and paste the contents of the Office clipboard (three separate items) with a single command.

Selected text is copied automatically to the Office clipboard regardless of whether you use the Copy command in the Edit menu, the Copy button on the Standard toolbar, or the Ctrl+C shortcut. You must, however, use the Clipboard toolbar to paste items from the Office clipboard into a document.

UNDO, REDO, AND REPEAT COMMANDS

The **Undo command** was introduced in Chapter 1, but it is repeated here because it is so valuable. The command is executed from the Edit menu or by clicking the Undo button on the Standard toolbar. Word enables you to undo multiple changes to a document. You just click the down arrow next to the Undo button on the Standard toolbar to display a reverse-order list of your previous commands, then you click the command you want to undo, which also undoes all of the preceding commands. Undoing the fifth command in the list, for example, will also undo the preceding four commands.

The **Redo command** redoes (reverses) the last command that was undone. As with the Undo command, the Redo command redoes all of the previous commands prior to the command you select. Redoing the fifth command in the list, for example, will also redo the preceding four commands. The Undo and Redo commands work in conjunction with one another; that is, every time a command is undone it can be redone at a later time. The **Repeat command** does what its name implies and repeats the last action or command. It is executed from the Edit menu.

FIND, REPLACE, AND GO TO COMMANDS

The Find, Replace, and Go To commands share a common dialog box with different tabs for each command as shown in Figure 2.1. The **Find command** locates one or more occurrences of specific text (e.g., a word or phrase). The **Replace command** goes one step further in that it locates the text, and then enables you to optionally replace (one or more occurrences of) that text with different text. The **Go To command** goes directly to a specific place (e.g., a specific page) in the document.

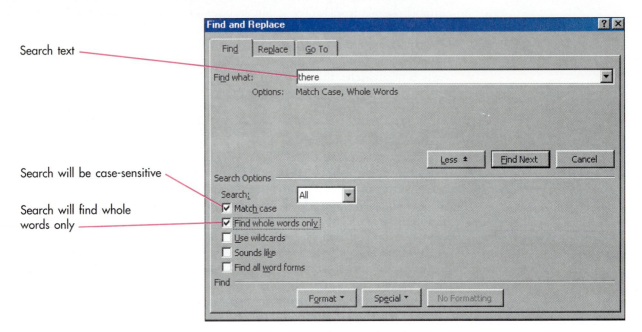

(a) Find Command

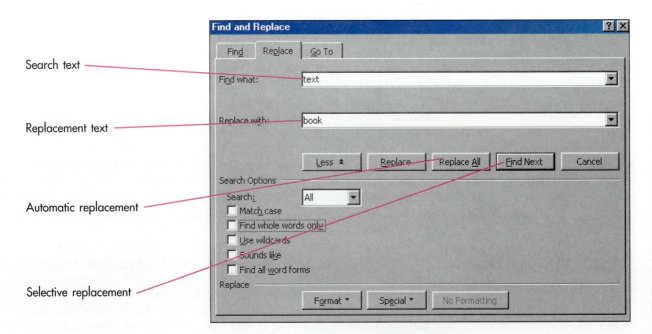

(b) Replace Command

FIGURE 2.1   The Find, Replace, Go To Commands

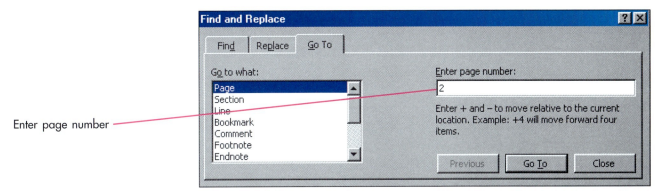

Enter page number

(c) Go To Command

FIGURE 2.1 The Find, Replace, and Go To Commands (continued)

The search in both the Find and Replace commands is case-sensitive or case-insensitive. A *case-sensitive search* (where Match Case is selected as in Figure 2.1a) matches not only the text, but also the use of upper- and lowercase letters. Thus, *There* is different from *there*, and a search on one will not identify the other. A *case-insensitive search* (where Match Case is *not* as selected in Figure 2.1b) is just the opposite and finds both *There* and *there*. A search may also specify **whole words only** to identify *there*, but not *therefore* or *thereby*. And finally, the search and replacement text can also specify different numbers of characters; for example, you could replace *16* with *sixteen*.

The Replace command in Figure 2.1b implements either **selective replacement,** which lets you examine each occurrence of the character string in context and decide whether to replace it, or **automatic replacement,** where the substitution is made automatically. Selective replacement is implemented by clicking the Find Next command button, then clicking (or not clicking) the Replace button to make the substitution. Automatic replacement (through the entire document) is implemented by clicking the Replace All button. This often produces unintended consequences and is not recommended; for example, if you substitute the word *text* for *book*, the phrase *text book* would become *text text,* which is not what you had in mind.

The Find and Replace commands can include formatting and/or special characters. You can, for example, change all italicized text to boldface, or you can change five consecutive spaces to a tab character. You can also use special characters in the character string such as the "any character" (consisting of ^?). For example, to find all four-letter words that begin with "f" and end with "l" (such as *fall, fill,* or *fail*), search for f^?^?l. (The question mark stands for any character, just like a wild card in a card game.) You can also search for all forms of a word; for example, if you specify *am,* it will also find *is* and *are.* You can even search for a word based on how it sounds. When searching for *Marion,* for example, check the Sounds Like check box, and the search will find both *Marion* and *Marian.*

SCROLLING

Scrolling occurs when a document is too large to be seen in its entirety. Figure 2.2a displays a large printed document, only part of which is visible on the screen as illustrated in Figure 2.2b. In order to see a different portion of the document, you need to scroll, whereby new lines will be brought into view as the old lines disappear.

To: Our Students
From: Robert Grauer and Maryann Barber

Welcome to the wonderful world of word processing and desktop publishing. Over the next several chapters we will build a foundation in the basics of Microsoft Word, then teach you to format specialized documents, create professional looking tables and charts, publish well-designed newsletters, and create Web pages. Before you know it, you will be a word processing and desktop publishing wizard!

The first chapter presented the basics of word processing and showed you how to create a simple document. You learned how to insert, replace, and/or delete text. This chapter will teach you about fonts and special effects (such as **boldfacing** and *italicizing*) and how to use them effectively — how too little is better than too much.

You will go on to experiment with margins, tab stops, line spacing, and justification, learning first to format simple documents and then going on to longer, more complex ones. It is with the latter that we explore headers and footers, page numbering, widows and orphans (yes, we really did mean widows and orphans). It is here that we bring in graphics, working with newspaper-type columns, and the elements of a good page design. And without question, we will introduce the tools that make life so much easier (and your writing so much more impressive) — the Spell Check, Grammar Check, Thesaurus, and Styles.

If you are wondering what all these things are, read on in the text and proceed with the hands-on exercises. We will show you how to create a simple newsletter, and then improve it by adding graphics, fonts, and WordArt. You will create a simple calendar using the Tables feature, and then create more intricate forms that will rival anything you have seen. You will learn how to create a résumé with your beginner's skills, and then make it look like so much more with your intermediate (even advanced) skills. You will learn how to download resources from the Internet and how to create your own Web page. Last, but not least, run a mail merge to produce the cover letters that will accompany your resume as it is mailed to companies across the United States (and even the world).

It is up to you to practice for it is only through working at the computer, that you will learn what you need to know. Experiment and don't be afraid to make mistakes. Practice and practice some more.

Our goal is for you to learn and to enjoy what you are learning. We have great confidence in you, and in our ability to help you discover what you can do. Visit the home page for the Exploring Windows series. You can also send us e-mail. Bob's address is rgrauer@sba.miam.edu. Maryann's address is mbarber@sba.miami.edu. As you read the last sentence, notice that Word 2000 is Web-enabled and that the Internet and e-mail references appear as hyperlinks in this document. Thus, you can click the address of our home page from within Word, then view the page immediately, provided you have an Internet connection. You can also click the e-mail address to open your mail program, provided it has been configured correctly.

We look forward to hearing from you and hope that you will like our textbook. You are about to embark on a wonderful journey toward computer literacy. Be patient and inquisitive.

(a) Printed Document

FIGURE 2.2   Scrolling

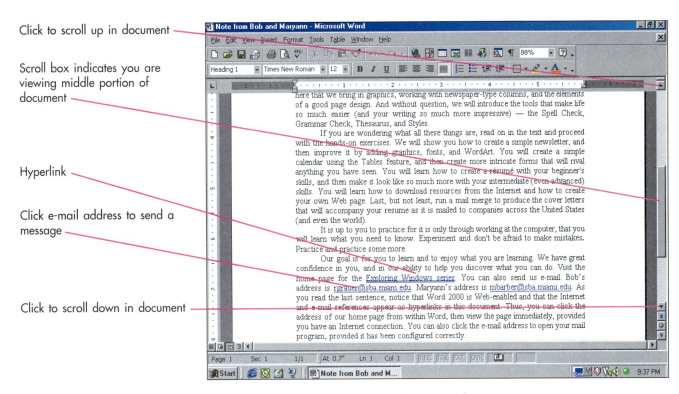

(b) Screen Display

FIGURE 2.2 Scrolling (continued)

Scrolling comes about automatically as you reach the bottom of the screen. Entering a new line of text, clicking on the down arrow within the scroll bar, or pressing the down arrow key brings a new line into view at the bottom of the screen and simultaneously removes a line at the top. (The process is reversed at the top of the screen.)

Scrolling can be done with either the mouse or the keyboard. Scrolling with the mouse (e.g., clicking the down arrow in the scroll bar) changes what is displayed on the screen, but does not move the insertion point, so that you must click the mouse after scrolling prior to entering the text at the new location. Scrolling with the keyboard, however (e.g., pressing Ctrl+Home or Ctrl+End to move to the beginning or end of a document, respectively), changes what is displayed on the screen as well as the location of the insertion point, and you can begin typing immediately.

Scrolling occurs most often in a vertical direction as shown in Figure 2.2. It can also occur horizontally, when the length of a line in a document exceeds the number of characters that can be displayed horizontally on the screen.

IT'S WEB-ENABLED

Every document in Office 2000 is Web-enabled, which means that Internet and e-mail references appear as hyperlinks within a document. Thus you can click the address of any Web page from within Word to display the page, provided you have an Internet connection. You can also click the e-mail address to open your mail program, provided it has been configured correctly.

VIEW MENU

The *View menu* provides different views of a document. Each view can be displayed at different magnifications, which in turn determine the amount of scrolling necessary to see remote parts of a document.

The *Normal view* is the default view and it provides the fastest way to enter text. The *Print Layout* view more closely resembles the printed document and displays the top and bottom margins, headers and footers, page numbers, graphics, and other features that do not appear in the Normal view. The Normal view tends to be faster because Word spends less time formatting the display.

The *Zoom command* displays the document on the screen at different magnifications; for example, 75%, 100%, or 200%. (The Zoom command does not affect the size of the text on the printed page.) A Zoom percentage (magnification) of 100% displays the document in the approximate size of the text on the printed page. You can increase the percentage to 200% to make the characters appear larger. You can also decrease the magnification to 75% to see more of the document at one time.

Word will automatically determine the magnification if you select one of four additional Zoom options—Page Width, Text Width, Whole Page, or Many Pages (Whole Page and Many Pages are available only in the Print Layout view). Figure 2.3a, for example, displays a two-page document in Print Layout view. Figure 2.3b shows the corresponding settings in the Zoom command. (The 37% magnification is determined automatically once you specify the number of pages as shown in the figure.)

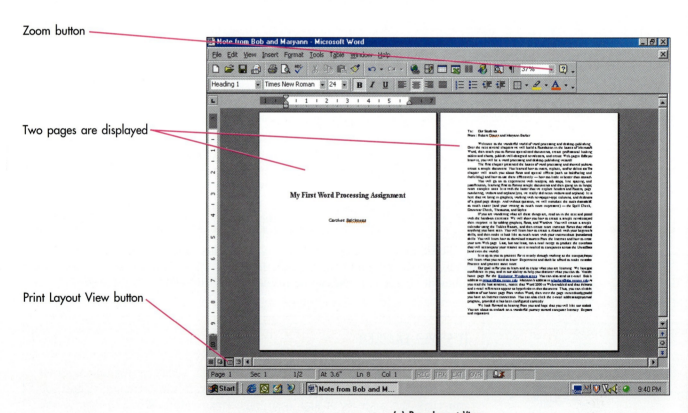

(a) Page Layout View

FIGURE 2.3 View Menu and Zoom Command

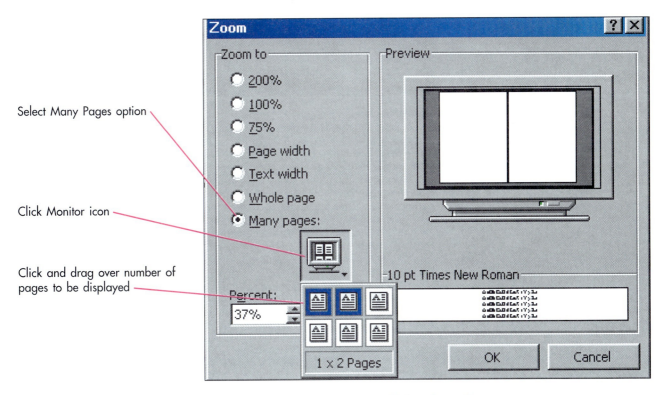

(b) Zoom Command

FIGURE 2.3 View Menu and Zoom Command (continued)

HANDS-ON EXERCISE 1

Editing a Document

Objective: To edit an existing document; to change the view and magnification of a document; to scroll through a document. To use the Find and Replace commands; to move and copy text using the clipboard and the drag-and-drop facility. Use Figure 2.4 as a guide in the exercise.

STEP 1: The View Menu
➤ Start Word as described in the hands-on exercises from Chapter 1. Pull down the **File menu** and click **Open** (or click the **Open button** on the toolbar).
  • Click the **drop-down arrow** on the Look In list box. Click the appropriate drive, drive C or drive A, depending on the location of your data.
  • Double click the **Exploring Word folder** to make it the active folder (the folder in which you will save the document).
  • Scroll in the Name list box (if necessary) until you can click the **Note from Bob and Maryann** to select this document. Double click the **document icon** or click the **Open command button** to open the file.
➤ The document should appear on the screen as shown in Figure 2.4a.
➤ Change to the Print Layout view at Page Width magnification:
  • Pull down the **View menu** and click **Print Layout** (or click the **Print Layout View button** above the status bar) as shown in Figure 2.4a.
  • Click the **down arrow** in the Zoom box to change to **Page Width.**

CHAPTER 2: GAINING PROFICIENCY

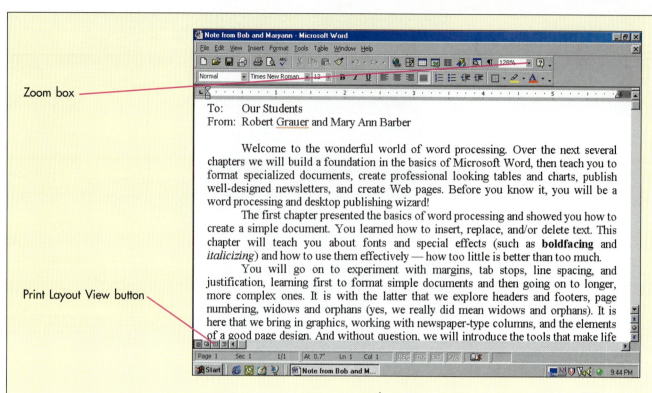

(a) The View Menu (step 1)

FIGURE 2.4   Hands-on Exercise 1

- Click and drag the mouse to select the phrase **Our Students,** which appears at the beginning of the document. Type your name to replace the selected text.
- Pull down the **File menu,** click the **Save As** command, then save the document as **Modified Note.** (This creates a second copy of the document.)

CREATE A BACKUP COPY

Microsoft Word enables you to automatically create a backup copy of a document in conjunction with the Save command. Pull down the Tools menu, click the Options button, click the Save tab, then check the box to always create a backup copy. The next time you save the file, the previously saved version is renamed "Backup of document" after which the document in memory is saved as the current version. In other words, the disk will contain the two most recent versions of the document.

STEP 2: Scrolling

- Click and drag the **scroll box** within the vertical scroll bar to scroll to the end of the document as shown in Figure 2.4b. Click immediately before the period at the end of the last sentence.
- Type a **comma** and a space, then insert the phrase **but most of all, enjoy.**
- Drag the **scroll box** to the top of the scroll bar to get back to the beginning of the document. Click immediately before the period ending the first sentence, press the **space bar,** then add the phrase **and desktop publishing.**

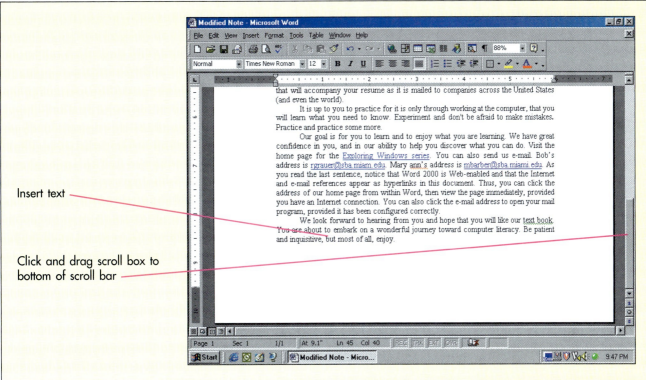

(b) Scrolling (step 2)

FIGURE 2.4 Hands-on Exercise 1 (continued)

THE MOUSE AND THE SCROLL BAR

Scroll quickly through a document by clicking above or below the scroll box to scroll up or down an entire screen. Move to the top, bottom, or an approximate position within a document by dragging the scroll box to the corresponding position in the scroll bar; for example, dragging the scroll box to the middle of the bar moves the mouse pointer to the middle of the document. Scrolling with the mouse does not change the location of the insertion point, however, and thus you must click the mouse at the new location prior to entering text at that location.

STEP 3: The Replace Command

➤ Press **Ctrl+Home** to move to the beginning of the document. Pull down the **Edit menu.** Click **Replace** to produce the dialog box of Figure 2.4c. Click the **More button** to display the available options.

- Type **text** in the Find what text box.
- Press the **Tab key.** Type **book** in the Replace with text box.

➤ Click the **Find Next button** to find the first occurrence of the word *text*. The dialog box remains on the screen and the first occurrence of *text* is selected. This is *not* an appropriate substitution; that is, you should not substitute *book* for *text* at this point.

➤ Click the **Find Next button** to move to the next occurrence without making the replacement. This time the substitution is appropriate.

CHAPTER 2: GAINING PROFICIENCY

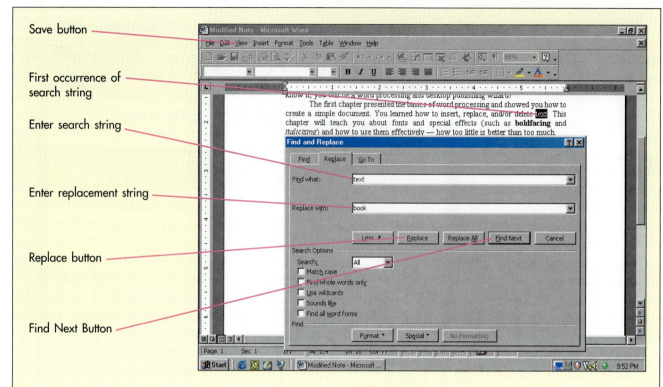

(c) The Replace Command (step 3)

FIGURE 2.4 Hands-on Exercise 1 (continued)

➤ Click **Replace** to make the change and automatically move to the next occurrence where the substitution is again inappropriate. Click **Find Next** a final time. Word will indicate that it has finished searching the document. Click **OK**.

➤ Change the Find and Replace strings to **Mary Ann** and **Maryann,** respectively. Click the **Replace All** button to make the substitution globally without confirmation. Word will indicate that it has finished searching and that two replacements were made. Click **OK**.

➤ Click the **Close command button** to close the dialog box. Click the **Save button** to save the document. Scroll through the document to review your changes.

SCROLLING WITH THE KEYBOARD

Press Ctrl+Home and Ctrl+End to move to the beginning and end of a document, respectively. Press Home and End to move to the beginning and end of a line. Press PgUp or PgDn to scroll one screen in the indicated direction. The advantage of scrolling via the keyboard (instead of the mouse) is that the location of the insertion point changes automatically and you can begin typing immediately.

STEP 4: The Windows Clipboard

➤ Press **PgDn** to scroll toward the end of the document until you come to the paragraph beginning **It is up to you.** Select the sentence **Practice and practice some more** by dragging the mouse over the sentence. (Be sure to include the period.) The sentence will be selected as shown in Figure 2.4d.

➤ Pull down the **Edit menu** and click the **Copy command** or click the **Copy button** on the Standard toolbar.

➤ Press **Ctrl+End** to scroll to the end of the document. Press the **space bar.** Pull down the **Edit menu** and click the **Paste command** (or click the **Paste button** on the Standard toolbar).

➤ Move the insertion point to the end of the first paragraph (following the exclamation point after the word *wizard*). Press the **space bar.** Click the **Paste button** on the Standard toolbar to paste the sentence a second time.

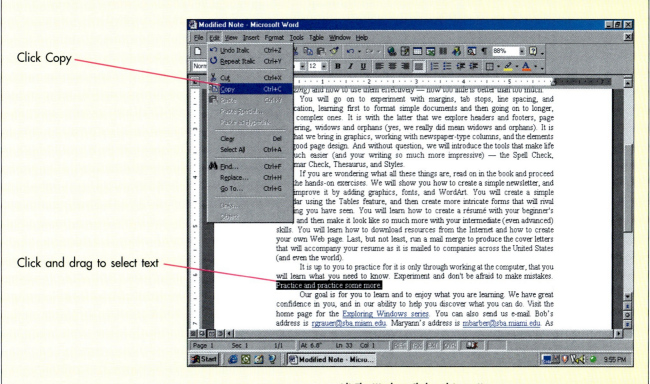

(d) The Windows Clipboard (step 4)

FIGURE 2.4   Hands-on Exercise 1 (continued)

CUT, COPY, AND PASTE

Ctrl+X, Ctrl+C, and Ctrl+V are keyboard shortcuts to cut, copy, and paste, respectively. (The shortcuts are easier to remember when you realize that the operative letters X, C, and V are next to each other at the bottom left side of the keyboard.) You can also use the Cut, Copy, and Paste buttons on the Standard toolbar.

STEP 5: The Office Clipboard

➤ Pull down the **View menu,** click (or point to) the **Toolbars command,** then click **Clipboard** to display the Clipboard toolbar as shown in Figure 2.4e.

➤ Scroll down in the document until you can click and drag to select the two sentences that indicate you can send us e-mail, and that contain our e-mail addresses. Click the **Copy button** to copy these sentences to the Office clipboard, which now contains the icons for two Word documents.

➤ Press **Ctrl+End** to move to the end of the document, press **enter** to begin a new paragraph, and press the **Tab key** to indent the paragraph. Click the **Paste All button** on the Office clipboard to paste both items at the end of the document. (You may have to add a space between the two sentences.)

➤ Close the Clipboard toolbar.

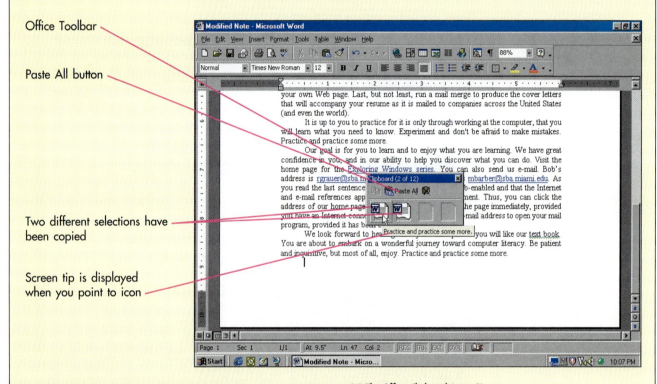

(e) The Office Clipboard (step 5)

FIGURE 2.4   Hands-on Exercise 1 (continued)

TWO DIFFERENT CLIPBOARDS

The Office clipboard is different from the Windows clipboard. Each successive copy operation adds an object to the Office clipboard (up to a maximum of 12 objects), whereas it replaces the contents of the Windows clipboard. Execution of the Paste command (via the Edit menu, Paste button, or Ctrl+V shortcut) pastes the contents of the Windows clipboard or the last item on the Office clipboard. The Office clipboard, however, lets you paste multiple objects. Note, too, that clearing the Office clipboard also clears the Windows clipboard.

STEP 6: Undo and Redo Commands

➤ Click the **drop-down arrow** next to the Undo button to display the previously executed actions as in Figure 2.4f. The list of actions corresponds to the editing commands you have issued since the start of the exercise. (Your list will be different from ours if you deviated from any instructions in the hands-on exercise.)

➤ Click **Paste** (the first command on the list) to undo the last editing command; the sentence asking you to send us e-mail disappears from the last paragraph.

➤ Click the **Undo** button a second time and the sentence, Practice and practice some more, disappears from the end of the first paragraph.

➤ Click the remaining steps on the undo list to retrace your steps through the exercise one command at a time. Alternatively, you can scroll to the bottom of the list and click the last command, which automatically undoes all of the preceding commands.

➤ Either way, when the undo list is empty, you will have the document as it existed at the start of the exercise.

➤ Click the **drop-down arrow** for the Redo command to display the list of commands you have undone.

➤ Click each command in sequence (or click the command at the bottom of the list) and you will restore the document.

➤ Save the document.

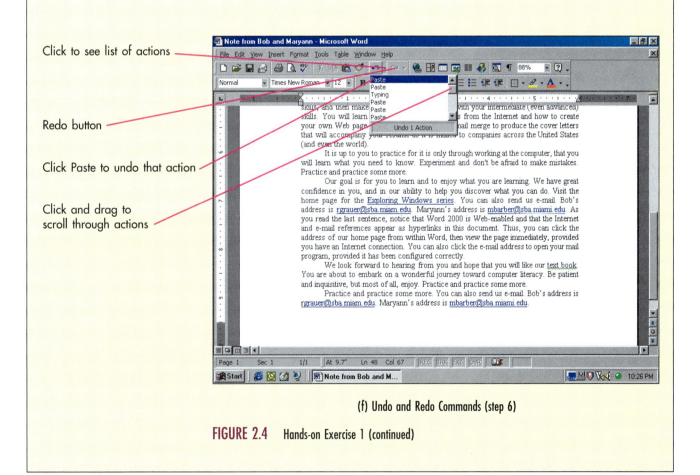

(f) Undo and Redo Commands (step 6)

FIGURE 2.4 Hands-on Exercise 1 (continued)

STEP 7: Drag and Drop

➤ Click and drag to select the phrase **format specialized documents** (including the comma and space) as shown in Figure 2.4g, then drag the phrase to its new location immediately before the word *and*. (A dotted vertical bar appears as you drag the text, to indicate its new location.)

➤ Release the mouse button to complete the move.

➤ Click the **drop-down arrow** for the Undo command; click **Move** to undo the move.

➤ To copy the selected text to the same location (instead of moving it), press and hold the **Ctrl key** as you drag the text to its new location. (A plus sign appears as you drag the text, to indicate it is being copied rather than moved.)

➤ Practice the drag-and-drop procedure several times until you are confident you can move and copy with precision.

➤ Click anywhere in the document to deselect the text. Save the document.

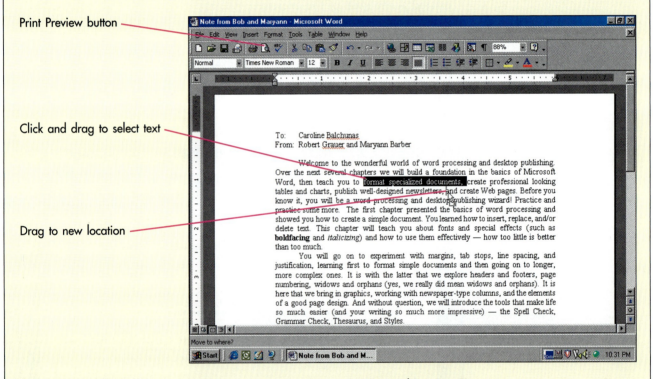

(g) Drag and Drop (step 7)

FIGURE 2.4 Hands-on Exercise 1 (continued)

STEP 8: The Print Preview Command

➤ Pull down the **File menu** and click **Print Preview** (or click the **Print Preview button** on the Standard toolbar). You should see your entire document as shown in Figure 2.4h.

➤ Check that the entire document fits on one page—that is, check that you can see all three lines in the last paragraph. If not, click the **Shrink to Fit button** on the toolbar to automatically change the font size in the document to force it on one page.

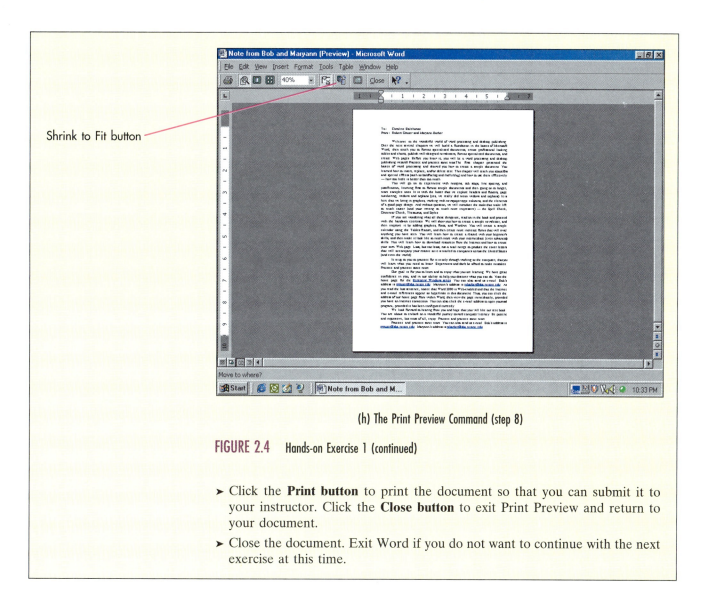

(h) The Print Preview Command (step 8)

FIGURE 2.4 Hands-on Exercise 1 (continued)

➤ Click the **Print button** to print the document so that you can submit it to your instructor. Click the **Close button** to exit Print Preview and return to your document.

➤ Close the document. Exit Word if you do not want to continue with the next exercise at this time.

TYPOGRAPHY

Typography is the process of selecting typefaces, type styles, and type sizes. The importance of these decisions is obvious, for the ultimate success of any document depends greatly on its appearance. Type should reinforce the message without calling attention to itself and should be consistent with the information you want to convey.

Typeface

A *typeface* or *font* is a complete set of characters (upper- and lowercase letters, numbers, punctuation marks, and special symbols). Figure 2.5 illustrates three typefaces—***Times New Roman, Arial,*** and ***Courier New***—that are supplied with Windows, and which in turn are accessible from any Windows application.

A definitive characteristic of any typeface is the presence or absence of tiny cross lines that end the main strokes of each letter. A *serif* typeface has these lines. A *sans serif* typeface (*sans* from the French for *without*) does not. Times New Roman and Courier New are examples of a serif typeface. Arial is a sans serif typeface.

CHAPTER 2: GAINING PROFICIENCY 67

Typography is the process of selecting typefaces, type styles, and type sizes. A serif typeface has tiny cross strokes that end the main strokes of each letter. A sans serif typeface does not have these strokes. Serif typefaces are typically used with large amounts of text. Sans serif typefaces are used for headings and limited amounts of text. A proportional typeface allocates space in accordance with the width of each character and is what you are used to seeing. A monospaced typeface uses the same amount of space for every character. A well-designed document will limit the number of typefaces so as not to overwhelm the reader.

(a) Times New Roman (serif and proportional)

Typography is the process of selecting typefaces, type styles, and type sizes. A serif typeface has tiny cross strokes that end the main strokes of each letter. A sans serif typeface does not have these strokes. Serif typefaces are typically used with large amounts of text. Sans serif typefaces are used for headings and limited amounts of text. A proportional typeface allocates space in accordance with the width of each character and is what you are used to seeing. A monospaced typeface uses the same amount of space for every character. A well-designed document will limit the number of typefaces so as not to overwhelm the reader.

(b) Arial (sans serif and proportional)

```
Typography is the process of selecting typefaces, type styles,
and type sizes. A serif typeface has tiny cross strokes that end
the main strokes of each letter. A sans serif typeface does not
have these strokes. Serif typefaces are typically used with large
amounts of text. Sans serif typefaces are used for headings and
limited amounts of text. A proportional typeface allocates space
in accordance with the width of each character and is what you
are used to seeing. A monospaced typeface uses the same amount of
space for every character. A well-designed document will limit
the number of typefaces so as not to overwhelm the reader.
```

(c) Courier New (serif and monospaced)

FIGURE 2.5 Typefaces

Serifs help the eye to connect one letter with the next and are generally used with large amounts of text. This book, for example, is set in a serif typeface. A sans serif typeface is more effective with smaller amounts of text and appears in headlines, corporate logos, airport signs, and so on.

A second characteristic of a typeface is whether it is monospaced or proportional. A ***monospaced typeface*** (e.g., Courier New) uses the same amount of space for every character regardless of its width. A ***proportional typeface*** (e.g., Times New Roman or Arial) allocates space according to the width of the character. Monospaced fonts are used in tables and financial projections where text must be precisely lined up, one character underneath the other. Proportional typefaces create a more professional appearance and are appropriate for most documents. Any typeface can be set in different ***type styles*** (such as regular, **bold,** or *italic*).

> ### TYPOGRAPHY TIP—USE RESTRAINT
>
> More is not better, especially in the case of too many typefaces and styles, which produce cluttered documents that impress no one. Try to limit yourself to a maximum of two typefaces per document, but choose multiple sizes and/or styles within those typefaces. Use boldface or italics for emphasis; but do so in moderation, because if you emphasize too many elements, the effect is lost.

Type Size

Type size is a vertical measurement and is specified in points. One ***point*** is equal to 1/72 of an inch; that is, there are 72 points to the inch. The measurement is made from the top of the tallest letter in a character set (for example, an uppercase T) to the bottom of the lowest letter (for example, a lowercase y). Most documents are set in 10 or 12 point type. Newspaper columns may be set as small as 8 point type, but that is the smallest type size you should consider. Conversely, type sizes of 14 points or higher are ineffective for large amounts of text.

Figure 2.6 shows the same phrase set in varying type sizes. Some typefaces appear larger (smaller) than others even though they may be set in the same point size. The type in Figure 2.6a, for example, looks smaller than the corresponding type in Figure 2.6b even though both are set in the same point size. Note, too, that you can vary the type size of a specific font within a document for emphasis. The eye needs at least two points to distinguish between different type sizes.

Format Font Command

The ***Format Font command*** gives you complete control over the typeface, size, and style of the text in a document. Executing the command before entering text will set the format of the text you type from that point on. You can also use the command to change the font of existing text by selecting the text, then executing the command. Either way, you will see the dialog box in Figure 2.7, in which you specify the font (typeface), style, and point size.

You can choose any of the special effects (e.g., ~~strikethrough~~ or SMALL CAPS) and/or change the underline options (whether or not spaces are to be underlined). You can even change the color of the text on the monitor, but you need a color printer for the printed document. (The Character Spacing and Text Effects tabs produce different sets of options in which you control the spacing and appearance of the characters and are beyond the scope of our discussion.)

This is Arial 8 point type

This is Arial 10 point type

This is Arial 12 point type

This is Arial 18 point type

This is Arial 24 point type

This is Arial 30 point type

(a) Sans Serif Typeface

This is Times New Roman 8 point type

This is Times New Roman 10 point type

This is Times New Roman 12 point type

This is Times New Roman 18 point type

This is Times New Roman 24 point type

This is Times New Roman 30 point

(b) Serif Typeface

FIGURE 2.6 Type Size

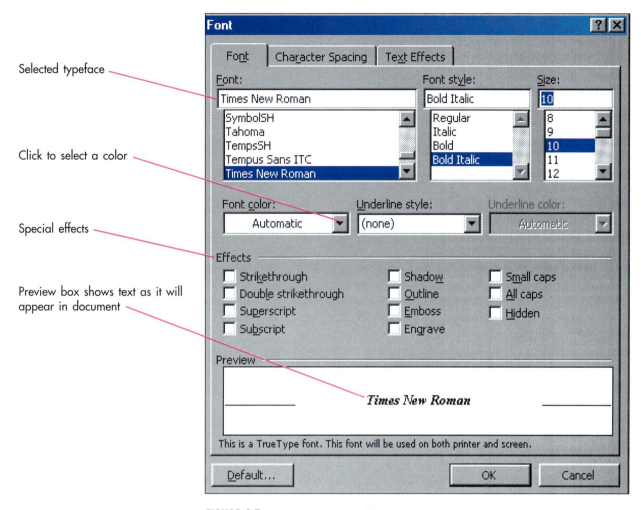

FIGURE 2.7 Format Font Command

The Preview box shows the text as it will appear in the document. The message at the bottom of the dialog box indicates that Times New Roman is a TrueType font and that the same font will be used on both the screen and the monitor. TrueType fonts ensure that your document is truly WYSIWYG (What You See Is What You Get) because the fonts you see on the monitor will be identical to those in the printed document.

PAGE SETUP COMMAND

The ***Page Setup command*** in the File menu lets you change margins, paper size, orientation, paper source, and/or layout. All parameters are accessed from the dialog box in Figure 2.8 by clicking the appropriate tab within the dialog box.

The default margins are indicated in Figure 2.8a and are one inch on the top and bottom of the page, and one and a quarter inches on the left and right. You can change any (or all) of these settings by entering a new value in the appropriate text box, either by typing it explicitly or clicking the up/down arrow. All of the settings in the Page Setup command apply to the whole document regardless of the position of the insertion point. (Different settings for any option in the Page Setup dialog box can be established for different parts of a document by creating sections. Sections also affect column formatting, as discussed later in the chapter.)

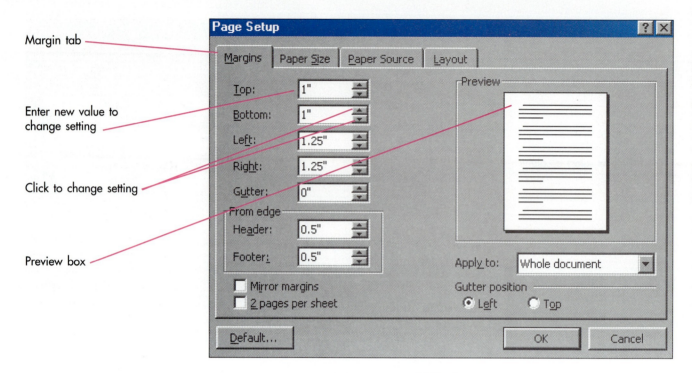

(a) Margins

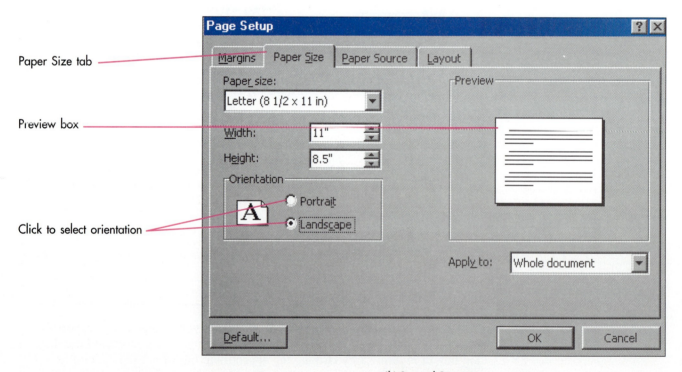

(b) Size and Orientation

FIGURE 2.8   Page Setup Command

The Paper Size tab within the Page Setup command enables you to change the orientation of a page as shown in Figure 2.8b. ***Portrait orientation*** is the default. ***Landscape orientation*** flips the page 90 degrees so that its dimensions are 11 × 8½ rather than the other way around. Note, too, the Preview area in both Figures 2.8a and 2.8b, which shows how the document will appear with the selected parameters.

The Paper Source tab is used to specify which tray should be used on printers with multiple trays, and is helpful when you want to load different types of paper simultaneously. The Layout tab is used to specify options for headers and footers (text that appears at the top or bottom of each page in a document), and/or to change the vertical alignment of text on the page.

Page Breaks

One of the first concepts you learned was that of word wrap, whereby Word inserts a soft return at the end of a line in order to begin a new line. The number and/or location of the soft returns change automatically as you add or delete text within a document. Soft returns are very different from the hard returns inserted by the user, whose number and location remain constant.

In much the same way, Word creates a ***soft page break*** to go to the top of a new page when text no longer fits on the current page. And just as you can insert a hard return to start a new paragraph, you can insert a ***hard page break*** to force any part of a document to begin on a new page. A hard page break is inserted into a document using the Break command in the Insert menu or more easily through the Ctrl+enter keyboard shortcut. (You can prevent the occurrence of awkward page breaks through the Format Paragraph command as described later in the chapter.)

AN EXERCISE IN DESIGN

The following exercise has you retrieve an existing document from the set of practice files, then experiment with various typefaces, type styles, and point sizes. The original document uses a monospaced (typewriter style) font, without boldface or italics, and you are asked to improve its appearance. The first step directs you to save the document under a new name so that you can always return to the original if necessary.

There is no right and wrong with respect to design, and you are free to choose any combination of fonts that appeals to you. The exercise takes you through various formatting options but lets you make the final decision. It does, however, ask you to print the final document and submit it to your instructor. Experiment freely and print multiple versions with different designs.

IMPOSE A TIME LIMIT

A word processor is supposed to save time and make you more productive. It will do exactly that, provided you use the word processor for its primary purpose—writing and editing. It is all too easy, however, to lose sight of that objective and spend too much time formatting the document. Concentrate on the content of your document rather than its appearance. Impose a time limit on the amount of time you will spend on formatting. End the session when the limit is reached.

HANDS-ON EXERCISE 2

Character Formatting

Objective: To experiment with character formatting; to change fonts and to use boldface and italics; to copy formatting with the format painter; to insert a page break and see different views of a document. Use Figure 2.9 as a guide in the exercise.

STEP 1: Open the Existing Document

➤ Start Word. Pull down the **File menu** and click **Open** (or click the **Open button** on the toolbar). To open a file:
- Click the **drop-down arrow** on the Look In list box. Click the appropriate drive, drive C or drive A, depending on the location of your data.
- Double click the **Exploring Word folder** to make it the active folder (the folder in which you will open and save the document).
- Scroll in the **Open list box** (if necessary) until you can click **Tips for Writing** to select this document.

➤ Double click the **document icon** or click the **Open command button** to open the file.

➤ Pull down the **File menu.** Click the **Save As command** to save the document as **Modified Tips.**

➤ Pull down the **View menu** and click **Normal** (or click the **Normal View button** above the status bar).

➤ Set the magnification (zoom) to **Page Width.**

SELECTING TEXT

The selection bar, a blank column at the far left of the document window, makes it easy to select a line, paragraph, or the entire document. To select a line, move the mouse pointer to the selection bar, point to the line and click the left mouse button. To select a paragraph, move the mouse pointer to the selection bar, point to any line in the paragraph, and double click the mouse. To select the entire document, move the mouse pointer to the selection bar and press the Ctrl key while you click the mouse.

STEP 2: The Right Mouse Button

➤ Select the first tip as shown in Figure 2.9a. Point to the selected text and click the **right mouse button** to display a context-sensitive or shortcut menu.

➤ Click outside the menu to close the menu without executing a command.

➤ Press the **Ctrl key** as you click the selection bar to select the entire document, then click the **right mouse button** to display the shortcut menu.

➤ Click **Font** to execute the Format Font command.

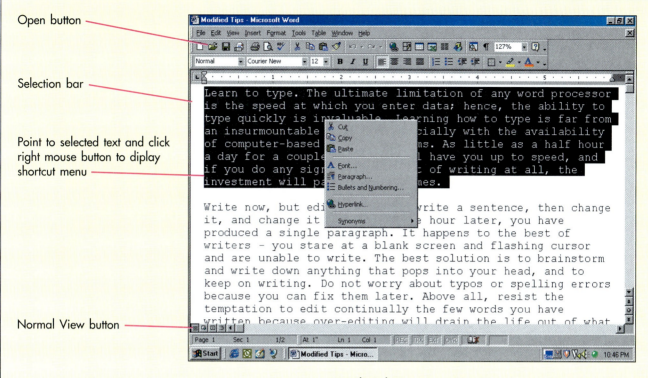

(a) The Right Mouse Button (step 2)

FIGURE 2.9 Hands-on Exercise 2

STEP 3: The Format Font Command
- Click the **down arrow** on the Font list box of Figure 2.9b to scroll through the available fonts. Select a different font, such as Times New Roman.
- Click the **down arrow** in the Font Size list box to choose a point size.
- Click **OK** to change the font and point size for the selected text.
- Pull down the **Edit menu** and click **Undo** (or click the **Undo button** on the Standard toolbar) to return to the original font.
- Experiment with different fonts and/or different point sizes until you are satisfied with the selection. We chose 12 point Times New Roman.

FIND AND REPLACE FORMATTING

The Replace command enables you to replace formatting as well as text. To replace any text set in bold with the same text in italics, pull down the Edit menu, and click the Replace command. Click the Find what text box, but do *not* enter any text. Click the More button to expand the dialog box. Click the Format command button, click Font, click Bold in the Font Style list, and click OK. Click the Replace with text box and again do *not* enter any text. Click the Format command button, click Font, click Italic in the Font Style list, and click OK. Click the Find Next or Replace All command button to do selective or automatic replacement. Use a similar technique to replace one font with another.

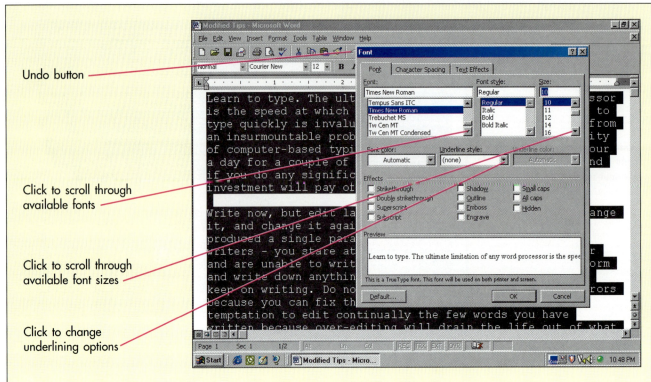

(b) The Format Command (step 3)

FIGURE 2.9   Hands-on Exercise 2 (continued)

STEP 4: Boldface and Italics

➤ Select the sentence **Learn to type** at the beginning of the document.

➤ Click the **Italic button** on the Formatting toolbar to italicize the selected phrase, which will remain selected after the italics take effect.

➤ Click the **Bold button** to boldface the selected text. The text is now in bold italic.

➤ Experiment with different styles (bold, italics, underlining, or bold italic) until you are satisfied. The Italic, Bold, and Underline buttons function as toggle switches; that is, clicking the Italic button when text is already italicized returns the text to normal.

➤ Save the document

UNDERLINING TEXT

Underlining is less popular than it was, but Word provides a complete range of underlining options. Select the text to underline, pull down the Format menu, click Font to display the Font dialog box, and click the Font tab if necessary. Click the down arrow on the Underline Style list box to choose the type of underlining you want. You can choose whether to underline the words only (i.e., the underline does not appear in the space between words). You can also choose the type of line you want—solid, dashed, thick, or thin.

STEP 5: The Format Painter

➤ Click anywhere within the sentence Learn to Type. **Double click** the **Format Painter button** on the Standard toolbar. The mouse pointer changes to a paintbrush as shown in Figure 2.9c.

➤ Drag the mouse pointer over the next title, **Write now, but edit later,** and release the mouse. The formatting from the original sentence (bold italic as shown in Figure 2.9c) has been applied to this sentence as well.

➤ Drag the mouse pointer (in the shape of a paintbrush) over the remaining titles (the first sentence in each paragraph) to copy the formatting.

➤ Click the **Format Painter button** after you have painted the title of the last tip to turn the feature off.

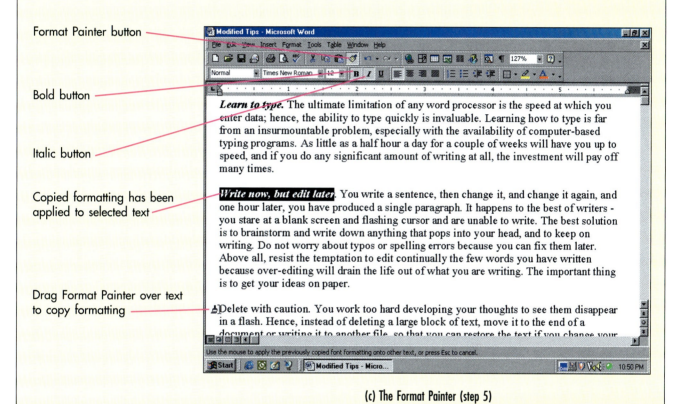

(c) The Format Painter (step 5)

FIGURE 2.9 Hands-on Exercise 2 (continued)

THE FORMAT PAINTER

The Format Painter copies the formatting of the selected text to other places in a document. Select the text with the formatting you want to copy, then click or double click the Format Painter button on the Standard toolbar. Clicking the button will paint only one selection. Double clicking the button will paint multiple selections until the feature is turned off by again clicking the Format Painter button. Either way, the mouse pointer changes to a paintbrush, which you can drag over text to give it the identical formatting characteristics as the original selection.

STEP 6: Change Margins

➤ Press **Ctrl+End** to move to the end of the document as shown in Figure 2.9d. You will see a dotted line indicating a soft page break. (If you do not see the page break, it means that your document fits on one page because you used a different font and/or a smaller point size. We used 12 point Times New Roman.)

➤ Pull down the **File menu.** Click **Page Setup.** Click the **Margins tab** if necessary. Change the bottom margin to **.75** inch. Check that these settings apply to the **Whole Document.** Click **OK.**

➤ The page break disappears because more text fits on the page.

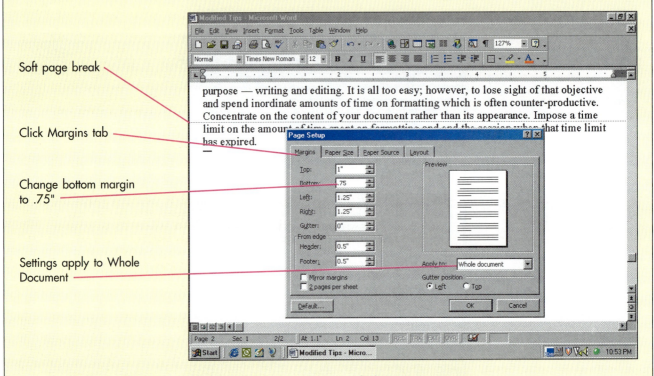

(d) Change Margins (step 6)

FIGURE 2.9 Hands-on Exercise 2 (continued)

DIALOG BOX SHORTCUTS

You can use keyboard shortcuts to select options in a dialog box. Press Tab (Shift+Tab) to move forward (backward) from one field or command button to the next. Press Alt plus the underlined letter to move directly to a field or command button. Press enter to activate the selected command button. Press Esc to exit the dialog box without taking action. Press the space bar to toggle check boxes on or off. Press the down arrow to open a drop-down list box once the list has been accessed, then press the up or down arrow to move between options in a list box.

STEP 7: Create the Title Page

➤ Press **Ctrl+Home** to move to the beginning of the document. Press **enter** three or four times to add a few blank lines.

➤ Press **Ctrl+enter** to insert a hard page break. You will see the words "Page Break" in the middle of a dotted line as shown in Figure 2.9e.

➤ Press the **up arrow key** three times. Enter the title **Tips for Writing.** Select the title, and format it in a larger point size, such as 24 points.

➤ Enter your name on the next line and format it in a different point size, such as 14 points. Select both the title and your name as shown in the figure. Click the **Center button** on the Formatting toolbar. Save the document.

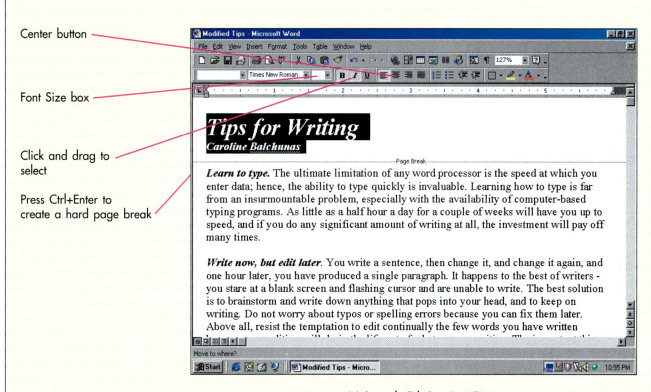

Center button

Font Size box

Click and drag to select

Press Ctrl+Enter to create a hard page break

(e) Create the Title Page (step 7)

FIGURE 2.9 Hands-on Exercise 2 (continued)

DOUBLE CLICK AND TYPE

Creating a title page is a breeze if you take advantage of the (double) click and type feature in Word 2000. Pull down the View menu and change to the Print Layout view, then look closely at the mouse pointer and notice the horizontal lines that surround the I-beam shape. Double click anywhere on the page and you can begin typing immediately at that location, without having to type several blank lines, or set tabs. The feature does not work in the Normal view or in a document that has columns. To enable (disable) the feature, pull down the Tools menu, click the Options command, click the Edit tab, then check (clear) the Enable Click and Type check box.

STEP 8: The Completed Document

➤ Pull down the **View menu** and click **Print Layout** (or click the **Print Layout button** above the status bar).

➤ Click the **Zoom Control arrow** on the Standard toolbar and select **Two Pages**. Release the mouse to view the completed document in Figure 2.9f. You may want to add additional blank lines at the top of the title page to move the title further down on the page.

➤ Save the document a final time. Exit Word if you do not want to continue with the next exercise at this time.

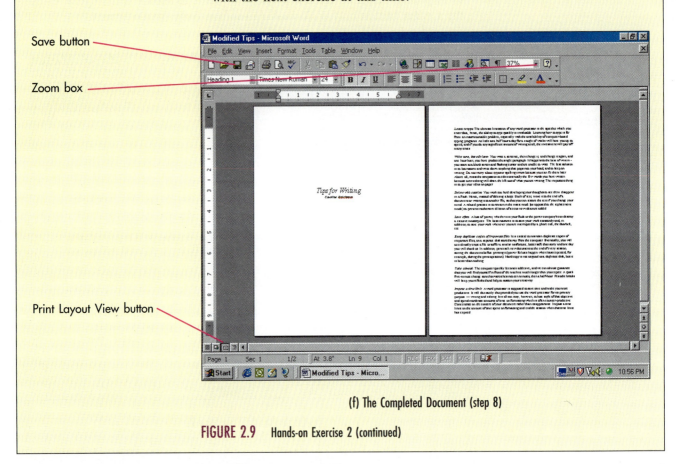

(f) The Completed Document (step 8)

FIGURE 2.9 Hands-on Exercise 2 (continued)

PARAGRAPH FORMATTING

A change in typography is only one way to alter the appearance of a document. You can also change the alignment, indentation, tab stops, or line spacing for any paragraph(s) within the document. You can control the pagination and prevent the occurrence of awkward page breaks by specifying that an entire paragraph has to appear on the same page, or that a one-line paragraph (e.g., a heading) should appear on the same page as the next paragraph. You can include borders or shading for added emphasis around selected paragraphs.

All of these features are implemented at the paragraph level and affect all selected paragraphs. If no paragraphs are selected, the commands affect the entire current paragraph (the paragraph containing the insertion point), regardless of the position of the insertion point when the command is executed.

Alignment

Text can be aligned in four different ways as shown in Figure 2.10. It may be justified (flush left/flush right), left aligned (flush left with a ragged right margin), right aligned (flush right with a ragged left margin), or centered within the margins (ragged left and right).

Left aligned text is perhaps the easiest to read. The first letters of each line align with each other, helping the eye to find the beginning of each line. The lines themselves are of irregular length. There is uniform spacing between words, and the ragged margin on the right adds white space to the text, giving it a lighter and more informal look.

Justified text produces lines of equal length, with the spacing between words adjusted to align at the margins. It may be more difficult to read than text that is left aligned because of the uneven (sometimes excessive) word spacing and/or the greater number of hyphenated words needed to justify the lines.

Type that is centered or right aligned is restricted to limited amounts of text where the effect is more important than the ease of reading. Centered text, for example, appears frequently on wedding invitations, poems, or formal announcements. Right aligned text is used with figure captions and short headlines.

Indents

Individual paragraphs can be indented so that they appear to have different margins from the rest of a document. Indentation is established at the paragraph level; thus different indentation can be in effect for different paragraphs. One paragraph may be indented from the left margin only, another from the right margin only, and a third from both the left and right margins. The first line of any paragraph may be indented differently from the rest of the paragraph. And finally, a paragraph may be set with no indentation at all, so that it aligns on the left and right margins.

The indentation of a paragraph is determined by three settings: the *left indent,* the *right indent,* and a *special indent* (if any). There are two types of special indentation, first line and hanging, as will be explained shortly. The left and right indents are set to zero by default, as is the special indent, and produce a paragraph with no indentation at all as shown in Figure 2.11a. Positive values for the left and right indents offset the paragraph from both margins as shown in Figure 2.11b.

The *first line indent* (Figure 2.11c) affects only the first line in the paragraph and is implemented by pressing the Tab key at the beginning of the paragraph. A *hanging indent* (Figure 2.11d) sets the first line of a paragraph at the left indent and indents the remaining lines according to the amount specified. Hanging indents are often used with bulleted or numbered lists.

INDENTS VERSUS MARGINS

Indents measure the distance between the text and the margins. Margins mark the distance from the text to the edge of the page. Indents are determined at the paragraph level, whereas margins are established at the section (document) level. The left and right margins are set (by default) to 1.25 inches each; the left and right indents default to zero. The first line indent is measured from the setting of the left indent.

We, the people of the United States, in order to form a more perfect Union, establish justice, insure domestic tranquillity, provide for the common defense, promote the general welfare, and secure the blessings of liberty to ourselves and our posterity, do ordain and establish this Constitution for the United States of America.

(a) Justified (flush left/flush right)

We, the people of the United States, in order to form a more perfect Union, establish justice, insure domestic tranquillity, provide for the common defense, promote the general welfare, and secure the blessings of liberty to ourselves and our posterity, do ordain and establish this Constitution for the United States of America.

(b) Left Aligned (flush left/ragged right)

We, the people of the United States, in order to form a more perfect Union, establish justice, insure domestic tranquillity, provide for the common defense, promote the general welfare, and secure the blessings of liberty to ourselves and our posterity, do ordain and establish this Constitution for the United States of America.

(c) Right Aligned (ragged left/flush right)

We, the people of the United States, in order to form a more perfect Union, establish justice, insure domestic tranquillity, provide for the common defense, promote the general welfare, and secure the blessings of liberty to ourselves and our posterity, do ordain and establish this Constitution for the United States of America.

(d) Centered (ragged left/ragged right)

FIGURE 2.10 Alignment

The left and right indents are defined as the distance between the text and the left and right margins, respectively. Both parameters are set to zero in this paragraph and so the text aligns on both margins. Different indentation can be applied to different paragraphs in the same document.

(a) No Indents

> Positive values for the left and right indents offset a paragraph from the rest of a document and are often used for long quotations. This paragraph has left and right indents of one-half inch each. Different indentation can be applied to different paragraphs in the same document.

(b) Left and Right Indents

    A first line indent affects only the first line in the paragraph and is implemented by pressing the Tab key at the beginning of the paragraph. The remainder of the paragraph is aligned at the left margin (or the left indent if it differs from the left margin) as can be seen from this example. Different indentation can be applied to different paragraphs in the same document.

(c) First Line Indent

A hanging indent sets the first line of a paragraph at the left indent and indents the remaining
    lines according to the amount specified. Hanging indents are often used with bulleted
    or numbered lists. Different indentation can be applied to different paragraphs in the
    same document.

(d) Hanging (Special) Indent

FIGURE 2.11 Indents

Tabs

Anyone who has used a typewriter is familiar with the function of the Tab key; that is, press Tab and the insertion point moves to the next **tab stop** (a measured position to align text at a specific place). The Tab key is much more powerful in Word as you can choose from four different types of tab stops (left, center, right, and decimal). You can also specify a **leader character,** typically dots or hyphens, to draw the reader's eye across the page. Tabs are often used to create columns of text within a document.

The default tab stops are set every ½ inch and are left aligned, but you can change the alignment and/or position with the Format Tabs command. Figure 2.12 illustrates a dot leader in combination with a right tab to produce a Table of Contents. The default tab stops have been cleared in Figure 2.12a, in favor of a single right tab at 5.5 inches. The option button for a dot leader has also been checked. The resulting document is shown in Figure 2.12b.

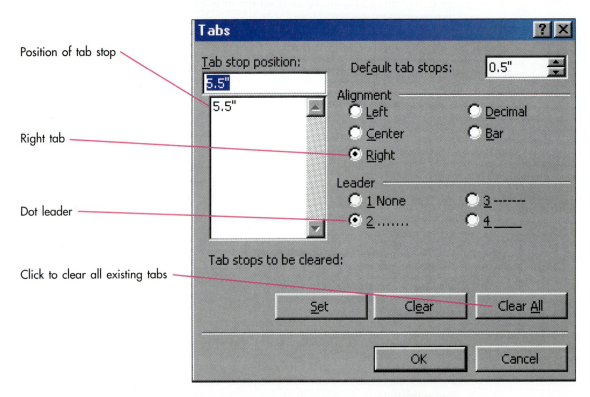

(a) Tab Stops

Chapter 1: Introduction	3
Chapter 2: Gaining Proficiency	32
Chapter 3: The Tools	61
Chapter 4: The Professional Document	99
Chapter 5: Desktop Publishing	124

(b) Table of Contents

FIGURE 2.12 Tabs

Hyphenation

Hyphenation gives a document a more professional look by eliminating excessive gaps of white space. It is especially useful in narrow columns and/or justified text. Hyphenation is implemented through the Language command in the Tools menu. You can choose to hyphenate a document automatically, in which case the hyphens are inserted as the document is created. (Microsoft Word will automatically rehyphenate the document to adjust for subsequent changes in editing.)

You can also hyphenate a document manually, to have Word prompt you prior to inserting each hyphen. Manual hyphenation does not, however, adjust for changes that affect the line breaks, and so it should be done only after the document is complete. And finally, you can fine-tune the use of hyphenation by preventing a hyphenated word from breaking if it falls at the end of a line. This is done by inserting a ***nonbreaking hyphen*** (press Ctrl+Shift+Hyphen) when the word is typed initially.

Line Spacing

Line spacing determines the space between the lines in a paragraph. Word provides complete flexibility and enables you to select any multiple of line spacing (single, double, line and a half, and so on). You can also specify line spacing in terms of points (there are 72 points per inch).

Line spacing is set at the paragraph level through the Format Paragraph command, which sets the spacing within a paragraph. The command also enables you to add extra spacing before the first line in a paragraph or after the last line. (Either technique is preferable to the common practice of single spacing the paragraphs within a document, then adding a blank line between paragraphs.)

FORMAT PARAGRAPH COMMAND

The ***Format Paragraph command*** is used to specify the alignment, indentation, line spacing, and pagination for the selected paragraph(s). As indicated, all of these features are implemented at the paragraph level and affect all selected paragraphs. If no paragraphs are selected, the command affects the entire current paragraph (the paragraph containing the insertion point).

The Format Paragraph command is illustrated in Figure 2.13. The Indents and Spacing tab in Figure 2.13a calls for a hanging indent, line spacing of 1.5 lines, and justified alignment. The preview area within the dialog box enables you to see how the paragraph will appear within the document.

The Line and Page Breaks tab in Figure 2.13b illustrates an entirely different set of parameters in which you control the pagination within a document. The check boxes in Figure 2.13b enable you to prevent the occurrence of awkward soft page breaks that detract from the appearance of a document.

You might, for example, want to prevent widows and orphans, terms used to describe isolated lines that seem out of place. A ***widow*** refers to the last line of a paragraph appearing by itself at the top of a page. An ***orphan*** is the first line of a paragraph appearing by itself at the bottom of a page.

You can also impose additional controls by clicking one or more check boxes. Use the Keep Lines Together option to prevent a soft page break from occurring within a paragraph and ensure that the entire paragraph appears on the same page. (The paragraph is moved to the top of the next page if it doesn't fit on the bottom of the current page.) Use the Keep with Next option to prevent a soft page break between the two paragraphs. This option is typically used to keep a heading (a one-line paragraph) with its associated text in the next paragraph.

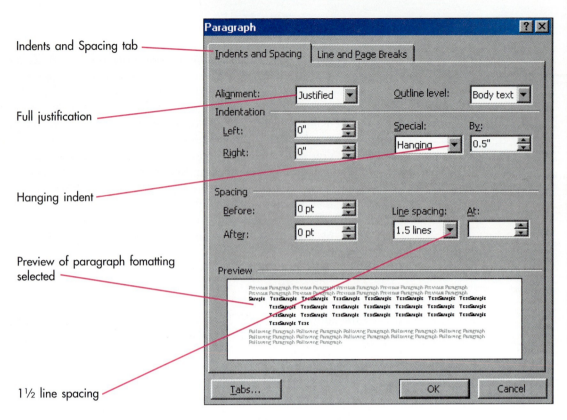

(a) Indents and Spacing

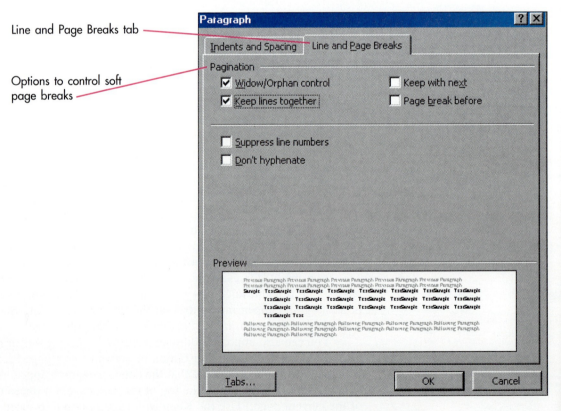

(b) Line and Page Breaks

FIGURE 2.13 Format Paragraph Command

Borders and Shading

The **Borders and Shading command** puts the finishing touches on a document and is illustrated in Figure 2.14. The command is applied to selected text within a paragraph or to the entire paragraph if no text is selected. Thus, you can create boxed and/or shaded text as well as place horizontal or vertical lines around a paragraph. You can choose from several different line styles in any color (assuming you have a color printer). You can place a uniform border around a paragraph (choose Box), or you can choose a shadow effect with thicker lines at the right and bottom. You can also apply lines to selected sides of a paragraph(s) by selecting a line style, then clicking the desired sides as appropriate.

Shading is implemented independently of the border. Clear (no shading) is the default. Solid (100%) shading creates a solid box where the text is turned white so you can read it. Shading of 10 or 20 percent is generally most effective to add emphasis to the selected paragraph. The Borders and Shading command is implemented on the paragraph level and affects the entire paragraph—either the current or selected paragraph(s).

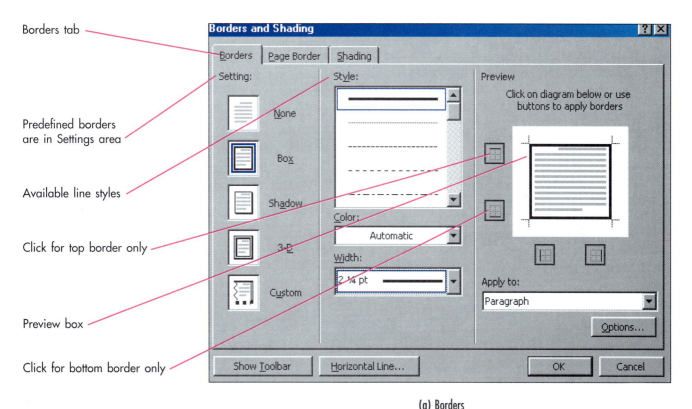

(a) Borders

FIGURE 2.14   Paragraph Borders and Shading

FORMATTING AND THE PARAGRAPH MARK

The paragraph mark ¶ at the end of a paragraph does more than just indicate the presence of a hard return. It also stores all of the formatting in effect for the paragraph. Hence in order to preserve the formatting when you move or copy a paragraph, you must include the paragraph mark in the selected text. Click the Show/Hide ¶ button on the toolbar to display the paragraph mark and make sure it has been selected.

COLUMN FORMATTING

Columns add interest to a document and are implemented through the **Columns command** in the Format menu as shown in Figure 2.15. You specify the number of columns and, optionally, the space between columns. Microsoft Word does the rest, calculating the width of each column according to the left and right margins on the page and the specified (default) space between columns.

The dialog box in Figure 2.15 implements a design of three equal columns. The 2-inch width of each column is computed automatically based on left and right page margins of 1 inch each and the ¼-inch spacing between columns. The width of each column is determined by subtracting the sum of the margins and the space between the columns (a total of 2½ inches in this example) from the page width of 8½ inches. The result of the subtraction is 6 inches, which is divided by 3, resulting in a column width of 2 inches.

There is, however, one subtlety associated with column formatting, and that is the introduction of the **section,** which controls elements such as the orientation of a page (landscape or portrait), margins, page numbers, and/or the number of columns. All of the documents in the text thus far have consisted of a single section, and therefore section formatting was not an issue. It becomes important only when you want to vary an element that is formatted at the section level. You could, for example, use section formatting to create a document that has one column on its title page and two columns on the remaining pages. This requires you to divide the document two sections through insertion of a **section break.** You then format each section independently and specify the number of columns in each section.

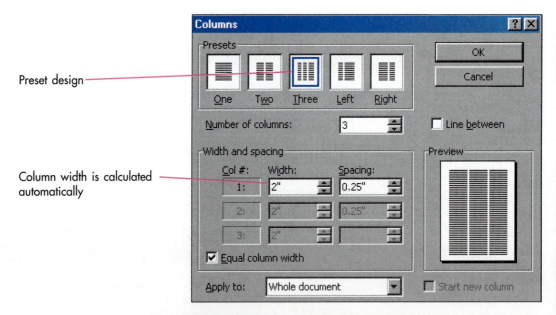

FIGURE 2.15 The Format Columns Command

THE SECTION VERSUS THE PARAGRAPH

Line spacing, alignment, tabs, and indents are implemented at the paragraph level. Change any of these parameters anywhere within the current (or selected) paragraph(s) and you change *only* those paragraph(s). Margins, page numbering, orientation, and columns are implemented at the section level. Change these parameters anywhere within a section and you change the characteristics of every page within that section.

HANDS-ON EXERCISE 3

Paragraph Formatting

Objective: To implement line spacing, alignment, and indents; to implement widow and orphan protection; to box and shade a selected paragraph.

STEP 1: Select-Then-Do

➤ Open the **Modified Tips** document from the previous exercise. If necessary, change to the Print Layout view. Click the **Zoom drop-down arrow** and click **Two Pages** to match the view in Figure 2.16a.

➤ Select the entire second page as shown in the figure. Point to the selected text and click the **right mouse button** to produce the shortcut menu. Click **Paragraph.**

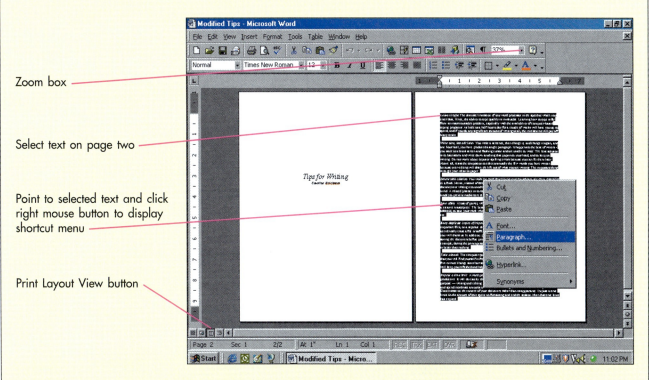

Zoom box

Select text on page two

Point to selected text and click right mouse button to display shortcut menu

Print Layout View button

(a) Select-Then-Do (step 1)

FIGURE 2.16 Hands-on Exercise 3

SELECT TEXT WITH THE F8 EXTEND KEY

Move to the beginning of the text you want to select, then press the F8 (extend) key. The letters EXT will appear in the status bar. Use the arrow keys to extend the selection in the indicated direction; for example, press the down arrow key to select the line. You can also press any character—for example, a letter, space, or period—to extend the selection to the first occurrence of that character. Press Esc to cancel the selection mode.

STEP 2: Line Spacing, Justification, and Pagination

➤ If necessary, click the **Indents and Spacing tab** to view the options in Figure 2.16b.
  • Click the **down arrow** on the list box for Line Spacing and select **1.5 Lines.**
  • Click the **down arrow** on the Alignment list box and select **Justified** as shown in Figure 2.16b.
  • The Preview area shows the effect of these settings.
➤ Click the tab for **Line and Page Breaks.**
  • Check the box for **Keep Lines Together.** If necessary, check the box for **Widow/Orphan Control.**
➤ Click **OK** to accept all of the settings in the dialog box.
➤ Click anywhere in the document to deselect the text and see the effects of the formatting changes:
  • The document is fully justified and the line spacing has increased.
  • The document now extends to three pages, with the fifth, sixth, and seventh paragraphs appearing on the last page.
  • There is a large bottom margin on the second page as a consequence of keeping the lines together in paragraph five.
➤ Save the document.

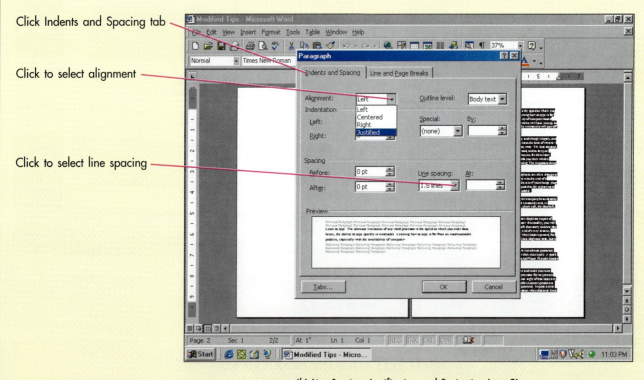

(b) Line Spacing, Justification, and Pagination (step 2)

FIGURE 2.16 Hands-on Exercise 3 (continued)

STEP 3: Indents

➤ Select the second paragraph as shown in Figure 2.16c. (The second paragraph will not yet be indented.)

➤ Pull down the **Format menu** and click **Paragraph** (or press the **right mouse button** to produce the shortcut menu and click **Paragraph**).

➤ If necessary, click the **Indents and Spacing tab** in the Paragraph dialog box. Click the **up arrow** on the Left Indentation text box to set the **Left Indent** to **.5** inch. Set the **Right indent** to **.5** inch. Click **OK.** Your document should match Figure 2.16c.

➤ Save the document.

Click and drag to set right indent

Click and drag to set left indent and first line indent at same time

Select paragraph two

(c) Indents (step 3)

FIGURE 2.16 Hands-on Exercise 3 (continued)

INDENTS AND THE RULER

Use the ruler to change the special, left, and/or right indents. Select the paragraph (or paragraphs) in which you want to change indents, then drag the appropriate indent markers to the new location(s). If you get a hanging indent when you wanted to change the left indent, it means you dragged the bottom triangle instead of the box. Click the Undo button and try again. (You can always use the Format Paragraph command rather than the ruler if you continue to have difficulty.)

STEP 4: Borders and Shading

- Pull down the **Format menu.** Click **Borders and Shading** to produce the dialog box in Figure 2.16d.
- If necessary, click the **Borders tab.** Select a style and width for the line around the box. Click the rectangle labeled **Box** under Setting.
- Click the **Shading Tab.** Click the **down arrow** on the Style list box. Click **10%**.
- Click **OK** to accept the settings for both Borders and Shading. Click outside the paragraph.
- Save the document.

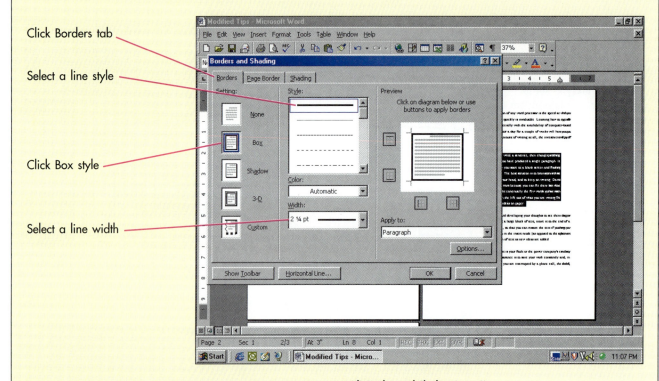

(d) Borders and Shading (step 4)

FIGURE 2.16 Hands-on Exercise 3 (continued)

THE PAGE BORDER COMMAND

You can apply a border to the title page of your document, to every page except the title page, or to every page including the title page. Pull down the Format menu, click Borders and Shading, and click the Page Borders tab. First design the border by selecting a style, color, width, and art (if any). Then choose the page(s) to which you want to apply the border by clicking the drop-down arrow in the Apply to list box. Close the Borders and Shading dialog box. See practice exercise 5 at the end of the chapter.

STEP 5: Help with Formatting

➤ Pull down the **Help menu** and click the **What's This command** (or press **Shift+F1**). The mouse pointer changes to an arrow with a question mark.

➤ Click anywhere inside the boxed paragraph to display the formatting information shown in Figure 2.16e.

➤ Click in a different paragraph to see its formatting. Press the **Esc key** to return the pointer to normal.

> **DISPLAY THE HARD RETURNS**
>
> Many formattting commands are implemented at the paragraph level, and thus it helps to know where a paragraph ends. Click the Show/Hide ¶ button on the Standard toolbar to display the hard returns (paragraph marks) and other nonprinting characters (such as tab characters or blank spaces) contained within a document. The Show/Hide ¶ functions as a toggle switch; the first time you click it the hard returns are displayed, the second time you press it the returns are hidden, and so on.

STEP 6: The Zoom Command

➤ Pull down the **View menu.** Click **Zoom** to produce the dialog box in Figure 2.16f. Click the **Many Pages** option button.

➤ Click the **monitor icon** to display a sample selection box, then click and drag to display three pages across. Release the mouse. Click **OK**.

STEP 7: Help for Word 2000

➤ Display the Office Assistant if it is not already visible on your screen. Pull down the **Help menu** and click the command to **Show the Office Assistant.**

➤ Ask the Assistant a question, then press the **Search button** in the Assistant's balloon to look for the answer. Select (click) the appropriate topic from the list of suggested topics provided by the Assistant.

➤ Click the **Show button** in the Help window that is displayed by the Assistant, then use either the **Contents** or **Index tab** to search for additional information. Close the Help window.

➤ If you have an Internet connection, pull down the **Help menu** and click **Microsoft on the Web** to connect to the Microsoft Web site for additional information. Explore the site, then close the browser and return to your document.

> **ADVICE FROM THE OFFICE ASSISTANT**
>
> The Office Assistant indicates it has a suggestion by displaying a lightbulb. Click the lightbulb to display the tip, then click the OK button to close the balloon and continue working. The Assistant will not, however, repeat a tip from an earlier session unless you reset it at the start of a new session. This is especially important in a laboratory situation where you are sharing a computer with many students. To reset the tips, click the Assistant to display a balloon asking what you want to do, click the Options button in the balloon, click the Options tab, then click the button to Reset my Tips.

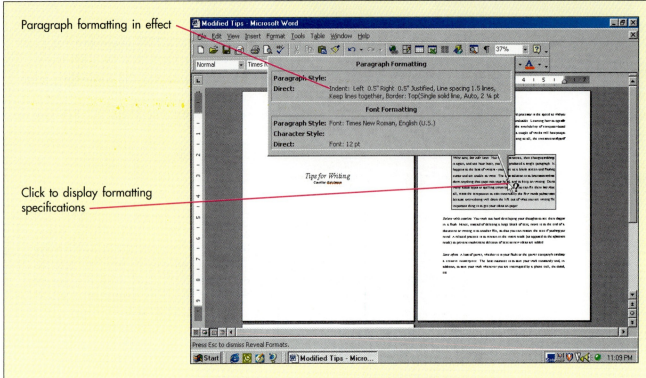

(e) Help with Formatting (step 5)

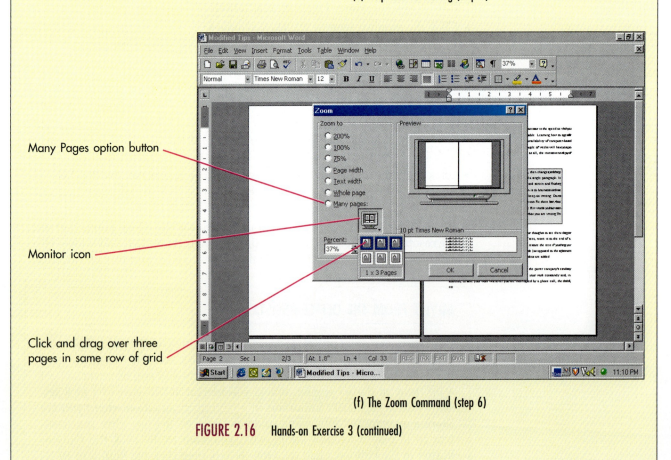

(f) The Zoom Command (step 6)

FIGURE 2.16 Hands-on Exercise 3 (continued)

STEP 8: The Completed Document

➤ Your screen should match the one in Figure 2.16g, which displays all three pages of the document.

➤ The Print Layout view displays both a vertical and a horizontal ruler. The boxed and indented paragraph is clearly shown in the second page.

➤ The soft page break between pages two and three occurs between tips rather than within a tip; that is, the text of each tip is kept together on the same page.

➤ Save the document a final time. Print the completed document and submit it to your instructor.

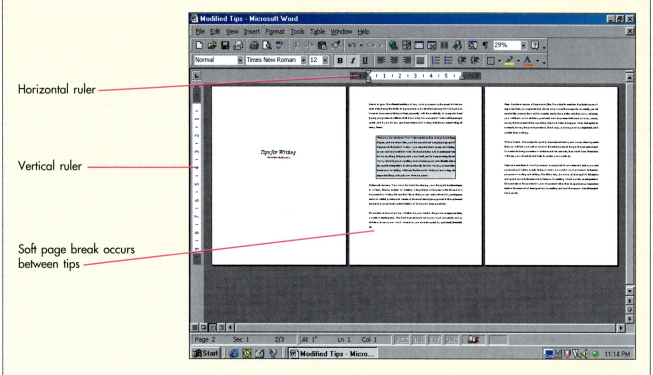

(g) The Completed Document (step 8)

FIGURE 2.16 Hands-on Exercise 3 (continued)

PRINT SELECTED PAGES

Why print an entire document if you want only a few pages? Pull down the File menu and click Print as you usually do to initiate the printing process. Click the Pages option button, then enter the page numbers and/or page ranges you want; for example, 3, 6–8 will print page three and pages six through eight. You can also print multiple copies by entering the appropriate number in the Number of copies list box.

STEP 9: Change the Column Structure

- Click the **down arrow** on the Zoom list box and return to **Page Width.** Press the **PgDn key** to scroll until the second page comes into view.
- Pull down the **File menu** and click the **Page Setup command** to display the Page Setup dialog box. Click the **Margins tab,** then change the Left and Right margins to 1″ each. Click **OK** to accept the settings and close the dialog box.
- Click anywhere in the paragraph, "Write Now but Edit Later". Pull down the **Format menu,** click the **Paragraph command,** click the Indents and Spacing tab if necessary, then change the left and right indents to 0.
- All paragraphs in the document should have the same indentation as shown in Figure 2.16h. Pull down the **Format menu** and click the **Columns command** to display the Columns dialog box.
- Click the icon for **three columns.** The default spacing between columns is .5″, which leads to a column width of 1.83″. Click in the Spacing list box and change the spacing to **.25″,** which automatically changes the column width to 2″.
- Check the box for the **Line Between** columns. Click **OK.**

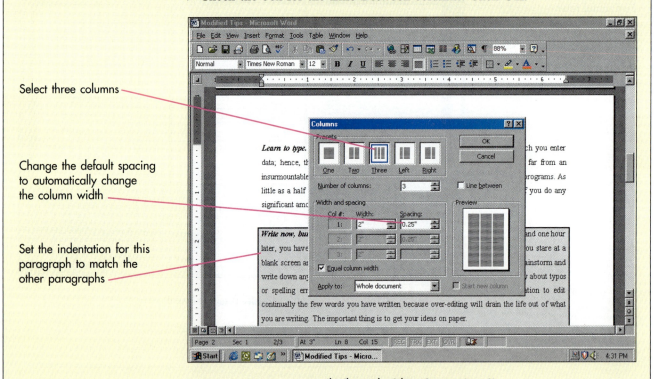

Select three columns

Change the default spacing to automatically change the column width

Set the indentation for this paragraph to match the other paragraphs

(h) Change the Column Structure (step 9)

FIGURE 2.16   Hands-on Exercise 3 (continued)

USE THE RULER TO CHANGE COLUMN WIDTH

Click anywhere within the column whose width you want to change, then point to the ruler and click and drag the right margin (the mouse pointer changes to a double arrow) to change the column width. Changing the width of one column in a document with equal-sized columns changes the width of all other columns so that they remain equal. Changing the width in a document with unequal columns changes only that column.

STEP 10: Insert a Section Break

- Pull down the **View menu,** click the **Zoom command,** then click the **Many Pages** option button. The document has switched to column formatting.
- Click at the beginning of the second page, immediately to the left of the first paragraph. Pull down the **Insert menu** and click **Break** to display the dialog box in Figure 2.16i.
- Click the **Continuous option button,** then click **OK** to accept the settings and close the dialog box.
- Click anywhere on the title page (before the section break you just inserted). Click the **Columns button,** then click the first column.
- The formatting for the first section of the document (the title page) should change to one column; the title of the document and your name are centered across the entire page.
- Print the document in this format for your instructor. Decide in which format you want to save the document—i.e., as it exists now, or as it existed at the end of step 8. Exit Word.

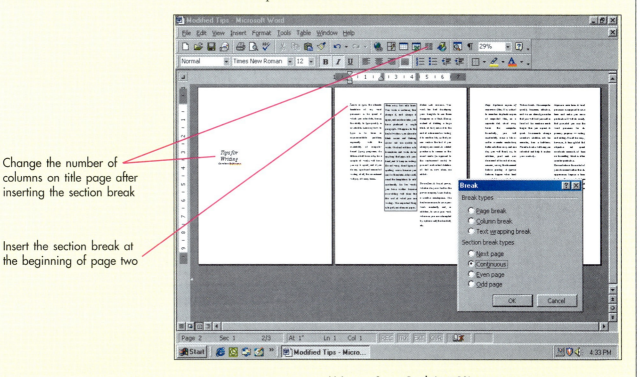

Change the number of columns on title page after inserting the section break

Insert the section break at the beginning of page two

(i) Insert a Section Break (step 10)

FIGURE 2.16 Hands-on Exercise 3 (continued)

THE COLUMNS BUTTON

The Columns button on the Standard toolbar is the fastest way to create columns in a document. Click the button, drag the mouse to choose the number of columns, then release the mouse to create the columns. The toolbar lets you change the number of columns, but not the spacing between columns. The toolbar is also limited, in that you cannot create columns of different widths or select a line between the columns.

SUMMARY

Many operations in Word are done within the context of select-then-do; that is, select the text, then execute the necessary command. Text may be selected by dragging the mouse, by using the selection bar to the left of the document, or by using the keyboard. Text is deselected by clicking anywhere within the document.

The Find and Replace commands locate a designated character string and optionally replace one or more occurrences of that string with a different character string. The search may be case-sensitive and/or restricted to whole words as necessary.

Text is moved or copied through a combination of the Cut, Copy, and Paste commands and/or the drag-and-drop facility. The contents of the Windows clipboard are modified by any subsequent Cut or Copy command, but are unaffected by the Paste command; that is, the same text can be pasted into multiple locations.

The Undo command reverses the effect of previous commands. The Undo and Redo commands work in conjunction with one another; that is, every command that is undone can be redone at a later time.

Scrolling occurs when a document is too large to be seen in its entirety. Scrolling with the mouse changes what is displayed on the screen, but does not move the insertion point; that is, you must click the mouse to move the insertion point. Scrolling via the keyboard (for example, PgUp and PgDn) changes what is seen on the screen as well as the location of the insertion point.

The Print Layout view displays top and bottom margins, headers and footers, and other elements not seen in the Normal view. The Normal view is faster because Word spends less time formatting the display. Both views can be seen at different magnifications.

TrueType fonts are scaleable and accessible from any Windows application. The Format Font command enables you to choose the typeface (e.g., Times New Roman or Arial), style (e.g., bold or italic), point size, and color of text.

The Format Paragraph command determines the line spacing, alignment, indents, and text flow, all of which are set at the paragraph level. Borders and shading are also set at the paragraph level. Margins, page size, and orientation, are set in the Page Setup command and affect the entire document (or section).

KEY WORDS AND CONCEPTS

Alignment
Arial
Automatic replacement
Borders and Shading command
Case-insensitive replacement
Case-sensitive replacement
Clipboard toolbar
Columns command
Copy command
Courier New
Cut command
Drag and drop

Find command
First line indent
Font
Format Font command
Format Painter
Format Paragraph command
Go To command
Hanging indent
Hard page break
Hyphenation
Indents
Landscape orientation
Leader character
Left indent

Line spacing
Margins
Monospaced typeface
Nonbreaking hyphen
Normal view
Office clipboard
Page break
Page Setup command
Paste command
Point size
Portrait orientation
Print Layout view
Proportional typeface
Redo command
Repeat command

Replace command	Serif typeface	Typography
Right indent	Shortcut menu	Underlining
Sans serif typeface	Soft page break	Undo command
Scrolling	Special indent	View menu
Section	Tab stop	Whole word replacement
Section break	Times New Roman	Widows and orphans
Select-Then-Do	Typeface	Wild card
Selection bar	Type size	Windows clipboard
Selective replacement	Type style	Zoom command

MULTIPLE CHOICE

1. Which of the following commands does *not* place data onto the clipboard?
   (a) Cut
   (b) Copy
   (c) Paste
   (d) All of the above

2. What happens if you select a block of text, copy it, move to the beginning of the document, paste it, move to the end of the document, and paste the text again?
   (a) The selected text will appear in three places: at the original location, and at the beginning and end of the document
   (b) The selected text will appear in two places: at the beginning and end of the document
   (c) The selected text will appear in just the original location
   (d) The situation is not possible; that is, you cannot paste twice in a row without an intervening cut or copy operation

3. What happens if you select a block of text, cut it, move to the beginning of the document, paste it, move to the end of the document, and paste the text again?
   (a) The selected text will appear in three places: at the original location and at the beginning and end of the document
   (b) The selected text will appear in two places: at the beginning and end of the document
   (c) The selected text will appear in just the original location
   (d) The situation is not possible; that is, you cannot paste twice in a row without an intervening cut or copy operation

4. Which of the following are set at the paragraph level?
   (a) Alignment
   (b) Tabs and indents
   (c) Line spacing
   (d) All of the above

5. How do you change the font for *existing* text within a document?
   (a) Select the text, then choose the new font
   (b) Choose the new font, then select the text
   (c) Either (a) or (b)
   (d) Neither (a) nor (b)

6. The Page Setup command can be used to change:
   (a) The margins in a document
   (b) The orientation of a document
   (c) Both (a) and (b)
   (d) Neither (a) nor (b)

7. Which of the following is a true statement regarding indents?
   (a) Indents are measured from the edge of the page rather than from the margin
   (b) The left, right, and first line indents must be set to the same value
   (c) The insertion point can be anywhere in the paragraph when indents are set
   (d) Indents must be set with the Format Paragraph command

8. The spacing in an existing multipage document is changed from single spacing to double spacing throughout the document. What can you say about the number of hard and soft page breaks before and after the formatting change?
   (a) The number of soft page breaks is the same, but the number and/or position of the hard page breaks is different
   (b) The number of hard page breaks is the same, but the number and/or position of the soft page breaks is different
   (c) The number and position of both hard and soft page breaks is the same
   (d) The number and position of both hard and soft page breaks is different

9. The default tab stops are set to:
   (a) Left indents every ½ inch
   (b) Left indents every ¼ inch
   (c) Right indents every ½ inch
   (d) Right indents every ¼ inch

10. Which of the following describes the Arial and Times New Roman fonts?
    (a) Arial is a sans serif font, Times New Roman is a serif font
    (b) Arial is a serif font, Times New Roman is a sans serif font
    (c) Both are serif fonts
    (d) Both are sans serif fonts

11. The find and replacement strings must be
    (a) The same length
    (b) The same case, either upper or lower
    (c) The same length and the same case
    (d) None of the above

12. Assume that you are in the middle of a multipage document. How do you scroll to the beginning of the document and simultaneously change the insertion point?
    (a) Press Ctrl+Home
    (b) Drag the scroll bar to the top of the scroll box
    (c) Both (a) and (b)
    (d) Neither (a) nor (b)

13. Which of the following substitutions can be accomplished by the Find and Replace command?
    (a) All occurrences of the words "Times New Roman" can be replaced with the word "Arial"
    (b) All text set in the Times New Roman font can be replaced by the Arial font
    (c) Both (a) and (b)
    (d) Neither (a) nor (b)

14. Which of the following deselects a selected block of text?
    (a) Clicking anywhere outside the selected text
    (b) Clicking any alignment button on the toolbar
    (c) Clicking the Bold, Italic, or Underline button
    (d) All of the above

15. Which view, and which magnification, lets you see the whole page, including top and bottom margins?
    (a) Print Layout view at 100% magnification
    (b) Print Layout view at Whole Page magnification
    (c) Normal view at 100% magnification
    (d) Normal view at Whole Page magnification

Answers

1. c	6. c	11. d
2. a	7. c	12. a
3. b	8. b	13. c
4. d	9. a	14. a
5. a	10. a	15. b

PRACTICE WITH MICROSOFT WORD

1. Formatting a Document: Open the *Chapter 2 Practice 1* document that is displayed in Figure 2.17 and make the following changes.
    a. Copy the sentence *Discretion is the better part of valor* to the beginning of the first paragraph.
    b. Move the second paragraph to the end of the document.
    c. Change the typeface of the entire document to 12 point Arial.
    d. Change all whole word occurrences of *feel* to *think*.
    e. Change the spacing of the entire document from single spacing to 1.5. Change the alignment of the entire document to justified.
    f. Set the phrases *Format Font command* and *Format Paragraph command* in italics.
    g. Indent the second paragraph .25 inch on both the left and right.
    h. Box and shade the last paragraph.
    i. Create a title page that precedes the document. Set the title, *Discretion in Design,* in 24 point Arial bold and center it approximately two inches from the top of the page. Right align your name toward the bottom of the title page in 12 point Arial regular.
    j. Print the revised document and submit it to your instructor.

It is not difficult, especially with practice, to learn to format a document. It is not long before the mouse goes automatically to the Format Font command to change the selected text to a sans-serif font, to increase the font size, or to apply a boldface or italic style. Nor is it long before you go directly to the Format Paragraph command to change the alignment or line spacing for selected paragraphs.

What is not easy, however, is to teach discretion in applying formats. Too many different formats on one page can be distracting, and in almost all cases, less is better. Be conservative and never feel that you have to demonstrate everything you know how to do in each and every document that you create. Discretion is the better part of valor. No more than two different typefaces should be used in a single document, although each can be used in a variety of different styles and sizes.

It is always a good idea to stay on the lookout for what you feel are good designs and then determine exactly what you like and don't like about each. In that way, you are constantly building ideas for your own future designs.

FIGURE 2.17 Formatting a Document (Exercise 1)

2. **Typography:** Figure 2.18 displays a completed version of the *Chapter 2 Practice 2* document that exists on the data disk. We want you to retrieve the original document from the data disk, then change the document so that it matches Figure 2.18. No editing is required as the text in the original document is identical to the finished document.

    The only changes are in formatting, but you will have to compare the documents in order to determine the nature of the changes. Color is a nice touch (which depends on the availability of a color printer) and is not required. Add your name somewhere in the document, then print the revised document and submit it to your instructor.

3. **The Preamble:** Create a simple document containing the text of the Preamble to the Constitution as shown in Figure 2.19.
    a. Set the Preamble in 12 point Times New Roman.
    b. Use single spacing and left alignment.
    c. Copy the Preamble to a new page, then change to a larger point size and more interesting typeface.
    d. Create a title page for your assignment, containing your name, course name, and appropriate title.
    e. Use a different typeface for the title page than in the rest of the document, and set the title in at least 24 points.
    f. Submit all three pages (the title page and both versions of the Preamble) to your instructor.

TYPOGRAPHY

The art of formatting a document is more than just knowing definitions, but knowing the definitions is definitely a starting point. A ***typeface*** is a complete set of characters with the same general appearance, and can be *serif* (cross lines at the end of the main strokes of each letter) or *sans serif* (without the cross lines). A ***type size*** is a vertical measurement, made from the top of the tallest letter in the character set to the bottom of the lowest letter in the character set. ***Type style*** refers to variations in the typeface, such as boldface and italics.

Several typefaces are shipped with Windows, including ***Times New Roman***, a serif typeface, and ***Arial***, a sans serif typeface. Times New Roman should be used for large amounts of text, whereas Arial is best used for titles and subtitles. It is best not to use too many different typefaces in the same document, but rather to use only one or two and then make the document interesting by varying their size and style.

FIGURE 2.18 Typography (Exercise 2)

We, the people of the United States, in order to form a more perfect Union, establish justice, insure domestic tranquillity, provide for the common defense, promote the general welfare, and secure the blessings of liberty to ourselves and our posterity, do ordain and establish this Constitution for the United States of America.

FIGURE 2.19 The Preamble (Exercise 3)

4. Tab Stops: Anyone who has used a typewriter is familiar with the function of the Tab key; that is, press Tab and the insertion point moves to the next tab stop (a measured position to align text at a specific place). The Tab key is more powerful in Word because you can choose from four different types of tab stops (left, center, right, and decimal). You can also specify a leader character, typically dots or hyphens, to draw the reader's eye across the page.

Create the document in Figure 2.20 and add your name in the indicated position. (Use the Help facility to discover how to work with tab stops.) Submit the completed document to your instructor as proof that you have mastered the Tab key.

EXAMPLES OF TAB STOPS

Example 1 - Right tab at 6":

CIS 120   **Maryann Barber**
Fall 1999   **September 21, 1999**

Example 2 - Right tab with a dot leader at 6":

Chapter 1..1
Chapter 2..31
Chapter 3..56

Example 3 - Right tab at 1" and left tab at 1.25":

          To: Maryann Barber
     From: Joel Stutz
Department: Computer Information Systems
  Subject: Exams

Example 4 - Left tab at 2" and a decimal tab at 3.5":

          Rent $375.38
          Utilities $125.59
          Phone $56.92
          Cable $42.45

FIGURE 2.20   Tab Stops (Exercise 4)

5. **The Page Borders Command:** Figure 2.21 illustrates a hypothetical title page for a paper describing the capabilities of borders and shading. The Borders and Shading command is applied at the paragraph level as indicated in the chapter. You can, however, select the Page Border tab within the Borders and Shading dialog box to create an unusual and attractive document. Experiment with the command to create a title page similar to Figure 2.21. Submit the document to your instructor as proof you did the exercise.

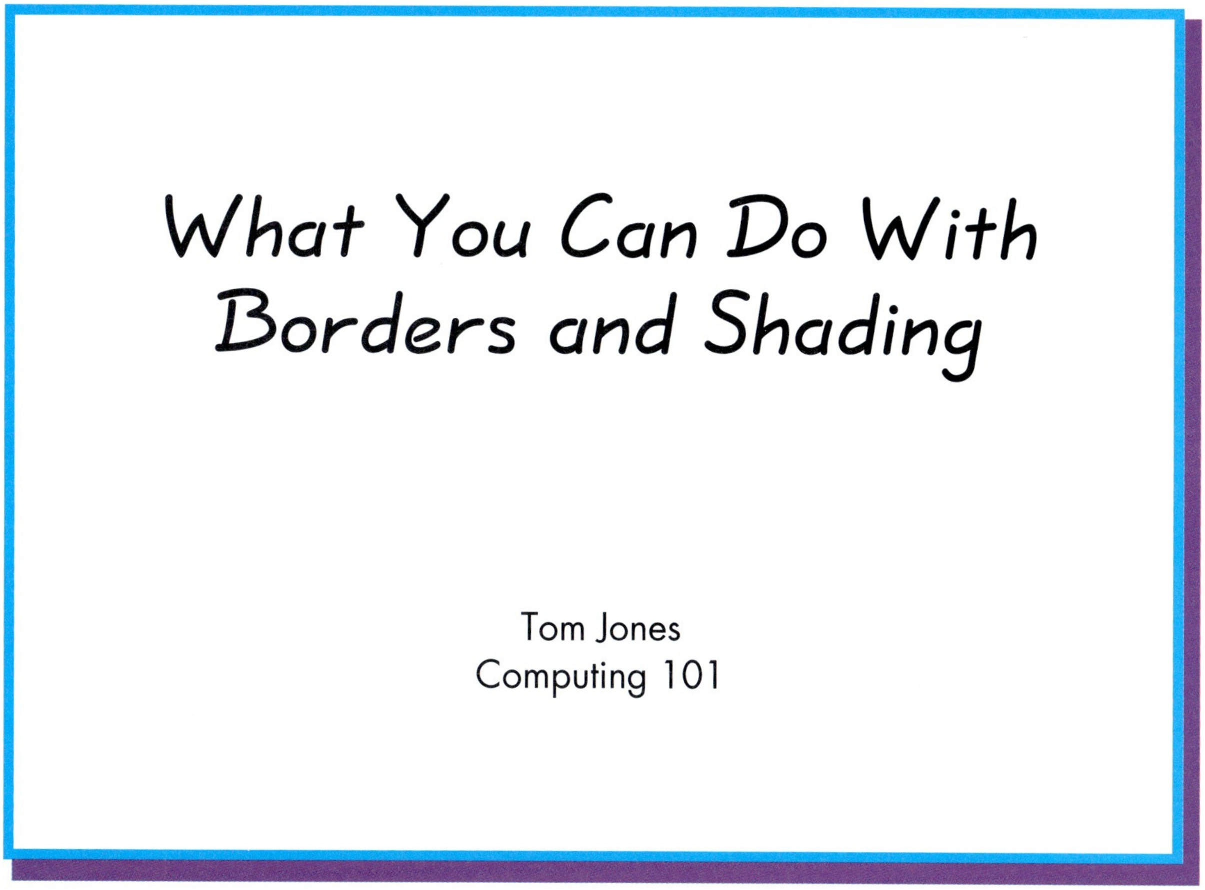

What You Can Do With Borders and Shading

Tom Jones
Computing 101

FIGURE 2.21   The Page Borders Command (Exercise 5)

6. **Exploring Fonts:** The Font Folder within the Control Panel displays the names of the fonts available on a system and enables you to obtain a printed sample of any specific font. Click the Start button, click (or point to) the Settings command, click (or point to) Control Panel, then double click the Fonts icon to open the font folder and display the fonts on your system.
    a. Double click a font you want to view, then click the Print button to print a sample of the selected font.
    b. Click the Fonts button on the Taskbar to return to the Fonts window and open a different font. Print a sample page of this font as well.
    c. Start Word. Create a title page containing your name, class, date, and the title of this assignment (My Favorite Fonts). Center the title. Use boldface or italics as you see fit. Be sure to use appropriate type sizes.
    d. Staple the three pages together (the title page and two font samples), then submit them to your instructor.

7. Inserting the Date and Time: Create a document similar to Figure 2.22 that describes the Insert Date and Time command. You need not duplicate our document exactly, but you are asked to print the dates in several formats. Use the columns feature to separate the two sets of dates. Note the keyboard shortcut that is described in the document to go to the next column. You will also have to insert a section break before and after the dates to change the number of columns in the document. Create your document on one day, then open it a day later, to be sure that the dates that were entered as fields were updated appropriately.

Inserting the Date and Time

The *Insert Date and Time command* puts the date (and/or time) into a document. The date can be inserted as a specific value (the date and time on which the command is executed) or as a *field*. The latter is updated automatically from the computer's internal clock whenever the document is opened or when the document is printed. You can also update a field manually, by selecting the appropriate command from a shortcut menu. Either way, the date may be printed in a variety of formats as shown below.

Update field box is clear	Update field box is checked
January 21, 1999	February 15, 1999
Thursday, January 21, 1999	Monday, February 15, 1999
1/21/99	2/15/99
21 January 1999	15 February 1999
1/21/99 10:08 AM	2/15/1999

Any date that is entered as a field is shaded by default. You can change that, however, by using the Options command in the Tools menu. (Select the View tab and click the drop-down arrow in the Field Shading list box to choose the option you want.) Note, too, that I created this document using the columns feature. My document has three sections, with the section in the middle containing two columns. (I pressed **Ctrl+Shift+Enter** to go from the bottom of one column to the top of the next.)

Maryann Coulter
January 21, 1999

FIGURE 2.22 Inserting the Date and Time (Exercise 7)

CASE STUDIES

Computers Past and Present

The ENIAC was the scientific marvel of its day and the world's first operational electronic computer. It could perform 5,000 additions per second, weighed 30 tons, and took 1,500 square feet of floor space. The price was a modest $486,000 in 1946 dollars. The story of the ENIAC and other influential computers of the author's choosing is found in the file *History of Computers*, which we forgot to format, so we are asking you to do it for us.

Be sure to use appropriate emphasis for the names of the various computers. Create a title page in front of the document, then submit the completed assignment to your instructor. If you are ambitious, you can enhance this assignment by using your favorite search engine to look for computer museums on the Web. Visit one or two sites, and include this information on a separate page at the end of the document. One last task, and that is to update the description of Today's PC (the last computer in the document).

Your First Consultant's Job

Go to a real installation, such as a doctor's or an attorney's office, the company where you work, or the computer lab at school. Determine the backup procedures that are in effect, then write a one-page report indicating whether the policy is adequate and, if necessary, offering suggestions for improvement. Your report should be addressed to the individual in charge of the business, and it should cover all aspects of the backup strategy—that is, which files are backed up and how often, and what software is used for the backup operation. Use appropriate emphasis (for example, bold italics) to identify any potential problems. This is a professional document (it is your first consultant's job), and its appearance must be perfect in every way.

To Hyphenate or Not to Hyphenate

The best way to learn about hyphenation is to experiment with an existing document. Open the *To Hyphenate or Not to Hyphenate* document that is on the data disk. The document is currently set in 12-point type with hyphenation in effect. Experiment with various formatting changes that will change the soft line breaks to see the effect on the hyphenation within the document. You can change the point size, the number of columns, and/or the right indent. You can also suppress hyphenation altogether, as described within the document. Summarize your findings in a short note to your instructor.

Paper Makes a Difference

Most of us take paper for granted, but the right paper can make a significant difference in the effectiveness of the document. Reports and formal correspondence are usually printed on white paper, but you would be surprised how many different shades of white there are. Other types of documents lend themselves to colored paper for additional impact. In short, which paper you use is far from an automatic decision. Walk into a local copy store and see if they have any specialty papers available. Our favorite source for paper is a company called *Paper Direct* (1-800-APAPERS). Ask for a catalog, then consider the use of a specialty paper the next time you have an important project.

The Invitation

Choose an event and produce the perfect invitation. The possibilities are endless and limited only by your imagination. You can invite people to your wedding or to a fraternity party. Your laser printer and abundance of fancy fonts enable you to do anything a professional printer can do. Special paper (see previous case study) will add the finishing touch. Go to it—this assignment is a lot of fun.

One Space After a Period

Touch typing classes typically teach the student to place two spaces after a period. The technique worked well in the days of the typewriter and monospaced fonts, but it creates an artificially large space when used with proportional fonts and a word processor. Select any document that is at least several paragraphs in length and print the document with the current spacing. Use the Find and Replace commands to change to the alternate spacing, then print the document a second time. Which spacing looks better to you? Submit both versions of the document to your instructor with a brief note summarizing your findings.

The Contest

Almost everyone enjoys some form of competition. Ask your instructor to choose a specific type of document, such as a flyer or résumé, and declare a contest in the class to produce the "best" document. Submit your entry, but write your name on the back of the document so that it can be judged anonymously. Your instructor may want to select a set of semifinalists and then distribute copies of those documents so that the class can vote on the winner.

chapter 3

ENHANCING A DOCUMENT: THE WEB AND OTHER RESOURCES

OBJECTIVES

After reading this chapter you will be able to:

1. Describe object linking and embedding; explain how it is used to create a compound document.
2. Describe the resources in the Microsoft Clip Gallery; insert clip art and/or a photograph into a document.
3. Use the Format Picture command to wrap text around a clip art image.
4. Use WordArt to insert decorative text into a document.
5. Describe the Internet and World Wide Web; download resources from the Web for inclusion in a Word document.
6. Insert a hyperlink into a Word document; save a Word document as a Web page.
7. Use the Drawing toolbar to create and modify lines and objects.
8. Insert a footnote or endnote into a document to cite a reference.
9. Use wizards and templates to create a document.

OVERVIEW

This chapter describes how to enhance a document using applications within Microsoft Office Professional as well as resources on the Internet and World Wide Web. We begin with a discussion of the Microsoft Clip Gallery, a collection of clip art, sound files, and motion clips that can be inserted into any office document. We describe how Microsoft WordArt can be used to create special effects with text and how to create lines and objects through the Drawing toolbar.

These resources pale, however, in comparison to what is available via the Internet. Thus, we also show you how to download an object from the Web and include it in an Office document. We describe how to add footnotes to give appropriate credit to your sources and how to further enhance a document through inclusion of hyperlinks. We also explain how to save a Word document as a Web page so that you can post the documents you create to a Web server or local area network.

The chapter also describes the various wizards and templates that are built into Microsoft Word to help you create professionally formatted documents. We believe this to be a very enjoyable chapter that will add significantly to your capability in Microsoft Word. As always, learning is best accomplished by doing, and the hands-on exercises are essential to master the material.

A COMPOUND DOCUMENT

The applications in Microsoft Office are thoroughly integrated with one another. Equally important, they share information through a technology known as ***Object Linking and Embedding (OLE),*** which enables you to create a ***compound document*** containing data (objects) from multiple applications.

Consider, for example, the compound document in Figure 3.1, which was created in Microsoft Word but contains objects (data) from other applications. The ***clip art*** (a graphic as opposed to a photograph) was taken from the Microsoft Clip Gallery. The title of the document was created using Microsoft WordArt. The document also illustrates the Insert Symbol command to insert special characters such as the Windows logo.

Enhancing a Document

Clip art is available from a variety of sources, including the Microsoft Clip Gallery, which is part of Microsoft Office. The Clip Gallery contains clip art as well as sound bites and motion clips, although the latter are more common in PowerPoint presentations. Once the object has been inserted into a document, it can be moved and sized using various options in the Format Picture command. You can wrap text around a picture, place a border around the picture or even crop (cut out part of) the picture if necessary.

In addition to clip art, you can use WordArt to create artistic effects to enhance any document. WordArt enables you to create special effects with text. It lets you rotate and/or flip text, display it vertically on the page, shade it, slant it, arch it, or even print it upside down. Best of all, WordArt is intuitive and easy to use. In essence, you enter text into a dialog box, and then you choose a shape for the text from a dialog box. You can create special effects by choosing one of several different shadows. You can vary the image even further by using any TrueType font on your system. It's fun, it's easy, and you can create some truly dynamite documents.

The Insert Symbol command enables you to insert special symbols into a document to give it a professional look. You can, for example, use ™ rather than TM, © rather than (C), or ½ and ¼ rather than 1/2 and 1/4. It also enables you to insert accented characters as appropriate in English, as in the word *résumé*, or in a foreign language to create properly accented words and phrases—for example, *¿Cómo está usted?*

You can insert clip art or WordArt into any Office document using the same commands that you will learn in this chapter. Indeed, that is one of the benefits of the Office suite because the same commands are executed from the same menus as you go from one application to another. In addition, each application also contains a Standard toolbar and a Formatting toolbar.

Eric Simon created this document using Microsoft Windows ®

WordArt

Clip art

Windows logo added through Insert Symbol command

FIGURE 3.1 A Compound Document

Microsoft Clip Gallery

The *Microsoft Clip Gallery* contains clip art, sound files, and motion clips and it is accessible from any application in Microsoft Office. Clip art is inserted into a document in one of two ways—through the *Insert Object command* or more directly through the *Insert Picture command* as shown in Figure 3.2. Choose the type of object and the category (such as a picture in the Animals category in Figure 3.2a), then select the image (the lion in Figure 3.2b) and insert it into the document. After a picture has been placed into a document, it can be moved and sized just like any Windows object.

(a) Choose the Category

(b) Choose the Image

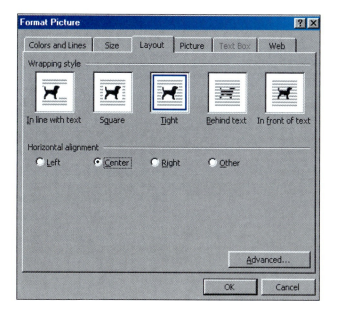

(c) Format the Picture

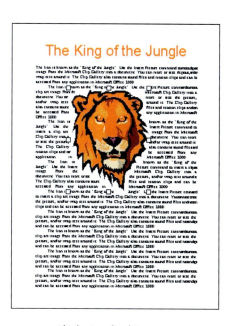

(d) The Completed Document

FIGURE 3.2 Microsoft Clip Gallery

The ***Format Picture command*** enables you to further customize the picture. The Layout tab in Figure 3.2c determines the position of the picture with respect to the text. We chose the tight wrapping style, which means that the text comes to the border of the picture. You can also use the ***Picture Toolbar*** (not shown in Figure 3.2) to ***crop*** (cut out part of) the picture if necessary. Figure 3.2d shows how the selected object appears in the completed document. Note, too, the ***sizing handles*** on the graphic that enable you to move and size the picture within the document.

The Insert Symbol Command

One characteristic of a professional document is the use of typographic symbols in place of ordinary typing—for example, ® rather than (R), © rather than (C), or ½ and ¼ rather than 1/2 and 1/4. Much of this formatting is implemented automatically by Word through substitutions built into the ***AutoCorrect*** feature. Other characters, especially accented characters such as the "é" in résumé, or those in a foreign language (e.g., ¿Cómo está usted?), have to be inserted manually into a document.

Look carefully at the last line of Figure 3.1, and notice the Windows logo at the end of the sentence. The latter was created through the ***Insert Symbol command,*** as shown in Figure 3.3. You select the font containing the desired character (e.g., Wingdings in Figure 3.3), then you select the character, and finally you click the Insert command button to place the character in the document.

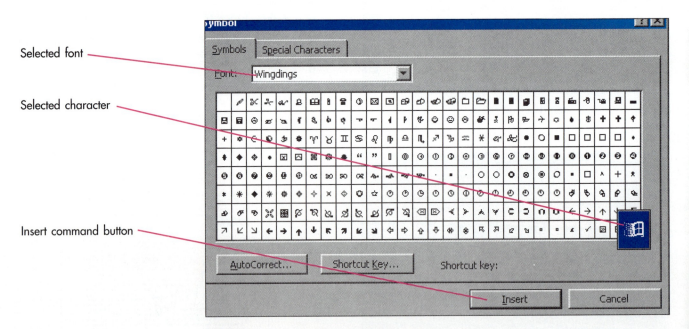

FIGURE 3.3 The Insert Symbol Command

THE WINGDINGS AND SYMBOLS FONTS

The Wingdings and Symbols fonts are two of the best-kept secrets in Windows 95. Both fonts contain a variety of special characters that can be inserted into a document through the Insert Symbol command. These fonts are scaleable to any point size, enabling you to create some truly unusual documents. (See practice exercise 3 at the end of the chapter.)

Microsoft WordArt

Microsoft WordArt is an application within Microsoft Office that creates decorative text to add interest to a document. You can use WordArt in addition to clip art, as was done in Figure 3.1, or in place of clip art if the right image is not available. You're limited only by your imagination, as you can rotate text in any direction, add three-dimensional effects, display the text vertically down the page, shade it, slant it, arch it, or even print it upside down.

WordArt is intuitive and easy to use. In essence, you choose a style for the text from among the selections in the dialog box of Figure 3.4a, then you enter your specific text as shown in Figure 3.4b. You can modify the style through various special effects, you can use any TrueType font on your system, and you can change the color or shading. Figure 3.4c shows the completed WordArt object. It's fun, it's easy, and you can create some truly dynamite documents.

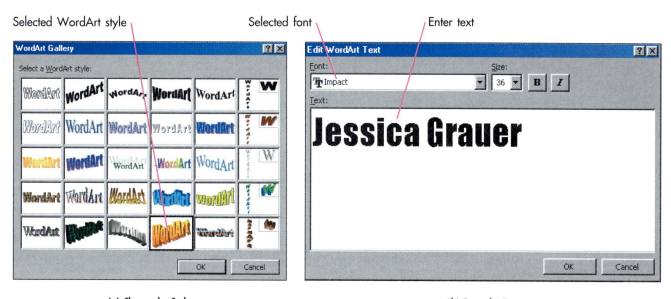

(a) Choose the Style   (b) Enter the Text

(c) Completed WordArt

FIGURE 3.4   Microsoft WordArt

THE DRAWING TOOLBAR

Did you ever stop to think how the images in the Clip Gallery were developed? Undoubtedly they were drawn by someone with artistic ability who used basic shapes, such as lines and curves in various combinations, to create the images. The ***Drawing toolbar*** in Figure 3.5 contains all of the tools necessary to create original clip art. As with any toolbar, you can point to a button to display a ScreenTip containing the name of the button that is indicative of its function.

To draw an object, select the appropriate tool, then click and drag in the document to create the object. Select the Line tool, for example, then draw the line. After the line has been created, you can select it and change its properties (such as thickness, style, or color) by using other tools on the Drawing toolbar. To create a drawing, you add other objects such as lines and curves, and soon you have a piece of original clip art.

Once you learn the basics, there are other techniques to master. The Shift key, for example, has special significance when used in conjunction with the Line, Rectangle, and Oval tools. Press and hold the Shift key as you drag the line tool horizontally or vertically to create a perfectly straight line in either direction. Press and hold the Shift key as you drag the Rectangle and Oval tool to create a square or circle, respectively. We don't expect you to create clip art comparable to the images within the Clip Gallery, but you can use the tools on the Drawing toolbar to modify an existing image and/or create simple shapes of your own that can enhance any document.

One tool that is especially useful is the ***AutoShapes button*** that displays a series of selected shapes such as the callout or banner. And, as with any object, you can change the thickness, color, or fill by selecting the object and choosing the appropriate tool. It's fun, it's easy—just be flexible and willing to experiment. We think you will be pleased at what you will be able to do.

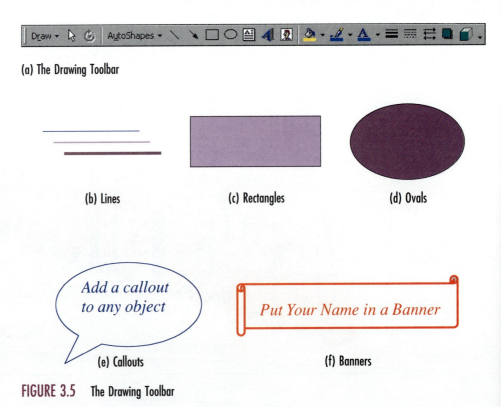

FIGURE 3.5   The Drawing Toolbar

HANDS-ON EXERCISE 1

Creating a Compound Document

Objective: To create a compound document containing clip art and WordArt; to illustrate the Insert Symbol command to place typographical symbols into a document. Use Figure 3.6 as a guide in the exercise.

STEP 1: Insert the Clip Art

➤ Start Word. Open the **Clip Art and WordArt** document in the Exploring Word folder. Save the document as **Modified Clip Art and WordArt.**

➤ Check that the insertion point is at the beginning of the document. Pull down the **Insert menu,** click **Picture,** then click **Clip Art** to display the Insert Clip Art dialog box as shown in Figure 3.6a.

➤ If necessary, click the **Pictures tab** and select (click) the **Science and Technology category.** Select the **Computers graphic** (or a different image if you prefer), then click the **Insert Clip button** on the shortcut menu.

➤ The picture should appear in the document where it can be moved and sized as described in the next several steps.

➤ Click the **Close button** on the Insert Clip Art dialog box.

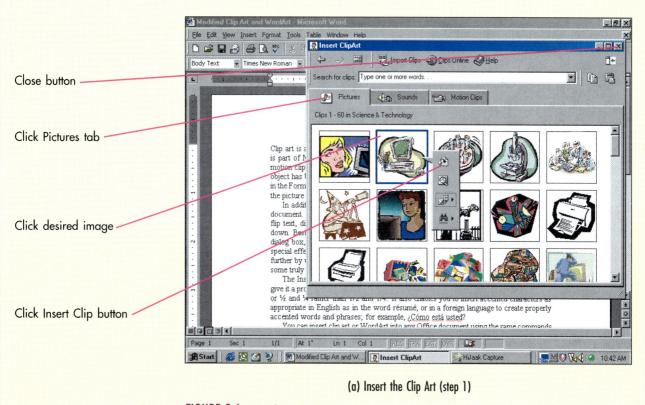

(a) Insert the Clip Art (step 1)

FIGURE 3.6 Hands-on Exercise 1

CHAPTER 3: ENHANCING A DOCUMENT

STEP 2: Move and Size the Picture

➤ Change to the Print Layout view in Figure 3.6b. Move and size the image.
➤ To size an object:
- Click the object to display the sizing handles.
- Drag a corner handle (the mouse pointer changes to a double arrow) to change the length and width of the picture simultaneously; this keeps the graphic in proportion as it sizes it.
- Drag a handle on the horizontal or vertical border to change one dimension only; this distorts the picture.

➤ To move an object:
- Click the object to display the sizing handles.
- Point to any part of the image except a sizing handle (the mouse pointer changes to a four-sided arrow), then click and drag to move the image elsewhere in the document. You cannot wrap text around the image until you execute the Format Picture command in step 3.

➤ Save the document.

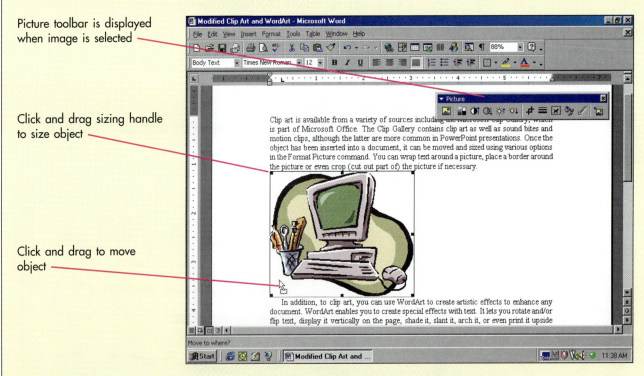

Picture toolbar is displayed when image is selected

Click and drag sizing handle to size object

Click and drag to move object

(b) Move and Size the Picture (step 2)

FIGURE 3.6 Hands-on Exercise 1 (continued)

FIND THE RIGHT CLIP ART

Use the search capability within the Clip Gallery to find the right image. Pull down the Insert menu, click Picture, then click Clip Art to display the Insert Clip Art dialog box. Click in the Search for text box, enter a key word such as "women," then press the enter key to display all of the images, regardless of category, that list "women" as a key word.

STEP 3: Format the Picture

➤ Be sure the clip art is still selected, then pull down the **Format menu** and select the **Picture command** to display the Format Picture dialog box in Figure 3.6c.

➤ Click the **Layout tab,** select **Square** as the wrapping style, and choose the **left option button** under horizontal alignment.

➤ The text should be wrapped to the right of the image. Move and size the image until you are satisfied with its position. Note, however, that the image will always be positioned (wrapped) according to the settings in the Format Picture command.

➤ Save the document.

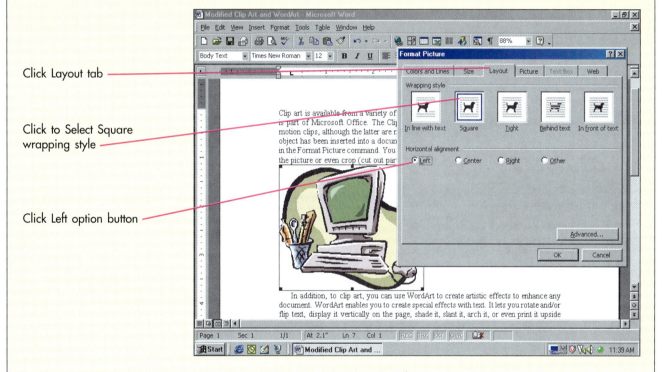

(c) Format the Picture (step 3)

FIGURE 3.6 Hands-on Exercise 1 (continued)

CLIP PROPERTIES

Every clip art image has multiple properties that determine the category (or categories) in which it is listed as well as key words that are reflected in a search of the Clip Gallery. Right click any image within the Insert Clip Art dialog box and click the Click Properties command to display the Clip Properties dialog box. Click the Categories tab, then check any additional categories under which the image should appear. Click the Keywords tab to add (delete) the entries for this item. Click OK to accept the changes and close the Properties dialog box. Check the additional categories or search on a new key word within the Insert Clip Art dialog box to verify the effect of your changes.

STEP 4: WordArt

➤ Press **Ctrl+End** to move to the end of the document. Pull down the **Insert menu,** click **Picture,** then click **WordArt** to display the WordArt Gallery dialog box.

➤ Select the WordArt style you like (you can change it later). Click **OK.** You will see a second dialog box in which you enter the text. Enter **Enhancing a Document.** Click **OK.**

➤ The WordArt object appears in your document in the style you selected. Point to the WordArt object and click the **right mouse button** to display the shortcut menu in Figure 3.6d. Click **Format WordArt** to display the Format WordArt dialog box.

➤ Click the **Layout tab,** then select **Square** as the Wrapping style. Click **OK.** It is important to select this wrapping option to facilitate placing the WordArt at the top of the document. Save the document.

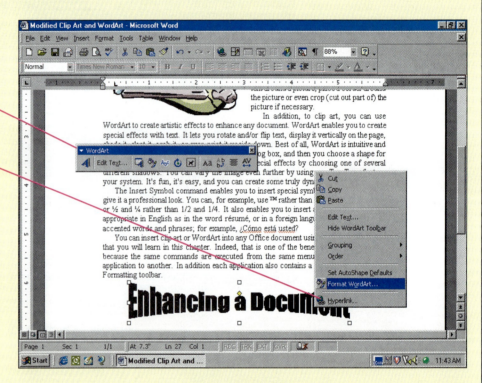

WordArt toolbar is displayed when WordArt object is selected

Point to WordArt object and click right mouse button to display shortcut menu

(d) WordArt (step 4)

FIGURE 3.6 Hands-on Exercise 1 (continued)

FORMATTING WORDART

The WordArt toolbar offers the easiest way to execute various commands associated with a WordArt object. It is displayed automatically when a WordArt object is selected, and suppressed otherwise. As with any toolbar, you can point to a button to display a ScreenTip containing the name of the button, which is indicative of its function. You will find buttons to display the text vertically, change the style or shape, and/or edit the text.

STEP 5: WordArt (continued)

➤ Click and drag the WordArt object to move it the top of the document as shown in Figure 3.6e. (The Format WordArt dialog box is not yet visible.)

➤ Point to the WordArt object, click the **right mouse button** to display a shortcut menu, then click **Format WordArt** to display the Format WordArt dialog box.

➤ Click the **Colors and Lines tab,** then click the **Fill Color drop-down arrow** to display the available colors. Select a different color (e.g., blue). Click **OK.**

➤ Move and/or size the WordArt object as necessary.

➤ Save the document.

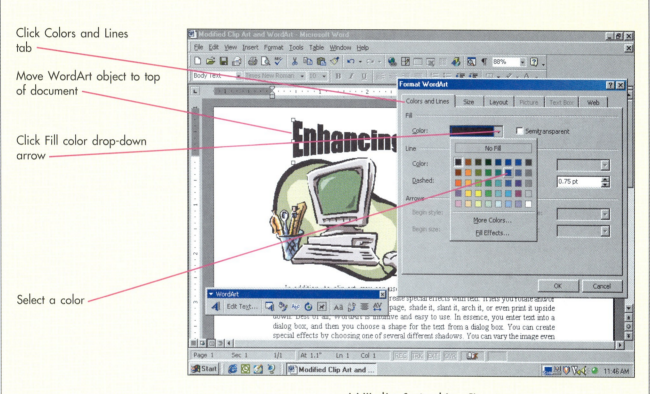

Click Colors and Lines tab

Move WordArt object to top of document

Click Fill color drop-down arrow

Select a color

(e) WordArt, Continued (step 5)

FIGURE 3.6 Hands-on Exercise 1 (continued)

THE THIRD DIMENSION

You can make your WordArt images even more dramatic by adding 3-D effects. You can tilt the text up or down, right or left, increase or decrease the depth, and change the shading. Pull down the View menu, click Toolbars, click Customize to display the complete list of available toolbars, click the Toolbars tab, check the box to display the 3-D Settings toolbar, and click the Close button. Select the WordArt object, then experiment with various tools and special effects. The results are even better if you have a color printer.

STEP 6: The Insert Symbol Command

➤ Press **Ctrl+End** to move to the end of the document as shown in Figure 3.6f. Press the **enter key** to insert a blank line at the end of the document.

➤ Type the sentence, **Eric Simon created this document using Microsoft Windows,** substituting your name for Eric Simon. Click the **Center button** on the Formatting toolbar to center the sentence.

➤ Pull down the **Insert menu,** click **Symbol,** then choose **Wingdings** from the Font list box. Click the **Windows logo** (the last character in the last line), click **Insert,** then close the Symbol dialog box.

➤ Click and drag to select the newly inserted symbol, click the **drop-down arrow** on the **Font Size box,** then change the font to **24** points. Press the **right arrow key** to deselect the symbol.

➤ Click the **drop-down arrow** on the **Font Size box** and change to **10 point type** so that subsequent text is entered in this size. Type **(r)** after the Windows logo and try to watch the monitor as you enter the text. The (r) will be converted automatically to ® because of the AutoFormat command.

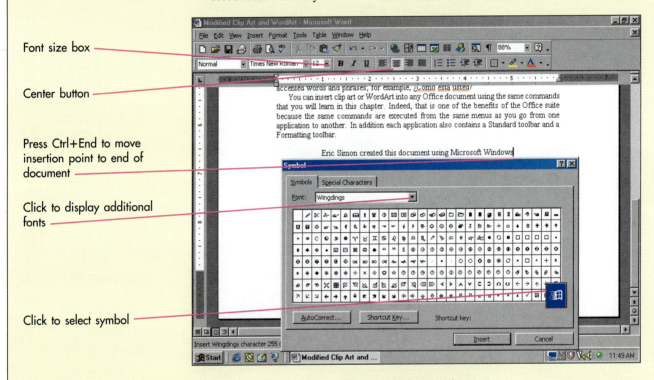

Font size box

Center button

Press Ctrl+End to move insertion point to end of document

Click to display additional fonts

Click to select symbol

(f) Insert Symbol Command (step 6)

FIGURE 3.6   Hands-on Exercise 1 (continued)

AUTOCORRECT AND AUTOFORMAT

The AutoCorrect feature not only corrects mistakes as you type by substituting one character string for another (e.g., *the* for *teh*), but it will also substitute symbols for typewritten equivalents such as © for (c), provided the entries are included in the table of substitutions. The AutoFormat feature is similar in concept and replaces common fractions such as 1/2 or 1/4 with ½ or ¼. It also converts ordinal numbers such as 1st to 1st.

STEP 7: Create the AutoShape

➤ Pull down the **View menu,** click (or point to) the **Toolbars command** to display the list of available toolbars, then click the **Drawing toolbar**.

➤ Press **Ctrl+End** to move to the end of the document. Move up one line and press **enter** to create a blank line. Click the **down arrow** on the AutoShapes button to display the AutoShapes menu. Click the **Stars and Banners submenu** and select (click) the **Horizontal scroll.**

➤ The mouse pointer changes to a tiny crosshair. Click and drag the mouse over the last sentence (that has Eric Simon's name) to create the scroll as shown in Figure 3.6g (the shortcut menus are not yet visible). Release the mouse.

➤ The scroll is still selected but the underlying text has disappeared. Click the **right mouse button** to display a context-sensitive menu, click the **Order command,** then click **Send Behind Text.** The text is now visible.

➤ Click the **Line Style** and/or **Line Color** tools to change the thickness and color of the line, respectively.

➤ Click elsewhere in the document to deselect the scroll. Save the document.

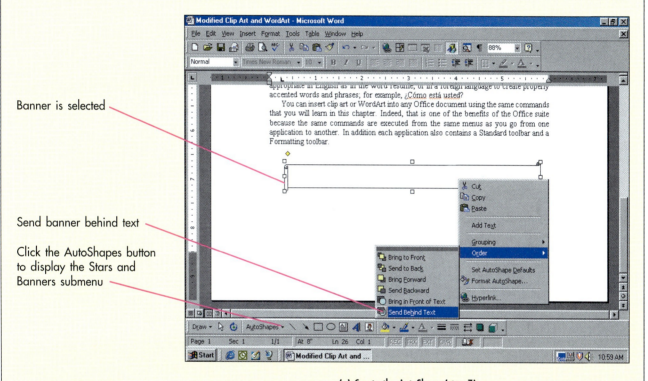

(g) Create the AutoShape (step 7)

FIGURE 3.6 Hands-on Exercise 1 (continued)

DISPLAY THE AUTOSHAPE TOOLBAR

Click the down arrow on the AutoShapes button on the Drawing toolbar to display a cascaded menu listing the various types of AutoShapes, then click and drag the menu's title bar to display the menu as a floating toolbar. Click any tool on the AutoShapes toolbar (such as Stars and Banners), then click and drag its title bar to display the various stars and banners in their own floating toolbar.

STEP 8: The Completed Document

➤ Pull down the **File menu** and click the **Page Setup command** to display the Page Setup dialog box. Click the **Margins tab** and change the top margin to **1.5 inches** (to accommodate the WordArt at the top of the document). Click **OK**.

➤ Click the **drop-down arrow** on the Zoom box and select **Whole Page** to preview the completed document as shown in Figure 3.6h. You can change the size and position of the objects from within this view. For example:

- Click the WordArt to select the object and display the sizing handles and WordArt toolbar.
- Click the banner to deselect the WordArt and display the sizing handles for the banner.

➤ Move and size either object as necessary; then save the document a final time.

➤ Print the document and submit it to your instructor as proof that you did the exercise. Close the document. Exit Word if you do not want to continue with the next exercise at this time.

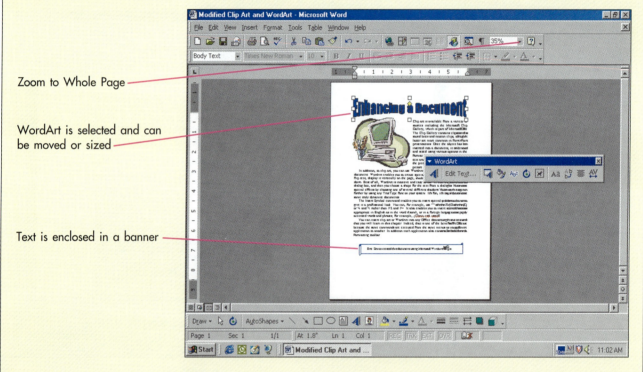

(h) The Completed Document (step 8)

FIGURE 3.6 Hands-on Exercise 1 (continued)

HIGHLIGHT IMPORTANT TEXT

You will love the Highlight text tool, especially if you are in the habit of highlighting text in with a pen. Click the tool to turn the feature on (the button is depressed and the mouse pointer changes to a pen), then paint as many sections as you like. Click the tool a second time to turn the feature off. Click the drop-down arrow on the tool to change the highlighting color.

WORD 2000 AND THE INTERNET

The emergence of the Internet and World Wide Web has totally changed our society. Perhaps you are already familiar with the basic concepts that underlie the Internet, but if not, a brief review is in order. The **Internet** is a network of networks that connects computers anywhere in the world. The **World Wide Web** (WWW or simply, the Web) is a very large subset of the Internet, consisting of those computers that store a special type of document known as a **Web page** or **HTML document.**

The interesting thing about a Web page is that it contains references called **hyperlinks** to other Web pages, which may in turn be stored on a different computer that may be located anywhere in the world. And therein lies the fascination of the Web, in that you simply click on link after link to go effortlessly from one document to the next. You can start your journey on your professor's home page, then browse through any set of links you wish to follow.

The Internet and World Wide Web are thoroughly integrated into Office 2000 in three important ways. First, you can download resources from any Web page for inclusion in an Office document. Second, you can insert hyperlinks into an Office document, then click those links within Office to display the associated Web page. And finally, you can convert any Office document into a Web page as we will do in Figure 3.7.

All Web pages are developed in a special language called **HTML (HyperText Markup Language).** Initially, the only way to create a Web page was to learn HTML. As indicated, Office 2000 simplifies the process because you can create the document in Word, then simply save it as a Web page. In other words, you start Word in the usual fashion and enter the text of the document with basic formatting. However, instead of saving the document in the default format (as a Word document), you use the **Save As Web Page command** to convert the document to HTML. Microsoft Word does the rest and generates the HTML statements for you.

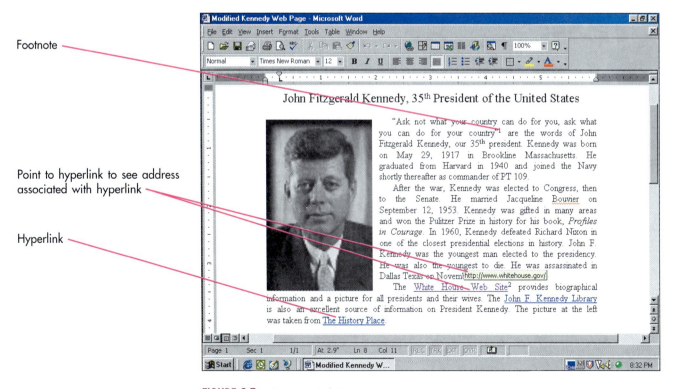

FIGURE 3.7   Creating a Web Page

Figure 3.7 contains the Web page you will create in the next hands-on exercise. The exercise begins by having you search the Web to locate a suitable photograph of President Kennedy for inclusion into the document. You then download the picture to your PC and use the Insert Picture command to insert the photograph into your document. You add formatting, hyperlinks, and footnotes as appropriate, then you save the document as a Web page. The exercise is easy to do and it will give you an appreciation for the various Web capabilities that are built into Office 2000.

Realize, however, that even if you do not place your page on the Web, you can still view it locally on your PC. This is the approach we follow in the next hands-on exercise, which shows you how to save a Word document as a Web page, then see the results of your effort in a Web browser. The Web page is stored on a local drive (e.g., on drive A or drive C) rather than on an Internet server, but it can still be viewed through Internet Explorer (or any other browser).

The ability to create links to local documents and to view those pages through a Web browser has created an entirely new way to disseminate information. Organizations of every size are taking advantage of this capability to develop an *intranet,* in which Web pages are placed on a local area network for use within the organizations. The documents on an intranet are available only to individuals with access to the local area network on which the documents are stored. This is in contrast to loading pages onto a Web server, where they can be viewed by anyone with access to the Web.

THE WEB PAGE WIZARD

The Save As Web Page command converts a Word document to the equivalent HTML document for posting on a Web server. The Web Page Wizard extends the process to create a multipage Web site, complete with navigation and a professionally designed theme. The navigation options let you choose between horizontal and vertical frames so that the user can see the links and content at the same time. The design themes are quite varied and include every element on a Web page. The Wizard is an incredibly powerful tool that rivals any Web-authoring tool we have seen. Try it if a Web project is in your future!

Copyright Protection

A *copyright* provides legal protection for a written or artistic work, giving the author exclusive rights to its use and reproduction, except as governed under the fair use exclusion as explained below. Anything on the Internet or World Wide Web should be considered copyrighted unless the document specifically says it is in the *public domain,* in which case the author is giving everyone the right to freely reproduce and distribute the material.

Does copyright protection mean you cannot quote in your term papers statistics and other facts you find while browsing the Web? Does it mean you cannot download an image to include in your report? The answer to both questions depends on the amount of the material and on your intended use of the information. It is considered *fair use,* and thus not an infringement of copyright, to use a portion of the work for educational, nonprofit purposes, or for the purpose of critical review or commentary. In other words, you can use a quote, downloaded image, or other information from the Web *if* you cite the original work in your footnotes and/or bibliography. Facts themselves are not covered by copyright, so you can use statistical and other data without fear of infringement. You should, however, cite the original source in your document.

Footnotes and Endnotes

A *footnote* provides additional information about an item, such as its source, and appears at the bottom of the page where the reference occurs. An *endnote* is similar in concept but appears at the end of a document. A horizontal line separates the notes from the rest of the document.

The **Insert Footnote command** inserts a note into a document, and automatically assigns the next sequential number to that note. To create a note, position the insertion point where you want the reference, pull down the Insert menu, click Footnote to display the dialog box in Figure 3.8a, then choose either the Footnote or Endnote option button. A superscript reference is inserted into the document, and you will be positioned at the bottom of the page (a footnote) or at the end of the document (an endnote) where you enter the text of the note.

The Options command button in the Footnote and Endnote dialog box enables you to modify the formatting of either type of note as shown in Figure 3.8b. You can change the numbering format (e.g., to Roman numerals) and/or start numbering from a number other than 1. You can also convert footnotes to endnotes or vice versa.

The Insert Footnote command adjusts for last-minute changes, either in your writing or in your professor's requirements. It will, for example, renumber all existing notes to accommodate the addition or deletion of a footnote or endnote. Existing notes are moved (or deleted) within a document by moving (deleting) the reference mark rather than the text of the footnote.

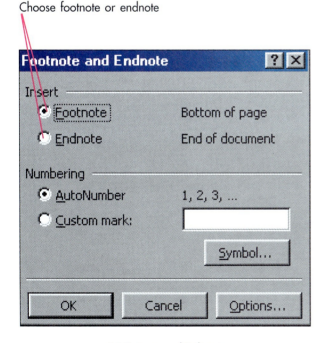

(a) Footnotes and Endnotes

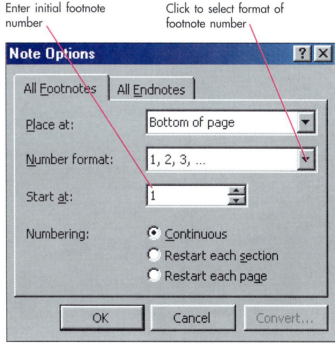

(b) Options

FIGURE 3.8 Footnotes and Endnotes

HANDS-ON EXERCISE 2

Word 2000 and the Web

Objective: To download a picture from the Internet for use in a Word document; to insert a hyperlink into a Word document; to save a Word document as a Web page. The exercise requires an Internet connection.

STEP 1: Search the Web

➤ Start **Internet Explorer.** Click the **Maximize button** so that Internet Explorer takes the entire screen.

➤ Click the **Search button** on the Internet Explorer toolbar to open the Explorer bar. The option button to find a Web page is selected by default. Enter **John Kennedy** in the text box, then click the **Search button.**

➤ The results of the search are displayed in the left pane. You can follow any of the links returned by your search engine, or you can attempt to duplicate our results using **Yahoo.** Click the **down arrow** on the **Next button,** then select **Yahoo** as the search engine.

➤ The list of hits is displayed at the bottom of the left pane as shown in Figure 3.9a. (Your list may be different from ours.) Click any link and the associated page is displayed in the right pane. We chose the first category. The links for that category are displayed in the right pane, where we chose the link to **Photo History of JFK.**

➤ Close the left pane to give yourself more room to browse through the site containing the Kennedy photographs. (You can click the **Search button** at any time to reopen the Explorer bar to choose a different site.)

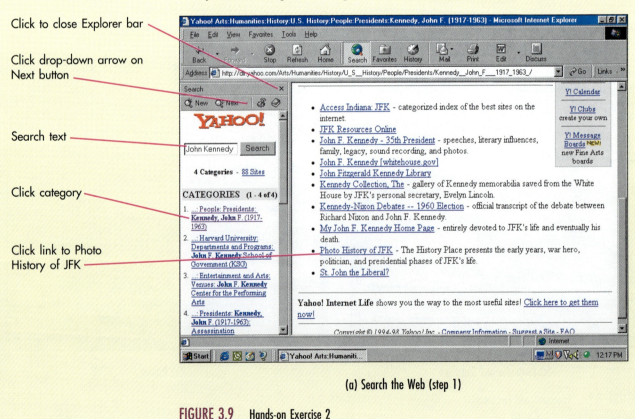

(a) Search the Web (step 1)

FIGURE 3.9   Hands-on Exercise 2

STEP 2: Save the Picture

➤ Point to the picture of President Kennedy you want to use in your document. Click the **right mouse button** to display a shortcut menu, then click the **Save Picture As command** to display the Save As dialog box in Figure 3.9b.

- Click the **drop-down arrow** in the Save in list box to specify the drive and folder in which you want to save the graphic.
- Internet Explorer supplies the file name and file type for you. You may change the name, but you cannot change the file type.
- Click the **Save button** to download the image. Remember the file name and location, as you will need to access the file in the next step.

➤ The Save As dialog box will close automatically after the picture has been downloaded. Click the **Minimize button** in the Internet Explorer window, since you are temporarily finished using the browser.

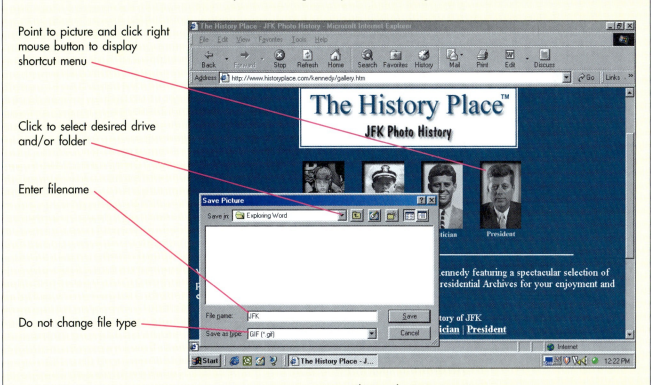

(b) Save the Picture (step 2)

FIGURE 3.9 Hands-on Exercise 2 (continued)

MINIMIZING VERSUS CLOSING AN APPLICATION

Minimizing an application is different from closing it, and you should understand the difference. Minimizing an application leaves the application open in memory, but shrinks its window to a button on the Windows taskbar so that you can return to it later in the session. Closing an application removes the application from memory, so that you have to restart the application if you need it. The advantage to closing an application, however, is that you free system resources, so that your remaining applications will run more efficiently.

STEP 3: Insert the Picture

➤ Start Word and open the **Kennedy document** in the **Exploring Word folder.** Save the document as **Modified Kennedy.**

➤ Pull down the **View menu** to be sure that you are in the **Print Layout view** (or else you will not see the picture after it is inserted into the document). Pull down the **Insert menu,** point to (or click) **Picture command,** then click **From File** to display the Insert Picture dialog box shown in Figure 3.9c.

➤ Click the **drop-down arrow** on the Look in text box to select the drive and folder where you previously saved the picture.

➤ Select (click) **JFK,** which is the file containing the picture of President Kennedy. Click the **drop-down arrow** on the **Views button** to switch to the **Preview button** and display the picture prior to inserting it into the document. Click **Insert.**

➤ Save the document.

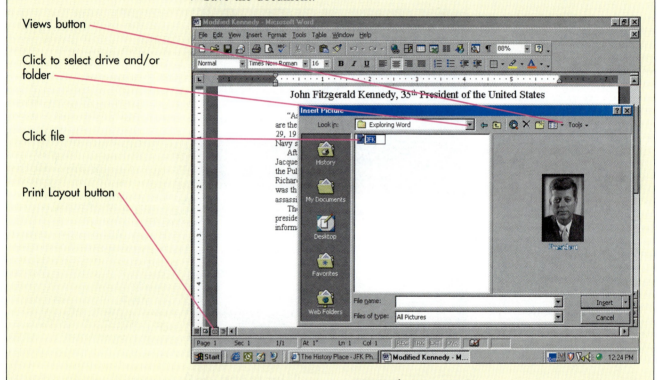

(c) Insert the Picture (step 3)

FIGURE 3.9 Hands-on Exercise 2 (continued)

THE VIEWS BUTTON

Click the Views button to cycle through the four available views, each with a flavor of its own. The Details view shows the file size as well as the date and time the file was last modified. The Preview view displays the beginning of the file without having to open it. The Properties view shows additional characteristics about the file, such as the author's name. The List view displays only icons and file names, but enables you to see the largest number of files without having to scroll. Choose the view that is appropriate for your current task.

STEP 4: Move and Size the Picture

➤ Point to the picture after it is inserted into the document, click the **right mouse button** to display a shortcut menu, then click the **Format Picture command** to display the Format Picture dialog box.

➤ Click the **Layout tab,** choose **Square** as the Wrapping Style, then click the **Left option button** under Horizontal Alignment. Click **OK** to accept the settings and close the Format Picture dialog box. Move and/or size the picture so that it approximates the position in Figure 3.9d.

➤ Check that the picture is still selected, then click the **Crop tool** on the Picture toolbar. The mouse pointer changes to interlocking lines. Click and drag the sizing handle on the bottom of the picture upward to delete the label in the picture. Resize the picture as necessary.

➤ Save the document.

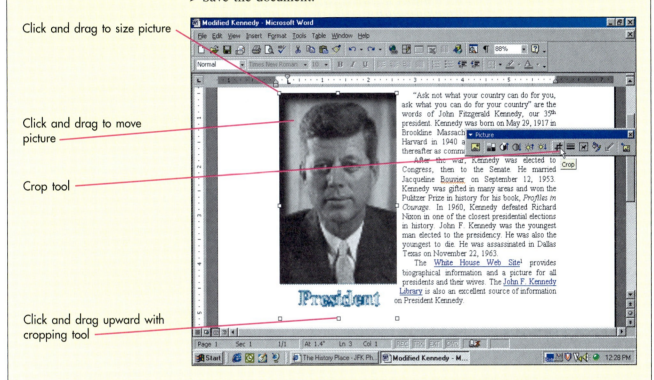

(d) Move and Size the Picture (step 4)

FIGURE 3.9 Hands-on Exercise 2 (continued)

THE PICTURE TOOLBAR

The Picture Toolbar is displayed automatically when a picture is selected, and suppressed otherwise. As with any toolbar, it may be docked along the edge of the application window or floating within the window. You can move a floating toolbar by dragging its title bar. You can move a docked toolbar by dragging the move handle (the line at the left of the toolbar). If by chance you do not see the Picture toolbar when a picture is selected, pull down the View menu, click the Toolbars command, and check the Picture toolbar. Point to any toolbar button to display a ScreenTip that is indicative of its function.

STEP 5: Insert a Hyperlink

➤ Press **Ctrl+End** to move to the end of the document, where you will add a sentence to identify the photograph. Enter the text, **The picture at the left was taken from** (the sentence will end with a hyperlink).

➤ Pull down the **Insert menu** and click the **Hyperlink command** (or click the **Insert Hyperlink button** on the Standard toolbar) to display the Insert Hyperlink dialog box as shown in Figure 3.9e.

➤ Click in the **Text to display** text box and enter **The History Place.** Press **Tab.** Enter **www.historyplace.com/kennedy/gallery.htm.** Click **OK.** The hyperlink should appear as an underlined entry in the document. Type a period after the hyperlink. Save the document.

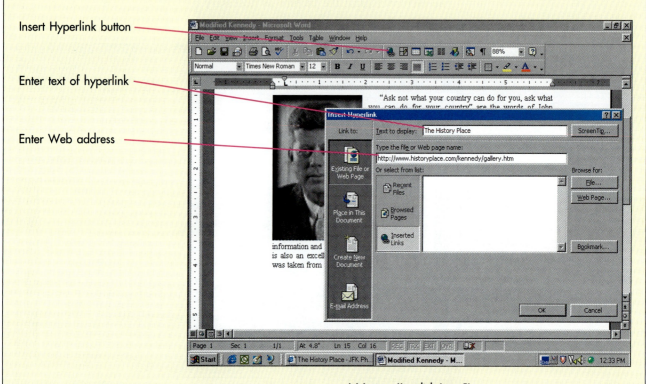

(e) Insert a Hyperlink (step 5)

FIGURE 3.9 Hands-on Exercise 2 (continued)

COPY THE WEB ADDRESS

Use the Copy command to enter a Web address from Internet Explorer into a Word document or dialog box. Not only do you save time by not having to type the address yourself, but you also ensure that it is entered correctly. Click in the Address bar of Internet Explorer to select the URL, then pull down the Edit menu and click the Copy command (or use the Ctrl+C keyboard shortcut). Switch to the Word document, click at the place in the document where you want to insert the URL, pull down the Edit menu and click the Paste command (or use the Ctrl+V keyboard shortcut). You must, however, use the keyboard shortcut if you are pasting the address into a dialog box.

STEP 6: Insert a Footnote

➤ Press **Ctrl+Home** to move to the beginning of the document. Click at the end of the quotation in the first paragraph, where you will insert a new footnote.

➤ Pull down the **Insert menu.** Click **Footnote** to display the Footnote and Endnote dialog as shown in Figure 3.9f. Check that the option buttons for **Footnote** and **AutoNumber** are selected, then click **OK**.

➤ The insertion point moves to the bottom of the page, where you type the text of the footnote. Enter **Inaugural Address, John F. Kennedy, January 20, 1961.** You can expand the footnote to include a Web site that contains the text at **www.cc.columbia.edu/acis/bartleby/inaugural/pres56.html.**

➤ Press **Ctrl+Home** to move to the beginning of the page, where you will see a reference for the footnote you just created. If necessary, you can move (or delete) a footnote by moving (deleting) the reference mark. Save the document.

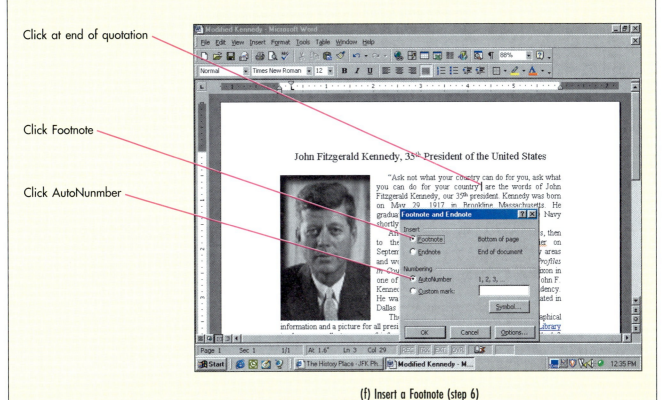

(f) Insert a Footnote (step 6)

FIGURE 3.9 Hands-on Exercise 2 (continued)

CREATE A HYPERLINK AUTOMATICALLY

Type any Internet path (i.e., any text that begins with http:// or www) or e-mail address, and Word will automatically convert the entry to a hyperlink. (If this does not work on your system, pull down the Tools menu, click AutoCorrect, then click the AutoFormat as you Type tab. Check the box in the Replace as you type area for Internet and Network paths, and click OK.) To modify the hyperlink after it is created, right click the link to display a shortcut menu, click the Hyperlink command, then select the Edit Hyperlink command to display the associated dialog box.

STEP 7: Create the Web Page

➤ Pull down the **File menu** and click the **Save as Web Page** command to display the Save as dialog box as shown in Figure 3.9g. Click the drop-down arrow in the Save In list box to select the appropriate drive, then open the **Exploring Word folder** that contains the documents you are using.

➤ Change the name of the Web page to **Modified Kennedy Web Page** (to differentiate it from the Word document). Click the **Save button.**

➤ The title bar changes to reflect the name of the Web page. There are now two versions of this document in the Exploring Word folder—Modified Kennedy, and Modified Kennedy Web Page. The latter has been saved as a Web page (in HTML format).

➤ Print this page for your instructor.

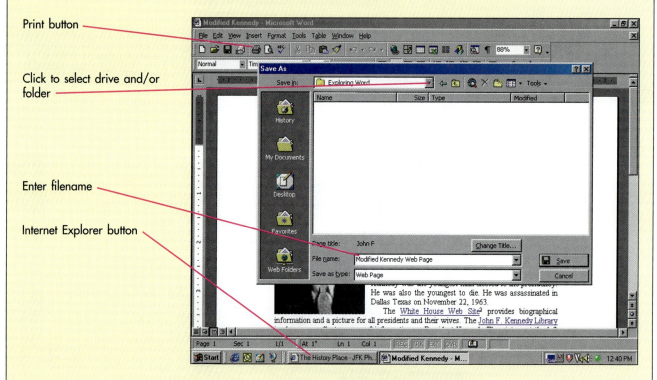

(g) Create the Web Page (step 7)

FIGURE 3.9   Hands-on Exercise 2 (continued)

CHANGE THE DEFAULT FILE LOCATION

The default file location is the folder Word uses to open and save a document unless it is otherwise instructed. To change the default location, pull down the Tools menu, click Options, click the File Locations tab, click the desired File type (documents), then click the Modify command button to display the Modify Location dialog box. Click the drop-down arrow in the Look In box to select the new folder (e.g., C:\Exploring Word). Click OK to accept this selection. Click OK to close the Options dialog box. The next time you access the Open or Save command from the File menu, the Look In text box will reflect the change.

STEP 8: Preview the Web Page

➤ The easiest way to start Internet Explorer is to pull down the **File menu** and click the **Web Page Preview command.** However, we want you to see the extra folder that was created with your Web page. Thus, click the button for Internet Explorer on the Windows taskbar.

➤ Pull down the **File menu** and click the **Open command** to display the Open dialog box. Click the **Browse button,** then select the folder (e.g., Exploring Word) where you saved the Web page. Select (click) the **Modified Kennedy as Web Page** document, click **Open,** then click **OK** to open the document.

➤ You should see the Web page that was created earlier as shown in Figure 3.9h, except that you are viewing the page in Internet Explorer.

➤ Click the **Print button** on the Internet Explorer toolbar to print this page for your instructor. Does this printed document differ from the version that was printed at the end of step 7? Close Internet Explorer.

➤ Exit Word if you do not want to continue with the next exercise at this time.

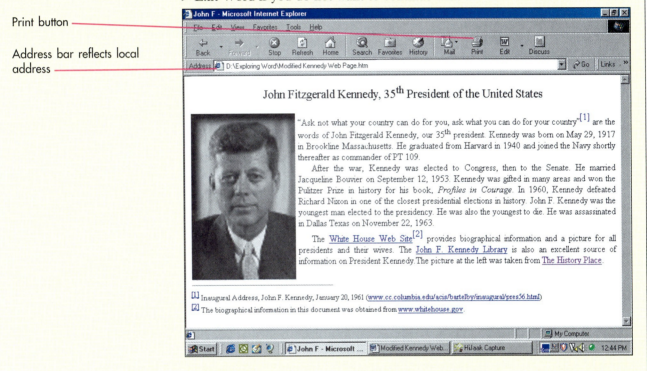

Print button

Address bar reflects local address

(h) Preview the Web Page (step 8)

FIGURE 3.9 Hands-on Exercise 2 (continued)

AN EXTRA FOLDER

Look carefully at the contents of the Exploring Word folder within the Open dialog box. You see the HTML document you just created, as well as a folder that was created automatically by the Save as Web page command. The latter folder contains the objects that are referenced by the page such as the Kennedy picture and a horizontal line above the footnotes. Be sure to copy the contents of this folder to the Web server in addition to your Web page if you decide to post the page.

WIZARDS AND TEMPLATES

We have created some very interesting documents throughout the text, but in every instance we have formatted the document entirely on our own. It is time now to see what is available to "jump start" the process by borrowing professional designs from others. Accordingly, we discuss the wizards and templates that are built into Microsoft Word.

A *template* is a partially completed document that contains formatting, text, and/or graphics. It may be as simple as a memo or as complex as a résumé or newsletter. Microsoft Word provides a variety of templates for common documents including a résumé, agenda, and fax cover sheet. You simply open the template, then modify the existing text as necessary, while retaining the formatting in the template. A *wizard* makes the process even easier by asking a series of questions, then creating a customized document based on your answers. A template or wizard creates the initial document for you. It's then up to you to complete the document by entering the appropriate information.

Figure 3.10 illustrates the use of wizards and templates in conjunction with a résumé. You can choose from one of three existing templates (contemporary, elegant, and professional) to which you add personal information. Alternatively, you can select the **Résumé Wizard** to create a customized résumé, as was done in Figure 3.10a.

After the Résumé Wizard is selected, it prompts you for the information it needs to create a basic résumé. You specify the style in Figure 3.10b, enter the requested information in Figure 3.10c, and choose the headings in Figure 3.10d. The wizard continues to ask additional questions (not shown in Figure 3.10), after which it displays the (partially) completed résumé based on your responses. You then complete the résumé by entering the specifics of your employment and/or additional information. As you edit the document, you can copy and paste information within the résumé, just as you would with a regular document. It takes a little practice, but the end result is a professionally formatted résumé in a minimum of time.

Microsoft Word contains templates and wizards for a variety of other documents. (Look carefully at the tabs within the dialog box of Figure 3.10a and you can infer that Word will help you to create letters, faxes, memos, reports, legal pleadings, publications, and even Web pages.) Consider, too, Figure 3.11, which displays four attractive documents that were created using the respective wizards. Realize, however, that while wizards and templates will help you to create professionally designed documents, they are only a beginning. *The content is still up to you.*

THIRTY SECONDS IS ALL YOU HAVE

Thirty seconds is the average amount of time a personnel manager spends skimming your résumé and deciding whether or not to call you for an interview. It doesn't matter how much training you have had or how good you are if your résumé and cover letter fail to project a professional image. Know your audience and use the vocabulary of your targeted field. Be positive and describe your experience from an accomplishment point of view. Maintain a separate list of references and have it available on request. Be sure that all information is accurate. Be conscientious about the design of your résumé, and proofread the final documents very carefully.

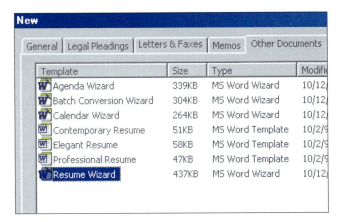
(a) Résumé Wizard

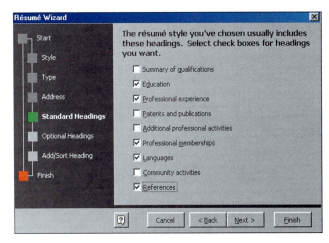
(d) Choose the Headings

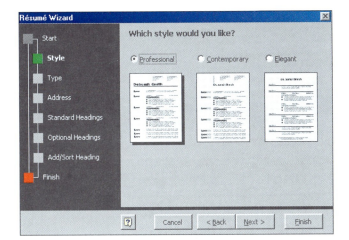
(b) Choose the Style

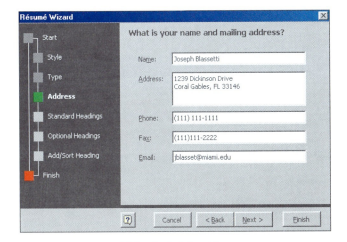
(c) Supply the Information

(e) The Completed Résumé

FIGURE 3.10   Creating a Résumé

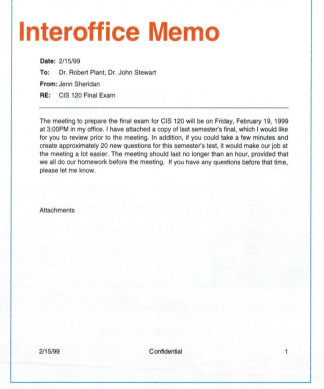

(a) Calendar (b) Agenda

(c) Fax Cover Sheet (d) Memo

FIGURE 3.11 What You Can Do With Wizards

HANDS-ON EXERCISE 3

Wizards and Templates

Objective: To use the Agenda Wizard to create an agenda for a study group, then use the Fax Wizard to fax the agenda to your group. Use Figure 3.12 as a guide in the exercise.

STEP 1: The File New Command

➤ Start Word. Pull down the **File menu.** Click **New** to display the New dialog box shown in Figure 3.12a. Click the **Other Documents tab.**

➤ Click the **Details button** to switch to the Details view to see the file name, type, size, and date of last modification. Click and drag the vertical line between the Template and Size columns, to increase the size of the Template column, so that you can see the complete document name.

➤ Select (click) **Agenda Wizard.** If necessary, click the option button to **Create New Document** (as opposed to a template). Click **OK.**

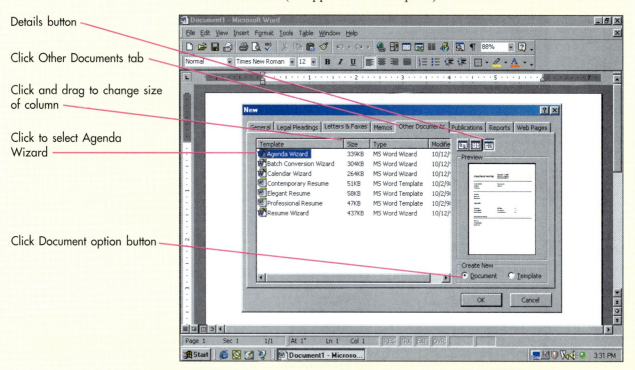

Details button
Click Other Documents tab
Click and drag to change size of column
Click to select Agenda Wizard
Click Document option button

(a) The File New Command (step 1)

FIGURE 3.12 Hands-on Exercise 3

SORT BY NAME, DATE, OR FILE SIZE

The files in the Save As, Open, and New dialog boxes can be displayed in ascending or descending sequence by name, date modified, or size. Change to the Details view, then click the heading of the desired column; e.g., click the Type column to list the files according to file type (to separate the documents from the templates).

CHAPTER 3: ENHANCING A DOCUMENT 137

STEP 2: The Agenda Wizard

➤ You should see the main screen of the Agenda Wizard as shown in Figure 3.12b. Click **Next** to begin. The Wizard will take you through a series of questions, from start to finish. To create the desired agenda:

- Click **Modern** as the style of the agenda. Click **Next**.
- Enter the date and time of your meeting. Enter **Initial Study Group Session** as the title. Enter **Joe's Place** as the location. Click **Next**.
- The Wizard asks which headings you want and supplies a check box next to each heading. The check boxes function as toggle switches to select (deselect) each heading. We suggest you clear all entries except **Please bring.** Click **Next**.
- The Wizard asks which names you want in the agenda. Clear all headings except **Note Taker** and **Attendees.** Click **Next**.
- Enter at least three topics for the agenda. Press the **Tab key** to move from one text box to the next (e.g., from Agenda topic, to Person, to Minutes). Click the **Add** button when you have completed the information for one topic.
- If necessary, reorder the topics by clicking the desired topic, then clicking the **Move Up** or **Move Down** command button. Click **Next** when you are satisfied with the agenda.
- Click **No** when asked whether you want a form to record the minutes of the meeting. Click **Next**.

➤ The final screen of the Agenda Wizard indicates that the Wizard has all the information it needs. Click the **Finish button**.

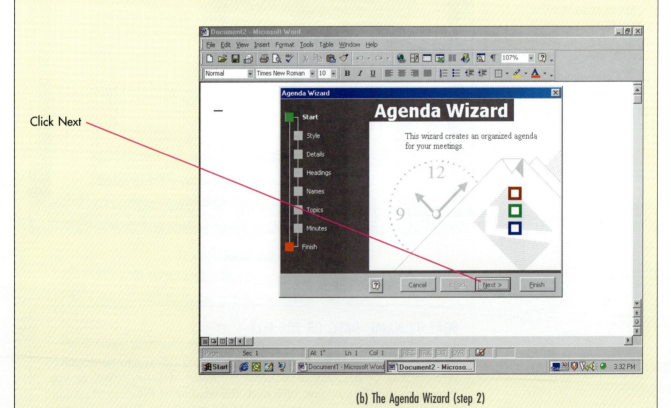

Click Next

(b) The Agenda Wizard (step 2)

FIGURE 3.12   Hands-on Exercise 3 (continued)

STEP 3: Complete the Agenda

➤ You should see an initial agenda similar to the document in Figure 3.12c. Cancel the Office Assistant if it appears (or you can leave it open and request help as necessary).

➤ Save the agenda as **Initial Study Group Session** in the **Exploring Word** folder. If necessary, change to the **Print Layout view** and zoom to **Page Width** so that your document more closely matches ours.

➤ Complete the Agenda by entering the additional information, such as the names of the note taker and attendees as well as the specifics of what to read or bring, as shown in the figure. Click at the indicated position on the figure prior to entering the text, so that your entries align properly.

➤ Click the **Spelling and Grammar button** to check the agenda for spelling.

➤ Save the document but do not close it.

➤ Click the **Print button** on the Standard toolbar to print the completed document and submit it to your instructor.

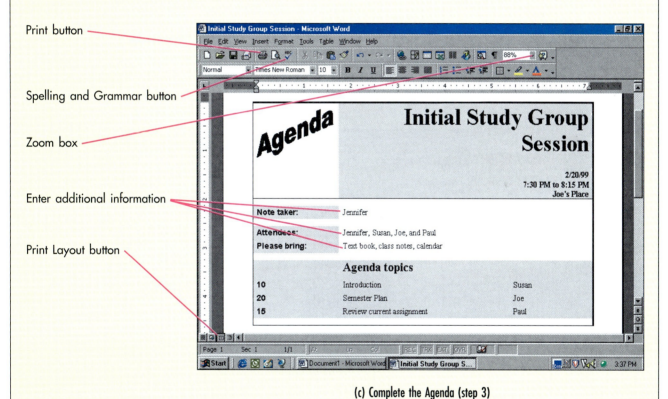

(c) Complete the Agenda (step 3)

FIGURE 3.12 Hands-on Exercise 3 (continued)

RETRACE YOUR STEPS

The Agenda Wizard guides you every step of the way, but what if you make a mistake or change your mind? Click the Back command button at any time to return to a previous screen in order to enter different information, then continue working with the Wizard.

STEP 4: The Fax Wizard

➤ Pull down the **File menu** and click **New** to display the New dialog box. Click the **Letters & Faxes tab** to display the indicated wizards and templates. Check that the **Document option button** is selected. Double click the **Fax Wizard** to start it.

➤ You should see the main screen of the Fax Wizard as shown in Figure 3.12d. Click **Next** to begin.

- The Fax Wizard suggests Initial Study Group as the name of the document you want to fax (because the document is still open). The option button **With a Cover Sheet** is selected. Click **Next.**

- Do not be concerned about the fax software that is installed on your computer, because you're not going to send the fax. Thus, click the option button to print the document (as though you were going to send it from a fax machine). Click **Next.**

- Enter the name and fax number of one person in your group. Complete this entry even if you do not intend to send an actual fax. Click **Next.**

- Choose the style of the cover sheet. We selected **Professional.** Click **Next.**

- If necessary, complete and/or modify the information about the sender so that it reflects your name and telephone number. Click **Next.**

- Read the last screen reminding you about how to list phone numbers correctly. Click **Finish.**

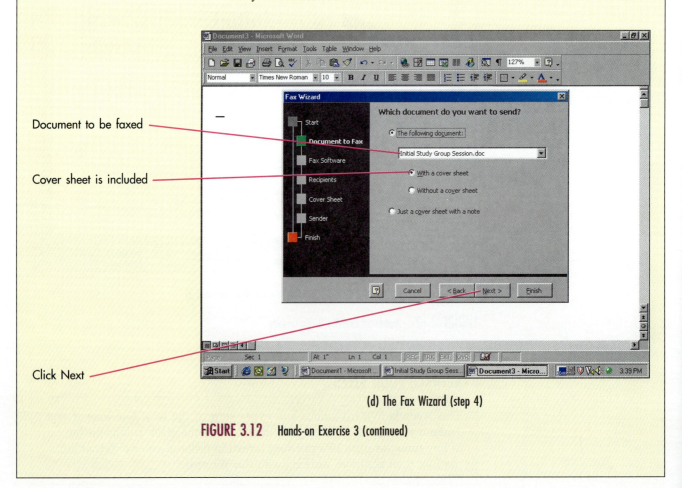

(d) The Fax Wizard (step 4)

FIGURE 3.12 Hands-on Exercise 3 (continued)

STEP 5: Complete the Fax

➤ You should see a fax cover sheet similar to the document in Figure 3.12e.

➤ Save the cover sheet as **Fax Cover Sheet** in the **Exploring Word** folder. If necessary, change to the **Normal view** and zoom to **Page Width** so that your document more closely matches ours.

➤ Complete the cover sheet by entering the additional information as appropriate. Click at the indicated position in Figure 3.12e prior to entering the text, so that your entries align properly.

➤ Click the **Spelling and Grammar button** to check the agenda for spelling.

➤ Save the document a final time. Click the **Print button** on the Standard toolbar to print the completed document, and submit it to your instructor.

➤ Exit Word. Congratulations on a job well done.

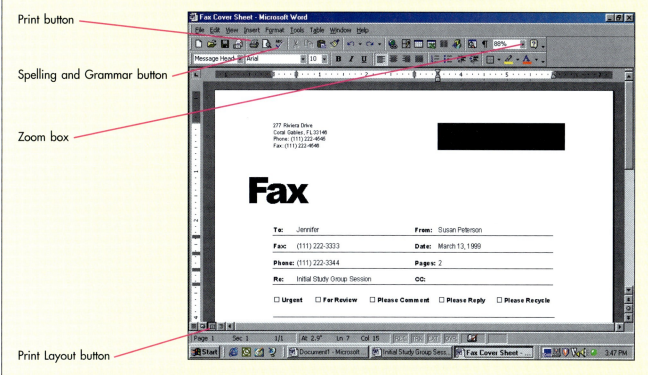

(e) Complete the Fax (step 5)

FIGURE 3.12 Hands-on Exercise 3 (continued)

CHANGING THE VIEW

Word provides different views of a document and different magnifications of each view. The Normal view suppresses the margins, giving you more room in which to work. The Print Layout view, on the other hand, displays the margins, so that what you see on the monitor more closely resembles the printed page. The easiest way to change from one view to the other is by clicking the appropriate icon above the status bar. The easiest way to change the magnification is to click the drop-down arrow in the Zoom box on the Standard toolbar.

SUMMARY

The applications in Microsoft Office are thoroughly integrated with one another. They look alike and work alike. Equally important, they share information through a technology known as Object Linking and Embedding (OLE), which enables you to create a compound document containing data (objects) from multiple applications.

The Microsoft Clip Gallery contains clip art, sound files, and motion clips and it is accessible from any application in Microsoft Office. Clip art is inserted into a document in one of two ways—through the Insert Object command or more directly through the Insert Picture command. Either way, you choose the type of object and the category, then select the image and insert it into the document. Microsoft WordArt is an application within Microsoft Office that creates decorative text, which can be used to add interest to a document.

The Insert Symbol command provides access to special characters, making it easy to place typographic characters into a document. The symbols can be taken from any TrueType font and can be displayed in any point size.

The Internet is a network of networks. The World Wide Web (WWW, or simply the Web) is a very large subset of the Internet, consisting of those computers containing hypertext and/or hypermedia documents. Resources (e.g., clip art or photographs) can be downloaded from the Web for inclusion in a Word document. All Web pages are written in a language called HTML (HyperText Markup Language). The Save As Web Page command saves a Word document as a Web page.

A copyright provides legal protection to a written or artistic work, giving the author exclusive rights to its use and reproduction except as governed under the fair use exclusion. Anything on the Internet or World Wide Web should be considered copyrighted unless the document specifically says it is in the public domain. The fair use exclusion enables you to use a portion of the work for educational, nonprofit purposes, or for the purpose of critical review or commentary.

A footnote provides additional information about an item, such as its source, and appears at the bottom of the page where the reference occurs. The Insert Footnote command inserts a footnote into a document and automatically assigns the next sequential number to that note.

Wizards and templates help create professionally designed documents with a minimum of time and effort. A template is a partially completed document that contains formatting and other information. A wizard is an interactive program that creates a customized template based on the answers you supply.

OBJECT LINKING AND EMBEDDING

Object Linking and Embedding (OLE) enables you to create a compound document containing objects (data) from multiple Windows applications. Each of the techniques, linking and embedding, can be implemented in various ways. Althogh OLE is one of the major benefits of working in the Windows environment, it would be impossible to illustrate all of the techniques in a single exercise. Accordingly, we have created the icon at the left to help you identify the many OLE examples that appear throughout the *Exploring Windows* series.

KEY WORDS AND CONCEPTS

Agenda Wizard
AutoCorrect
AutoFormat
Clip art
Clipboard
Compound document
Copyright
Crop
Drawing toolbar
Endnote
Fair use exclusion
Fax Wizard
Footnote
Format Picture command

HTML document
Hyperlink
Insert Footnote command
Insert Hyperlink command
Insert Picture command
Insert Symbol command
Internet
Intranet
Microsoft Clip Gallery
Microsoft WordArt
Object Linking and Embedding (OLE)

Picture toolbar
Public domain
Résumé Wizard
Save as Web Page command
Sizing handle
Template
Web page
Wizard
WordArt
WordArt toolbar
World Wide Web

MULTIPLE CHOICE

1. How do you change the size of a selected object so that the height and width change in proportion to one another?
    (a) Click and drag any of the four corner handles in the direction you want to go
    (b) Click and drag the sizing handle on the top border, then click and drag the sizing handle on the left side
    (c) Click and drag the sizing handle on the bottom border, then click and drag the sizing handle on the right side
    (d) All of the above

2. The Microsoft Clip Galley:
    (a) Is accessed through the Insert Picture command
    (b) Is available to every application in the Microsoft Office
    (c) Enables you to search for a specific piece of clip art by specifying a key word in the description of the clip art
    (d) All of the above

3. Which view, and which magnification, offers the most convenient way to position a graphic within a document?
    (a) Page Width in the Print Layout view
    (b) Full Page in the Print Layout view
    (c) Page Width in the Normal view
    (d) Full Page in the Normal view

4. Which of the following can be inserted from the Microsoft Clip Gallery?
    (a) Clip art
    (b) Sound
    (c) Motion clips
    (d) All of the above

5. How do you insert special characters such as the accented letters or typographical symbols into a Word document?
   (a) Use the Insert WordArt command to draw the character
   (b) Use the Insert Picture command to draw the character
   (c) Use the Insert Symbol command
   (d) All of the above

6. How do you format a document so that text in the document wraps around a clip art image?
   (a) Select the text, then use the Format Text command or the Format Text toolbar to specify the desired layout
   (b) Select the picture, then use the Format Picture command or the Format Picture toolbar to specify the desired layout
   (c) Select the text, then click and drag a sizing handle to obtain the desired layout
   (d) You cannot wrap the text around the picture

7. Which of the following is true about footnotes or endnotes?
   (a) The addition of a footnote or endnote automatically renumbers the notes that follow
   (b) The deletion of a footnote or endnote automatically renumbers the notes that follow
   (c) Both (a) and (b)
   (d) Neither (a) nor (b)

8. Which of the following is true about the Insert Symbol command?
   (a) It can insert a symbol in different type sizes
   (b) It can access any TrueType font installed on the system
   (c) Both (a) and (b)
   (d) Neither (a) nor (b)

9. Which of the following is a true statement regarding objects and the toolbars associated with those objects?
   (a) Clicking on a WordArt object displays the WordArt toolbar
   (b) Clicking on a Picture displays the Picture Toolbar
   (c) Both (a) and (b)
   (d) Neither (a) nor (b)

10. How do you insert a hyperlink into a Word document?
    (a) Pull down the Insert menu and click the Hyperlink command
    (b) Click the Insert Hyperlink button on the Standard toolbar
    (c) Both (a) and (b)
    (d) Neither (a) nor (b)

11. A Web browser such as Internet Explorer can display a page from:
    (a) A local drive such as drive A or drive C
    (b) A drive on a local area network
    (c) The World Wide Web
    (d) All of the above

12. What happens if you enter the text *www.intel.com* into a document?
    (a) The entry is converted to a hyperlink, and the text will be underlined and displayed in a different color
    (b) The associated page will be opened, provided your computer has access to the Internet
    (c) Both (a) and (b)
    (d) Neither (a) nor (b)

13. Which of the following is a true statement about wizards?
    (a) They are accessed through the New command in the File menu
    (b) They always produce a finished document
    (c) Both (a) and (b)
    (d) Neither (a) nor (b)

14. How do you access the wizards built into Microsoft Word?
    (a) Pull down the Wizards and Templates menu
    (b) Pull down the Insert menu and choose the Wizards and Templates command
    (c) Pull down the File menu and choose the New command
    (d) None of the above

15. Which of the following is true regarding wizards and templates?
    (a) A wizard may create a template
    (b) A template may create a wizard
    (c) Both (a) and (b)
    (d) Neither (a) nor (b)

Answers

1. a	**6.** b	**11.** d
2. d	**7.** c	**12.** a
3. b	**8.** c	**13.** a
4. d	**9.** c	**14.** c
5. c	**10.** c	**15.** a

PRACTICE WITH MICROSOFT WORD

1. Inserting Objects: Figure 3.13 illustrates a flyer that we created for a hypothetical computer sale. We embedded clip art and WordArt and created what we believe is an attractive flyer. Try to duplicate our advertisement, or better yet, create your own. Include your name somewhere in the document as a sales associate. Be sure to spell check your ad, then print the completed flyer and submit it to your instructor.

2. Exploring TrueType: The installation of Microsoft Windows and/or Office 2000 also installs several TrueType fonts, which in turn are accessible from any application. Two of the fonts, Symbols and Wingdings, contain a variety of special characters that can be used to create some unusual documents. Use the Insert Symbol command, your imagination, and the fact that TrueType fonts are scaleable to any point size to re-create the documents in Figure 3.14. Better yet, use your imagination to create your own documents.

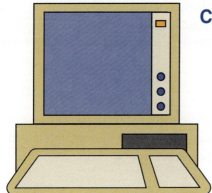

Computer World's Annual Pre-Inventory Sale

When: June 21, 1999
8:00AM - 10:00PM

Where: 13640 South Dixie Highway

Computer World

Computers
Printers
Fax/Modems
CD-ROM drives
Sound Systems
Software
Etc.

Pre-Inventory Sale

Sales Associate: Bianca Costo

FIGURE 3.13 Inserting Objects (Exercise 1)

Valentine's Day
We'll serenade your sweetheart
Call 284-LOVE

STUDENT COMPUTER LAB
Fall Semester Hours

FIGURE 3.14   Exploring TrueType (Exercise 2)

3. **Automatic Formatting:** The document in Figure 3.15 was created to illustrate the automatic formatting and correction facilities that are built into Microsoft Word. We want you to create the document, include your name at the bottom, then submit the completed document to your instructor as proof that you did the exercise. All you have to do is follow the instructions within the document and let Word do the formatting and correcting for you.

   The only potential difficulty is that the options on your system may be set to negate some of the features to which we refer. Accordingly, you need to pull down the Tools menu, click the AutoCorrect command, and click the AutoFormat As You Type tab. Verify that the options referenced in the document are in effect. You also need to review the table of predefined substitutions on the AutoCorrect tab to learn the typewritten characters that will trigger the smiley faces, copyright, and registered trademark substitutions.

It's Easier Than It Looks

This document was created to demonstrate the AutoCorrect and AutoFormat features that are built into Microsoft Word. In essence, you type as you always did and enter traditional characters, then let Word perform its "magic" by substituting symbols and other formatting for you. Among the many features included in these powerful commands are the:

1. Automatic creation of numbered lists by typing a number followed by a period, tab, or right parenthesis. Just remember to press the return key twice to turn off this feature.
2. Symbols for common fractions such as ½ or ¼.
3. Ordinal numbers with superscripts created automatically such as 1st, 2nd, or 3rd.
4. Copyright © and Registered trademark ® symbols.

AutoFormat will even add a border to a paragraph any time you type three or more hyphens, equal signs, or underscores on a line by itself.

===
_____

And finally, the AutoCorrect feature has built-in substitution for smiley faces that look best when set in a larger point size such as 72 points.

FIGURE 3.15   Automatic Formatting (Exercise 3)

4. **Create an Envelope:** The Résumé Wizard will take you through the process of creating a résumé, but you need an envelope in which to mail it. Pull down the Tools menu, click the Envelopes and Labels command, click the Envelopes command, then enter the indicated information. Look closely at the dialog box and note that Word will even append a bar code to the envelope if you request it.

   You can print the envelope and/or include it permanently in the document as shown in Figure 3.16. *Do not, however, do this exercise in a Computer Lab at school unless envelopes are available for the printer.*

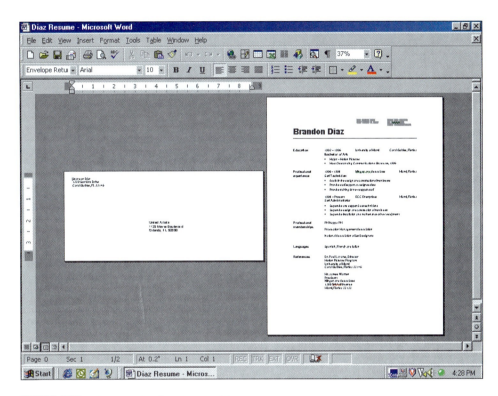

FIGURE 3.16 Create an Envelope (Exercise 4)

5. **Presidential Anecdotes:** Figure 3.17 displays the finished version of a document containing 10 presidential anecdotes. The anecdotes were taken from the book *Presidential Anecdotes,* by Paul F. Boller, Jr., published by Penguin Books (New York, NY, 1981). Open the *Chapter 3 Practice 5* document that is found on the data disk, then make the following changes:

   a. Add a footnote after Mr. Boller's name, which appears at the end of the second sentence, citing the information about the book. This, in turn, renumbers all existing footnotes in the document.

   b. Switch the order of the anecdotes for Lincoln and Jefferson so that the presidents appear in order. The footnotes for these references are changed automatically.

   c. Convert all of the footnotes to endnotes, as shown in the figure.

   d. Go to the White House Web site and download a picture of any of the 10 presidents, then incorporate that picture into a cover page. Remember to cite the reference with an appropriate footnote.

   e. Submit the completed document to your instructor.

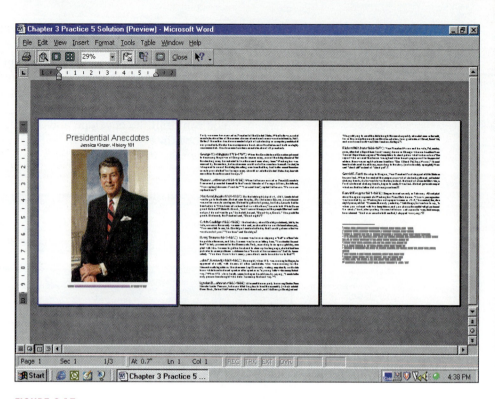

FIGURE 3.17 Presidential Anecdotes (Exercise 5)

6. **Photographs Online:** The Smithsonian Institution is a priceless resource. Go to the home page of the Smithsonian (www.si.edu), select photography from the subject area, then go to Smithsonian Photographs online to display the page in Figure 3.18. (You can also go to this page directly at photo2.si.edu). Click the link to search the image database, then choose one or two photographs on any subject that you find interesting.

    Use the technique described in the chapter to download those photographs to your PC, then use the Insert Picture command to incorporate those pictures into a Word document. Write a short paper (250 to 500 words) describing those photographs and submit the paper to your professor as proof you did this exercise. Be sure to include an appropriate footnote to cite the source of the photographs.

7. **Music on the Web:** The World Wide Web is a source of infinite variety, including music from your favorite rock group. You can find biographical information and/or photographs such as the one in Figure 3.19. You can even find music, which you can download and play, provided you have the necessary hardware. It's fun, it's easy, so go to it. Use any search engine to find documents about your favorite rock group. Try to find biographical information as well as a picture, then incorporate the results of your research into a short paper to submit to your instructor.

8. **The iCOMP Index:** The iCOMP index was developed by Intel to compare the speeds of various microprocessors. We want you to search the Web and find a chart showing values in the current iCOMP index. (The chart you find need not be the same as the one in Figure 3.20.) Once you find the chart, download the graphic and incorporate it into a memo to your instructor. Add a paragraph or two describing the purpose of the index as shown in Figure 3.20.

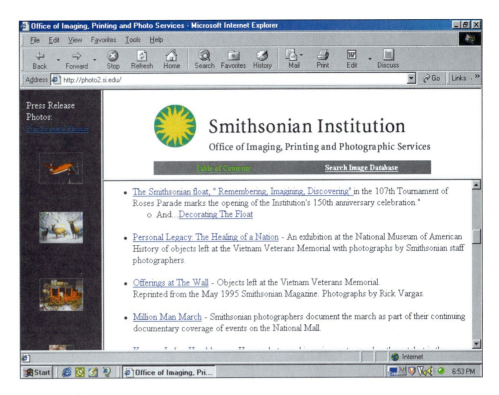

FIGURE 3.18 Photographs Online (Exercise 6)

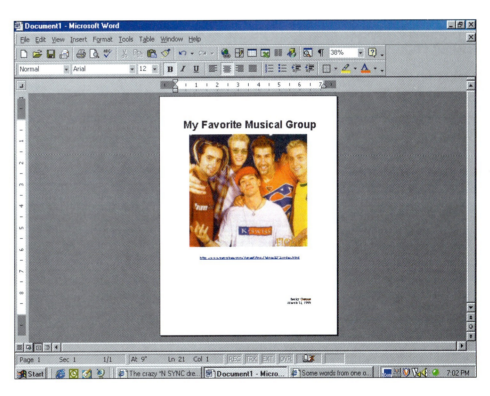

FIGURE 3.19 Music on the Web (Exercise 7)

A Comparison of Microcomputers

James Warren, CIS 120
(http://pentium.intel.com/procs/perf/icomp/index.htm)

The capability of a PC depends on the microprocessor on which it is based. Intel microprocessors are currently in their sixth generation, with each generation giving rise to increasingly powerful personal computers. All generations are upward compatible; that is, software written for one generation will automatically run on the next. This upward compatibility is crucial because it protects your investment in software when you upgrade to a faster computer.

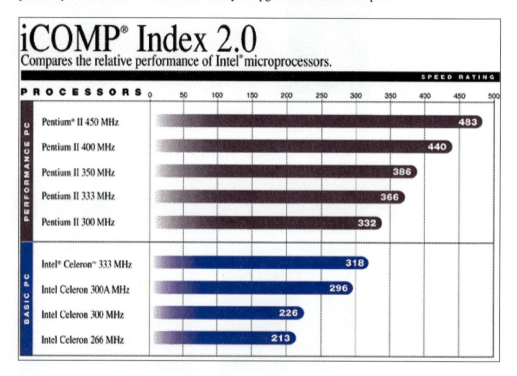

Each generation has multiple microprocessors which are differentiated by *clock speed*, an indication of how fast instructions are executed. Clock speed is measured in *megahertz* (MHz). The higher the clock speed the faster the machine. Thus, all Pentiums are not created equal, because they operate at different clock speeds. The *Intel CPU Performance Index* (see chart) was created to compare the performance of one microprocessor to another. The index consists of a single number to indicate the relative performance of the microprocessor; the higher the number, the faster the processor.

FIGURE 3.20   The iCOMP Index (Exercise 8)

9. **Create a Home Page:** Creating a home page has never been easier. Start Word, click the File menu, then click the New command to display the New Page dialog box. Select the Web Pages tab, then open the Personal Web page template in Figure 3.21. Add your personal information to the appropriate sections in the template and you have your home page. Pull down the Format menu, click the Themes command, then select a professionally chosen design for your Web page. You can view the completed page locally, or better yet, ask your instructor whether the page can be posted to a Web server.

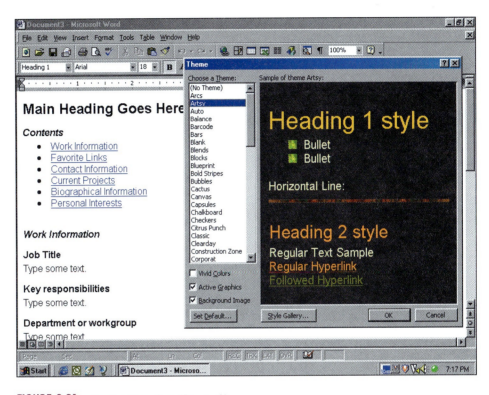

FIGURE 3.21 Create a Home Page (Exercise 9)

CASE STUDIES

The Letterhead

Collect samples of professional stationery, then design your own letterhead, which includes your name, address, phone, and any other information you deem relevant. Try different fonts and/or the Format Border command to add horizontal line(s) under the text. Consider a graphic logo, but keep it simple. You might also want to decrease the top margin so that the letterhead prints closer to the top of the page.

The Cover Page

Use WordArt and/or the Clip Gallery to create a truly original cover page that you can use with all of your assignments. The cover page should include the title of the assignment, your name, course information, and date. (Use the Insert Date and Time command to insert the date as a field so that it will be updated automatically every time you retrieve the document.) The formatting is up to you

CHAPTER 3: ENHANCING A DOCUMENT   153

The Résumé

Use your imagination to create a résumé for Benjamin Franklin or Leonardo da Vinci, two acknowledged geniuses. The résumé is limited to one page and will be judged for content (yes, you have to do a little research on the Web) as well as appearance. You can intersperse fact and fiction as appropriate; for example, you may want to leave space for a telephone and/or a fax number, but could indicate that these devices have not yet been invented. You can choose a format for the résumé using the Résumé Wizard, or better yet, design your own.

File Compression

Photographs add significantly to the appearance of a document, but they also add to its size. Accordingly, you might want to consider acquiring a file compression program to facilitate copying large documents to a floppy disk in order to transport your documents to and from school, home, or work. You can download an evaluation copy of the popular WinZip program at *www.winzip.com*. Investigate the subject of file compression, then submit a summary of your findings to your instructor.

Copyright Infringement

It's fun to download images from the Web for inclusion in a document, but is it legal? Copyright protection (infringement) is one of the most pressing legal issues on the Web. Search the Web for sites that provide information on current copyright law. One excellent site is the copyright page at the Institute for Learning Technologies at *www.ilt.columbia.edu/projects/copyright*. Another excellent reference is the page at *www.benedict.com*. Research these and other sites, then summarize your findings in a short note to your instructor.

Macros

The Insert Symbol command can be used to insert foreign characters into a document, but this technique is too slow if you use these characters with any frequency. It is much more efficient to develop a series of macros (keyboard shortcuts) that will insert the characters for you. You could, for example, create a macro to insert an accented *e*, then invoke that macro through the Ctrl+e keyboard shortcut. Parallel macros could be developed for the other vowels or special characters that you use frequently. Use the Help menu to learn about macros, then summarize your findings in a short note to your instructor.

chapter 1

INTRODUCTION TO MICROSOFT EXCEL: WHAT IS A SPREADSHEET?

OBJECTIVES

After reading this chapter you will be able to:

1. Describe a spreadsheet and suggest several potential applications; explain how the rows and columns of a spreadsheet are identified, and how its cells are labeled.
2. Distinguish between a formula and a constant; explain the use of a predefined function within a formula.
3. Open an Excel workbook; insert and delete rows and columns of a worksheet; save and print the modified worksheet.
4. Distinguish between a pull-down menu, a shortcut menu, and a toolbar.
5. Describe the three-dimensional nature of an Excel workbook; distinguish between a workbook and a worksheet.
6. Print a worksheet two ways: to show the computed values or the cell formulas.
7. Use the Page Setup command to print a worksheet with or without gridlines and/or row and column headings; preview a worksheet before printing.

OVERVIEW

This chapter provides a broad-based introduction to spreadsheets in general, and to Microsoft Excel in particular. The spreadsheet is the microcomputer application that is most widely used by managers and executives. Our intent is to show the wide diversity of business and other uses to which the spreadsheet model can be applied. For one example, we draw an analogy between the spreadsheet and the accountant's ledger. For a second example, we create an instructor's grade book.

The chapter covers the fundamentals of spreadsheets as implemented in Excel, which uses the term worksheet rather than spreadsheet. It discusses how the rows and columns of an Excel worksheet are labeled, the difference between a formula and a constant, and the ability of a worksheet to recalculate itself after a change is made. We also distinguish between a worksheet and a workbook.

The hands-on exercises in the chapter enable you to apply all of the material at the computer, and are indispensable to the learn-by-doing philosophy we follow throughout the text. As you do the exercises, you may recognize many commands from other Windows applications, all of which share a common user interface and consistent command structure. Excel will be even easier to learn if you already know another application in Microsoft Office.

INTRODUCTION TO SPREADSHEETS

A *spreadsheet* is the computerized equivalent of an accountant's ledger. As with the ledger, it consists of a grid of rows and columns that enables you to organize data in a readily understandable format. Figures 1.1a and 1.1b show the same information displayed in ledger and spreadsheet format, respectively.

"What is the big deal?" you might ask. The big deal is that after you change an entry (or entries), the spreadsheet will, automatically and almost instantly, recompute all of the formulas. Consider, for example, the profit projection spreadsheet shown in Figure 1.1b. As the spreadsheet is presently constructed, the unit price is $20 and the projected sales are 1,200 units, producing gross sales of $24,000 ($20/unit × 1,200 units). The projected expenses are $19,200, which yields a profit of $4,800 ($24,000 − $19,200). If the unit price is increased to $22 per unit, the spreadsheet recomputes the formulas, adjusting the values of gross sales and net profit. The modified spreadsheet of Figure 1.1c appears automatically.

With a calculator and bottle of correction fluid or a good eraser, the same changes could also be made to the ledger. But imagine a ledger with hundreds of entries and the time that would be required to make the necessary changes to the ledger by hand. The same spreadsheet will be recomputed automatically by the computer. And the computer will not make mistakes. Herein lies the advantage of a spreadsheet—the ability to make changes, and to have the computer carry out the recalculation faster and more accurately than could be accomplished manually.

		1	2	3	4	5	6	
1	UNIT PRICE		20					1
2	UNIT SALES		1,200					2
3	GROSS PROFIT		24,000					3
4								4
5	EXPENSES							5
6	PRODUCTION		10,000					6
7	DISTRIBUTION		1,200					7
8	MARKETING		5,000					8
9	OVERHEAD		3,000					9
10	TOTAL EXPENSES		19,200					10
11								11
12	NET PROFIT		4,800					12

(a) The Accountant's Ledger

FIGURE 1.1 The Accountant's Ledger

Unit price is increased to $22

Formulas recompute automatically

	A	B
1	Profit Projection	
2		
3	Unit Price	$20
4	Unit Sales	1,200
5	Gross Sales	$24,000
6		
7	Expenses	
8	Production	$10,000
9	Distribution	$1,200
10	Marketing	$5,000
11	Overhead	$3,000
12	Total Expenses	$19,200
13		
14	Net Profit	$4,800

(b) Original Spreadsheet

	A	B
1	Profit Projection	
2		
3	Unit Price	$22
4	Unit Sales	1,200
5	Gross Sales	$26,400
6		
7	Expenses	
8	Production	$10,000
9	Distribution	$1,200
10	Marketing	$5,000
11	Overhead	$3,000
12	Total Expenses	$19,200
13		
14	Net Profit	$7,200

(c) Modified Spreadsheet

FIGURE 1.1 The Accountant's Ledger (continued)

The Professor's Grade Book

A second example of a spreadsheet, one with which you can easily identify, is that of a professor's grade book. The grades are recorded by hand in a notebook, which is nothing more than a different kind of accountant's ledger. Figure 1.2 contains both manual and spreadsheet versions of a grade book.

Figure 1.2a shows a handwritten grade book as it has been done since the days of the little red schoolhouse. For the sake of simplicity, only five students are shown, each with three grades. The professor has computed class averages for each exam, as well as a semester average for every student, in which the final counts *twice* as much as either test; for example, Adams's average is equal to $(100+90+81+81)/4 = 88$.

Figure 1.2b shows the grade book as it might appear in a spreadsheet, and is essentially unchanged from Figure 1.2a. Walker's grade on the final exam in Figure 1.2b is 90, giving him a semester average of 85 and producing a class average on the final of 75.2 as well. Now consider Figure 1.2c, in which the grade on Walker's final has been changed to 100, causing Walker's semester average to change from 85 to 90, and the class average on the final to go from 75.2 to 77.2. As with the profit projection, a change to any entry within the grade book automatically recalculates all other dependent formulas as well. Hence, when Walker's final exam was regraded, all dependent formulas (the class average for the final as well as Walker's semester average) were recomputed.

As simple as the idea of a spreadsheet may seem, it provided the first major reason for managers to have a personal computer on their desks. Essentially, anything that can be done with a pencil, a pad of paper, and a calculator can be done faster and far more accurately with a spreadsheet. The spreadsheet, like the personal computer, has become an integral part of every type of business. Indeed, it is hard to imagine that these calculations were ever done by hand.

Final counts twice so average is computed as (100 + 90 + 81 + 81)/4

	TEST 1	TEST 2	FINAL	AVERAGE
ADAMS	100	90	81	88
BAKER	90	76	87	85
GLASSMAN	90	78	78	81
MOLDOF	60	60	40	50
WALKER	80	80	90	85
CLASS AVERAGE	84.0	76.8	75.2	

NOTE: FINAL COUNTS DOUBLE

(a) The Professor's Grade Book

	A	B	C	D	E
1	Student	Test 1	Test 2	Final	Average
2					
3	Adams	100	90	81	88.0
4	Baker	90	76	87	85.0
5	Glassman	90	78	78	81.0
6	Moldof	60	60	40	50.0
7	Walker	80	80	90	85.0
8					
9	Class Average	84.0	76.8	75.2	

Walker's original grade is 90

(b) Original Grades

	A	B	C	D	E
1	Student	Test 1	Test 2	Final	Average
2					
3	Adams	100	90	81	88.0
4	Baker	90	76	87	85.0
5	Glassman	90	78	78	81.0
6	Moldof	60	60	40	50.0
7	Walker	80	80	100	90.0
8					
9	Class Average	84.0	76.8	77.2	

Grade on Walker's final is changed to 100

Formulas recompute automatically

(c) Modified Spreadsheet

FIGURE 1.2 The Professor's Grade Book

Row and Column Headings

A spreadsheet is divided into rows and columns, with each row and column assigned a heading. Rows are given numeric headings ranging from 1 to 65,536 (the maximum number of rows allowed). Columns are assigned alphabetic headings from column A to Z, then continue from AA to AZ and then from BA to BZ and so on, until the last of 256 columns (column IV) is reached.

The intersection of a row and column forms a *cell*, with the number of cells in a spreadsheet equal to the number of rows times the number of columns. The professor's grade book in Figure 1.2, for example, has 5 columns labeled A through E, 9 rows numbered from 1 to 9, and a total of 45 cells. Each cell has a unique *cell reference;* for example, the cell at the intersection of column A and row 9 is known as cell A9. The column heading always precedes the row heading in the cell reference.

Formulas and Constants

Figure 1.3 is an alternate view of the professor's grade book that shows the cell contents rather than the computed values. Cell E3, for example, does not contain the number 88 (Adams' average for the semester), but rather the formula to compute the average from the exam grades. Indeed, it is the existence of the formula that lets you change the value of any cell containing a grade for Adams (cells B3, C3, or D3), and have the computed average in cell E3 change automatically.

To create a spreadsheet, one goes from cell to cell and enters either a *constant* or a *formula*. A *constant* is an entry that does not change. It may be a number, such as a student's grade on an exam, or it may be descriptive text (a label), such as a student's name. A *formula* is a combination of numeric constants, cell references, arithmetic operators, and/or functions (described below) that displays the result of a calculation. You can *edit* (change) the contents of a cell, by returning to the cell and reentering the constant or formula.

A formula always begins with an equal sign. Consider, for example, the formula in cell E3, =(B3+C3+2*D3)/4, which computes Adams's semester average. The formula is built in accordance with the professor's rules for computing a student's semester average, which counts the final twice as much as the other tests. Excel uses symbols +, −, *, /, and ^ to indicate addition, subtraction, multiplication, division, and exponentiation, respectively, and follows the normal rules of arithmetic precedence. Any expression in parentheses is evaluated first, then within an expression exponentiation is performed first, followed by multiplication or division in left to right order, then finally addition or subtraction.

The formula in cell E3 takes the grade on the first exam (in cell B3), plus the grade on the second exam (in cell C3), plus two times the grade on the final (in cell D3), and divides the result by four. Thus, should any of the exam grades change, the semester average (a formula whose results depend on the individual exam grades) will also change. This, in essence, is the basic principle behind the spreadsheet and explains why, when one number changes, various other numbers throughout the spreadsheet change as well.

A formula may also include a *function*, or predefined computational task, such as the **AVERAGE function** in cells B9, C9, and D9. The function in cell B9, for example, =AVERAGE(B3:B7), is interpreted to mean the average of all cells starting at cell B3 and ending at cell B7 and is equivalent to the formula =(B3+B4+B5+B6+B7)/5. You can appreciate that functions are often easier to use than the corresponding formulas, especially with larger spreadsheets (and classes with many students). Excel contains a wide variety of functions that help you to create very powerful spreadsheets. Financial functions, for example, enable you to calculate the interest payments on a car loan or home mortgage.

Constant (entry that does not change)

Function (predefined computational task)

Formula (displays the result of a calculation)

	A	B	C	D	E
1	Student	Test 1	Test 2	Final	Average
2					
3	Adams	100	90	81	=(B3+C3+2*D3)/4
4	Baker	90	76	87	=(B4+C4+2*D4)/4
5	Glassman	90	78	78	=(B5+C5+2*D5)/4
6	Moldof	60	60	40	=(B6+C6+2*D6)/4
7	Walker	80	80	90	=(B7+C7+2*D7)/4
8					
9	Class Average	=AVERAGE(B3:B7)	=AVERAGE(C3:C7)	=AVERAGE(D3:D7)	

FIGURE 1.3 The Professor's Grade Book (cell formulas)

INTRODUCTION TO MICROSOFT EXCEL

Figure 1.4 displays the professor's grade book as it is implemented in Microsoft Excel. Microsoft Excel is a Windows application, and thus shares the common user interface with which you are familiar. (It's even easier to learn Excel if you already know another Office application such as Microsoft Word.) You should recognize, therefore, that the desktop in Figure 1.4 has two open windows—an application window for Microsoft Excel and a document window for the workbook, which is currently open.

Each window has its own Minimize, Maximize (or Restore), and Close buttons. Both windows have been maximized and thus the title bars have been merged into a single title bar that appears at the top of the application window. The title bar reflects the application (Microsoft Excel) as well as the name of the workbook (Grade Book) on which you are working. A menu bar appears immediately below the title bar. Two toolbars, which are discussed in depth on page 8, appear below the menu bar. Vertical and horizontal scroll bars appear at the right and bottom of the document window. The Windows taskbar appears at the bottom of the screen and shows the open applications.

The terminology is important, and we distinguish between spreadsheet, worksheet, and workbook. Excel refers to a spreadsheet as a ***worksheet***. Spreadsheet is a generic term; *workbook* and *worksheet* are unique to Excel. An Excel ***workbook*** contains one or more worksheets. The professor's grades for this class are contained in the CIS120 worksheet within the Grade Book workbook. This workbook also contains additional worksheets (CIS223 and CIS316) as indicated by the worksheet tabs at the bottom of the window. These worksheets contain the professor's grades for other courses that he or she is teaching this semester. (See practice exercise 1 at the end of the chapter.)

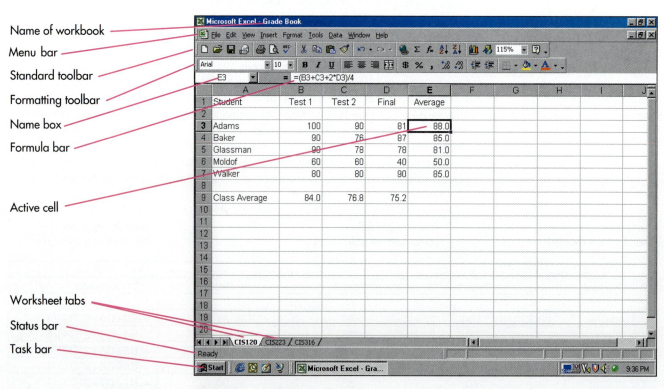

FIGURE 1.4 Professor's Grade Book

Figure 1.4 resembles the grade book shown earlier, but it includes several other elements that enable you to create and/or edit the worksheet. The heavy border around cell E3 indicates that it (cell E3) is the *active cell*. Any entry made at this time is made into the active cell, and any commands that are executed affect the contents of the active cell. The active cell can be changed by clicking a different cell, or by using the arrow keys to move to a different cell.

The displayed value in cell E3 is 88.0, but as indicated earlier, the cell contains a formula to compute the semester average rather than the number itself. The contents of the active cell, =(B3+C3+2*D3)/4, are displayed in the *formula bar* near the top of the worksheet. The cell reference for the active cell, cell E3 in Figure 1.4, appears in the *Name box* at the left of the formula bar.

The *status bar* at the bottom of the worksheet keeps you informed of what is happening as you work within Excel. It displays information about a selected command or an operation in progress.

THE EXCEL WORKBOOK

An Excel workbook is the electronic equivalent of the three-ring binder. A workbook contains one or more worksheets (or chart sheets), each of which is identified by a tab at the bottom of the workbook. The worksheets in a workbook are normally related to one another; for example, each worksheet may contain the sales for a specific division within a company. The advantage of a workbook is that all of its worksheets are stored in a single file, which is accessed as a unit.

Toolbars

Excel provides several different ways to accomplish the same task. Commands may be accessed from a pull-down menu, from a shortcut menu (which is displayed by pointing to an object and clicking the right mouse button), and/or through keyboard equivalents. Commands can also be executed from one of many *toolbars* that appear immediately below the menu bar. The Standard and Formatting toolbars are displayed by default. The toolbars appear initially on the same line, but can be separated as described in the hands-on exercise that follows.

The *Standard toolbar* contains buttons corresponding to the most basic commands in Excel—for example, opening and closing a workbook, printing a workbook, and so on. The icon on the button is intended to be indicative of its function (e.g., a printer to indicate the Print command). You can also point to the button to display a *ScreenTip* showing the name of the button.

The *Formatting toolbar* appears under the Standard toolbar, and provides access to common formatting operations such as boldface, italics, or underlining. It also enables you to change the alignment of entries within a cell and/or change the font or color. The easiest way to master the toolbars is to view the buttons in groups according to their general function, as shown in Figure 1.5.

The toolbars may appear overwhelming at first, but there is absolutely no need to memorize what the individual buttons do. That will come with time. Indeed, if you use another office application such as Microsoft Word, you may already recognize many of the buttons on the Standard and Formatting toolbars. Note, too, that many of the commands in the pull-down menus are displayed with an image that corresponds to a button on a toolbar.

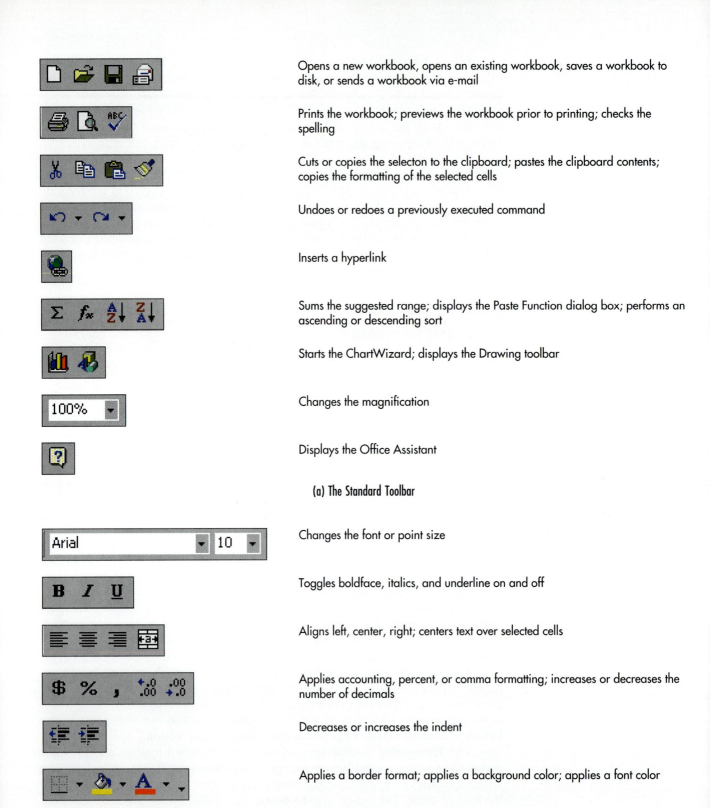

FIGURE 1.5 Toolbars

THE FILE MENU

The *File Menu* is a critically important menu in virtually every Windows application. It contains the Save and Open commands to save a workbook on disk, then subsequently retrieve (open) that workbook at a later time. The File Menu also contains the **Print command** to print a workbook, the **Close command** to close the current workbook but continue working in the application, and the **Exit command** to quit the application altogether.

The **Save command** copies the workbook that you are working on (i.e., the workbook that is currently in memory) to disk. The command functions differently the first time it is executed for a new workbook, in that it displays the Save As dialog box as shown in Figure 1.6a. The dialog box requires you to specify the name of the workbook, the drive (and an optional folder) in which the workbook is to be stored, and its file type. All subsequent executions of the command save the workbook under the assigned name, replacing the previously saved version with the new version.

The *file name* (e.g., My First Spreadsheet) can contain up to 255 characters including spaces, commas, and/or periods. (Periods are discouraged, however, since they are too easily confused with DOS extensions.) The Save In list box is used to select the drive (which is not visible in Figure 1.6a) and the optional folder (e.g., Exploring Excel). The **Places Bar** provides shortcuts to any of its folders without having to search through the Save In list box. Click the Desktop icon, for example, and the file is saved on the Windows desktop. You can also use the Favorites folder, which is accessible from every application in Office 2000.

The *file type* defaults to an Excel 2000 workbook. You can, however, choose a different format such as Excel 95 to maintain compatibility with earlier versions of Microsoft Excel. You can also save any Excel workbook as a Web page or HTML document. (Long-time DOS users will remember the three-character extension at the end of a filename such as XLS to indicate an Excel workbook. The extension is generally hidden in Windows 95/98, according to options that are set through the View menu in My Computer or Windows Explorer.)

The **Open command** is the opposite of the Save command as it brings a copy of an existing workbook into memory, enabling you to work with that workbook. The Open command displays the Open dialog box in which you specify the file name, the drive (and optionally the folder) that contains the file, and the file type. Microsoft Excel will then list all files of that type on the designated drive (and folder), enabling you to open the file you want.

The Save and Open commands work in conjunction with one another. The Save As dialog box in Figure 1.6a, for example, saves the file My First Spreadsheet in the Exploring Excel folder. The Open dialog box in Figure 1.6b loads that file into memory so that you can work with the file, after which you can save the revised file for use at a later time.

The toolbars in the Save As and Open dialog boxes have several buttons in common that facilitate the execution of either command. The Views button lets you display the files in one of four different views. The Details view shows the file size as well as the date and time a file was last modified. The Preview view shows the beginning of a workbook, without having to open the workbook. The List view displays only the file names, and thus lets you see more files at one time. The Properties view shows information about the workbook including the date of creation and number of revisions.

Other buttons provide limited file management without having to go to My Computer or Windows Explorer. You can for example, delete a file, create a new folder, or start your Web browser from either dialog box. The Tools button provides access to additional commands that are well worth exploring as you gain proficiency in Microsoft Office.

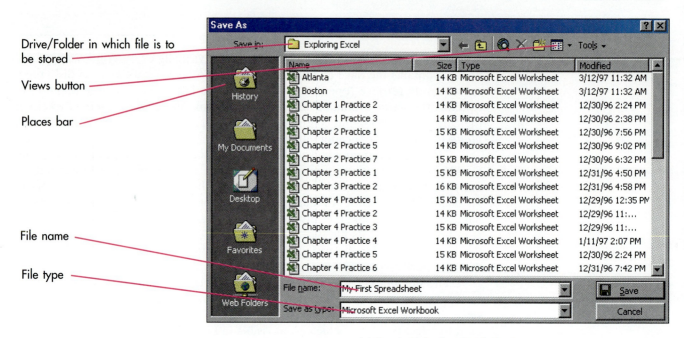

(a) Save As Dialog Box (Details View)

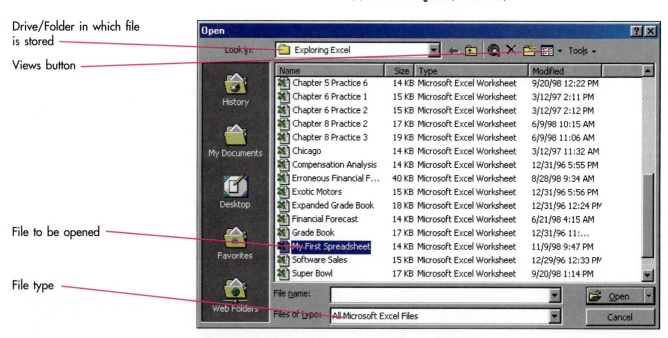

(b) Open Dialog Box (Details Views)

FIGURE 1.6 The Save and Open Commands

SORT BY NAME, DATE, OR FILE SIZE

The files in the Save As and Open dialog boxes can be displayed in ascending or descending sequence by name, date modified, or size. Change to the Details view, then click the heading of the desired column; e.g., click the Modified column to list the files according to the date they were last changed. Click the column heading a second time to reverse the sequence; that is, to switch from ascending to descending, and vice versa.

HANDS-ON EXERCISE 1

Introduction to Microsoft Excel

Objective: To start Microsoft Excel; to open, modify, and print an existing workbook. Use Figure 1.7 as a guide in the exercise.

STEP 1: Welcome to Windows

➤ Turn on the computer and all of its peripherals. The floppy drive should be empty prior to starting your machine. This ensures that the system starts by reading from the hard disk, which contains the Windows files, as opposed to a floppy disk, which does not.

➤ Your system will take a minute or so to get started, after which you should see the desktop in Figure 1.7a. Do not be concerned if the appearance of your desktop is different from ours.

➤ You may see additional objects on the desktop in Windows 95 and/or the active desktop in Windows 98. It doesn't matter which operating system you are using because Office 2000 runs equally well under both Windows 95 and Windows 98, as well as Windows NT.

➤ You may also see a Welcome to Windows dialog box with commands to take a tour of the operating system. If so, click the appropriate button(s) or close the dialog box.

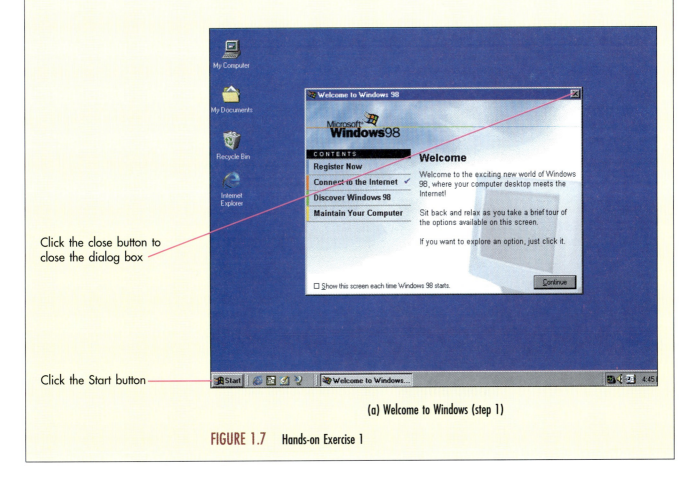

(a) Welcome to Windows (step 1)

FIGURE 1.7 Hands-on Exercise 1

CHAPTER 1: INTRODUCTION TO MICROSOFT EXCEL

STEP 2: Obtain the Practice Files

➤ We have created a series of practice files (also called a "data disk") for you to use throughout the text. Your instructor will make these files available to you in a variety of ways:

- The files may be on a network drive, in which case you use Windows Explorer to copy the files from the network to a floppy disk.
- There may be an actual "data disk" that you are to check out from the lab in order to use the Copy Disk command to duplicate the disk.

➤ You can also download the files from our Web site provided you have an Internet connection. Start Internet Explorer, then go to the Exploring Windows home page at **www.prenhall.com/grauer.**

- Click the book for **Office 2000,** which takes you to the Office 2000 home page. Click the **Student Resources tab** (at the top of the window) to go to the Student Resources page as shown in Figure 1.7b.
- Click the link to **Student Data Disk** (in the left frame), then scroll down the page until you can select Excel 2000. Click the link to download the student data disk.
- You will see the File Download dialog box asking what you want to do. The option button to save this program to disk is selected. Click **OK.** The Save As dialog box appears.
- Click the down arrow in the Save In list box to enter the drive and folder where you want to save the file. It's best to save the file to the Windows desktop or to a temporary folder on drive C
- Double click the file after it has been downloaded to your PC, then follow the onscreen instructions.

➤ Check with your instructor for additional information.

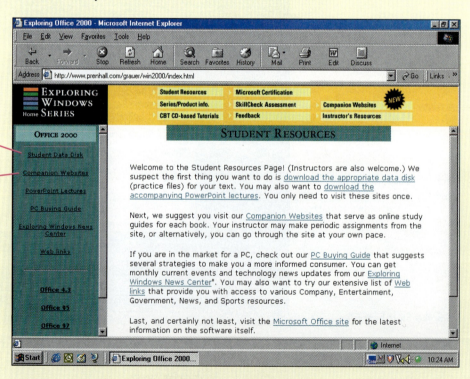

Click here for student data disk

Click here for Companion Web site (see problem 8 at the end of the chapter)

(b) Download the Data Disk (step 2)

FIGURE 1.7 Hands-on Exercise 1 (continued)

STEP 3: Start Excel

➤ Click the **Start button** to display the Start menu. Click (or point to) the **Programs menu,** then click **Microsoft Excel** to start the program.

➤ Click and drag the Office Assistant out of the way. (The Office Assistant is illustrated in step 7 of this exercise.)

➤ If necessary, click the **Maximize button** in the application window so that Excel takes the entire desktop as shown in Figure 1.7c. Click the **Maximize button** in the document window (if necessary) so that the document window is as large as possible.

Click and drag the Office Assistant out of the way

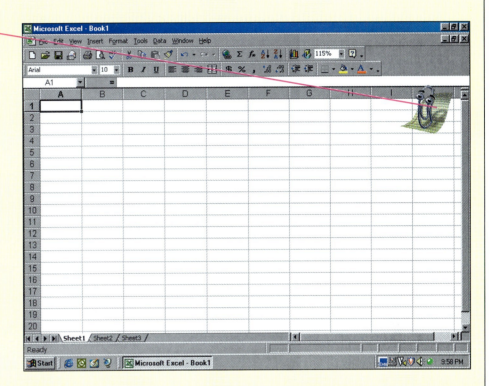

(c) Start Excel (step 3)

FIGURE 1.7 Hands-on Exercise 1 (continued)

ABOUT THE ASSISTANT

The Assistant is very powerful and hence you want to experiment with various ways to use it. To ask a question, click the Assistant's icon to toggle its balloon on or off. To change the way in which the Assistant works, click the Options button within the balloon and experiment with the various check boxes to see their effects. If you find the Assistant distracting, click and drag the character out of the way or hide it altogether by pulling down the Help menu and clicking the Hide the Office Assistant command. Pull down the Help menu and click the Show the Office Assistant command to return the Assistant to the desktop.

STEP 4: Open the Workbook

➤ Pull down the **File menu** and click **Open** (or click the **Open button** on the Standard toolbar). You should see a dialog box similar to the one in Figure 1.7d.

➤ Click the down-drop arrow on the Views button, then click **Details** to change to the Details view. Click and drag the vertical border between two columns to increase (or decrease) the size of a column.

➤ Click the **drop-down arrow** on the Look In list box. Click the appropriate drive, drive C or drive A, depending on the location of your data. Double click the **Exploring Excel folder** to make it the active folder (the folder from which you will retrieve and into which you will save the workbook).

➤ Click the **down scroll arrow** if necessary in order to click **Grade Book** to select the professor's grade book. Click the **Open command button** to open the workbook and begin the exercise.

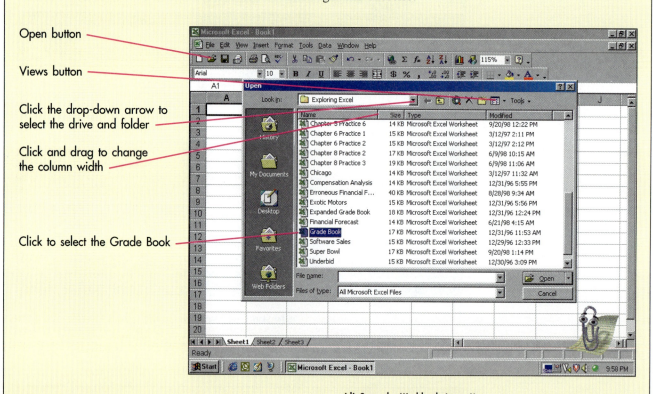

(d) Open the Workbook (step 4)

FIGURE 1.7 Hands-on Exercise 1 (continued)

SEPARATE THE TOOLBARS

Office 2000 displays the Standard and Formatting toolbars on the same row to save space within the application window. The result is that only a limited number of buttons are visible on each toolbar, and hence you may need to click the double arrow (More Buttons) tool at the end of the toolbar to view additional buttons. You can, however, separate the toolbars. Pull down the Tools menu, click the Customize command, click the Options tab, then clear the check box that has the toolbars share one row.

STEP 5: The Active Cell, Formula Bar, and Worksheet Tabs

➤ You should see the workbook in Figure 1.7e. Click in **cell B3,** the cell containing Adams's grade on the first test. Cell B3 is now the active cell and is surrounded by a heavy border. The Name box indicates that cell B3 is the active cell, and its contents are displayed in the formula bar.

➤ Click in **cell B4** (or press the **down arrow key**) to make it the active cell. The Name box indicates cell B4 while the formula bar indicates a grade of 90.

➤ Click in **cell E3,** the cell containing the formula to compute Adams's semester average; the worksheet displays the computed average of 88.0, but the formula bar displays the formula, =(B3+C3+2*D3)/4, to compute that average based on the test grades.

➤ Click the **CIS223 tab** to view a different worksheet within the same workbook. This worksheet contains the grades for a different class.

➤ Click the **CIS316 tab** to view this worksheet. Click the **CIS120 tab** to return to this worksheet and continue with the exercise.

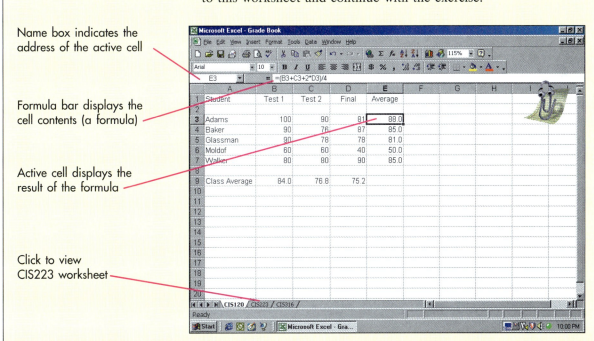

Name box indicates the address of the active cell

Formula bar displays the cell contents (a formula)

Active cell displays the result of the formula

Click to view CIS223 worksheet

(e) The Active Cell, Formula Bar, and Worksheet Tabs (step 5)

FIGURE 1.7 Hands-on Exercise 1 (continued)

THE MENUS CHANGE

All applications in Office 2000 display a series of short menus that contain only basic commands to simplify the application for the new user. There is, however, a double arrow at the bottom of each menu that you can click to display the additional commands. In addition, each time you execute a command it is added to the menu, and conversely, commands are removed from a menu if they are not used after a period of time. You can, however, display the full menus through the Customize command in the Tools menu by clearing the check boxes in the Personalized Menus and Toolbars section.

STEP 6: Experiment (What If?)

➤ Click in **cell C4,** the cell containing Baker's grade on the second test. Enter a corrected value of **86** (instead of the previous entry of 76). Press **enter** (or click in another cell).

➤ The effects of this change ripple through the worksheet, automatically changing the computed value for Baker's average in cell E4 to 87.5. The class average on the second test in cell C9 changes to 78.8.

➤ Change Walker's grade on the final from 90 to **100.** Press **enter** (or click in another cell). Walker's average in cell E7 changes to 90.0, while the class average in cell D9 changes to 77.2.

➤ Your worksheet should match Figure 1.7f.

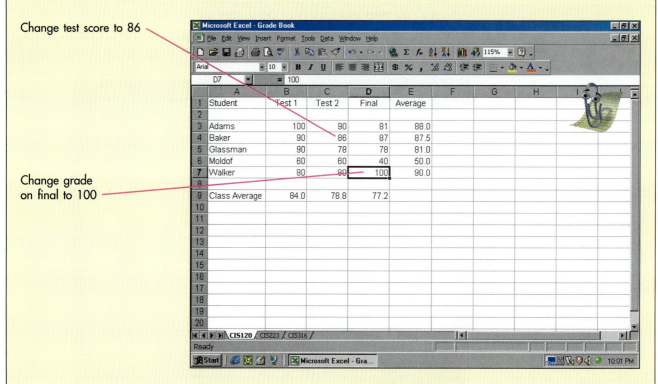

(f) What If? (step 6)

FIGURE 1.7 Hands-on Exercise 1 (continued)

THE UNDO AND REDO COMMANDS

The Undo Command lets you undo the last several changes to a workbook. Click the down arrow next to the Undo button on the Standard toolbar to display a reverse-order list of your previous commands, then click the command you want to undo, which also cancels all of the preceding commands. Undoing the fifth command in the list, for example, will also undo the preceding four commands. The Redo commands redoes (reverses) the last command that was undone. It, too, displays a reverse-order list of commands, so that redoing the fifth command in the list will also redo the preceding four commands.

STEP 7: The Office Assistant

➤ If necessary, pull down the **Help menu** and click the comand to **Show the Office Assistant.** You may see a different character than the one we have selected. Click the Assistant, then enter the question, **How do I use the Office Assistant?** as shown in Figure 1.7g.

➤ Click the **Search button** in the Assistant's balloon to look for the answer. The size of the Assistant's balloon expands as the Assistant suggests several topics that may be appropriate.

➤ Select (click) any topic, which in turn diplays a Help window with multiple links associated with the topic you selected.

➤ Click the Office Assistant to hide the balloon, then click any of the links in the Help window to read the information. You can print the contents of any topic by clicking the **Print button** in the Help window.

➤ Close the Help window when you are finished. If necessary, click the Excel button on the taskbar to return to the workbook.

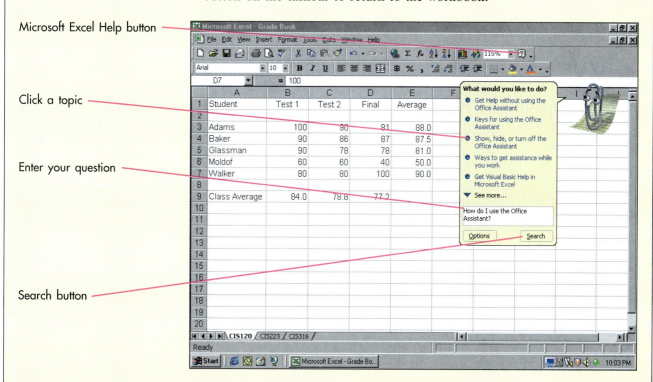

(g) The Office Assistant (step 7)

FIGURE 1.7 Hands-on Exercise 1 (continued)

ABOUT MICROSOFT EXCEL

Pull down the Help menu and click About Microsoft Excel to display the specific release number as well as other licensing information, including the Product ID. This help screen also contains two very useful command buttons, System Info and Technical Support. The first button displays information about the hardware installed on your system, including the amount of memory and available space on the hard drive. The Technical Support button provides information on obtaining technical assistance.

STEP 8: Print the Workbook

➤ Pull down the **File menu** and click **Save** (or click the **Save button** on the Standard toolbar).

➤ Pull down the **File menu.** Click **Print** to display a dialog box requesting information for the Print command as shown in Figure 1.7h. Click **OK** to accept the default options (you want to print only the selected worksheet).

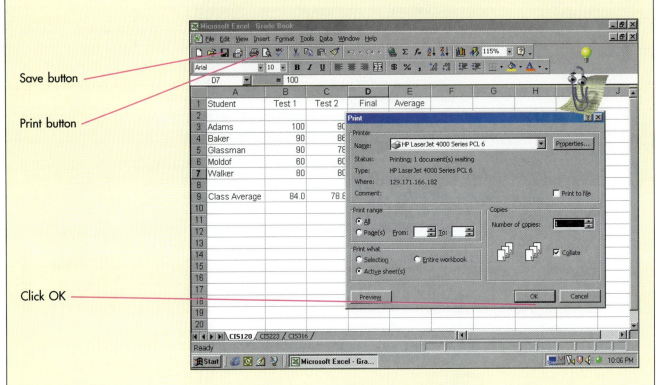

(h) Print the Workbook (step 8)

FIGURE 1.7 Hands-on Exercise 1 (continued)

THE PRINT PREVIEW COMMAND

The Print Preview command displays the worksheet as it will appear when printed. The command is invaluable and will save you considerable time as you don't have to rely on trial and error to obtain the perfect printout. The Print Preview command can be executed from the File menu, via the Print Preview button on the Standard toolbar, or from the Print Preview command button within the Page Setup command.

STEP 9: Close the Workbook

➤ Pull down the **File menu.** Click **Close** to close the workbook but leave Excel open.

➤ Pull down the **File menu** a second time. Click **Exit** if you do not want to continue with the next exercise at this time.

MODIFYING THE WORKSHEET

We trust that you completed the hands-on exercise without difficulty and that you are more confident in your ability than when you first began. The exercise was not complicated, but it did accomplish several objectives and set the stage for a second exercise, which follows shortly.

Consider now Figure 1.8, which contains a modified version of the professor's grade book. Figure 1.8a shows the grade book at the end of the first hands-on exercise and reflects the changes made to the grades for Baker and Walker. Figure 1.8b shows the worksheet as it will appear at the end of the second exercise. Several changes bear mention:

1. One student has dropped the class and two other students have been added. Moldof appeared in the original worksheet in Figure 1.8a, but has somehow managed to withdraw; Coulter and Courier did not appear in the original grade book but have been added to the worksheet in Figure 1.8b.
2. A new column containing the students' majors has been added.

The implementation of these changes is accomplished through a combination of the **Insert Command** (to add individual cells, rows, or columns) and/or the **Delete command** (to remove individual cells, rows, or columns). Execution of either command automatically adjusts the cell references in existing formulas to reflect the insertion or deletion of the various cells. The Insert and Delete commands can also be used to insert or delete a worksheet. The professor could, for example, add a new sheet to a workbook to include grades for another class and/or delete a worksheet for a class that was no longer taught. We focus initially, however, on the insertion and deletion of rows and columns within a worksheet.

	A	B	C	D	E
1	Student	Test 1	Test 2	Final	Average
2					
3	Adams	100	90	81	88.0
4	Baker	90	86	87	87.5
5	Glassman	90	78	78	81.0
6	Moldof	60	60	40	50.0
7	Walker	80	80	100	90.0
8					
9	Class Average	84.0	78.8	77.2	

Moldof will be dropped from class

(a) After Hands-on Exercise 1

	A	B	C	D	E	F
1	Student	Major	Test 1	Test 2	Final	Average
2						
3	Adams	CIS	100	90	81	88.0
4	Baker	MKT	90	86	87	87.5
5	Coulter	ACC	85	95	100	95.0
6	Courier	FIN	75	75	85	80.0
7	Glassman	CIS	90	78	78	81.0
8	Walker	CIS	80	80	100	90.0
9						

A new column has been added (Major)

Two new students have been added

Moldof has been deleted

(b) After Hands-on Exercise 2

FIGURE 1.8 The Modified Grade Book

Figure 1.9 displays the cell formulas in the professor's grade book and corresponds to the worksheets in Figure 1.8. The "before" and "after" worksheets reflect the insertion of a new column containing the students' majors, the addition of two new students, Coulter and Courier, and the deletion of an existing student, Moldof.

Let us consider the formula to compute Adams's semester average, which is contained in cell E3 of the original grade book, but in cell F3 in the modified grade book. The formula in Figure 1.9a referenced cells B3, C3, and D3 (the grades on test 1, test 2, and the final). The corresponding formula in Figure 1.9b reflects the fact that a new column has been inserted, and references cells C3, D3, and E3. The change in the formula is made automatically by Excel, without any action on the part of the user other than to insert the new column. The formulas for all other students have been adjusted in similar fashion.

Some students (all students below Baker) have had a further adjustment to reflect the addition of the new students through insertion of new rows in the worksheet. Glassman, for example, appeared in row 5 of the original worksheet, but appears in row 7 of the revised worksheet. Hence the formula to compute Glassman's semester average now references the grades in row 7, rather than in row 5 as in the original worksheet.

Finally, the formulas to compute the class averages have also been adjusted. These formulas appeared in row 9 of Figure 1.9a and averaged the grades in rows 3 through 7. The revised worksheet has a net increase of one student, which automatically moves these formulas to row 10, where the formulas are adjusted to average the grades in rows 3 through 8.

Formula references grades in B3, C3, and D3

	A	B	C	D	E
1	Student	Test1	Test2	Final	Average
2					
3	Adams	100	90	81	=(B3+C3+2*D3)/4
4	Baker	90	86	87	=(B4+C4+2*D4)/4
5	Glassman	90	78	78	=(B5+C5+2*D5)/4
6	Moldof	60	60	40	=(B6+C6+2*D6)/4
7	Walker	80	80	100	=(B7+C7+2*D7)/4
8					
9	Class Average	=AVERAGE(B3:B7)	=AVERAGE(C3:C7)	=AVERAGE(D3:D7)	

Function references grades in rows 3–7

(a) Before

	A	B	C	D	E	F
1	Student	Major	Test1	Test2	Final	Average
2						
3	Adams	CIS	100	90	81	=(C3+D3+2*E3)/4
4	Baker	MKT	90	86	87	=(C4+D4+2*E4)/4
5	Coulter	ACC	85	95	100	=(C5+D5+2*E5)/4
6	Courier	FIN	75	75	85	=(C6+D6+2*E6)/4
7	Glassman	CIS	90	78	78	=(C7+D7+2*E7)/4
8	Walker	CIS	80	80	100	=(C8+D8+2*E8)/4
9						
10	Class Average		=AVERAGE(C3:C8)	=AVERAGE(D3:D8)	=AVERAGE(E3:E8)	

Function changes to reference grades in rows 3–8 (due to addition of 2 new students and deletion of 1)

Formula changes to reference grades in C3, D3, and E3 due to addition of new column

(b) After

FIGURE 1.9 The Insert and Delete Commands

THE PAGE SETUP COMMAND

The Print command was used at the end of the first hands-on exercise to print the completed workbook. The **Page Setup command** gives you complete control of the printed worksheet as illustrated in Figure 1.10. Many of the options may not appear important now, but you will appreciate them as you develop larger and more complicated worksheets later in the text.

The Page tab in Figure 1.10a determines the orientation and scaling of the printed page. **Portrait orientation** (8½ × 11) prints vertically down the page. **Landscape orientation** (11 × 8½) prints horizontally across the page and is used

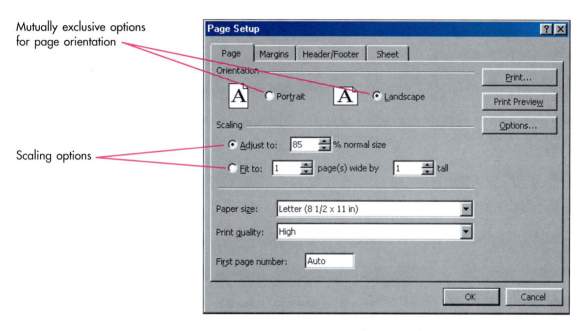

(a) The Page Tab

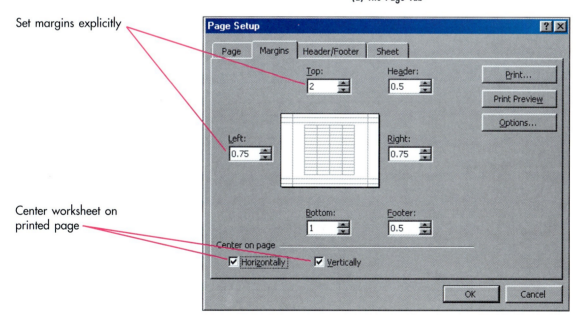

(b) The Margins Tab

FIGURE 1.10 The Page Setup Command

when the worksheet is too wide to fit on a portrait page. The option buttons indicate mutually exclusive items, one of which *must* be selected; that is, a worksheet must be printed in either portrait or landscape orientation. Option buttons are also used to choose the scaling factor. You can reduce (enlarge) the output by a designated scaling factor, or you can force the output to fit on a specified number of pages. The latter option is typically used to force a worksheet to fit on a single page.

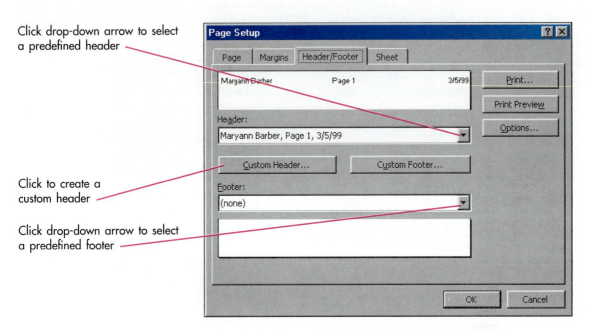

(c) The Header/Footer Tab

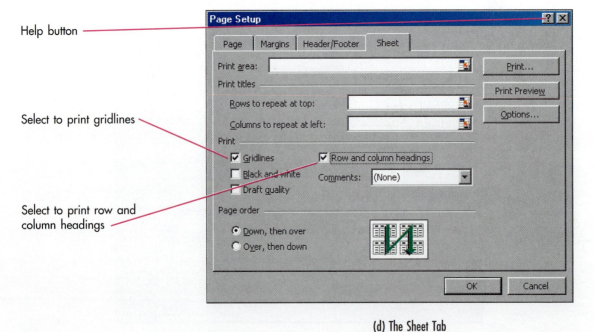

(d) The Sheet Tab

FIGURE 1.10 The Page Setup Command (continued)

The Margins tab in Figure 1.10b not only controls the margins, but will also center the worksheet horizontally and/or vertically. Check boxes are associated with the centering options and indicate that multiple options can be chosen; for example, horizontally and vertically are both selected. The Margins tab also determines the distance of the header and footer from the edge of the page.

The Header/Footer tab in Figure 1.10c lets you create a header (and/or footer) that appears at the top (and/or bottom) of every page. The pull-down list boxes let you choose from several preformatted entries, or alternatively, you can click the appropriate command button to customize either entry.

The Sheet tab in Figure 1.10d offers several additional options. The Gridlines option prints lines to separate the cells within the worksheet. The Row and Column Headings option displays the column letters and row numbers. Both options should be selected for most worksheets. Information about the additional entries can be obtained by clicking the Help button.

The Print Preview command button is available from all four tabs within the Page Setup dialog box. The command shows you how the worksheet will appear when printed and saves you from having to rely on trial and error.

HANDS-ON EXERCISE 2

Modifying a Worksheet

Objective: To open an existing workbook; to insert and delete rows and columns in a worksheet; to print cell formulas and displayed values; to use the Page Setup command to modify the appearance of a printed workbook. Use Figure 1.11 as a guide in doing the exercise.

STEP 1: Open the Workbook

➤ Open the grade book as you did in the previous exercise. Pull down the **File menu** and click **Open** (or click the **Open button** on the Standard toolbar) to display the Open dialog box.

➤ Click the **drop-down arrow** on the Look In list box. Click the appropriate drive, drive C or drive A, depending on the location of your data. Double click the **Exploring Excel folder** to make it the active folder (the folder from which you will open the workbook).

➤ Click the **down scroll arrow** until you can select (click) the **Grade Book** workbook. Click the **Open button** to open the workbook and begin the exercise.

THE MOST RECENTLY OPENED FILE LIST

The easiest way to open a recently used workbook is to select the workbook directly from the File menu. Pull down the File menu, but instead of clicking the Open command, check to see if the workbook appears on the list of the most recently opened workbooks located at the bottom of the menu. If it does, you can click the workbook name rather than having to make the appropriate selections through the Open dialog box.

STEP 2: The Save As Command

➤ Pull down the **File menu.** Click **Save As** to display the dialog box shown in Figure 1.11a.

➤ Enter **Finished Grade Book** as the name of the new workbook. (A filename may contain up to 255 characters. Spaces and commas are allowed in the filename.)

➤ Click the **Save button.** Press the **Esc key** or click the **Close button** if you see a Properties dialog box.

➤ There are now two identical copies of the file on disk: "Grade Book," which is the completed workbook from the previous exercise, and "Finished Grade Book," which you just created. The title bar shows the latter name, which is the workbook currently in memory.

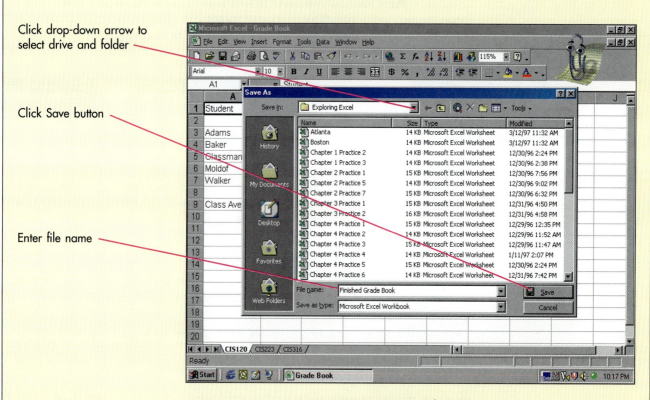

(a) Save As Command (step 2)

FIGURE 1.11 Hands-on Exercise 2

INCOMPATIBLE FILE TYPES

The file format for Excel 2000 is compatible with Excel 97, but incompatible with earlier versions such as Excel 95. The newer releases can open a workbook that was created using the older program (Excel 95), but the reverse is not true; that is, you cannot open a workbook that was created in Excel 2000 in Excel 95 unless you change the file type. Pull down the File menu, click the Save As command, then specify the earlier (Microsoft Excel 5.0/95 workbook) file type. You will be able to read the file in Excel 95, but will lose any formatting that is unique to the newer release.

STEP 3: Delete a Row

➤ Click any cell in **row 6** (the row you will delete). Pull down the **Edit menu.** Click **Delete** to display the dialog box in Figure 1.11b. Click **Entire Row.** Click **OK** to delete row 6.

➤ Moldof has disappeared from the grade book, and the class averages (now in row 8) have been updated automatically.

➤ Pull down the **Edit menu** and click **Undo Delete** (or click the **Undo button** on the Standard toolbar) to reverse the last command.

➤ The row for Moldof has been put back in the worksheet.

➤ Click any cell in **row 6,** and this time delete the entire row for good.

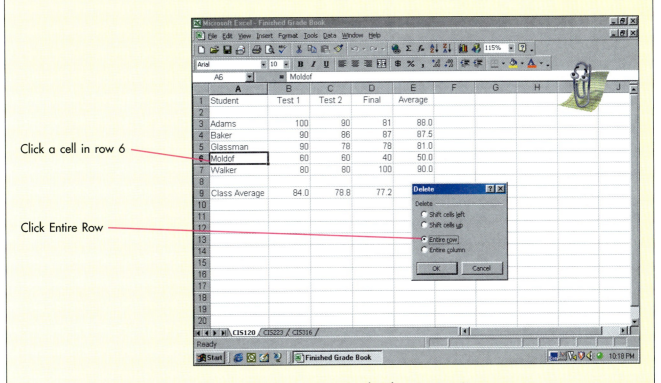

(b) Delete a Row (step 3)

FIGURE 1.11 Hands-on Exercise 2 (continued)

EDIT CLEAR VERSUS EDIT DELETE

The Edit Delete command deletes the selected cell, row, or column from the worksheet, and thus its execution will adjust cell references throughout the worksheet. It is very different from the Edit Clear command, which erases the contents (and/or formatting) of the selected cells, but does not delete the cells from the worksheet and hence has no effect on the cell references in other cells. Pressing the Del key erases the contents of a cell and thus corresponds to the Edit Clear command.

STEP 4: Insert a Row

➤ Click any cell in **row 5** (the row containing Glassman's grades).

➤ Pull down the **Insert menu.** Click **Rows** to add a new row above the current row. Row 5 is now blank (it is the newly inserted row), and Glassman (who was in row 5) is now in row 6.

➤ Enter the data for the new student in row 5 as shown in Figure 1.11c. Click in **cell A5.** Type **Coulter.** Press the **right arrow key** or click in **cell B5.** Enter the test grades of 85, 95, 100 in cells B5, C5, and D5.

➤ Enter the formula to compute the semester average, **=(B5+C5+2*D5)/4.** Be sure to begin the formula with an equal sign. Press **enter.**

➤ Click the **Save button** on the Standard toolbar, or pull down the **File menu** and click **Save** to save the changes made to this point.

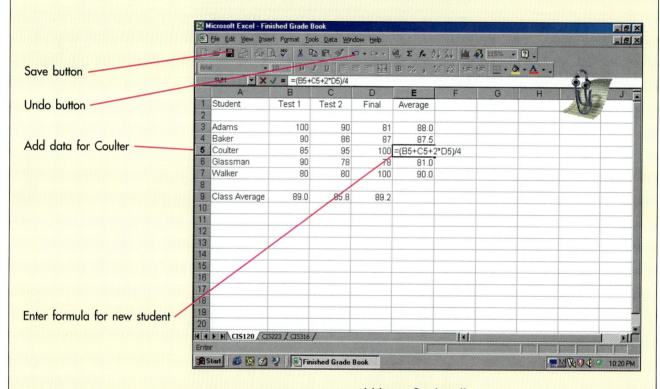

(c) Insert a Row (step 4)

FIGURE 1.11 Hands-on Exercise 2 (continued)

INSERTING (DELETING) ROWS AND COLUMNS

The fastest way to insert or delete a row is to point to the row number, then click the right mouse button to simultaneously select the row and display a shortcut menu. Click Insert to add a row above the selected row, or click Delete to delete the selected row. Use a similar technique to insert or delete a column, by pointing to the column heading, then clicking the right mouse button to display a shortcut menu from which you can select the appropriate command.

STEP 5: The AutoComplete Feature

➤ Point to the row heading for **row 6** (which now contains Glassman's grades), then click the **right mouse button** to select the row and display a shortcut menu. Click **Insert** to insert a new row 6, which moves Glassman to row 7 as shown in Figure 1.11d.

➤ Click in **cell A6**. Type **C,** the first letter in "Courier," which also happens to be the first letter in "Coulter," a previous entry in column A. If the Auto-Complete feature is on (see boxed tip), Coulter's name will be automatically inserted in cell A6 with "oulter" selected.

➤ Type **ourier** (the remaining letters in "Courier," which replace "oulter."

➤ Enter Courier's grades in the appropriate cells (75, 75, and 85 in cells B6, C6, and D6, respectively). Click in **cell E6**. Enter the formula to compute the semester average, **=(B6+C6+2*D6)/4.** Press **enter.**

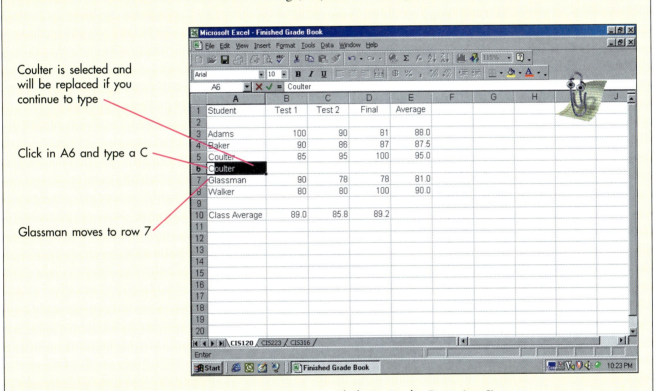

(d) The AutoComplete Feature (step 5)

FIGURE 1.11   Hands-on Exercise 2 (continued)

AUTOCOMPLETE

As soon as you begin typing a label into a cell, Excel searches for and (automatically) displays any other label in that column that matches the letters you typed. It's handy if you want to repeat a label, but it can be distracting if you want to enter a different label that just happens to begin with the same letter. To turn the feature on (off), pull down the Tools menu, click Options, then click the Edit tab. Check (clear) the box to enable the AutoComplete feature.

STEP 6: Insert a Column

➤ Point to the column heading for column B, then click the **right mouse button** to display a shortcut menu as shown in Figure 1.11e.

➤ Click **Insert** to insert a new column, which becomes the new column B. All existing columns have been moved to the right.

➤ Click in **cell B1.** Type **Major.**

➤ Click in **cell B3.** Enter **CIS** as Adams's major. Press the **down arrow** to move automatically to the major for the next student.

➤ Type **MKT** in cell B4. Press the **down arrow.** Type **ACC** in cell B5. Press the **down arrow.** Type **FIN** in cell B6.

➤ Press the **down arrow** to move to cell B7. Type **C** (AutoComplete will automatically enter "IS" to complete the entry). Press the **down arrow** to move to cell B8. Type **C** (the AutoComplete feature again enters "IS"), then press **enter** to complete the entry.

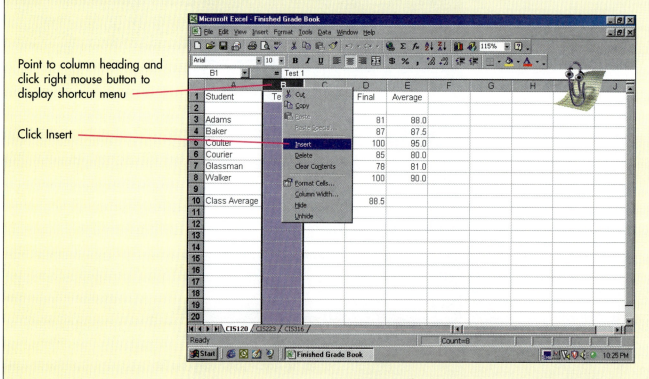

(e) Insert a Column (step 6)

FIGURE 1.11 Hands-on Exercise 2 (continued)

INSERTING AND DELETING INDIVIDUAL CELLS

You can insert and/or delete individual cells as opposed to an entire row or column. To insert a cell, click in the cell to the left or above of where you want the new cell to go, pull down the Insert menu, then click Cells to display the Insert dialog box. Click the appropriate option button to shift cells right or down and click OK. To delete a cell or cells, select the cell(s), pull down the Edit menu, click the Delete command, then click the option button to shift cells left or up.

STEP 7: Display the Cell Formulas

➤ Pull down the **Tools menu.** Click **Options** to display the Options dialog box. Click the **View tab.** Check the box for **Formulas.** Click **OK.**

➤ The worksheet should display the cell formulas as shown in Figure 1.11f. If necessary, click the **right scroll arrow** on the horizontal scroll bar until column F, the column containing the formulas to compute the semester averages, comes into view.

➤ If necessary (i.e., if the formulas are not completely visible), double click the border between the column headings for columns F and G. This increases the width of column F to accommodate the widest entry in that column.

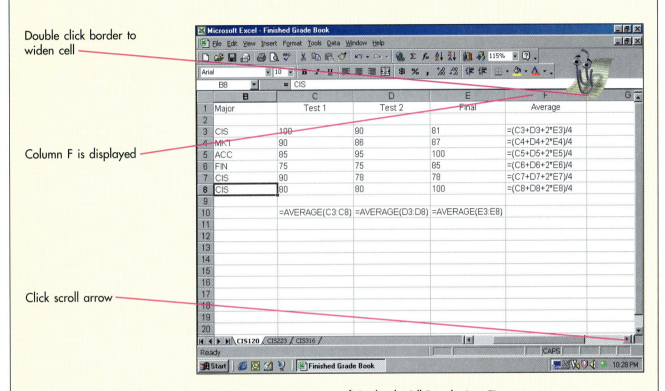

(f) Display the Cell Formulas (step 7)

FIGURE 1.11   Hands-on Exercise 2 (continued)

DISPLAY CELL FORMULAS

A worksheet should always be printed twice, once to show the computed results, and once to show the cell formulas. The fastest way to toggle (switch) between cell formulas and displayed values is to use the Ctrl+` keyboard shortcut. (The ` is on the same key as the ~ at the upper left of the keyboard.) Press Ctrl+` to switch from displayed values to cell formulas. Press Ctrl+` a second time and you are back to the displayed values.

STEP 8: The Page Setup Command

➤ Pull down the **File menu.** Click the **Page Setup command** to display the Page Setup dialog box as shown in Figure 1.11g.

- Click the **Page tab.** Click the **Landscape option button.** Click the option button to **Fit to 1 page.**
- Click the **Margins tab.** Check the box to center the worksheet horizontally.
- Click the **Header/Footer tab.** Click the **drop-down arrow** on the Footer list box. Scroll to the top of the list and click **(none)** to remove the footer.
- Click the **Sheet tab.** Check the boxes to print Row and Column Headings and Gridlines.

➤ Click **OK** to exit the Page Setup dialog box. Save the workbook.

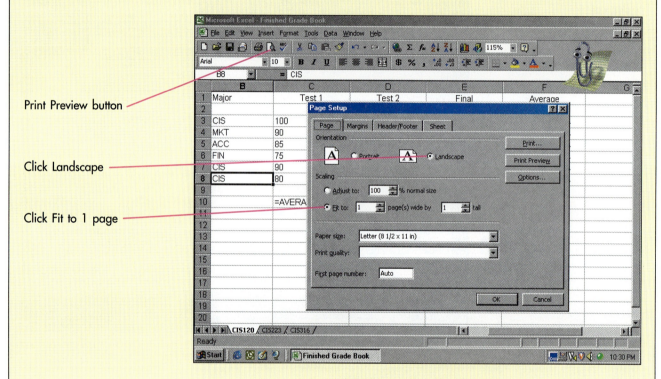

(g) The Page Setup Command (step 8)

FIGURE 1.11   Hands-on Exercise 2 (continued)

KEYBOARD SHORTCUTS—THE DIALOG BOX

Press Tab or Shift+Tab to move forward (backward) between fields in a dialog box, or press the Alt key plus the underlined letter to move directly to an option. Use the space bar to toggle check boxes on or off and the up (down) arrow keys to move between options in a list box. Press enter to activate the highlighted command button and Esc to exit the dialog box without accepting the changes.

STEP 9: The Print Preview Command

➤ Pull down the **File menu** and click **Print Preview** (or click the **Print Preview button** on the Standard toolbar). Your monitor should match the display in Figure 1.11h.

➤ Click the **Print command button** to display the Print dialog box, then click **OK** to print the worksheet.

➤ Press **Ctrl+`** to switch to displayed values rather than cell formulas. Click the **Print button** on the Standard toolbar to print the worksheet without displaying the Print dialog box.

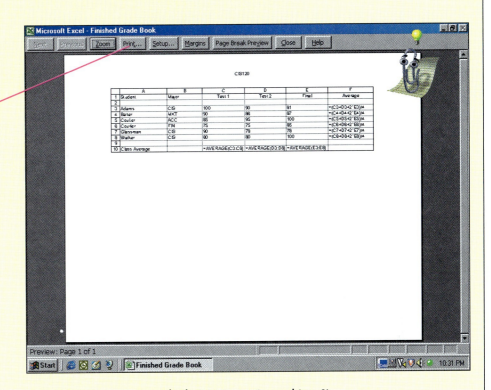

Click Print command button

(h) The Print Preview Command (step 9)

FIGURE 1.11 Hands-on Exercise 2 (continued)

CREATE A CUSTOM VIEW

Use the Custom View command to store the different column widths associated with printing cell formulas versus displayed values. Start with either view, pull down the View menu, and click Custom Views to display the Custom Views dialog box. Click the Add button, enter the name of the view (e.g., Cell formulas), and click OK to close the Custom View dialog box. Press Ctrl+` to switch to the other view, change the column widths as appropriate, then pull down the View menu a second time to create the second custom view (e.g., Displayed Values). You can then switch from one view to the other at any time by pulling down the View menu, clicking the Custom Views command, and double clicking the desired view.

STEP 10: Insert and Delete a Worksheet

➤ Pull down the **Insert menu** and click the **Worksheet command** to insert a new worksheet. The worksheet is inserted as Sheet1.

➤ Click in cell **A1,** type **Student,** and press **enter.** Enter the labels and student data as shown in Figure 1.11i. Enter the formulas to calculate the students' semester averages. (The midterm and final count equally.)

➤ Enter the formulas in row 7 to compute the class averages on each exam. If necessary, click and drag the column border between columns A and B to widen column A.

➤ Double click the name of the worksheet (Sheet1) to select the name. Type a new name, **CIS101,** to replace the selected text and press enter.

➤ Click the worksheet tab for **CIS223.** Pull down the **Edit menu** and click the **Delete Sheet command.** Click **OK** when you are warned that the worksheet will be permanently deleted.

➤ Save the workbook. Print the new worksheet. Exit Excel.

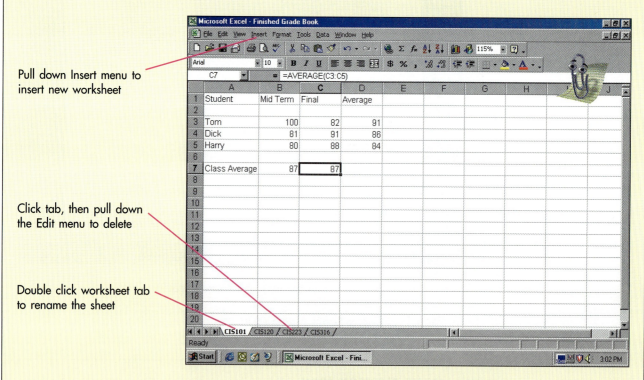

(i) Inserting and Deleting a Worksheet (step 10)

FIGURE 1.11 Hands-on Exercise 2 (continued)

MOVING, COPYING, AND RENAMING WORKSHEETS

The fastest way to move a worksheet is to click and drag the worksheet tab. You can copy a worksheet in similar fashion by pressing and holding the Ctrl key as you drag the worksheet tab. To rename a worksheet, double click its tab to select the current name, type the new name, and press the enter key.

SUMMARY

A spreadsheet is the computerized equivalent of an accountant's ledger. It is divided into rows and columns, with each row and column assigned a heading. The intersection of a row and column forms a cell. Spreadsheet is a generic term. Workbook and worksheet are Excel specific. An Excel workbook contains one or more worksheets.

Every cell in a worksheet (spreadsheet) contains either a formula or a constant. A formula begins with an equal sign; a constant does not. A constant is an entry that does not change and may be numeric or descriptive text. A formula is a combination of numeric constants, cell references, arithmetic operators, and/or functions that produces a new value from existing values.

The Insert and Delete commands add or remove individual cells, rows, or columns from a worksheet. The commands are also used to insert or delete worksheets within a workbook. The Open command brings a workbook from disk into memory. The Save command copies the workbook in memory to disk.

The Page Setup command provides complete control over the printed page, enabling you to print a worksheet with or without gridlines or row and column headings. The Page Setup command also controls margins, headers and footers, centering, and orientation. The Print Preview command shows the worksheet as it will print and should be used prior to printing.

A worksheet should always be printed twice, once with displayed values and once with cell formulas. The latter is an important tool in checking the accuracy of a worksheet, which is far more important than its appearance.

KEY WORDS AND CONCEPTS

Active cell	Formula	Save command
AutoComplete	Formula bar	ScreenTip
AVERAGE function	Function	Spreadsheet
Cell	Insert command	Standard toolbar
Cell contents	Landscape orientation	Status bar
Cell reference	Name box	Text box
Close command	Office Assistant	Toolbar
Constant	Open command	Undo command
Delete command	Page Setup command	Value
Exit command	Portrait orientation	Workbook
File menu	Print command	Worksheet
Formatting toolbar	Print Preview command	

MULTIPLE CHOICE

1. Which of the following is true?
   (a) A worksheet contains one or more workbooks
   (b) A workbook contains one or more worksheets
   (c) A spreadsheet contains one or more worksheets
   (d) A worksheet contains one or more spreadsheets

2. A worksheet is superior to manual calculation because:
   (a) The worksheet computes its entries faster
   (b) The worksheet computes its results more accurately
   (c) The worksheet recalculates its results whenever cell contents are changed
   (d) All of the above

3. The cell at the intersection of the second column and third row has the cell reference:
   (a) B3
   (b) 3B
   (c) C2
   (d) 2C

4. A right-handed person will normally:
   (a) Click the right and left mouse button to access a pull-down menu and shortcut menu, respectively
   (b) Click the left and right mouse button to access a pull-down menu and shortcut menu, respectively
   (c) Click the left mouse button to access both a pull-down menu and a shortcut menu
   (d) Click the right mouse button to access both a pull-down menu and a shortcut menu

5. What is the effect of typing F5+F6 into a cell without a beginning equal sign?
   (a) The entry is equivalent to the formula =F5+F6
   (b) The cell will display the contents of cell F5 plus cell F6
   (c) The entry will be treated as a text entry and display F5+F6 in the cell
   (d) The entry will be rejected by Excel, which will signal an error message

6. The Open command:
   (a) Brings a workbook from disk into memory
   (b) Brings a workbook from disk into memory, then erases the workbook on disk
   (c) Stores the workbook in memory on disk
   (d) Stores the workbook in memory on disk, then erases the workbook from memory

7. The Save command:
   (a) Brings a workbook from disk into memory
   (b) Brings a workbook from disk into memory, then erases the workbook on disk
   (c) Stores the workbook in memory on disk
   (d) Stores the workbook in memory on disk, then erases the workbook from memory

8. How do you open an Excel workbook?
   (a) Pull down the File menu and click the Open command
   (b) Click the Open button on the Standard toolbar
   (c) Either (a) or (b)
   (d) Neither (a) nor (b)

9. In the absence of parentheses, the order of operation is:
   (a) Exponentiation, addition or subtraction, multiplication or division
   (b) Addition or subtraction, multiplication or division, exponentiation
   (c) Multiplication or division, exponentiation, addition or subtraction
   (d) Exponentiation, multiplication or division, addition or subtraction

10. Given that cells A1, A2, and A3 contain the values 10, 20, and 40, respectively, what value will be displayed in a cell containing the cell formula =A1/A2*A3+1?
    (a) 1.125
    (b) 21
    (c) 20.125
    (d) Impossible to determine

11. The entry =AVERAGE(A4:A6):
    (a) Is invalid because the cells are not contiguous
    (b) Computes the average of cells A4 and A6
    (c) Computes the average of cells A4, A5, and A6
    (d) None of the above

12. Which of the following was suggested with respect to printing a workbook?
    (a) Print the displayed values only
    (b) Print the cell formulas only
    (c) Print both the displayed values and cell formulas
    (d) Print neither the displayed values nor the cell formulas

13. Which of the following is true regarding a printed worksheet?
    (a) It may be printed with or without the row and column headings
    (b) It may be printed with or without the gridlines
    (c) Both (a) and (b) above
    (d) Neither (a) nor (b)

14. Which options are mutually exclusive in the Page Setup menu?
    (a) Portrait and landscape orientation
    (b) Cell gridlines and row and column headings
    (c) Headers and footers
    (d) Left and right margins

15. Which of the following is controlled by the Page Setup command?
    (a) Headers and footers
    (b) Margins
    (c) Orientation
    (d) All of the above

ANSWERS

1. b	**6.** a	**11.** c
2. d	**7.** c	**12.** c
3. a	**8.** c	**13.** c
4. b	**9.** d	**14.** a
5. c	**10.** b	**15.** d

PRACTICE WITH EXCEL 2000

1. **The Grading Assistant:** Your professor is very impressed with the way you did the hands-on exercises in the chapter and has hired you as his grading assistant to handle all of his classes this semester. He would like you to take the Finished Grade Book that you used in the chapter, and save it as *Chapter 1 Practice 1 Solution*. Make the following changes in the new workbook:
   a. Click the worksheet tab for CIS120. Add Milgrom as a new student majoring in Finance with grades of 88, 80, and 84, respectively. Delete Baker. Be sure that the class averages adjust automatically for the insertion and deletion of these students.
   b. Click the worksheet tab for CIS316 to move to this worksheet. Insert a new column for the Final, then enter the following grades for the students in this class (Bippen, 90; Freeman, 75; Manni, 84; Peck, 93; Tanney, 87).
   c. Enter the formulas to compute the semester average for each student in the class. (Tests 1, 2, and 3 each count 20%. The final counts 40%.)
   d. Enter the formulas to compute the class average on each test and the final.
   e. Enter the label *Grading Assistant* followed by your name on each worksheet. Print the entire workbook and submit all three pages of the printout to your instructor as proof that you did this exercise.

2. **Exotic Gardens:** The worksheet in Figure 1.12 displays last week's sales from the Exotic Gardens Nurseries. There are four locations, each of which divides its sales into three general areas.
   a. Open the partially completed *Chapter 1 Practice 2* workbook on the data disk. Save the workbook as *Chapter 1 Practice 2 Solution*.
   b. Enter the appropriate formulas in row 5 of the worksheet to compute the total sales for each location. Use the SUM function to compute the total for each location; for example, type =SUM(B2:B4) in cell B5 (as opposed to =B2+B3+B4) to compute the total sales for the Las Olas location.
   c. Insert a new row 4 for a new category of product. Type *Insecticides* in cell A4, and enter $1,000 for each store in this category. The total sales for each store should adjust automatically to include the additional business.
   d. Enter the appropriate formulas in column F of the worksheet to compute the total sales for each category.
   e. Delete column D, the column containing sales for the Galleria location.
   f. Add your name somewhere in the worksheet as the bookkeeper.
   g. Print the completed worksheet two times, to show both displayed values and cell formulas. Submit both pages to your instructor.

	A	B	C	D	E	F
1		Las Olas	Coral Gables	Galleria	Miracle Mile	Total
2	Indoor Plants	$1,500	$3,000	$4,500	$800	$9,800
3	Accessories	$350	$725	$1,200	$128	$2,403
4	Landscaping	$3,750	$7,300	$12,000	$1,500	$24,550
5	Total	$5,600	$11,025	$17,700	$2,428	$36,753
6						
7						
8						

FIGURE 1.12 Exotic Gardens (Exercise 2)

3. **Residential Colleges:** Formatting is not covered until Chapter 2, but we think you are ready to try your hand at basic formatting now. Most formatting operations are done in the context of select-then-do. You select the cell or cells you want to format, then you execute the appropriate formatting command, most easily by clicking the appropriate button on the Formatting toolbar. The function of each button should be apparent from its icon, but you can simply point to a button to display a ScreenTip that is indicative of the button's function.

   Open the unformatted version of the *Chapter 1 Practice 3* workbook on the data disk, and save it as *Chapter 1 Practice 3 Solution*. Add a new row 6 and enter data for Hume Hall as shown in Figure 1.13. Enter formulas for totals. Format the remainder of the worksheet so that it matches the completed worksheet in Figure 1.13. Add your name in bold italics somewhere in the worksheet as the Residence Hall Coordinator, then print the completed worksheet and submit it to your instructor.

	A	B	C	D	E	F	G
1	Residential Colleges						
2							
3		Freshmen	Sophomores	Juniors	Seniors	Graduates	Totals
4	Broward Hall	176	143	77	29	13	438
5	Graham Hall	375	112	37	23	7	554
6	Hume Hall	212	108	45	43	12	420
7	Jennnings Hall	89	54	23	46	23	235
8	Rawlings Hall	75	167	93	145	43	523
9	Tolbert Hall	172	102	26	17	22	339
10	Totals	1099	686	301	303	120	2509

FIGURE 1.13 Residential Colleges (Exercise 3)

4. **Companion Web Sites:** A Companion Web site (or online study guide) accompanies each book in the *Exploring Microsoft Office 2000* series. Go to the Exploring Windows home page at www.prenhall.com/grauer, click the book to Office 2000, and click the Companion Web site tab at the top of the screen. Choose the appropriate text (Exploring Excel 2000) and the chapter within the text (e.g., Chapter 1).

   Each chapter contains a series of short-answer exercises (multiple-choice, true/false, and matching) to review the material in the chapter. You can take practice quizzes by yourself and/or e-mail the results to your instructor. You can try the essay questions for additional practice and engage in online chat sessions. We hope you will find the online guide to be a valuable resource.

5. **Student Budget:** Create a worksheet that shows your income and expenses for a typical semester according to the format in Figure 1.14. Enter your budget rather than ours by entering your name in cell A1.

   a. Enter at least five different expenses in consecutive rows, beginning in A6, and enter the corresponding amounts in column B.

   b. Enter the text *Total Expenses* in the row immediately below your last expense item and then enter the formula to compute the total in the corresponding cells in columns B through E.

   c. Skip one blank row and then enter the text *What's Left for Fun* in column A and the formula to compute how much money you have left at the end of the month in columns B through E.

d. Insert a new row 8. Add an additional expense that you left out, entering the text in A8 and the amount in cells B8 through E8. Do the formulas for total expenses reflect the additional expense? If not, change the formulas so they adjust automatically.

e. Save the workbook as *Chapter 1 Practice 5 Solution*. Center the worksheet horizontally, then print the worksheet two ways, to show cell formulas and displayed values. Submit both printed pages to your instructor.

	A	B	C	D	E
1	Maryann Barber's Budget				
2		Sept	Oct	Nov	Dec
3	Monthly Income	$1,000	$1,000	$1,000	$1,400
4					
5	Monthly Expenses				
6	Food	$250	$250	$250	$250
7	Rent	$350	$350	$350	$350
8	Cable	$40	$40	$40	$40
9	Utilities	$100	$100	$125	$140
10	Phone	$30	$30	$30	$20
11	Gas	$40	$40	$40	$75
12	Total Expenses	$810	$810	$835	$875
13					
14	What's Left for Fun	$190	$190	$165	$525

FIGURE 1.14 Student Budget (Exercise 5)

6. **Vacation to Europe:** Figure 1.15 displays a spreadsheet that plans for a summer vacation in Europe. The spreadsheet includes fixed costs such as airfare and a Euro Rail pass. It also has variable costs for each day of the vacation. Develop a spreadsheet similar to the one in Figure 1.15. You need not follow our format exactly, but you should include all expenses for your vacation. Add your name somewhere in the worksheet, then print it two ways, once with displayed values and once with the cell formulas. Create a title page, then submit all three pages to your instructor as proof you did this exercise.

	A	B	C	D
1	My Vacation to Europe			
2				
3	Daily Expenses	Cost	Number of Days	Amount
4	Hotel	$95	5	$475
5	Youth Hostel	$45	16	$720
6	Food	$30	21	$630
7	Touring/Shopping	$45	21	$945
8	One time expenses			
9	Round Trip Airfare			$750
10	EuroRail Pass			$200
11				
12	Subtotal			$3,720
13	Contingency (10% of total)			$372
14	Estimated cost			$4,092

FIGURE 1.15 Vacation to Europe (Exercise 6)

7. **E-mail Your Homework:** Sending an Excel workbook as an attached file as shown in Figure 1.16 has never been easier, but we suggest you check with your professor first. He or she may prefer that you print the assignment rather than mail it, and e-mail may not be available to you. If e-mail is an option, start Excel, open any workbook that you have created in this chapter, then click the E-mail button on the Standard toolbar. You should see a message from the Office Assistant indicating that you can send the entire workbook as an attachment or that you can send the current worksheet in the message body.

   Choose the option you want, then enter your professor's e-mail address and the subject of the message in the appropriate text boxes. Press the Tab key to move to the body of the message. Type a short note above the inserted document to your professor, then click the Send button to mail the message.

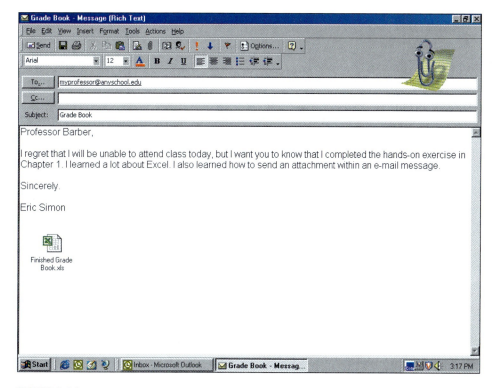

FIGURE 1.16   E-mail Your Homework (Exercise 7)

CASE STUDIES

Buying a PC

You have decided to buy a PC and have settled on a minimum configuration consisting of an entry-level Pentium II, 64MB of RAM, a CD-ROM, an 8GB hard drive, a 15-inch monitor, and a 56Kbps modem. You also need a printer and Microsoft Office 2000. You can spend up to $2,500 and hope that at today's prices you can find a system that goes beyond your minimum requirements.

Create a spreadsheet based on real data that presents several alternatives. Show different configurations from the same vendor and/or comparable systems from different vendors. Include the vendor's telephone number with its estimate.

Bring the spreadsheet to class, together with the supporting documentation in the form of printed advertisements. The best place to obtain current information is the Web. Go to www.prenhall.com/grauer, click the Office 2000 text, then click the link to Student Resources to access our PC Buying Guide.

Portfolio Management

A spreadsheet is an ideal vehicle to track the progress of your investments. You need to maintain the name of the company, the number of shares purchased, the date of the purchase, and the purchase price. You can then enter the current price and see immediately the potential gain or loss on each investment as well as the current value of the portfolio. Retrieve the *Wishful Thinking Portfolio* workbook from the data disk, enter the closing prices of the listed investments, and compute the current value of the portfolio.

There are many sites on the Web where you can obtain the current price of each stock listed in the *Wishful Thinking Portfolio* workbook. Try starting at investor.msn.com or use your favorite search engine to locate a different site.

Accuracy Counts

The *Underbid* workbook on the data disk was the last assignment completed by your predecessor prior to his unfortunate dismissal. The worksheet contains a significant error, which caused your company to underbid a contract and assume a subsequent loss of $100,000. As you look for the error, don't be distracted by the attractive formatting. The shading, lines, and other touches are nice, but accuracy is more important than anything else. Write a memo to your instructor describing the nature of the error. Include suggestions in the memo on how to avoid similar mistakes in the future.

Changing Menus and Toolbars

Office 2000 implements one very significant change over previous versions of Office in that it displays a series of short menus that contain only basic commands. The additional commands are made visible by clicking the double arrow that appears at the bottom of the menu. New commands are added to the menu as they are used, and conversely, other commands are removed if they are not used. A similar strategy is followed for the Standard and Formatting toolbars which are displayed on a single row, and thus do not show all of the buttons at one time. The intent is to simplify Office 2000 for the new user by limiting the number of commands that are visible. The consequence, however, is that the individual is not exposed to new commands, and hence may not use Office to its full potential. Which set of menus do you prefer? How do you switch from one set to the other?

Microsoft Online

Help for Microsoft Excel is available from two primary sources, the Office Assistant, and the Microsoft Web site at www.microsoft.com/excel. The latter enables you to obtain more recent, and often more detailed information. You will find the answer to the most frequently asked questions and you can access the same knowledge base used by Microsoft support engineers. Experiment with both sources of help, then submit a summary of your findings to your instructor.

chapter 2

GAINING PROFICIENCY: COPYING, FORMATTING, AND ISOLATING ASSUMPTIONS

OBJECTIVES

After reading this chapter you will be able to:

1. Explain the importance of isolating assumptions within a worksheet.
2. Define a cell range; select and deselect ranges within a worksheet.
3. Copy and/or move cells within a worksheet; differentiate between relative, absolute, and mixed addresses.
4. Format a worksheet to include boldface, italics, shading, and borders; change the font and/or alignment of a selected entry.
5. Change the width of a column; explain what happens if a column is too narrow to display the computed result.
6. Insert a hyperlink into an Excel workbook; save a workbook as a Web page.

OVERVIEW

This chapter continues the grade book example of Chapter 1. It is perhaps the most important chapter in the entire text as it describes the basic commands to create a worksheet. We begin with the definition of a cell range and the commands to build a worksheet without regard to its appearance. We focus on the Copy command and the difference between relative and absolute addresses. We stress the importance of isolating the assumptions within a worksheet so that alternative strategies may be easily evaluated.

The second half of the chapter presents formatting commands to improve the appearance of a worksheet after it has been created. You will be pleased with the dramatic impact you can achieve with a few simple commands, but we emphasize that accuracy in a worksheet is much more important than appearance. The chapter also describes the relationship between Office 2000, the Internet, and the World Wide Web.

The hands-on exercises are absolutely critical if you are to master the material. As you do the exercises, you will realize that there are many different ways to accomplish the same task. Our approach is to present the most basic way first and the shortcuts later. You will like the shortcuts better, but you may not remember them all. Do not be concerned because it is much more important to understand the underlying concepts. You can always find the necessary command from the appropriate menu, and if you don't know which menu, you can always look to online help.

A BETTER GRADE BOOK

Figure 2.1 contains a much improved version of the professor's grade book over the one from the previous chapter. The most obvious difference is in the appearance of the worksheet, as a variety of formatting commands have been used to make it more attractive. The exam scores and semester averages are centered under the appropriate headings. The exam weights are formatted with percentages, and all averages are displayed with exactly one decimal point. Boldface and italics are used for emphasis. Shading and borders are used to highlight various areas of the worksheet. The title has been centered over the worksheet and is set in a larger typeface.

The most *significant* differences, however, are that the weight of each exam is indicated within the worksheet, and that the formulas to compute the students' semester averages reference these cells in their calculations. The professor can change the contents of the cells containing the exam weights and see immediately the effect on the student averages.

The isolation of cells whose values are subject to change is one of the most important concepts in the development of a spreadsheet. This technique lets the professor explore alternative grading strategies. He or she may notice, for example, that the class did significantly better on the final than on either of the first two exams. The professor may then decide to give the class a break and increase the weight of the final relative to the other tests. But before the professor says anything to the class, he or she wants to know the effect of increasing the weight of the final to 60%. What if the final should count 70%? The effect of these and other changes can be seen immediately by entering the new exam weights in the appropriate cells at the bottom of the worksheet.

Title is centered and in larger font size

Exam scores are centered

Boldface, italics, shading, and borders are used

Exam weights are used to calculate the Semester Average

	A	B	C	D	E
1		CIS120 - Spring 2000			
2					
3	**Student**	Test 1	Test 2	Final	Average
4	Costa, Frank	70	80	90	82.5
5	Ford, Judd	70	85	80	78.8
6	Grauer, Jessica	90	80	98	91.5
7	Howard, Lauren	80	78	98	88.5
8	Krein, Darren	85	70	95	86.3
9	Moldof, Adam	75	75	80	77.5
10					
11	**Class Averages**	78.3	78.0	90.2	
12					
13	**Exam Weights**	25%	25%	50%	

FIGURE 2.1 A Better Grade Book

CELL RANGES

Every command in Excel operates on a rectangular group of cells known as a *range*. A range may be as small as a single cell or as large as the entire worksheet. It may consist of a row or part of a row, a column or part of a column, or multiple rows and/or columns. The cells within a range are specified by indicating the diagonally opposite corners, typically the upper-left and lower-right corners of the rectangle. Many different ranges could be selected in conjunction with the worksheet of Figure 2.1. The exam weights, for example, are found in the range B13:D13. The students' semester averages are found in the range E4:E9. The student data is contained in the range A4:E9.

The easiest way to select a range is to click and drag—click at the beginning of the range, then press and hold the left mouse button as you drag the mouse to the end of the range where you release the mouse. Once selected, the range is highlighted and its cells will be affected by any subsequent command. The range remains selected until another range is defined or until you click another cell anywhere on the worksheet.

COPY COMMAND

The *Copy command* duplicates the contents of a cell, or range of cells, and saves you from having to enter the contents of every cell individually. It is much easier, for example, to enter the formula to compute the class average once (for test 1), then copy it to obtain the average for the remaining tests, rather than explicitly entering the formula for every test.

Figure 2.2 illustrates how the Copy command can be used to duplicate the formula to compute the class average. The cell(s) that you are copying from, cell B11, is called the *source range*. The cells that you are copying to, cells C11 and D11, are the *destination* (or target) *range*. The formula is not copied exactly, but is adjusted as it is copied, to compute the average for the pertinent test.

The formula to compute the average on the first test was entered in cell B11 as =AVERAGE(B4:B9). The range in the formula references the cell seven rows above the cell containing the formula (i.e., cell B4 is seven rows above cell B11) as well as the cell two rows above the formula (i.e., cell B9). When the formula in cell B11 is copied to C11, it is adjusted so that the cells referenced in the new formula are in the same relative position as those in the original formula; that is, seven and two rows above the formula itself. Thus, the formula in cell C11 becomes =AVERAGE(C4:C9). In similar fashion, the formula in cell D11 becomes =AVERAGE(D4:D9).

	A	B	C	D	E
1			CIS120 - Spring 2000		
2					
3	Student	Test 1	Test 2	Final	Average
4	Costa, Frank	70	80	90	=$B$13*B4+$C$13*C4+$D$13*D4
5	Ford, Judd	70	85	80	=$B$13*B5+$C$13*C5+$D$13*D5
6	Grauer, Jessica	90	80	98	=$B$13*B6+$C$13*C6+$D$13*D6
7	Howard, Lauren	80	78	98	=$B$13*B7+$C$13*C7+$D$13*D7
8	Krein, Darren	85	70	95	=$B$13*B8+$C$13*C8+$D$13*D8
9	Moldof, Adam	75	75	80	=$B$13*B9+$C$13*C9+$D$13*D9
10					
11	Class Averages	=AVERAGE(B4:B9)	=AVERAGE(C4:C9)	=AVERAGE(D4:D9)	
12					
13	Exam Weights	25%	25%	50%	

FIGURE 2.2 The Copy Command

Figure 2.2 also illustrates how the Copy command is used to copy the formula for a student's semester average, from cell E4 (the source range) to cells E5 through E9 (the destination range). This is slightly more complicated than the previous example because the formula is based on a student's grades, which vary from one student to the next, and on the exam weights, which do not. The cells referring to the student's grades should adjust as the formula is copied, but the addresses referencing the exam weights should not.

The distinction between cell references that remain constant versus cell addresses that change is made by means of a dollar sign. An *absolute reference* remains constant throughout the copy operation and is specified with a dollar sign in front of the column and row designation, for example, $B$13. A *relative reference*, on the other hand, adjusts during a copy operation and is specified without dollar signs; for example, B4. (A *mixed reference* uses a single dollar sign to make the column absolute and the row relative; for example, $A5. Alternatively, you can make the column relative and the row absolute as in A$5.)

Consider, for example, the formula to compute a student's semester average as it appears in cell E4 of Figure 2.2:

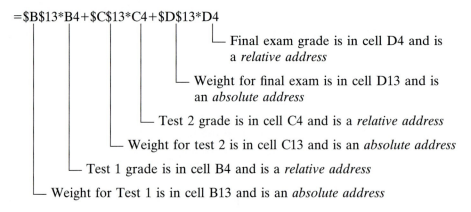

=$B$13*B4+$C$13*C4+$D$13*D4

- Final exam grade is in cell D4 and is a *relative address*
- Weight for final exam is in cell D13 and is an *absolute address*
- Test 2 grade is in cell C4 and is a *relative address*
- Weight for test 2 is in cell C13 and is an *absolute address*
- Test 1 grade is in cell B4 and is a *relative address*
- Weight for Test 1 is in cell B13 and is an *absolute address*

The formula in cell E4 uses a combination of relative and absolute addresses to compute the student's semester average. Relative addresses are used for the exam grades (found in cells B4, C4, and D4) and change automatically when the formula is copied to the other rows. Absolute addresses are used for the exam weights (found in cells B13, C13, and D13) and remain constant.

The copy operation is implemented by using the *clipboard* common to all Windows applications and a combination of the *Copy and Paste commands* from the Edit menu. (Office 2000 also supports the Office Clipboard that can hold 12 separate items. All references to the "clipboard" in this chapter, however, are to the Windows clipboard.) The contents of the source range are copied to the clipboard, from where they are pasted to the destination range. The contents of the clipboard are replaced with each subsequent Copy command but are unaffected by the Paste command. Thus, you can execute the Paste command several times in succession to paste the contents of the clipboard to multiple locations.

MIXED REFERENCES

Most spreadsheets can be developed using only absolute or relative references such as $A1$1 or A, respectively. Mixed references, where only the row ($A1) or column (A$1) changes, are more subtle, and thus are typically not used by beginners. Mixed references are necessary in more sophisticated worksheets and add significantly to the power of Excel. See practice exercise 4 at the end of the chapter.

MOVE OPERATION

The ***move operation*** is not used in the grade book, but its presentation is essential for the sake of completeness. The move operation transfers the contents of a cell (or range of cells) from one location to another. After the move is completed, the cells where the move originated (that is, the source range) are empty. This is in contrast to the Copy command, where the entries remain in the source range and are duplicated in the destination range.

A simple move operation is depicted in Figure 2.3a, in which the contents of cell A3 are moved to cell C3, with the formula in cell C3 unchanged after the move. In other words, the move operation simply picks up the contents of cell A3 (a formula that adds the values in cells A1 and A2) and puts it down in cell C3. The source range, cell A3, is empty after the move operation has been executed.

Figure 2.3b depicts a situation where the formula itself remains in the same cell, but one of the values it references is moved to a new location; that is, the

Source range is empty after move

	A	B	C
1	5		
2	2		
3	=A1+A2		

	A	B	C
1	5		
2	2		
3			=A1+A2

(a) Example 1 (only cell A3 is moved)

Cell reference is adjusted to follow moved entry

	A	B	C
1	5		
2	2		
3	=A1+A2		

	A	B	C
1			5
2	2		
3	=C1+A2		

(b) Example 2 (only cell A1 is moved)

Both cell references adjust to follow moved entries

	A	B	C
1	5		
2	2		
3	=A1+A2		

	A	B	C
1			5
2			2
3			=C1+C2

(c) Example 3 (all three cells in column A are moved)

Cell reference adjusts to follow moved entry

Moved formula is unchanged

	A	B	C
1	5	=A3*4	
2	2		
3	=A1+A2		

	A	B	C
1	5	=C3*4	
2	2		
3			=A1+A2

(d) Example 4 (dependent cells)

FIGURE 2.3 The Move Command

Cell reference adjusts to follow moved entry

Both cell references adjust to follow moved entries

	A	B	C
1		5	=$A$3*4
2		2	
3	=$A$1+$A$2		

	A	B	C
1		=$C$3*4	5
2			2
3			=$C$1+$C$2

(e) Example 5 (absolute cell addresses)

FIGURE 2.3 The Move Command (continued)

entry in A1 is moved to C1. The formula in cell A3 is adjusted to follow the moved entry to its new location; that is, the formula is now =C1+A2.

The situation is different in Figure 2.3c as the contents of all three cells—A1, A2, and A3—are moved. After the move has taken place, cells C1 and C2 contain the 5 and the 2, respectively, with the formula in cell C3 adjusted to reflect the movement of the contents of cells A1 and A2. Once again the source range (A1:A3) is empty after the move is completed.

Figure 2.3d contains an additional formula in cell B1, which is *dependent* on cell A3, which in turn is moved to cell C3. The formula in cell C3 is unchanged after the move because *only* the formula was moved, *not* the values it referenced. The formula in cell B1 changes because cell B1 refers to an entry (cell A3) that was moved to a new location (cell C3).

Figure 2.3e shows that the specification of an absolute reference has no meaning in a move operation, because the cell addresses are adjusted as necessary to reflect the cells that have been moved. Moving a formula that contains an absolute reference does not adjust the formula. Moving a value that is specified as an absolute reference, however, adjusts the formula to follow the cell to its new location. Thus all of the absolute references in Figure 2.3e are changed to reflect the entries that were moved.

The move operation is a convenient way to improve the appearance of a worksheet after it has been developed. It is subtle in its operation, and we suggest you think twice before moving cell entries because of the complexities involved.

The move operation is implemented by using the Windows clipboard and a combination of the **Cut** and **Paste commands** from the Edit menu. The contents of the source range are transferred to the clipboard, from which they are pasted to the destination range. (Executing a Paste command after a Cut command empties the clipboard. This is different from pasting after a Copy command, which does not affect the contents of the clipboard.)

LEARNING BY DOING

As we have already indicated, there are many different ways to accomplish the same task. You can execute commands using a pull-down menu, a shortcut menu, a toolbar, or the keyboard. In the exercise that follows we emphasize pull-down menus (the most basic technique) but suggest various shortcuts as appropriate.

Realize, however, that while the shortcuts are interesting, it is far more important to focus on the underlying concepts in the exercise, rather than specific key strokes or mouse clicks. The professor's grade book was developed to emphasize the difference between relative and absolute cell references. The grade book also illustrates the importance of isolating assumptions so that alternative strategies (e.g., different exam weights) can be considered.

HANDS-ON EXERCISE 1

Creating a Workbook

Objective: To create a new workbook; to develop a formula containing relative and absolute references; to use the Copy command within a worksheet. Use Figure 2.4 as a guide.

STEP 1: Create a New Workbook

➤ Click the **Start button,** click (or point to) the **Programs command,** then click **Microsoft Excel** to start the program. If Excel is already open, click the **New button** on the Standard toolbar to begin a new workbook.

➤ Click and drag the Office Assistant out of the way or hide it altogether. (Pull down the **Help menu** and click the **Hide the Office Assistant.**)

➤ If necessary, separate the Standard and Formatting toolbars. Pull down the **View menu,** click **Toolbars,** click **Customize,** and click the **Options tab.** Clear the check box that indicates the Standard and Formatting toolbars should share the same row.

➤ Click in **cell A1.** Enter the title of the worksheet, **CIS120 - Spring 2000** as in Figure 2.4a. (The Save As dialog box is not yet visible.)

➤ Press the **down arrow key** twice to move to cell A3. Type **Student.**

➤ Press the **right arrow key** to move to cell B3. Type **Test 1.**

➤ Press the **right arrow key** to move to cell C3. Type **Test 2.**

➤ Press the **right arrow key** to move to cell D3. Type **Final.**

➤ Press the **right arrow key** to move to cell E3. Type **Average.** Press **enter.**

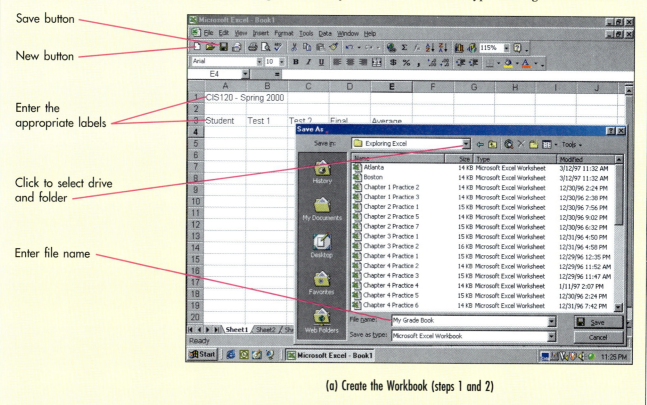

(a) Create the Workbook (steps 1 and 2)

FIGURE 2.4 Hands-on Exercise 1

CHAPTER 2: GAINING PROFICIENCY

STEP 2: Save the Workbook

- Pull down the **File menu** and click **Save** (or click the **Save button** on the Standard toolbar) to display the Save As dialog box as shown in Figure 2.4d.
- Click the **drop-down arrow** on the Save In list box. Click the appropriate drive, drive C or drive A, depending on where you are saving your Excel workbook.
- Double click the **Exploring Excel folder** to make it the active folder (the folder in which you will save the document).
- Click and drag to select **Book1** (the default entry) in the File name text box. Type **My Grade Book** as the name of the workbook. Press the **enter key**.
- The title bar changes to reflect the name of the workbook.

CREATE A NEW FOLDER

Do you work with a large number of workbooks? If so, it may be useful for you to store those workbooks in different folders. You could, for example, create one folder for school and one for work. Pull down the File menu, click the Save As command to display the Save As dialog box, then click the Create New Folder button to display the New Folder dialog box. Enter the name of the folder, then click OK to close the New Folder dialog box and create the folder. Once the folder has been created, use the Look In box to change to that folder the next time you open or save a workbook.

STEP 3: Enter Student Data

- Click in **cell A4** and type **Costa, Frank.** Move across row 4 and enter Frank's grades on the two tests and the final. Use Figure 2.4b as a guide.
  - Do *not* enter Frank's average in cell E4 as that will be entered as a formula in step 5.
  - Do *not* be concerned that you cannot see Frank's entire name because the default width of column A is not wide enough to display the entire name.
- Enter the names and grades for the other students in rows 5 through 9. Do *not* enter their averages.
- Complete the entries in column A by typing **Class Averages** and **Exam Weights** in cells **A11** and **A13,** respectively.

CHANGE THE ZOOM SETTING

You can increase or decrease the size of a worksheet as it appears on the monitor. If you find yourself squinting because the numbers are too small, click the down arrow on the Zoom box and choose a larger magnification. Conversely, if you are working with a large spreadsheet and cannot see it at one time, choose a number less than 100 percent. Changing the magnification on the screen does not affect printing; that is, worksheets are printed at 100% unless you change the scaling within the Page Setup command.

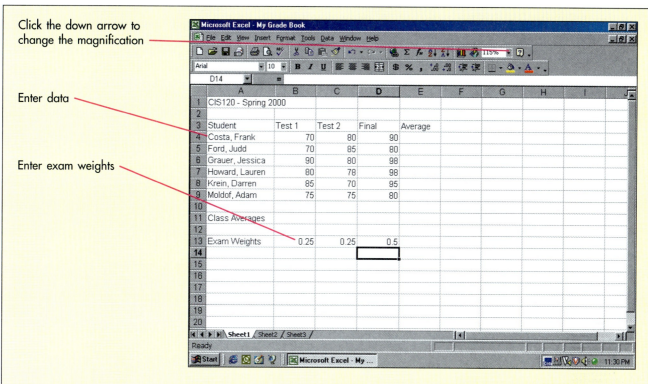

(b) Enter Student Data (steps 3 and 4)

FIGURE 2.4 Hands-on Exercise 1 (continued)

STEP 4: Enter Exam Weights

➤ Click in **cell B13** and enter **.25** (the weight for the first exam).

➤ Press the **right arrow key** to move to cell C13 and enter **.25** (the weight for the second exam).

➤ Press the **right arrow key** to move to cell D13 and enter **.5** (the weight for the final). Press **enter.** Do *not* be concerned that the exam weights do not appear as percentages; they will be formatted in the next exercise.

➤ The worksheet should match Figure 2.4b except that column A is too narrow to display the entire name of each student.

STEP 5: Compute the Semester Average

➤ Click in **cell E4** and type the formula **=$B$13*B4+$C$13*C4+$D$13*D4** as shown in Figure 2.4c. Press **enter** when you have completed the formula.

➤ Check that the displayed value in cell E4 is 82.5, which indicates you entered the formula correctly. Correct the formula if necessary. Save the workbook.

CORRECTING MISTAKES

The most basic way to correct an erroneous entry is to click in the cell, then re-enter the cell contents in their entirety. It's often faster, however, to edit the cell contents rather than retyping them. Click in the cell whose contents you want to change, then make the necessary changes in the formula bar near the top of the Excel window. Use the mouse or arrow keys to position the insertion point. Make the necessary correction(s), then press the enter key.

CHAPTER 2: GAINING PROFICIENCY   49

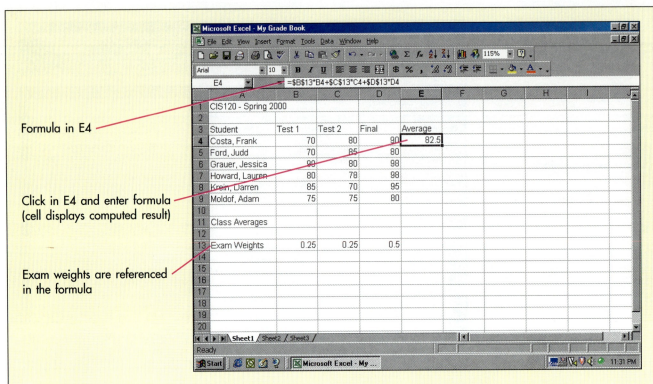

(c) Compute the Semester Average (step 5)

FIGURE 2.4 Hands-on Exercise 1 (continued)

STEP 6: Copy the Semester Average

➤ Click in **cell E4**. Pull down the **Edit menu** and click **Copy** (or click the **copy button** on the standard toolbar). A moving border will surround cell E4.

➤ Click **cell E5**. Drag the mouse over cells **E5** through **E9** to select the destination range as in Figure 2.4d.

➤ Pull down the **Edit menu** and click **Paste** to copy the contents of the clipboard to the destination range.

➤ Press **Esc** to remove the moving border around cell E4. Click anywhere in the worksheet to deselect cells E5 through E9.

➤ Click in **cell E5** and look at the formula. The cells that reference the grades have changed to B5, C5, and D5. The cells that reference the exam weights—$B$13, $C$13, and $D$13—are the same as in the formula in cell E4.

CUT, COPY, AND PASTE

Ctrl+X (the X is supposed to remind you of a pair of scissors), Ctrl+C, and Ctrl+V are keyboard equivalents to cut, copy, and paste, respectively, and apply to Excel, Word, PowerPoint and Access, as well as Windows applications in general. (The keystrokes are easier to remember when you realize that the operative letters, X, C, and V, are next to each other at the bottom-left side of the keyboard.) Alternatively, you can use the Cut, Copy, and Paste buttons on the Standard toolbar, which are also found on the Standard toolbar in the other Office applications.

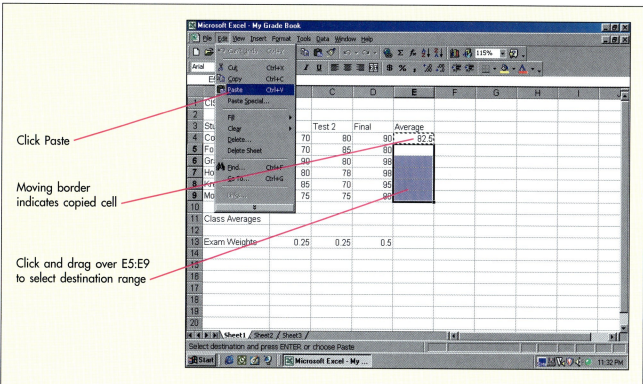

(d) Copy the Semester Average (step 6)

FIGURE 2.4 Hands-on Exercise 1 (continued)

STEP 7: Compute Class Averages

➤ Click in **cell B11** and type the formula **=AVERAGE(B4:B9)** to compute the class average on the first test. Press the **enter key** when you have completed the formula.

➤ Point to **cell B11,** then click the **right mouse button** to display the shortcut menu in Figure 2.4e. Click **Copy,** which produces the moving border around cell B11.

➤ Click **cell C11.** Drag the mouse over cells **C11** and **D11,** the destination range for the Copy command.

➤ Click the **Paste button** on the Standard toolbar (or press Ctrl+V) to paste the contents of the clipboard to the destination range.

➤ Press **Esc** to remove the moving border. Click anywhere in the worksheet to deselect cells C11 through D11.

THE RIGHT MOUSE BUTTON

Point to a cell (or cell range), a worksheet tab, or a toolbar, then click the right mouse button to display a context-sensitive menu with commands appropriate to the item you are pointing to. Right clicking a cell, for example, displays a menu with selected commands from the Edit, Insert, and Format menus. Right clicking a toolbar displays a menu that lets you display (hide) additional toolbars. Right clicking a worksheet tab enables you to rename, move, copy, or delete the worksheet.

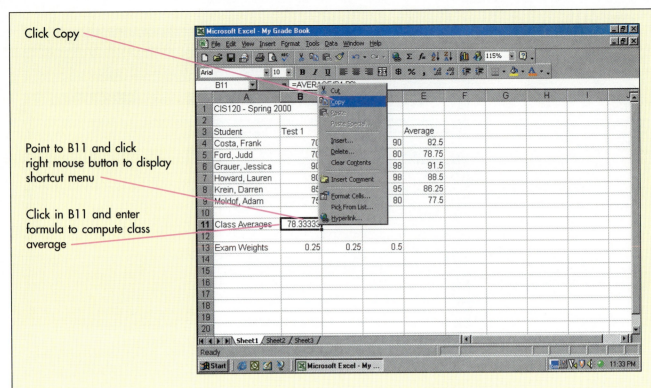

(e) Compute Class Averages (step 7)

FIGURE 2.4   Hands-on Exercise 1 (continued)

STEP 8: What If? Change Exam Weights

➤ Change the entries in cells B13 and C13 to **.20** and the entry in cell D13 to **.60**. The semester average for every student changes automatically; for example, Costa and Moldof change to 84 and 78, respectively.

➤ The professor decides this does not make a significant difference and wants to go back to the original weights. Click the **Undo button** three times to reverse the last three actions. You should see .25, .25, and .50 in cells B13, C13, and D13, respectively.

➤ Click the **Save button.**

STEP 9: Exit Excel

➤ Exit Excel if you are not ready to begin the next exercise at this time.

ISOLATE ASSUMPTIONS

The formulas in a worksheet should always be based on cell references rather than on specific values—for example, B13 or $B$13 rather than .25. The cells containing these values should be clearly labeled and set apart from the rest of the worksheet. You can then vary the inputs (or assumptions on which the worksheet is based) to see the effect within the worksheet. The chance for error is also minimized because you are changing the contents of a single cell rather than changing the multiple formulas that reference those values.

FORMATTING

Figure 2.5a shows the grade book as it exists at the end of the first hands-on exercise, without concern for its appearance. Figure 2.5b shows the grade book as it will appear at the end of the next exercise after it has been formatted. The differences between the two are due entirely to formatting. Consider:

- The exam weights are formatted as percentages in Figure 2.5b, as opposed to decimals in Figure 2.5a. The class and semester averages are displayed with a single decimal place in Figure 2.5b.
- Boldface and italics are used for emphasis, as are shading and borders.
- Exam grades and computed averages are centered under their respective headings, as are the exam weights.
- The worksheet title is centered across all five columns.
- The width of column A has been increased so that the students' names are completely visible. The other columns have been widened as well.

Column A is too narrow

	A	B	C	D	E
1	CIS120 - Spring 2000				
2					
3	Student	Test 1	Test 2	Final	Average
4	Costa, Fra	70	80	90	82.5
5	Ford, Judd	70	85	80	78.75
6	Grauer, Je	90	80	98	91.5
7	Howard, La	80	78	98	88.5
8	Krein, Darr	85	70	95	86.25
9	Moldof, Ad	75	75	80	77.5
10					
11	Class Aver	78.33333	78	90.16667	
12					
13	Exam Wei	0.25	0.25	0.5	

Class averages are not uniformly formatted

(a) At the End of Hands-on Exercise 1

Title is centered across columns and set in a larger font size

Boldface, italics, shading and borders are used for emphasis

Test scores are centered in cells

Results are displayed with 1 decimal place

Exam weights are formatted as a percentage

	A	B	C	D	E
1			CIS120 - Spring 2000		
2					
3	**Student**	**Test 1**	**Test 2**	**Final**	**Average**
4	Costa, Frank	70	80	90	82.5
5	Ford, Judd	70	85	80	78.8
6	Grauer, Jessica	90	80	98	91.5
7	Howard, Lauren	80	78	98	88.5
8	Krein, Darren	85	70	95	86.3
9	Moldof, Adam	75	75	80	77.5
10					
11	**Class Averages**	78.3	78.0	90.2	
12					
13	**Exam Weights**	25%	25%	50%	

(b) At the End of Hands-on Exercise 2

FIGURE 2.5 Developing the Grade Book

Column Widths

A column is often too narrow to display the contents of one or more cells in that column. When this happens, the display depends on whether the cell contains a text or numeric entry, and if it is a text entry, on whether or not the adjacent cell is empty.

The student names in Figure 2.5a, for example, are partially hidden because column A is too narrow to display the entire name. Cells A4 through A9 contain the complete names of each student, but because the adjacent cells in column B contain data, the displayed entries in column A are truncated (cut off) at the cell width. The situation is different for the worksheet title in cell A1. This time the adjacent cell (cell B1) is empty, so that the contents of cell A1 overflow into that cell and are completely visible.

Numbers are treated differently from text and do not depend on the contents of the adjacent cell. Excel will automatically increase the column width to accommodate a formatted number unless the column width has been previously adjusted. In that event, Excel displays a series of number signs (######) when a cell containing a numeric entry is too narrow to display the entry in its current format. You may be able to correct the problem by changing the format of the number (e.g., display the number with fewer decimal places). Alternatively, you can increase the column width by using the **Column command** in the Format menu.

Row Heights

The *row height* changes automatically as the font size is increased. Row 1 in Figure 2.5b, for example, has a greater height than the other rows to accommodate the larger font size in the title of the worksheet. The row height can also be changed manually through the **Row command** in the Format menu.

FORMAT CELLS COMMAND

The **Format Cells command** controls the formatting for numbers, alignment, fonts, borders, and patterns (color). Execution of the command produces a tabbed dialog box in which you choose the particular formatting category, then enter the desired options. All formatting is done within the context of **select-then-do**. You select the cells to which the formatting is to apply, then you execute the Format Cells command (or click the appropriate button on the Formatting toolbar).

Once a format has been assigned to a cell, the formatting remains in the cell and is applied to all subsequent values that are entered into that cell. You can, however, change the formatting by executing a new formatting command. You can also remove the formatting by using the Clear command in the Edit menu. Note, too, that changing the format of a number changes the way the number is displayed, but does not change its value. If, for example, you entered 1.2345 into a cell, but displayed the number as 1.23, the actual value (1.2345) would be used in all calculations involving that cell.

Numeric Formats

General format is the default format for numeric entries and displays a number according to the way it was originally entered. Numbers are shown as integers (e.g., 123), decimal fractions (e.g., 1.23), or in scientific notation (e.g., 1.23E+10) if the number exceeds 11 digits. You can also display a number in one of several built-in formats as shown in Figure 2.6a:

- ***Number format***, which displays a number with or without the 1000 separator (e.g., a comma) and with any number of decimal places. Negative numbers can be displayed with parentheses and/or can be shown in red.
- ***Currency format***, which displays a number with the 1000 separator and an optional dollar sign (which is placed immediately to the left of the number). Negative values can be preceded by a minus sign or displayed with parentheses and/or can be shown in red.
- ***Accounting format***, which displays a number with the 1000 separator, an optional dollar sign (at the left border of the cell, which vertically aligns the dollar signs within a column), negative values in parentheses, and zero values as hyphens.
- ***Date format***, which displays the date in different ways, such as March 4, 1998, 3/4/98, or 4-Mar-98.
- ***Time format***, which displays the time in different formats, such as 10:50 PM or the equivalent 22:50 (24-hour time).
- ***Percentage format***, whereby the number is multiplied by 100 for display purposes only, a percent sign is included, and any number of decimal places can be specified.
- ***Fraction format***, which displays a number as a fraction, and is appropriate when there is no exact decimal equivalent, for example, ⅓.
- ***Scientific format***, which displays a number as a decimal fraction followed by a whole number exponent of 10; for example, the number 12345 would

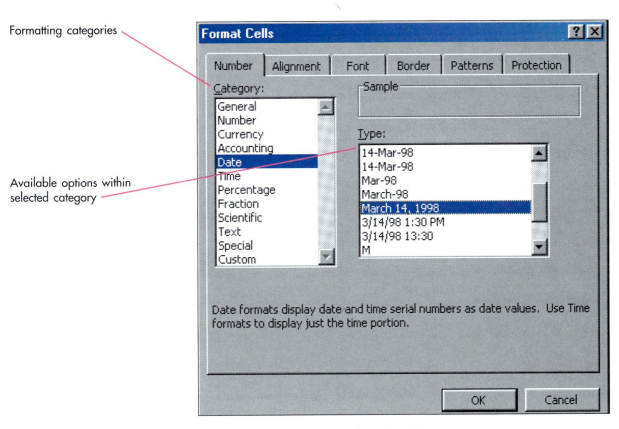

(a) The Number Tab

FIGURE 2.6   The Format Cells Command

appear as 1.2345E+04. The exponent, +04 in the example, is the number of places the decimal point is moved to the left (or right if the exponent is negative). Very small numbers have negative exponents; for example, the entry .0000012 would be displayed as 1.2E−06. Scientific notation is used only with very large or very small numbers.

- *Text format*, which left aligns the entry and is useful for numerical values that have leading zeros and should be treated as text, such as ZIP codes.
- *Special format*, which displays a number with editing characters, such as hyphens in a social security number or parentheses around the area code of a telephone number.
- *Custom format*, which allows you to develop your own formats.

DATES VERSUS FRACTIONS

A fraction may be entered into a cell by preceding the fraction with an equal sign, for example, =1/3. The fraction is converted to its decimal equivalent and displayed in that format in the worksheet. Omission of the equal sign causes Excel to treat the entry as a date; that is, 1/3 will be stored as January 3 (of the current year).

Alignment

The contents of a cell (whether text or numeric) may be aligned horizontally and/or vertically as indicated by the dialog box of Figure 2.6b. The default horizontal alignment is general, which left-aligns text and right-aligns date and numbers. You can also center an entry across a range of selected cells (or merge the selected cells), as in the professor's grade book, which centered the title in cell A1 across columns A through E. The Fill option duplicates the characters in the cell across the entire width of that cell.

Vertical alignment is important only if the row height is changed and the characters are smaller than the height of the row. Entries may be vertically aligned at the top, center, or bottom (the default) of a cell.

It is also possible to wrap the text within a cell to emulate the word wrap of a word processor. You select multiple cells and merge them together. And finally, you can achieve some very interesting effects by rotating text up to 90° in either direction.

Fonts

You can use the same fonts (typefaces) in Excel as you can in any other Windows application. Windows itself includes a limited number of fonts (Arial, Times New Roman, Courier New, Symbol, and Wingdings) to provide variety in creating documents. (Additional fonts are also installed with Microsoft Office.) All fonts are WYSIWYG (What You See Is What You Get), meaning that the worksheet you see on the monitor will match the worksheet produced by the printer.

Any entry in a worksheet may be displayed in any font, style, or point size as indicated by the dialog box of Figure 2.6c. The example shows Arial, Bold Italic, and 14 points, and corresponds to the selection for the worksheet title in the improved grade book. Special effects, such as subscripts or superscripts, are also possible. You can even select a different color, but you will need a color printer to see the effect on the printed page. The Preview box shows the text as it will appear in the worksheet.

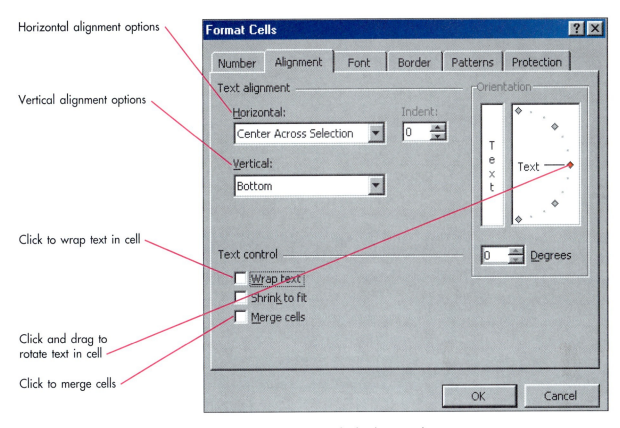

(b) The Alignment Tab

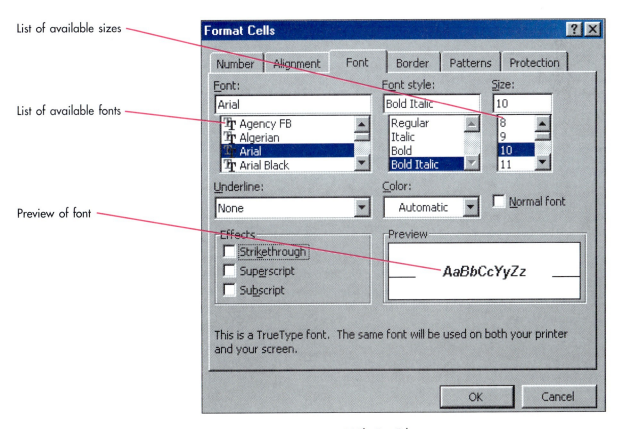

(c) The Font Tab

FIGURE 2.6 The Format Cells Command (continued)

Borders, Patterns, and Shading

The ***Border tab*** in Figure 2.6d enables you to create a border around a cell (or cells) for additional emphasis. You can outline the entire selection, or you can choose the specific side or sides; for example, thicker lines on the bottom and right sides produce a drop shadow, which is very effective. You can also specify a different line style and/or a different color for the border, but you will need a color printer to see the effect on the printed output.

The ***Patterns tab*** in Figure 2.6e lets you choose a different color in which to shade the cell and further emphasize its contents. The Pattern drop-down list box lets you select an alternate pattern, such as dots or slanted lines.

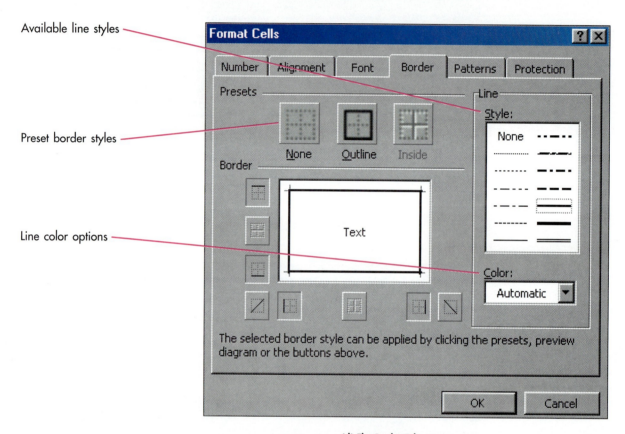

(d) The Border Tab

FIGURE 2.6 The Format Cells Command (continued)

USE RESTRAINT

More is not better, especially in the case of too many typefaces and styles, which produce cluttered worksheets that impress no one. Limit yourself to a maximum of two typefaces per worksheet, but choose multiple sizes and/or styles within those typefaces. Use boldface or italics for emphasis, but do so in moderation, because if you emphasize too many elements, the effect is lost.

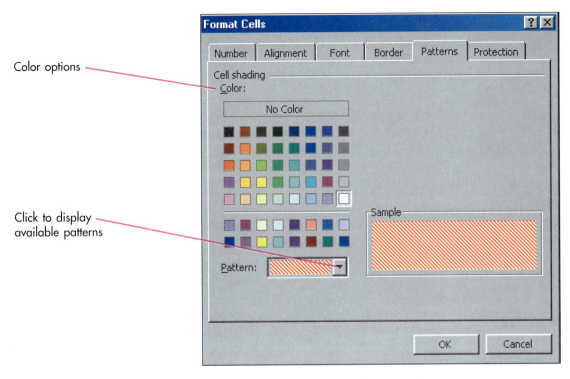

(e) The Patterns Tab

FIGURE 2.6 The Format Cells Command (continued)

HANDS-ON EXERCISE 2

Formatting a Worksheet

Objective: To format a worksheet using both pull-down menus and the Formatting toolbar; to use boldface, italics, shading, and borders; to change the font and/or alignment of a selected entry; to change the width of a column. Use Figure 2.7 as a guide in the exercise.

STEP 1: Center Across Selection

➤ Click the **Open button** on the Standard toolbar to display the Open dialog box, then click the **drop-down arrow** on the Look In list box and choose the appropriate drive. Double click the **Exploring Excel folder,** then double click the **My Grade Book** workbook that was created in the previous exercise.

➤ Click in **cell A1** to select the cell containing the title of the worksheet.

➤ Pull down the **Format menu.** Click **Cells.** If necessary, click the **Font tab.** Click **Arial** in the Font list box, **Bold Italic** in the Font Style box, and then scroll to select **14** from the Size box. Click **OK.**

➤ Click and drag to select cells **A1** through **E1,** which represents the width of the entire worksheet.

CHAPTER 2: GAINING PROFICIENCY **59**

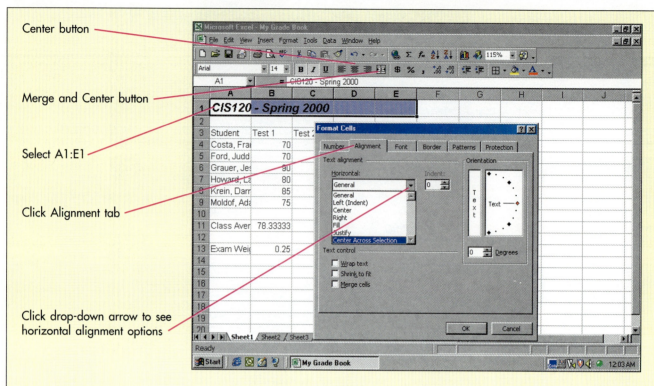

(a) Center Across Selection (step 1)

FIGURE 2.7 Hands-on Exercise 2

- Pull down the **Format menu** a second time. Click **Cells.** Click the **Alignment tab.** Click the **down arrow** in the Horizontal list box, then click **Center Across Selection** as in Figure 2.7a. Click **OK**.
- Click and drag over cells **B3** through **E13**. Click the **Center button** on the Formatting toolbar.

STEP 2: Increase the Width of Column A

- Click in **cell A4.** Drag the mouse over cells **A4** through **A13**.
- Pull down the **Format menu,** click **Column,** then click **AutoFit Selection** as shown in Figure 2.7b.
- The width of the selected cells increases to accommodate the longest entry in the selected range.
- Save the workbook.

COLUMN WIDTHS AND ROW HEIGHTS

Drag the border between column headings to change the column width; for example, to increase (decrease) the width of column A, drag the border between column headings A and B to the right (left). Double click the right boundary of a column heading to change the column width to accommodate the widest entry in that column. Use the same techniques to change the row heights.

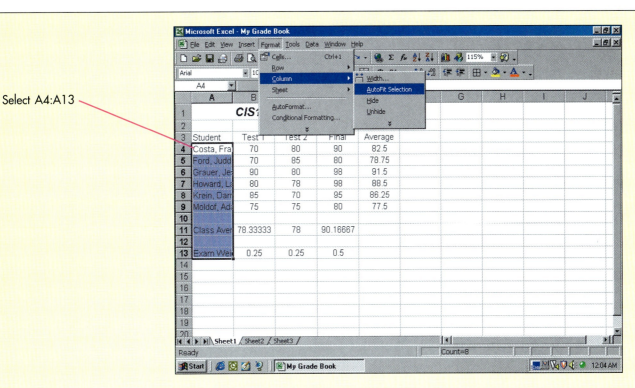

(b) Increase the Width of Column A (step 2)

FIGURE 2.7 Hands-on Exercise 2 (continued)

STEP 3: Format the Exam Weights

➤ Click and drag to select cells **B13** through **D13.** Point to the selected cells and click the **right mouse button** to display the shortcut menu in Figure 2.7c. Click **Format Cells** to produce the Format Cells dialog box.

➤ If necessary, click the **Number tab.** Click **Percentage** in the Category list box. Click the **down arrow** in the Decimal Places box to reduce the number of decimals to zero, then click **OK.** The exam weights are displayed with percent signs and no decimal places.

➤ Click the **Undo button** on the Standard toolbar to cancel the formatting command.

➤ Click the **% button** on the Formatting toolbar to reformat the exam weights as percentages. (This is an alternate and faster way to change to the percent format.)

AUTOMATIC FORMATTING

Excel converts any number entered with a beginning dollar sign to currency format, and any number entered with an ending percent sign to percentage format. The automatic formatting enables you to save a step by typing $100,000 or 7.5% directly into a cell, rather than entering 100000 or .075 and having to format the number. The formatting is applied to the cell and affects any subsequent numbers entered in that cell.

CHAPTER 2: GAINING PROFICIENCY 61

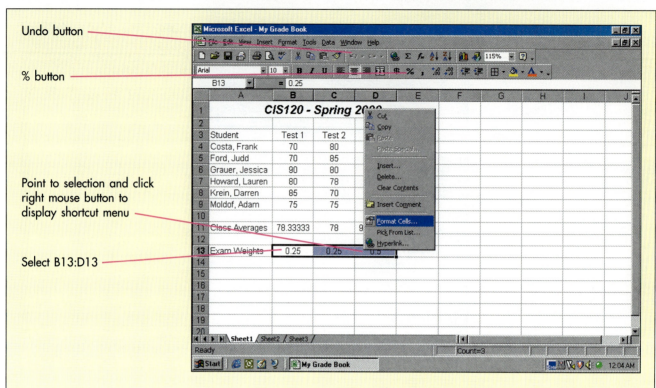

(c) Format the Exam Weights (step 3)

FIGURE 2.7 Hands-on Exercise 2 (continued)

STEP 4: Noncontiguous Ranges

➤ Select cells **B11** through **D11**. Press *and* hold the **Ctrl key** as you click and drag to select cells **E4** through **E9**. Release the **Ctrl key.**

➤ You will see two noncontiguous (nonadjacent) ranges highlighted, cells B11:D11 and cells E4:E9 as in Figure 2.7d. Format the selected cells using either the Formatting toolbar or the Format menu:

- To use the Formatting toolbar, click the appropriate button to increase or decrease the number of decimal places to one.
- To use the Format menu, pull down the **Format menu,** click **Cells,** click the **Number tab,** then click **Number** in the Category list box. Click the **down arrow** in the Decimal Places text box to reduce the decimal places to one. Click **OK.**

THE FORMAT PAINTER

The Format Painter copies the formatting of the selected cell to other cells in the worksheet. Click the cell whose formatting you want to copy, then double click the Format Painter button on the Standard toolbar. The mouse pointer changes to a paintbrush to indicate that you can copy the current formatting; just click and drag the paintbrush over the additional cells to which you want to apply the formatting. Repeat the painting process as often as necessary, then click the Format Painter button a second time to return to normal editing.

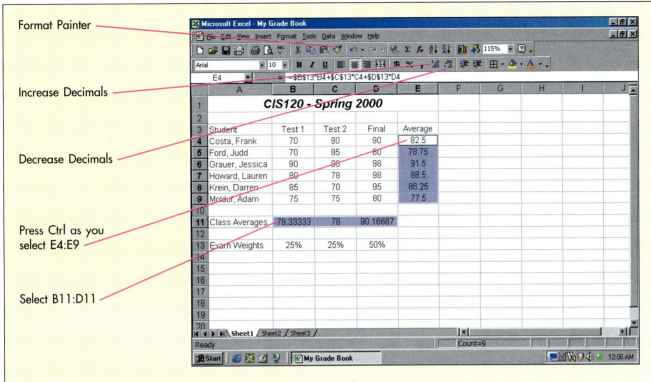

(d) Noncontiguous Ranges (step 4)

FIGURE 2.7 Hands-on Exercise 2 (continued)

STEP 5: The Border Command

➤ Click and drag to select cells **A3** through **E3.** Press *and* hold the **Ctrl key** as you click and drag to select the range **A11:E11.**

➤ Continue to press and hold the **Ctrl key** as you click and drag to select cells **A13:E13.**

➤ Pull down the **Format menu** and click **Cells** (or click the **right mouse button** to produce a shortcut menu, then click **Format Cells**). Click the **Border tab** to access the dialog box in Figure 2.7e.

➤ Choose a line width from the Style section. Click the **Top** and **Bottom** boxes in the Border section. Click **OK** to exit the dialog box and return to the worksheet.

> ### SELECTING NONCONTIGUOUS RANGES
>
> Dragging the mouse to select a range always produces some type of rectangle; that is, a single cell, a row or column, or a group of rows and columns. You can, however, select noncontiguous (nonadjacent) ranges by selecting the first range in the normal fashion, then pressing and holding the Ctrl key as you select the additional range(s). This is especially useful when the same command is to be applied to multiple ranges within a worksheet.

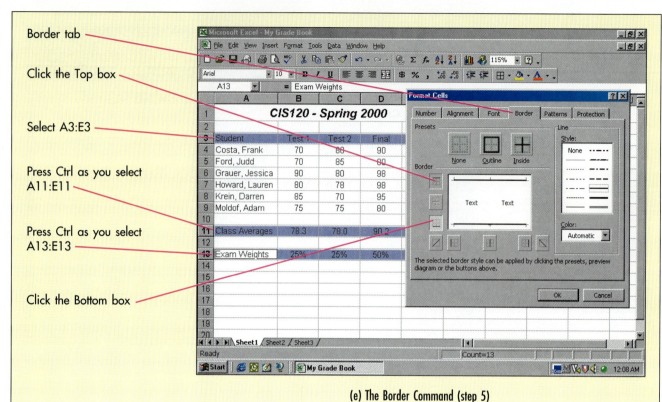

(e) The Border Command (step 5)

FIGURE 2.7 Hands-on Exercise 2 (continued)

STEP 6: Add Color

➤ Check that all three ranges are still selected (A3:E3, A11:E11, *and* A13:E13).

➤ Click the **down arrow** on the **Fill Color button** on the Formatting toolbar. Click yellow (or whatever color appeals to you) as shown in Figure 2.7f.

➤ Click the **boldface** and **italics buttons** on the Formatting toolbar. Click outside the selected cells to see the effects of the formatting change.

➤ Save the workbook.

THE FORMATTING TOOLBAR

The Formatting toolbar is the fastest way to implement most formatting operations. There are buttons for boldface, italics, and underlining, alignment (including merge and center), currency, percent, and comma formats, as well as buttons to increase or decrease the number of decimal places. There are also several list boxes to choose the font, point size, and font color as well as the type of border and shading. Be sure to separate the Formatting and Standard toolbars to see all of the available buttons, as described at the beginning of the first hands-on exercise.

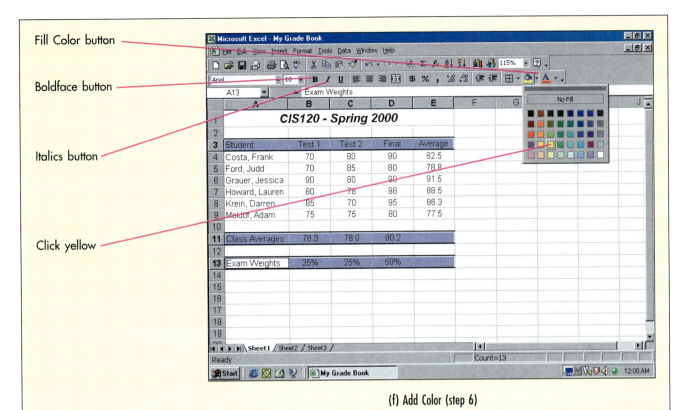

(f) Add Color (step 6)

FIGURE 2.7 Hands-on Exercise 2 (continued)

STEP 7: Enter Your Name and Social Security Number

➤ Click in **cell A15.** Type **Grading Assistant.** Press the **down arrow key.** Type your name, press the **down arrow key,** and enter your social security number *without* the hyphens. Press **enter.**

➤ Point to **cell A17,** then click the **right mouse button** to display a shortcut menu. Click **Format Cells** to display the dialog box in Figure 2.7g.

➤ Click the **Number tab,** click **Special** in the Category list box, then click **Social Security Number** in the Type list box. Click **OK.** Hyphens have been inserted into your social security number.

TIME STAMP YOUR SPREADSHEETS

The Now( ) function displays the current date and time and is continually updated throughout a session. The Today( ) function is similar in concept except it displays only the date. To change the format of either function, pull down the Format menu and click the Cells command to display the Format Cells dialog box. Click the Number tab, choose the Date category, select the desired format, then click OK to accept the setting and close the Format Cells dialog box.

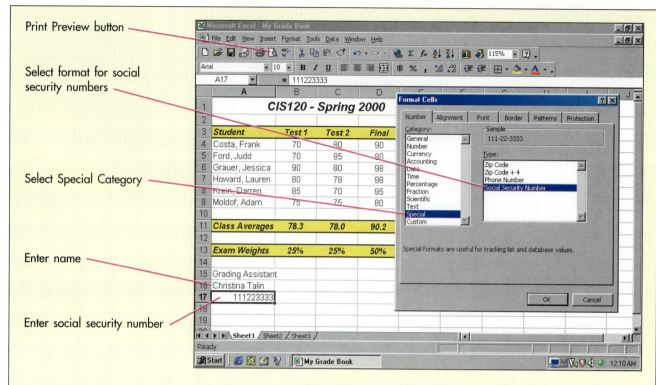

(g) Enter Your Name and Social Security Number (step 7)

FIGURE 2.7 Hands-on Exercise 2 (continued)

STEP 8: The Page Setup Command

➤ Pull down the **File menu.** Click **Page Setup** to display the Page Setup dialog box.
- Click the **Margins tab.** Check the box to center the worksheet Horizontally.
- Click the **Sheet tab.** Check the boxes to print Row and Column Headings and Gridlines.
- Click **OK** to exit the Page Setup dialog box.

➤ Click the **Print Preview button** to preview the worksheet before printing:
- If you are satisfied with the appearance of the worksheet, click the **Print button** within the Preview window, then click **OK** to print the worksheet.
- If you are not satisfied with the appearance of the worksheet, click the **Setup button** within the Preview window to make the necessary changes, after which you can print the worksheet.

➤ Save the workbook.

THE INSERT COMMENT COMMAND

You can add a comment, which displays a ScreenTip, to any cell in a worksheet. Click in the cell, pull down the Insert menu, and click Comment to display a box in which you enter the comment. Click outside the box when you have completed the entry. Point to the cell (which should have a tiny red triangle) and you will see the ScreenTip you just created. (If you do not see the triangle or the tip, pull down the Tools menu, click Options, click the View tab, then click the options button for Comment Indicator Only in the Comments area.)

STEP 9: Print the Cell Formulas

➤ Pull down the **Tools menu,** click **Options,** click the **View tab,** check the box for **Formulas,** then click **OK** (or use the keyboard shortcut **Ctrl+`**). The worksheet should display the cell formulas.

➤ If necessary, click the right arrow on the horizontal scroll bar so that column E, the column containing the cell formulas, comes into view.

➤ Double click the border between the column headings for columns E and F to increase the width of column E to accommodate the widest entry in the column.

➤ Pull down the **File menu.** Click the **Page Setup** command to display the Page Setup dialog box.
  • Click the **Page tab.** Click the **Landscape orientation button.**
  • Click the option button to **Fit to 1 page.** Click **OK** to exit the Page Setup dialog box.

➤ Click the **Print Preview button** to preview the worksheet before printing. It should match the display in Figure 2.7h:
  • If you are satisfied with the appearance of the worksheet, click the **Print button** within the Preview window, then click **OK** to print the worksheet.
  • If you are not satisfied with the appearance of the worksheet, click the **Setup button** within the Preview window to make the necessary changes, after which you can print the worksheet.

➤ Pull down the **File menu.** Click **Close.** Click **No** if prompted to save changes.
➤ Exit Excel if you do not want to continue with the next exercise at this time.

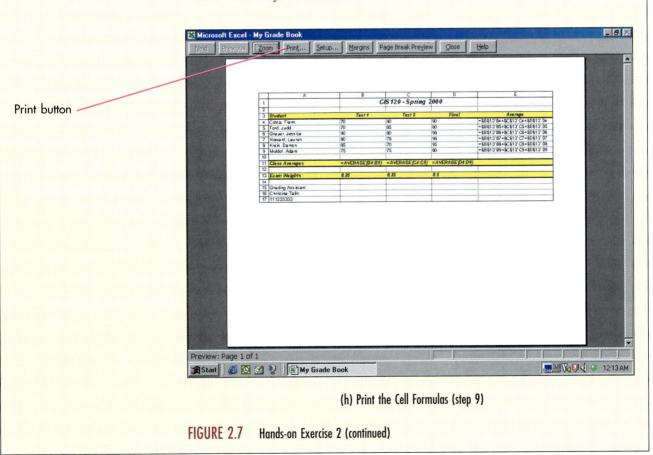

(h) Print the Cell Formulas (step 9)

FIGURE 2.7 Hands-on Exercise 2 (continued)

EXCEL 2000 AND THE INTERNET

The growth of the Internet and World Wide Web has been astounding and has totally changed our society. You may be familiar with the basic concepts that underlie the Internet, but we think a brief review is in order. The ***Internet*** is a network of networks that connects computers anywhere in the world. The ***World Wide Web*** (WWW, or simply, the Web) is a very large subset of the Internet, consisting of those computers that store a special type of document known as a ***Web page*** or ***HTML document***.

The interesting thing about a Web page or HTML document is that it contains references (called ***hyperlinks***) to other Web pages, which may be stored on the same computer, or even on a different computer, with the latter located anywhere in the world. And therein lies the fascination of the Web, in that you simply click on link after link to go effortlessly from one document to the next. You can start your journey on your professor's home page, then browse through any set of links you wish to follow.

The Internet and World Wide Web are thoroughly integrated into Office 2000 through two basic capabilities. You can insert a hyperlink into any Office document, then view the associated Web page by clicking the link without having to start your Web browser manually. You can also save any Office document as a Web page, which in turn can be stored on a Web server and displayed through a browser such as Internet Explorer or Netscape Navigator.

Consider, for example, Figure 2.8a, which displays a slightly modified version of the grade book that we have been using throughout the chapter. The grade book contains an additional column that identifies students by number (e.g., the last four digits of the Social Security number) rather than by name. In addition, a hyperlink to the professor's home page has been inserted into cell B15. You can click the link from within Excel, and provided you have an Internet connection, your Web browser will display the associated page.

Figure 2.8b displays the grade book using Internet Explorer rather than Excel. This was accomplished by saving the grade book in Excel as a Web page (or HTML document), then opening the document in Internet Explorer. The page can be posted to the professor's Web site, where it can be accessed by students connecting to the Internet. Alternatively, the HTML version of the grade book could be stored on a local area network to prevent access by individuals outside the organization. (Look carefully at the address bar in Figure 2.8b and you will see that we are viewing the document locally rather than from the Internet.)

Note, too, that the student names do not appear in Figure 2.8b because the professor elected to hide the column of student names prior to creating the Web page. (This is accomplished through the ***Hide Column command*** in the Format menu.) Hiding a column is different from deleting the column in that the information remains in the workbook but is hidden from view. The professor can display (unhide) the column at any time; for example, he can view the student names during data entry.

THE WEB TOOLBAR

The Web toolbar may be displayed from any application in Office 2000. It contains many of the same buttons as the Internet Explorer toolbar and can be used to display a document from a local or network drive as well as the World Wide Web. The Back, Forward, Stop, Home, Search, and Favorites buttons function identically in Office 2000 and Internet Explorer. The address bar is also similar and displays the address of the current document.

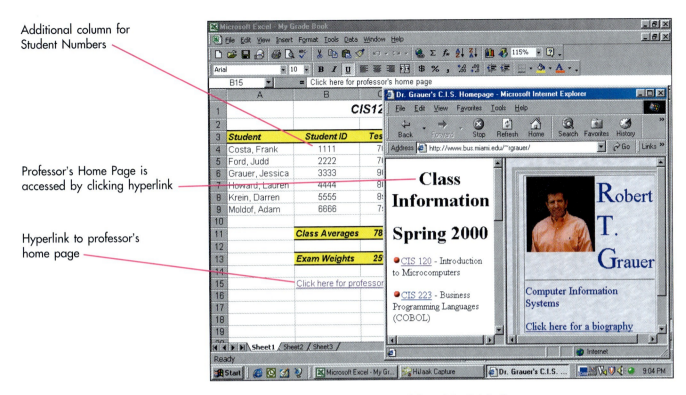

(a) Hyperlinks and the Web Toolbar

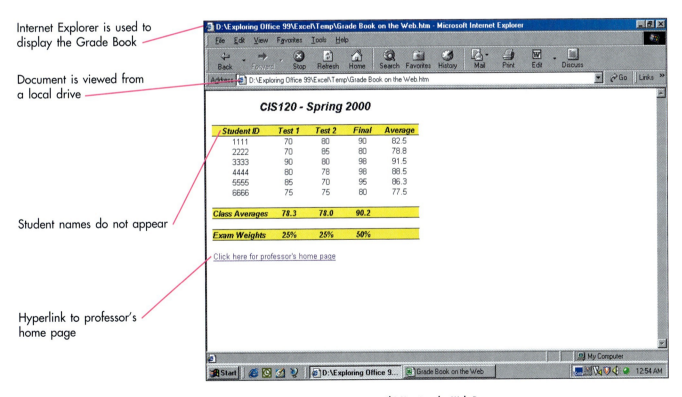

(b) Viewing the Web Page

FIGURE 2.8 Excel 2000 and the Internet

HANDS-ON EXERCISE 3

Excel 2000 and the Internet

Objective: To insert a hyperlink into an Excel workbook; to save a workbook as an HTML document. Use Figure 2.9 as a guide in the exercise. The exercise requires that you have an Internet connection to test the hyperlink.

STEP 1: Insert the Student IDs

➤ Open the **My Grade Book workbook** from the previous exercise. Move the contents of cell A1 to cell B1. Click the column header for column B.

➤ Pull down the **Insert menu** and click the **Columns command** to insert a new column to the left of column B; i.e., the grades for Test 1 are now in column C as shown in Figure 2.9a.

➤ Enter the label **Student ID** in cell B3, then enter the Student ID for each student as shown in the figure. Click and drag to select cells B3 through B9, then click the **Center button** on the Formatting toolbar.

➤ Click in cell **A11** to select this cell. Click and drag the top border (the mouse pointer changes from a cross to an arrow), to cell B11 to move the contents of cell A11 to B11. Move the contents of cell A13 to cell B13.

➤ Click the column header for column A to select the entire column as shown in Figure 2.9a. Pull down the **Format menu,** click (or point to) the **Column command** to display a cascaded menu, then click the **Hide command.** Column A (the student names) is no longer visible.

➤ Save the workbook.

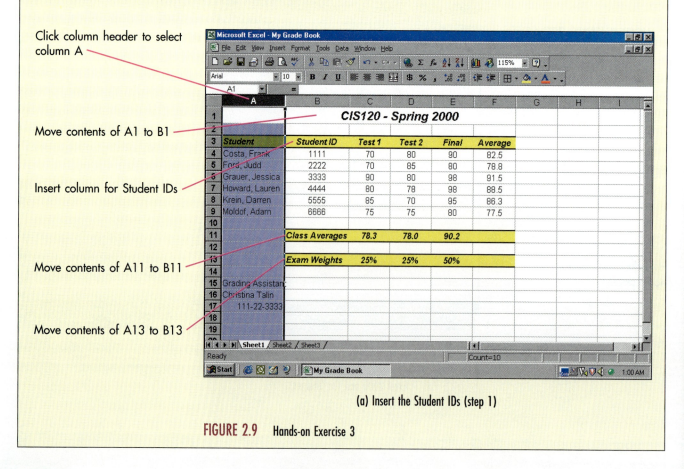

(a) Insert the Student IDs (step 1)

FIGURE 2.9 Hands-on Exercise 3

STEP 2: Insert a Hyperlink

➤ Click in cell **B15**. Pull down the **Insert menu** and click the **Hyperlink command** (or click the **Insert Hyperlink button** on the Standard toolbar) to display the Insert Hyperlink dialog box in Figure 2.9b.

➤ Click in the **Text to display** text box and enter **Click here for professor's home page.** Click in the second text box and enter the desired Web address; e.g., **www.bus.miami.edu/~rgrauer** (the http:// is assumed).

➤ Click **OK** to accept the settings and close the dialog box. The hyperlink should appear as an underlined entry in the worksheet.

➤ Save the workbook.

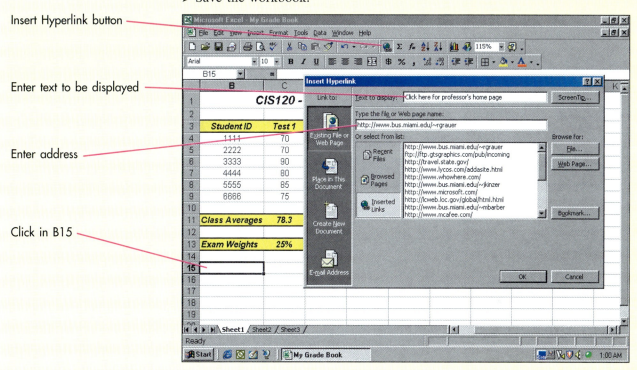

(b) Insert a Hyperlink (step 2)

FIGURE 2.9 Hands-on Exercise 3 (continued)

SELECTING (EDITING) A HYPERLINK

In an ideal world, you will enter all the information for a hyperlink correctly on the first attempt. But what if you make a mistake and need to edit the information? You cannot select a hyperlink by clicking it, because that displays the associated Web page. You can, however, right click the cell containing the hyperlink to display a context-sensitive menu. Click the Hyperlink command from that menu, then select the Edit Hyperlink command to display the associated dialog box in which to make the necessary changes.

STEP 3: Test the Hyperlink

➤ Point to the hyperlink (the Web address should appear as a ScreenTip), then click the link to start your browser and view the Web page. (You need an Internet connection to see the actual page.)

➤ If necessary, click the **maximize button** in your Web browser so that it takes the entire desktop as shown in Figure 2.9c. You are now running two applications, Excel and the Web browser, each of which has its own button on the Windows taskbar.

➤ Click the **Excel button** to continue working on the workbook.

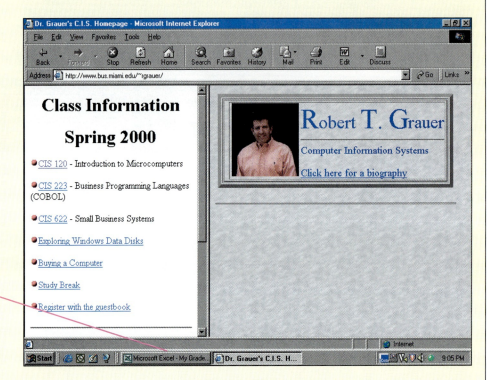

(c) Test the Hyperlink (step 3)

FIGURE 2.9 Hands-on Exercise 3 (continued)

MULTITASKING

Multitasking, the ability to run multiple applications at the same time, is one of the primary advantages of the Windows environment. Minimizing an application is different from closing it, and you want to minimize, rather than close, an application to take advantage of multitasking. Closing an application removes it from memory so that you have to restart the application if you want to return to it later in the session. Minimizing, however, leaves the application open in memory, but shrinks its window to a button on the Windows taskbar.

STEP 4: Save as a Web Page

➤ Pull down the **File menu** and click the **Save as Web Page** command to display the Save as dialog box in Figure 2.9d. (The Web page can be saved and viewed on a local drive prior to posting it on the Web.)

➤ Click the drop-down arrow in the Save In list box to select the appropriate drive, drive C or drive A, then open the **Exploring Excel folder**.

➤ Change the name of the Web page to **My Grade Book as Web Page** (to differentiate it from the Excel workbook of the same name). Click the **Save button** to save the page.

➤ The title bar changes to reflect the name of the Web page. There are now two versions of this workbook in the Exploring Excel folder, My Grade Book, and My Grade Book as Web Page. The latter has been saved as a Web page (in HTML format) and can be viewed by any Web browser.

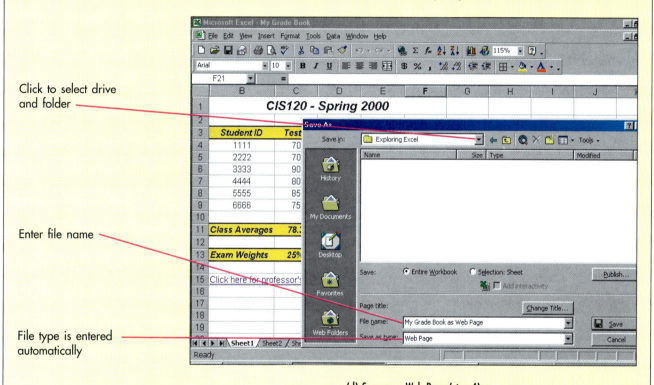

(d) Save as a Web Page (step 4)

FIGURE 2.9 Hands-on Exercise 3 (continued)

HIDING AND UNHIDING ROWS AND COLUMNS

Excel enables you to hide a column from view while retaining the data in the workbook. Select the column(s) you wish to hide, click the right mouse button, then select the Hide command from the shortcut menu. Reverse the process to unhide the column; i.e., right click the column header to the left of the hidden column, then click the Unhide command. To unhide column A, however, click in the Name box and enter A1. Pull down the Format menu, click Column, then click the Unhide command. Follow a similar process to hide and unhide a row.

STEP 5: View the Web Page

➤ You can preview the Web page by pulling down the **File menu** and clicking the **Web Page Preview command.** We prefer, however that you start Internet Explorer by clicking its button on the Windows taskbar to open the Web page explicitly.

➤ Pull down the **File menu** and click the **Open command** to display the Open dialog box in Figure 2.9e. Click the **Browse button,** then select the drive and folder where you saved the Web page in the previous step.

➤ Click the **Details button** on the Open toolbar to display the date and time the Web page was created.

➤ Select (click) **My Grade Book as Web Page,** then click **Open** to close the dialog box. Click **OK** to open the document. You should see the professor's grade book with the students listed by Student ID, rather than name.

➤ Close Excel and Internet Explorer.

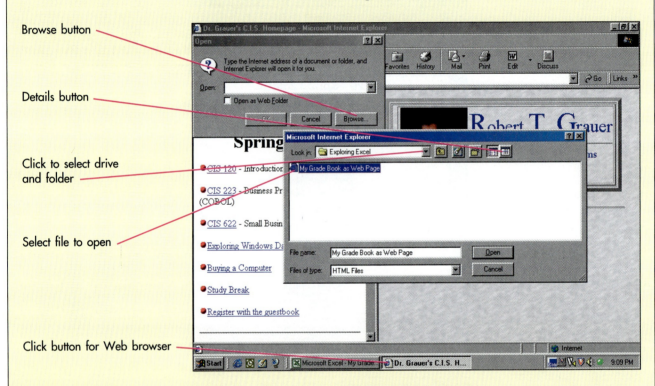

(e) View the Web Page (step 5)

FIGURE 2.9 Hands-on Exercise 3 (continued)

THE CORPORATE INTRANET

The ability to create links to local documents and to view those pages through a Web browser has created an entirely new way to disseminate information. Organizations of every size are taking advantage of this capability to develop a corporate intranet in which Web pages are placed on a local area network for use within the organizations. The documents on an intranet are available only to individuals with access to the local area network on which the documents are stored.

SUMMARY

All worksheet commands operate on a cell or group of cells known as a range. A range is selected by dragging the mouse to highlight the range. The range remains selected until another range is defined or you click another cell in the worksheet. Noncontiguous (nonadjacent) ranges may be selected in conjunction with the Ctrl key.

The formulas in a cell or range of cells may be copied or moved anywhere within a worksheet. An absolute reference remains constant throughout a copy operation, whereas a relative address is adjusted for the new location. Absolute and relative references have no meaning in a move operation. The copy and move operations are implemented through the Copy and Paste commands, and the Cut and Paste commands, respectively.

Formatting is done within the context of select-then-do; that is, select the cell or range of cells, then execute the appropriate command. The Format Cells command controls the formatting for Numbers, Alignment, Fonts, Borders, and Patterns (colors). The Formatting toolbar simplifies the formatting process.

A spreadsheet is first and foremost a tool for decision making, and as such, the subject of continual what-if speculation. It is critical, therefore, that the initial conditions and assumptions be isolated and clearly visible, and further that all formulas in the body of the spreadsheet be developed using these cells.

The Internet and World Wide Web are thoroughly integrated into Office 2000 through two basic capabilities. You can insert a hyperlink into any Office document, then view the associated Web page from within the document. You can also save any Office document as a Web page, which in turn can be displayed through a Web browser.

KEY WORDS AND CONCEPTS

Absolute reference
Accounting format
Alignment
Assumptions
Automatic formatting
Border tab
Cell formulas
Clipboard
Column command
Column width
Copy command
Currency format
Custom format
Cut command
Date format
Destination range
Format cells command
Format menu

Format Painter
Formatting toolbar
Fraction format
General format
Horizontal alignment
Hyperlink
Initial conditions
Insert Hyperlink command
Internet
Mixed reference
Move operation
Noncontiguous range
Now( ) function
Number format
Paste command
Patterns tab
Percentage format

Range
Relative reference
Row command
Row height
Save as Web Page command
Scientific format
Select-then-do
Source range
Special format
Text format
Time format
Today( ) function
Vertical alignment
Web toolbar
World Wide Web

MULTIPLE CHOICE

1. Cell F6 contains the formula =AVERAGE(B6:D6). What will be the contents of cell F7 if the entry in cell F6 is *copied* to cell F7?
   (a) =AVERAGE(B6:D6)
   (b) =AVERAGE(B7:D7)
   (c) =AVERAGE($B$6:$D$6)
   (d) =AVERAGE($B$7:$D$7)

2. Cell F6 contains the formula =AVERAGE(B6:D6). What will be the contents of cell F7 if the entry in cell F6 is *moved* to cell F7?
   (a) =AVERAGE(B6:D6)
   (b) =AVERAGE(B7:D7)
   (c) =AVERAGE($B$6:$D$6)
   (d) =AVERAGE($B$7:$D$7)

3. A formula containing the entry =$A$4 is copied to a cell one column over and two rows down. How will the entry appear in its new location?
   (a) Both the row and column will change
   (b) Neither the row nor column will change
   (c) The row will change but the column will remain the same
   (d) The column will change but the row will remain the same

4. Which commands are necessary to implement a move?
   (a) Cut and Paste commands
   (b) Move command from the Edit menu
   (c) Either (a) or (b)
   (d) Neither (a) nor (b)

5. A cell range may consist of:
   (a) A single cell
   (b) A row or set of rows
   (c) A column or set of columns
   (d) All of the above

6. Which command will take a cell, or group of cells, and duplicate them elsewhere in the worksheet, without changing the original cell references?
   (a) Copy command, provided relative addresses were specified
   (b) Copy command, provided absolute addresses were specified
   (c) Move command, provided relative addresses were specified
   (d) Move command, provided absolute addresses were specified

7. The contents of cell B4 consist of the formula =B2*B3, yet the displayed value in cell B4 is a series of pound signs. What is the most likely explanation for this?
   (a) Cells B2 and B3 contain text entries rather than numeric entries and so the formula in cell B4 cannot be evaluated
   (b) Cell B4 is too narrow to display the computed result
   (c) Both (a) and (b)
   (d) Neither (a) nor (b)

8. The Formatting toolbar contains buttons to
   (a) Change to percent format
   (b) Increase or decrease the number of decimal places
   (c) Center an entry across columns
   (d) All of the above

9. Given that the percentage format is in effect, and that the number .056 has been entered into the active cell, how will the contents of the cell appear?
   (a) .056
   (b) 5.6%
   (c) .056%
   (d) 56%

10. Which of the following entries is equivalent to the decimal number .2?
   (a) ⅕
   (b) =1/5
   (c) Both (a) and (b)
   (d) Neither (a) nor (b)

11. What is the effect of two successive Undo commands, one right after the other?
   (a) The situation is not possible because the Undo command is not available in Microsoft Excel
   (b) The situation is not possible because the Undo command cannot be executed twice in a row
   (c) The Undo commands cancel each other out; that is, the worksheet is as it was prior to the first Undo command
   (d) The last two commands prior to the first Undo command are reversed

12. A formula containing the entry =$B3 is copied to a cell one column over and two rows down. How will the entry appear in its new location?
   (a) =$B3
   (b) =B3
   (c) =$C5
   (d) =$B5

13. What will be stored in a cell if 2/5 is entered in it?
   (a) 2/5
   (b) .4
   (c) The date value February 5 of the current year
   (d) 2/5 or .4 depending on the format in effect

14. Which of the following is true regarding numeric formatting changes versus the numeric values?
   (a) When you change the numeric formatting the value will change
   (b) When you change the numeric formatting the value will not be changed
   (c) When you change the numeric formatting the value will be truncated
   (d) None of the above is true

15. Which of the following may be copied using the Copy command?
   (a) A cell
   (b) A range of cells
   (c) A function
   (d) All of the above

16. A numerical entry may be
    (a) Displayed in boldface and/or italics
    (b) Left, centered, or right aligned in a cell
    (c) Displayed in any TrueType font in any available point size
    (d) All of the above

17. How do you insert a hyperlink into an Excel workbook?
    (a) Pull down the Insert menu and click the Hyperlink command
    (b) Click the Insert Hyperlink button on the Standard toolbar
    (c) Right click a cell and click the Hyperlink command
    (d) All of the above

18. A Web browser such as Internet Explorer can display a page from
    (a) A local drive such as drive A or drive C
    (b) A drive on a local area network
    (c) The World Wide Web
    (d) All of the above

ANSWERS

1. b	**6.** b	**11.** d	**16.** d
2. a	**7.** b	**12.** d	**17.** d
3. b	**8.** d	**13.** c	**18.** d
4. a	**9.** b	**14.** b	
5. d	**10.** b	**15.** d	

PRACTICE WITH EXCEL 2000

1. **Coaches Realty:** Figure 2.10 contains a worksheet that was used to calculate the difference between the Asking Price and Selling Price on various real estate listings that were sold during June, as well as the commission paid to the real estate agency as a result of selling those listings. Complete the worksheet, following the steps on the next page.

	A	B	C	D	E	F
1	Coaches Realty - Sales for June					
2						
3						
4	Customer	Address	Asking Price	Selling Price	Difference	Commission
5	Landry	122 West 75 Terr.	450000	350000		
6	Spurrier	4567 S.W. 95 Street	750000	648500		
7	Shula	123 Alamo Road	350000	275000		
8	Lombardi	9000 Brickell Place	275000	250000		
9	Johnson	5596 Powerline Road	189000	189000		
10	Erickson	8900 N.W. 89 Street	456000	390000		
11	Bowden	75 Maynada Blvd.	300000	265000		
12						
13		Totals:				
14						
15	Commission %:		0.035			

FIGURE 2.10 Coaches Realty (Exercise 1)

a. Open the partially completed *Chapter 2 Practice 1* workbook on the data disk, then save the workbook as *Chapter 2 Practice 1 Solution.*
b. Click cell E5 and enter the formula to calculate the difference between the asking price and the selling price.
c. Click cell F5 and enter the formula to calculate the commission paid to the agency as a result of selling the property. (Pay close attention to the difference between relative and absolute cell references.)
d. Select cells E5:F5 and copy the formulas to E6:F11 to calculate the difference and commission for the rest of the properties.
e. Click cell C13 and enter the formula to calculate the total asking price, which is the sum of the asking prices for the individual listings.
f. Copy the formula in C13 to the range D13:F13.
g. Select the range C5:F13 and format the numbers so that they display with dollar signs and commas, and no decimal places (e.g., $450,000).
h. Click cell B15 and format the number as a percentage.
i. Click cell A1 and center the title across the width of the worksheet. With the cell still selected, select cells A2:F4 as well and change the font to 12 point Arial bold italic.
j. Select cells A4:F4 and create a bottom border to separate the headings from the data. Select cells F5:F11 and shade the commissions.
k. Add your name in cell A20. Print the worksheet.

2. **The Sales Invoice:** Use Figure 2.11 as the basis for a sales invoice that you will create and submit to your instructor. Your spreadsheet should follow the general format shown in the figure with respect to including a uniform discount for each item. Your spreadsheet should also include the sales tax. The discount percentage and sales tax percentage should be entered in a separate area so that they can be easily modified.

   Use your imagination and sell any product at any price. You must, however, include at least four items in your invoice. Formatting is important, but you need not follow our format exactly. See how creative you can be, then submit your completed invoice to your instructor for inclusion in a class contest for the best invoice. Be sure your name appears somewhere on the worksheet as a sales associate. If you are really ambitious, you might include an object from the Microsoft Clip Gallery.

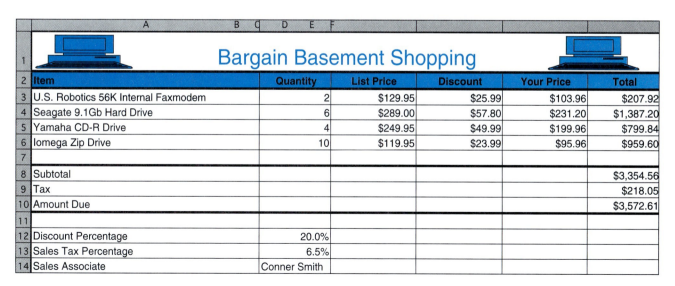

FIGURE 2.11 The Sales Invoice (Exercise 2)

3. The Checkbook: Figure 2.12 displays a worksheet that can be used to balance your checkbook. You can create the worksheet, and apply basic formatting by following these directions.

   a. Start Excel. If necessary, click the New button on the Standard toolbar to display a blank workbook. Click in cell A1 and enter the title with your name as shown. Enter the labels for cells A3 through F3. Do not worry about formatting at this time.

   b. Enter the initial balance in cell F4. Enter the data for your first check in row 5 and for your first deposit in row 6. (To enter a date, just type the date without an equal sign; e.g., enter 6/2/99 to enter June 2, 1999.) Use real or hypothetical data as you see fit.

   c. Click in cell F5 and enter the formula to compute your balance. Develop the formula in such a way that it can be copied to the remaining cells in column F; that is, the formula should compute the balance after the current transaction, regardless of whether the transaction is a check or deposit.

   d. Enter the data for at least four additional transactions in cells A through E of the appropriate row. Copy the formula to compute the balance for these transactions from cell F5.

   e. Skip one row after the last transaction, then enter the formulas to verify that the balance is correct. The formula for cell F12 (in our worksheet) is the initial balance, minus the sum of all check amounts, plus the sum of all deposits. The displayed value should equal the balance after the last transaction.

   f. Format the completed worksheet as appropriate. Print the worksheet twice, once to show the displayed values and once to show the cell contents. Submit both printouts to your instructor as proof that you did this exercise.

	A	B	C	D	E	F
1			Jessica Benjamin's Checkbook			
2	Check #	Date	Description	Amount	Deposit	Balance
3						$1,000.00
4	1	2-Jun	Rent	$345.00		$655.00
5		2-Jun	DEPOSIT		$125.00	$780.00
6	2	3-Jun	Utilities	$45.43		$734.57
7			ATM Withdrawal	$50.00		$684.57
8	3	6-Jun	Computer Repair	$84.25		$600.32
9	4	6-Jun	AOL	$19.99		$580.33
10						
11	Verification			$544.67	$125.00	$580.33

FIGURE 2.12 The Checkbook (Exercise 3)

4. Mixed References: Develop the multiplication table for a younger sibling shown in Figure 2.13. Creating the row and column headings is easy in that you can enter the numbers manually, or you can use online help to learn about the AutoFill feature. The hard part is creating the formulas in the body of the worksheet (we don't want you to enter the numbers manually).

   The trick is to use mixed references for the formula in cell B4, then copy that single cell to the remainder of the table. The formula in cell B4 will be the product of two numbers. To develop the proper mixed reference, you need to think about what will vary and what will remain constant (e.g., you will always be using one value from column A and another value from row 3).

Add your name to the worksheet and submit it to your instructor. Remember, this worksheet is for a younger sibling, and so formatting is important. Print the cell formulas as well so that you can see how the mixed reference changes throughout the worksheet. Submit the complete assignment (title page, displayed values, and cell formulas) to your instructor. Using mixed references correctly is challenging, but once you arrive at the correct solution, you will have learned a lot about this very powerful spreadsheet feature.

	A	B	C	D	E	F	G	H	I	J	K	L	M
1		A Multiplication Table for My Younger Sister											
2													
3		1	2	3	4	5	6	7	8	9	10	11	12
4	1	1	2	3	4	5	6	7	8	9	10	11	12
5	2	2	4	6	8	10	12	14	16	18	20	22	24
6	3	3	6	9	12	15	18	21	24	27	30	33	36
7	4	4	8	12	16	20	24	28	32	36	40	44	48
8	5	5	10	15	20	25	30	35	40	45	50	55	60
9	6	6	12	18	24	30	36	42	48	54	60	66	72
10	7	7	14	21	28	35	42	49	56	63	70	77	84
11	8	8	16	24	32	40	48	56	64	72	80	88	96
12	9	9	18	27	36	45	54	63	72	81	90	99	108
13	10	10	20	30	40	50	60	70	80	90	100	110	120
14	11	11	22	33	44	55	66	77	88	99	110	121	132
15	12	12	24	36	48	60	72	84	96	108	120	132	144

FIGURE 2.13 Mixed References (Exercise 4)

5. **Payroll:** Figure 2.14 illustrates how a spreadsheet can be used to compute a payroll for hourly employees. A partially completed version of the worksheet can be found in the file *Chapter 2 Practice 5*. Your job is to complete the worksheet by developing the entries for the first employee, then copying those entries to the remaining rows. (An employee receives time and a half for overtime.)

To receive full credit for this assignment, the formulas for the withholding and Social Security taxes must reference the percentages in cells C12 and C13, respectively. Format the worksheet after it has been completed. Add your name anywhere in the worksheet, then print it two ways, once with displayed values and once with cell contents; then submit both pages to your instructor.

	A	B	C	D	E	F	G	H
1	Employee Name	Hourly Wage	Regular Hours	Overtime Hours	Gross Pay	Withholding Tax	Soc Sec Tax	Net Pay
2								
3	Jones	$8.00	40	10	$440.00	$123.20	$28.60	$288.20
4	Smith	$9.00	35	0	$315.00	$88.20	$20.48	$206.33
5	Baker	$7.20	40	0	$288.00	$80.64	$18.72	$188.64
6	Barnard	$7.20	40	8	$374.40	$104.83	$24.34	$245.23
7	Adams	$10.00	40	4	$460.00	$128.80	$29.90	$301.30
8								
9	Totals				$1,877.40	$525.67	$122.03	$1,229.70
10								
11	**Assumptions**							
12	Withholding tax		28.0%					
13	FICA		6.5%					

FIGURE 2.14 Payroll (Exercise 5)

6. **Exchange Rates:** The attractive worksheet in Figure 2.15 is based on a simple monetary conversion formula whereby specified dollar amounts are converted to British pounds and vice versa. Your assignment is to create the equivalent worksheet, based on today's rate of exchange for any foreign currency. The most important part of the assignment is to create an accurate spreadsheet. The inclusion of the flags is optional.

   a. Choose any foreign currency you like, then use your favorite search engine to locate today's rate of exchange. Enter the conversion factors in the appropriate cells in the worksheet.

   b. Enter the fixed amounts of the foreign currency in cells B4 through B7, then enter the appropriate formulas in cells C4 through C7.

   c. Enter the fixed amounts of the U.S. currency in cells B10 through B13, then enter the appropriate formulas in cells C10 through C13.

   d. Use the Currency category in the Format Cells command to display the symbol for your selected currency in the appropriate cells.

   e. Click in cell C15 and enter the label, "Click here to obtain today's rate of Exchange." Click the Insert Hyperlink button on the Standard toolbar to display the Insert Hyperlink dialog box in which you enter the Web address of the site you used to obtain the exchange rate.

   f. This step requires the installation of additional clip art from the Office 2000 CD. Pull down the Insert menu, click (or point to) the Picture command, then choose Clip Art to display the Microsoft Clip Gallery dialog box. Select the Flags category, then insert the appropriate flags into your worksheet.

   g. Click in cell B19 and enter =today( ) to display the current date. Add your name elsewhere in the worksheet. Save the workbook. Print the workbook with today's conversion rates.

   h. Open the workbook on a different day and note that the displayed value in cell B19 changes automatically. Click the hyperlink to go to the Web site containing the rates of exchange and enter the new values, which in turn should change the other values in the body of the spreadsheet. Print the workbook a second time to reflect these rates.

	A	B	C
1		**Currency Conversion**	
2			
3	**Pounds to Dollars**	Cost in Pounds	Cost in Dollars
4		£1.00	$1.63
5		£5.00	$8.15
6		£10.00	$16.30
7		£25.00	$40.75
8			
9	**Dollars to Pounds**	Cost in Dollars	Cost in Pounds
10		$1.00	£0.61
11		$5.00	£3.07
12		$10.00	£6.13
13		$25.00	£15.34
14			
15	Click here to obtain today's rate of exchange		
16	Convert dollars to pounds		1.63
17	Convert pounds to dollars		0.61
18			
19	Today's Date	2/4/99	
20	Your friendly banker	Andrea Carrion	

FIGURE 2.15 Exchange Rates (Exercise 6)

7. **Get Rich Quick:** Financial planning and budgeting is one of the most common business applications of spreadsheets. Figure 2.16 depicts one such illustration, in which the income and expenses of Get Rich Quick Enterprises are projected over a five-year period. Your assignment is to create the spreadsheet from the partially completed version, *Chapter 2 Practice 7* that is found on the data disk. You don't have to be an accountant to do the assignment, which computes an estimated profit by subtracting expenses from income.

   The projected income in 1999, for example, is $300,000 based on sales of 100,000 units at a price of $3.00 per unit. The variable costs for the same year are estimated at $150,000 (100,000 units times $1.50 per unit). The production facility costs an additional $50,000 and administrative expenses add another $25,000. Subtracting the total expenses from the estimated income yields a net income before taxes of $75,000. The estimated income and expenses for each succeeding year are based on an assumed percentage increase over the previous year. The projected rates of increase as well as the initial conditions are shown at the bottom of the worksheet.

   Open the partially completed spreadsheet in *Chapter 2 Practice 7*, then complete the spreadsheet so that it matches Figure 2.16. The assignment is not difficult, provided you follow these basic steps.

   a. Develop the formulas for the first year of the forecast based on the initial conditions at the bottom of the spreadsheet; e.g., the entry in cell B4 should be =B18 (or =$B$18).

   b. Develop the formulas for the second year based on the values in year one and the assumed rates of change. Use the appropriate combination of relative and absolute addresses; e.g., the entry in cell C4 should be =B4+B4*$D$18.

   c. Copy the formulas for year two to the remaining years of the forecast.

   d. Format the spreadsheet, then print the completed forecast. Add your name somewhere in the worksheet, then submit the completed spreadsheet to your instructor.

	A	B	C	D	E	F
1		**Get Rich Quick Enterprises**				
2		1999	2000	2001	2002	2003
3	**Income**					
4	Units Sold	100,000	110,000	121,000	133,100	146,410
5	Unit Price	$3.00	$3.15	$3.31	$3.47	$3.65
6	**Gross Revenue**	$300,000	$346,500	$400,208	$462,240	$533,887
7						
8	**Fixed costs**					
9	Production facility	$50,000	$54,000	$58,320	$62,986	$68,024
10	Administration	$25,000	$26,250	$27,563	$28,941	$30,388
11	**Variable cost**					
12	Unit mfg cost	$1.50	$1.65	$1.82	$2.00	$2.20
13	Variable mfg cost	$150,000	$181,500	$219,615	$265,734	$321,538
14						
15	**Earnings before taxes**	$75,000	$84,750	$94,710	$104,579	$113,936
16						
17	**Initial conditions**			**Annual increase**		
18	First year sales	100,000		10.0%		
19	Selling price	$3.00		5.0%		
20	Unit mfg cost	$1.50		10.0%		
21	Production facility	$50,000		8.0%		
22	Administration	$25,000		5.0%		
23	First year of forecast	1999				

FIGURE 2.16 Get Rich Quick (Exercise 7)

CASE STUDIES

Establishing a Budget

Create a detailed budget for your four years at school. Your worksheet should include all sources of income (scholarships, loans, summer jobs, work-study, etc.) as well as all expenses (tuition, books, room and board, and entertainment). Make the budget as realistic as possible by building in projected increases over the four-year period. Be sure to isolate the assumptions and initial conditions so that your spreadsheet is amenable to change. Print the spreadsheet twice, once to show displayed values, and once to show the cell formulas. Submit both pages to your instructor together with a cover page.

Two Different Clipboards

The Office clipboard is different from the Windows clipboard, but both clipboards share some functionality. Thus, whenever you copy an object to the Office clipboard, it is also copied to the Windows clipboard. However, each successive copy operation adds an object to the Office clipboard (up to a maximum of 12 objects), whereas it replaces the contents of the Windows clipboard. The Office clipboard also has its own toolbar. Experiment with the Office clipboard from different applications, then summarize your findings in a brief note to your instructor.

Break-even Analysis

Widgets of America has developed the perfect product and is ready to go into production, pending a review of a five-year break-even analysis. The manufacturing cost in the first year is $1.00 per unit and is estimated to increase at 5% annually. The projected selling price is $2.00 per unit and can increase at 10% annually. Overhead expenses are fixed at $100,000 per year over the life of the project. The advertising budget is $50,000 in the first year but will decrease 15% a year as the product gains acceptance. How many units have to be sold each year for the company to break even?

As in the previous case, your worksheet should be completely flexible and capable of accommodating a change in any of the initial conditions or projected rates of increase or decrease. Be sure to isolate all of the assumptions (i.e., the initial conditions and rates of increase) in one area of the worksheet, and then reference these cells as absolute references when building the formulas.

chapter 3

GRAPHS AND CHARTS: DELIVERING A MESSAGE

OBJECTIVES

After reading this chapter you will be able to:

1. Distinguish between the different types of charts, stating the advantages and disadvantages of each.
2. Distinguish between a chart embedded in a worksheet and one in a separate chart sheet; explain how many charts can be associated with the same worksheet.
3. Use the Chart Wizard to create and/or modify a chart.
4. Use the Drawing toolbar to enhance a chart by creating lines, objects, and 3-D shapes.
5. Differentiate between data series specified in rows and data series specified in columns.
6. Describe how a chart can be statistically accurate yet totally misleading.
7. Create a compound document consisting of a word processing memo, a worksheet, and a chart.

OVERVIEW

Business has always known that the graphic representation of data is an attractive, easy-to-understand way to convey information. Indeed, business graphics has become one of the most exciting Windows applications, whereby charts (graphs) are easily created from a worksheet, with just a few simple keystrokes or mouse clicks.

The chapter begins by emphasizing the importance of determining the message to be conveyed by a chart. It describes the different types of charts available within Excel and how to choose among them. It explains how to create a chart using the Chart Wizard, how to embed a chart within a worksheet, and how to create a chart in a separate chart sheet. It also describes how to use the Drawing toolbar to enhance a chart by creating lines, objects, and 3-D shapes.

The second half of the chapter explains how one chart can plot multiple sets of data, and how several charts can be based on the same worksheet. It also describes how to create a compound document, in which a chart and its associated worksheet are dynamically linked to a memo created by a word processor. All told, we think you will find this to be one of the most enjoyable chapters in the text.

CHART TYPES

A *chart* is a graphic representation of data in a worksheet. The chart is based on descriptive entries called ***category labels,*** and on numeric values called ***data points.*** The data points are grouped into one or more ***data series*** that appear in row(s) or column(s) on the worksheet. In every chart there is exactly one data point in each data series for each value of the category label.

The worksheet in Figure 3.1 will be used throughout the chapter as the basis for the charts we will create. Your manager believes that the sales data can be understood more easily from charts than from the strict numerical presentation of a worksheet. You have been given the assignment of analyzing the data in the worksheet and are developing a series of charts to convey that information.

	A	B	C	D	E	F
1	Superior Software Sales					
2						
3		Miami	Denver	New York	Boston	Total
4	Word Processing	$50,000	$67,500	$9,500	$141,000	$268,000
5	Spreadsheets	$44,000	$18,000	$11,500	$105,000	$178,500
6	Database	$12,000	$7,500	$6,000	$30,000	$55,500
7	Total	$106,000	$93,000	$27,000	$276,000	$502,000

FIGURE 3.1 Superior Software

The sales data in the worksheet can be presented several ways—for example, by city, by product, or by a combination of the two. Ask yourself which type of chart is best suited to answer the following questions:

- What percentage of total revenue comes from each city? from each product?
- What is the dollar revenue produced by each city? by each product?
- What is the rank of each city with respect to sales?
- How much revenue does each product contribute in each city?

In every instance, realize that a chart exists only to deliver a message, and that you cannot create an effective chart unless you are sure of what that message is. The next several pages discuss various types of business charts, each of which is best suited to a particular type of message.

KEEP IT SIMPLE

Keep it simple. This rule applies to both your message and the means of conveying that message. Excel makes it almost too easy to change fonts, styles, type sizes, and colors, but such changes will often detract from, rather than enhance, a chart. More is not necessarily better, and you do not have to use the features just because they are there. Remember that a chart must ultimately succeed on the basis of content, and content alone.

Pie Charts

A *pie chart* is the most effective way to display proportional relationships. It is the type of chart to select whenever words like *percentage* or *market share* appear in the message to be delivered. The pie, or complete circle, denotes the total amount. Each slice of the pie corresponds to its respective percentage of the total.

The pie chart in Figure 3.2a divides the pie representing total sales into four slices, one for each city. The size of each slice is proportional to the percentage of total sales in that city. The chart depicts a single data series, which appears in cells B7 through E7 on the associated worksheet. The data series has four data points corresponding to the total sales in each city.

To create the pie chart, Excel computes the total sales ($502,000 in our example), calculates the percentage contributed by each city, and draws each slice of the pie in proportion to its computed percentage. Boston's sales of $276,000 account for 55 percent of the total, and so this slice of the pie is allotted 55 percent of the area of the circle.

An *exploded pie chart,* as shown in Figure 3.2b, separates one or more slices of the pie for emphasis. Another way to achieve emphasis in a chart is to choose a title that reflects the message you are trying to deliver. The title in Figure 3.2a, for example, *Revenue by Geographic Area*, is neutral and leaves the reader to develop his or her own conclusion about the relative contribution of each area. By contrast, the title in Figure 3.2b, *New York Accounts for Only 5% of Revenue,* is more suggestive and emphasizes the problems in this office. Alternatively, the title could be changed to *Boston Exceeds 50% of Total Revenue* if the intent were to emphasize the contribution of Boston.

Three-dimensional pie charts may be created in exploded or nonexploded format as shown in Figures 3.2c and 3.2d, respectively. Excel also enables you to add arrows and text for emphasis.

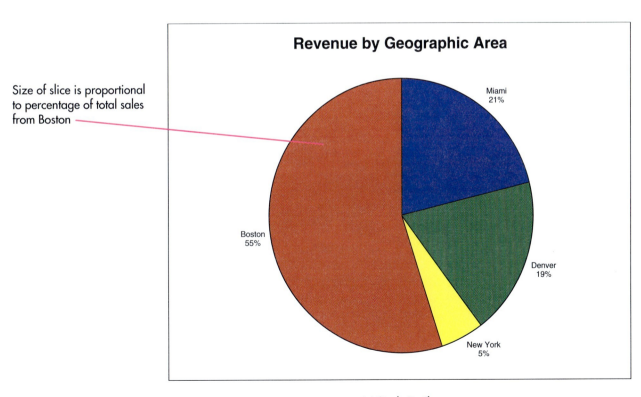

Size of slice is proportional to percentage of total sales from Boston

(a) Simple Pie Chart

FIGURE 3.2   Pie Charts

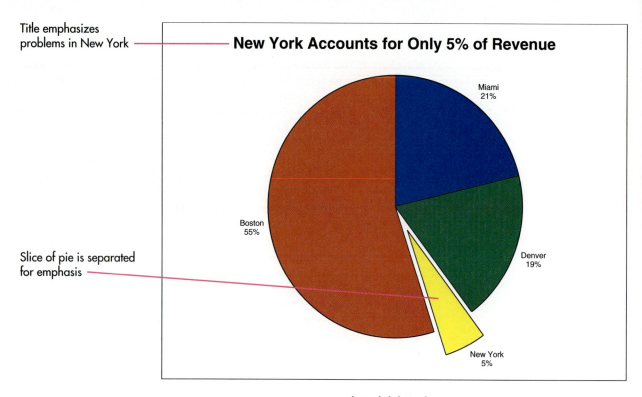

(b) Exploded Pie Chart

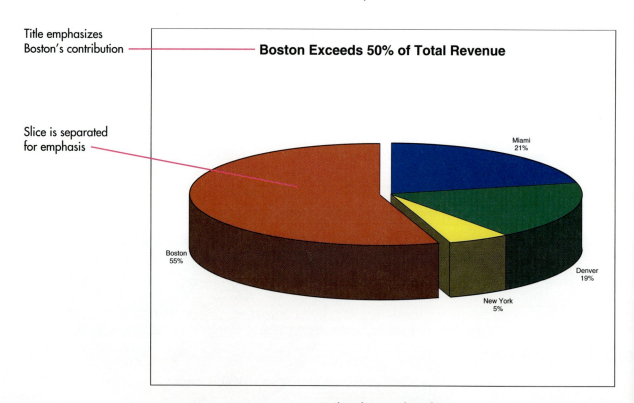

(c) Three-dimensional Pie Chart

FIGURE 3.2   Pie Charts (continued)

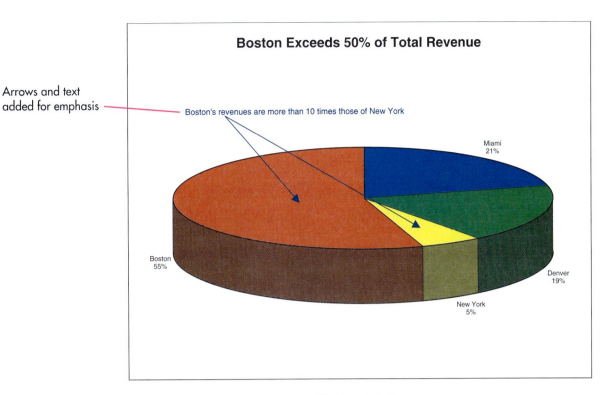

(d) Enhanced Pie Chart

FIGURE 3.2 Pie Charts (continued)

A pie chart is easiest to read when the number of slices is limited (i.e., not more than six or seven), and when small categories (percentages less than five) are grouped into a single category called "Other."

EXPLODED PIE CHARTS

Click and drag wedges out of a pie chart to convert an ordinary pie chart to an exploded pie chart. For best results pull the wedge out only slightly from the main body of the pie.

Column and Bar Charts

A *column chart* is used when there is a need to show actual numbers rather than percentages. The column chart in Figure 3.3a plots the same data series as the earlier pie chart, but displays it differently. The category labels (Miami, Denver, New York, and Boston) are shown along the *X* (horizontal) **axis.** The data points (monthly sales) are plotted along the *Y* (vertical) **axis,** with the height of each column reflecting the value of the data point.

A column chart can be given a horizontal orientation and converted to a ***bar chart*** as in Figure 3.3b. Some individuals prefer the bar chart over the corresponding column chart because the longer horizontal bars accentuate the difference between the items. Bar charts are also preferable when the descriptive labels are long, to eliminate the crowding that can occur along the horizontal axis of a

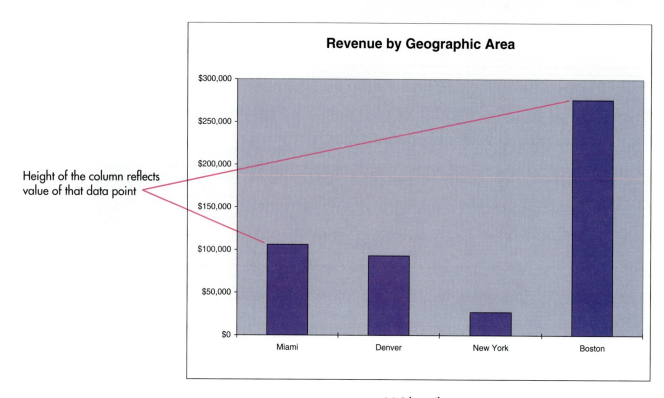

(a) Column Chart

(b) Horizontal Bar Chart

FIGURE 3.3   Column/Bar Charts

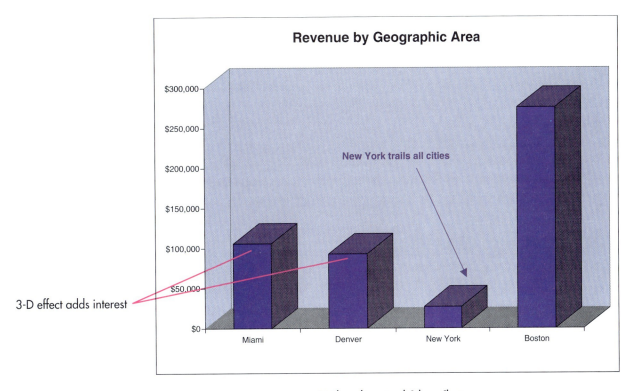

(c) Three-dimensional Column Chart

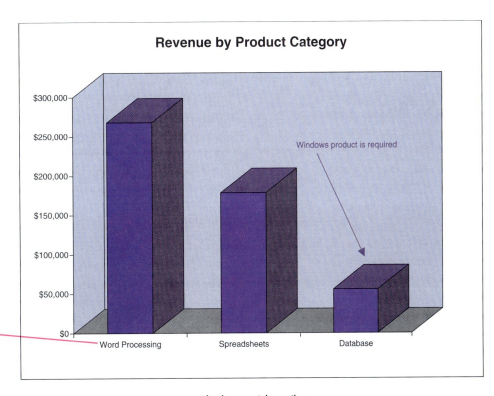

(d) Alternate Column Chart

FIGURE 3.3 Column/Bar Charts (continued)

column chart. As with the pie chart, a title can lead the reader and further emphasize the message, as with *Boston Leads All Cities* in Figure 3.3b.

A three-dimensional effect can produce added interest as shown in Figures 3.3c and 3.3d. Figure 3.3d plots a different set of numbers than we have seen so far (the sales for each product, rather than the sales for each city). The choice between the charts in Figures 3.3c and 3.3d depends on the message you want to convey—whether you want to emphasize the contribution of each city or each product. The title can be used to emphasize the message. Arrows, text, and 3-D shapes can be added to either chart to enhance the message.

As with a pie chart, column and bar charts are easiest to read when the number of categories is relatively small (seven or fewer). Otherwise, the columns (bars) are plotted so close together that labeling becomes impossible.

CREATING A CHART

There are two ways to create a chart in Excel. You can **embed** the chart in a worksheet, or you can create the chart in a separate **chart sheet.** Figure 3.4a displays an embedded column chart. Figure 3.4b shows a pie chart in its own chart sheet. Both techniques are valid. The choice between the two depends on your personal preference.

Regardless of where it is kept (embedded in a worksheet or in its own chart sheet), a chart is linked to the worksheet on which it is based. The charts in Figure 3.4 plot the same data series (the total sales for each city). Change any of these data points on the worksheet, and both charts will be updated automatically to reflect the new data.

Both charts are part of the same workbook (Software Sales) as indicated in the title bar of each figure. The tabs within the workbook have been renamed to indicate the contents of the associated sheet. Additional charts may be created and embedded in the worksheet and/or placed on their own chart sheets. And, as previously stated, if you change the worksheet, the chart (or charts) based upon it will also change.

Study the column chart in Figure 3.4a to see how it corresponds to the worksheet on which it is based. The descriptive names on the X axis are known as **category labels** and match the entries in cells B3 through E3. The quantitative values (data points) are plotted on the Y axis and match the total sales in cells B7 through E7. Even the numeric format matches; that is, the currency format used in the worksheet appears automatically on the scale of the Y axis.

The **sizing handles** on the embedded chart indicate it is currently selected and can be sized, moved, or deleted the same way as any other Windows object:

- To size the selected chart, point to a sizing handle (the mouse pointer changes to a double arrow), then drag the handle in the desired direction.
- To move the selected chart, point to the chart (the mouse pointer is a single arrow), then drag the chart to its new location.
- To copy the selected chart, click the Copy button to copy the chart to the clipboard, click in the workbook where you want the copied chart to go, then click the Paste button to paste the chart at that location.
- To delete the selected chart, press the Del key.

The same operations apply to any of the objects within the chart (e.g., its title), as will be discussed in the section on enhancing a chart. Note, too, that both figures contain a chart toolbar that enables you to modify a chart after it has been created.

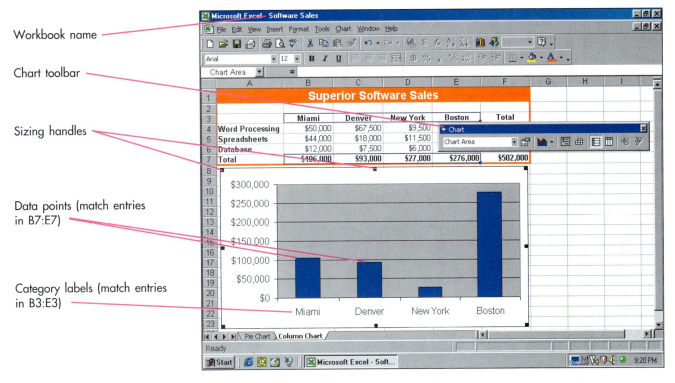

(a) Embedded Chart

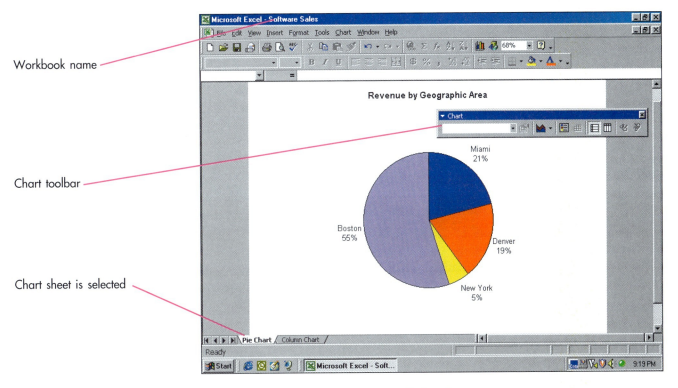

(b) Chart Sheet

FIGURE 3.4 Creating a chart

CHAPTER 3: GRAPHS AND CHARTS

The Chart Wizard

The **Chart Wizard** is the easiest way to create a chart. Just select the cells that contain the data as shown in Figure 3.5a, click the Chart Wizard button on the Standard toolbar, and let the wizard do the rest. The process is illustrated in Figure 3.5, which shows how the Wizard creates a column chart to plot total sales by geographic area (city).

The steps in Figure 3.5 appear automatically as you click the Next command button to move from one step to the next. You can retrace your steps at any time by pressing the Back command button, access the Office Assistant for help with the Chart Wizard, or abort the process with the Cancel command button.

Step 1 in the Chart Wizard (Figure 3.5b) asks you to choose one of the available chart types. Step 2 (Figure 3.5c) shows you a preview of the chart and enables you to confirm (and, if necessary, change) the category names and data series specified earlier. (Only one data series is plotted in this example. Multiple data series are illustrated later in the chapter.) Step 3 (Figure 3.5d) asks you to complete the chart by entering its title and specifying additional options (such as the position of a legend and gridlines). And finally, step 4 (Figure 3.5e) has you choose whether the chart is to be created as an embedded chart (an object) within a specific worksheet, or whether it is to be created in its own chart sheet. The entire process takes but a few minutes.

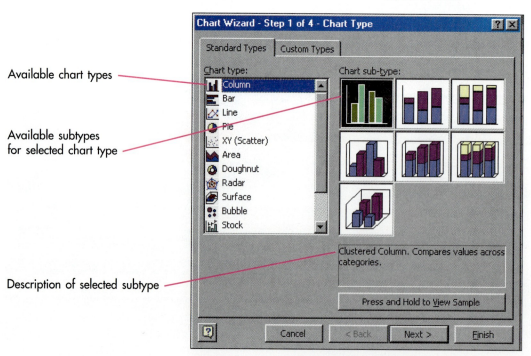

(a) The Worksheet

(b) Select the Chart Type (step 1)

FIGURE 3.5 The Chart Wizard

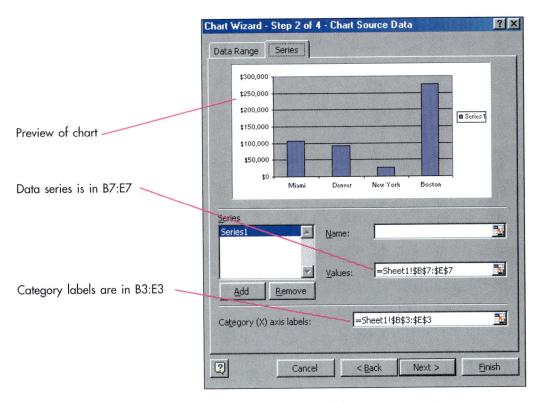

(c) Check the Data Series (step 2)

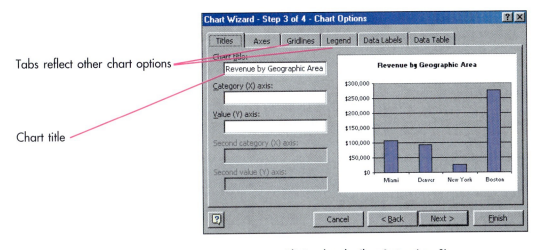

(d) Complete the Chart Options (step 3)

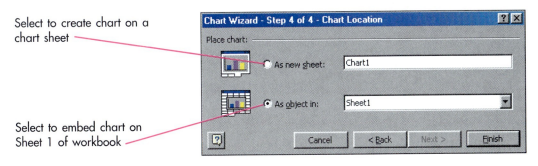

(e) Choose the Location (step 4)

FIGURE 3.5 The Chart Wizard (continued)

Modifying a Chart

A chart can be modified in several ways after it has been created. You can change the chart type and/or the color, shape, or pattern of the data series. You can add (or remove) gridlines and/or a legend. You can add labels to the data series. You can also change the font, size, color, and style of existing text anywhere in the chart by selecting the text, then changing its format. All of these features are implemented from the Chart menu or by using the appropriate button on the **Chart toolbar.**

You can also use the ***Drawing toolbar*** to add text boxes, arrows, and other objects for added emphasis. Figure 3.6, for example, contains a three-dimensional arrow with a text box within the arrow to call attention to the word processing sales. It also contains a second text box with a thin arrow in reference to the database product. Each of these objects is created separately using the appropriate tool from the Drawing toolbar. It's easy, as you will see in our next exercise.

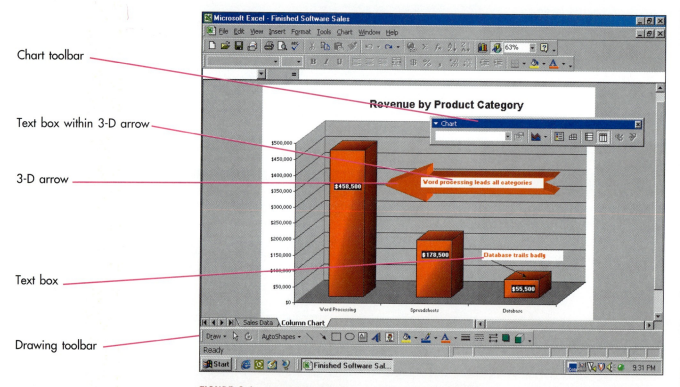

FIGURE 3.6 Enhancing a Chart

SET A TIME LIMIT

Excel enables you to customize virtually every aspect of every object within a chart. That is the good news. It's also the bad news, because you can spend inordinate amounts of time for little or no gain. It's fun to experiment, but set a time limit and stop when you reach the allocated time. The default settings are often adequate to convey your message, and further experimentation might prove counterproductive.

HANDS-ON EXERCISE 1

The Chart Wizard

Objective: To create and modify a chart by using the Chart Wizard; to embed a chart within a worksheet; to enhance a chart to include arrows and text. Use Figure 3.7 as a guide in the exercise.

STEP 1: The AutoSum Command

➤ Start Excel. Open the Software Sales workbook in the Exploring Excel folder. Save the workbook as **Finished Software Sales.**

➤ Click and drag to select the entries in cells **B7 through E7** (the cells that will contain the total sales for each location). Click the **AutoSum button** on the Standard toolbar.

➤ The totals are computed automatically as shown in Figure 3.7a. The formula bar shows that Cell B7 contains the Sum function to total all of the numeric entries immediately above the cell.

➤ Click and drag to select cells **F4 through F7,** then click the **AutoSum button.** The Sum function is entered automatically into these cells to total the entries to the left of the selected cells.

➤ Click and drag to select cells **B4 through F7** to format these cells with the currency symbol and no decimal places. Boldface the row and column headings and the totals. Add a red border and center the headings. Save the workbook.

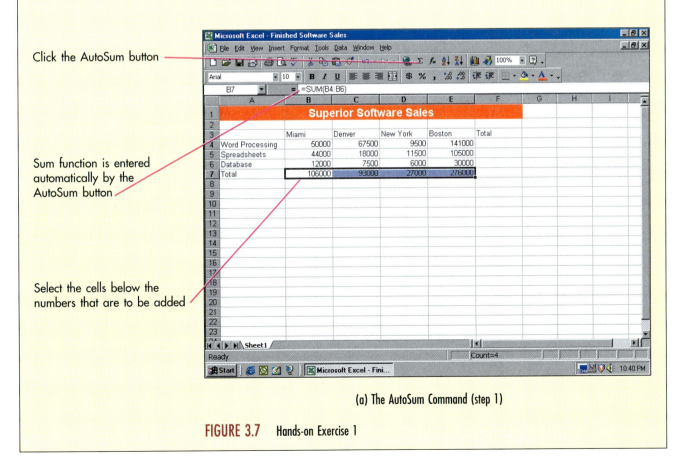

(a) The AutoSum Command (step 1)

FIGURE 3.7 Hands-on Exercise 1

THE AUTOFORMAT COMMAND

The AutoFormat command does not do anything that could not be done through individual formatting commands, but it does provide inspiration by suggesting several attractive designs. Select the cells you want to format, pull down the Format menu, and click the AutoFormat command to display the AutoFormat dialog box. Select (click) a design, then click the Options button to determine the formats to apply (font, column width, patterns, and so on). Click OK to close the dialog box and apply the formatting. Click the Undo button if you do not like the result.

STEP 2: Start the Chart Wizard

➤ Separate the toolbars if they occupy the same row. Pull down the **Tools menu,** click the **Customize command,** click the **Options tab,** then clear the check box that has the toolbars share one row.

➤ Drag the mouse over cells **B3 through E3** to select the category labels (the names of the cities). Press and hold the **Ctrl key** as you drag the mouse over cells **B7 through E7** to select the data series (the cells containing the total sales for the individual cities).

➤ Check that cells B3 through E3 and B7 through E7 are selected. Click the **Chart Wizard button** on the Standard toolbar to start the wizard. If you don't see the button, pull down the **Insert menu** and click the **Chart command.**

➤ You should see the dialog box for step 1 as shown in Figure 3.7b. The **Column** chart type and **Clustered column** subtype are selected. Click **Next.**

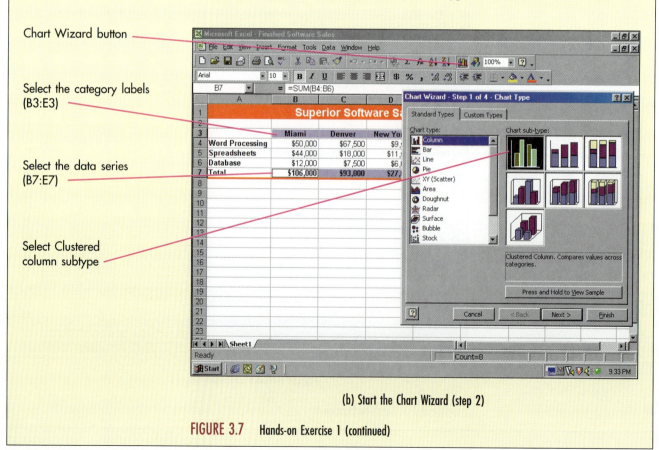

(b) Start the Chart Wizard (step 2)

FIGURE 3.7 Hands-on Exercise 1 (continued)

STEP 3: The Chart Wizard (continued)

➤ You should see step 2 of the Chart Wizard. Click the **Series tab** in the dialog box so that your screen matches Figure 3.7c. Note that the values (the data being plotted) are in cells B7 through E7, and that the Category labels for the X axis are in cells B3 through E3. Click **Next** to continue.

➤ You should see step 3 of the Chart Wizard. If necessary, click the **Titles tab,** then click in the text box for the Chart title. Type **Revenue by Geographic Area.** Click the **Legend tab** and clear the box to show a legend. Click **Next.**

➤ You should see step 4 of the Chart Wizard. If necessary, click the option button to place the chart **As object** in Sheet1 (the name of the worksheet in which you are working). Click **Finish.**

> ### RETRACE YOUR STEPS
>
> The Chart Wizard guides you every step of the way, but what if you make a mistake or change your mind? Click the Back command button at any time to return to a previous screen in order to enter different information, then continue working with the wizard.

STEP 4: Move and Size the Chart

➤ You should see the completed chart as shown in Figure 3.7d. The sizing handles indicate that the chart is selected and will be affected by subsequent commands. The Chart toolbar is displayed automatically whenever a chart is selected.

➤ Move and/or size the chart just as you would any other Windows object:
- To move the chart, click the chart (background) area to select the chart (a ScreenTip, "Chart Area," is displayed), then click and drag (the mouse pointer changes to a four-sided arrow) to move the chart.
- To size the chart, drag a corner handle (the mouse pointer changes to a double arrow) to change the length and width of the chart simultaneously, keeping the chart in proportion as it is resized.

➤ Click outside the chart to deselect it. The sizing handles disappear and the Chart toolbar is no longer visible.

> ### EMBEDDED CHARTS
>
> An embedded chart is treated as an object that can be moved, sized, copied, or deleted just as any other Windows object. To move an embedded chart, click the background of the chart to select the chart, then drag it to a new location in the worksheet. To size the chart, select it, then drag any of the eight sizing handles in the desired direction. To delete the chart, select it, then press the Del key. To copy the chart, select it, click the Copy button on the Standard toolbar to copy the chart to the clipboard, click elsewhere in the workbook where you want the copied chart to go, then click the Paste button.

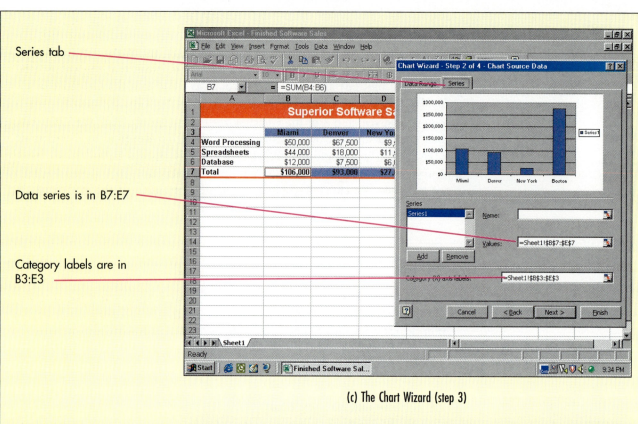

(c) The Chart Wizard (step 3)

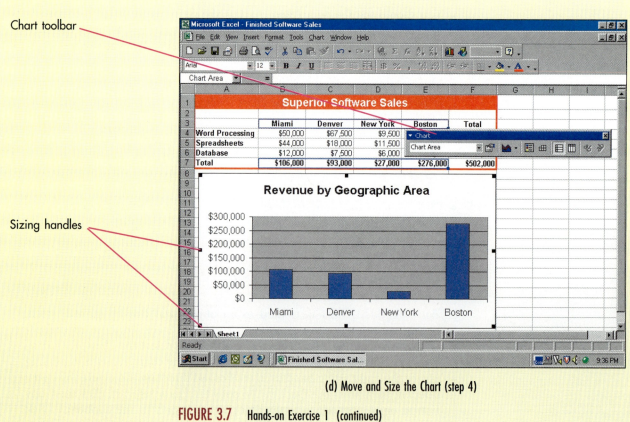

(d) Move and Size the Chart (step 4)

FIGURE 3.7   Hands-on Exercise 1 (continued)

STEP 5: Change the Worksheet

➤ Any changes in a worksheet are automatically reflected in the associated chart. Click in cell **B4,** change the entry to **$400,000,** and press the **enter key.**

➤ The total sales for Miami in cell B7 change automatically to reflect the increased sales for word processing, as shown in Figure 3.7e. The column for Miami also changes in the chart and is now larger than the column for Boston.

➤ Click in cell **B3.** Change the entry to **Chicago.** Press **enter.** The category label on the X axis changes automatically.

➤ Click the **Undo button** to change the city back to Miami. Click the **Undo button** a second time to return to the initial value of $50,000. The worksheet and chart are restored to their earlier values.

CREATE AN ATTRACTIVE CHART BORDER

Dress up an embedded chart by changing its border. Point to the chart area (the white background area near the border), click the right mouse button to display a shortcut menu, then click Format Chart Area to display the Format Chart Area dialog box. If necessary, click the Patterns tab, click the option button for a Custom border, then check the boxes for a Shadow and Round corners. Click the drop-down arrows in the style, color, and weight list boxes to specify a different border style, thickness (weight), or color. Click OK to accept these settings.

STEP 6: Change the Chart Type

➤ Click the chart (background) area to select the chart, click the **drop-down arrow** on the Chart type button on the Chart toolbar, then click the **3-D Pie Chart icon.** The chart changes to a three-dimensional pie chart.

➤ Point to the chart area, click the **right mouse button** to display a shortcut menu, then click the **Chart Options command** to display the Chart Options dialog box shown in Figure 3.7f.

➤ Click the **Data Labels tab,** then click the option button to **Show label and percent.** Click **OK** to accept the settings and close the Chart Options dialog box.

➤ The pie chart changes to reflect the options you just specified, although the chart may not appear exactly as you would like. Accordingly, you can modify each component as necessary:

- Select (click) the (gray) **Plot area.** Click and drag the sizing handles to increase the size of the plot area within the embedded chart.
- Point to any of the labels, click the **right mouse button** to display a shortcut menu, and click **Format Data Labels** to display a dialog box. Click the **Font tab,** and select a smaller point size. It may also be necessary to click and drag each label away from the plot area.

➤ Make other changes as necessary. Save the workbook.

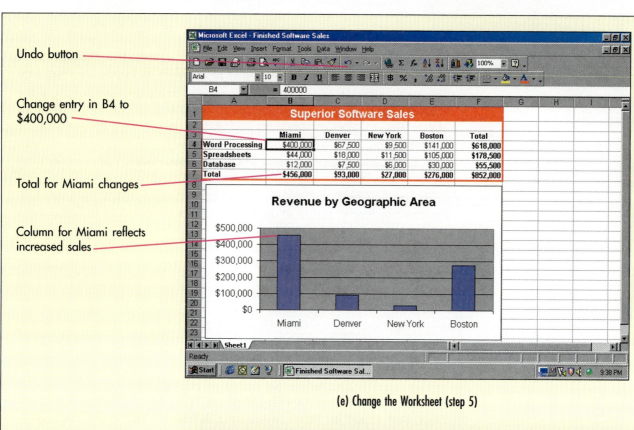

(e) Change the Worksheet (step 5)

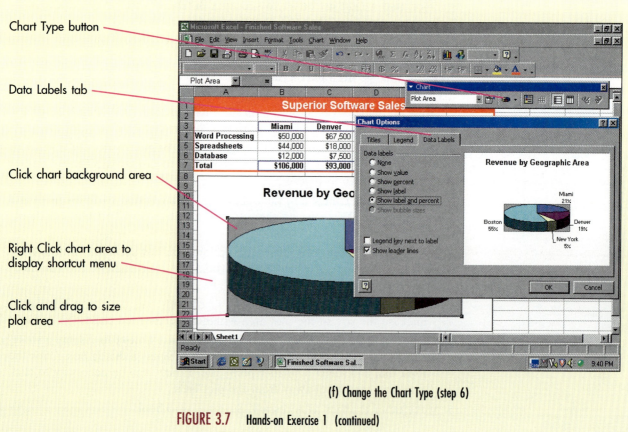

(f) Change the Chart Type (step 6)

FIGURE 3.7 Hands-on Exercise 1 (continued)

STEP 7: Create a Second Chart

- Click and drag to select cells **A4 through A6** in the worksheet. Press and hold the **Ctrl key** as you drag the mouse over cells **F4 through F6** to select the data series.
- Click the **Chart Wizard button** on the Standard toolbar to start the Chart Wizard and display the dialog box for step 1 as shown in Figure 3.7g. The Column Chart type is already selected. Click the **Clustered column with a 3-D visual effect subtype.** Press and hold the indicated button to preview the chart with your data. Click **Next.**
- Click the **Series tab** in the dialog box for step 2 to confirm that you selected the correct data points. The values for series1 should consist of cells F4 through F6. The Category labels for the X axis should be cells A4 through A6. Click **Next.**
- You should see step 3 of the Chart Wizard. Click the **Titles tab,** then click in the text box for the Chart title. Type **Revenue by Product Category.** Click the **Legend tab** and clear the box to show a legend. Click **Next.**
- You should see step 4 of the Chart Wizard. Select the option button to create the chart **As new sheet** (Chart1). Click **Finish.**
- The 3-D column chart has been created in the chart sheet labeled Chart1. Save the workbook.

ANATOMY OF A CHART

A chart is composed of multiple components (objects), each of which can be selected and changed separately. Point to any part of a chart to display a ScreenTip indicating the name of the component, then click the mouse to select that component and display the sizing handles. You can then click and drag the object within the chart and/or click the right mouse button to display a shortcut menu with commands pertaining to the selected object.

STEP 8: Add a Text Box

- Point to any visible toolbar, click the **right mouse button** to display a shortcut menu listing the available toolbars, then click **Drawing** to display the Drawing toolbar as shown in Figure 3.7h. Your toolbar may be in a different position from ours.
- Click the **TextBox button** on the Drawing toolbar. Click in the chart (the mouse pointer changes to a thin crosshair), then click and drag to create a text box. Release the mouse, then enter the text, **Word Processing leads all categories.**
- Point to the thatched border around the text box, then right click the border to display a context-sensitive menu. Click **Format Text Box** to display the Format Text dialog box. Click the **Font tab** and change the font to **12 point bold.** Choose **Red** as the font color.

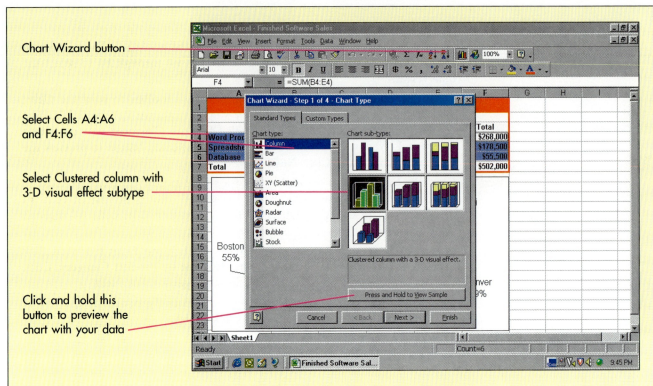

(g) Create a Second Chart (step 7)

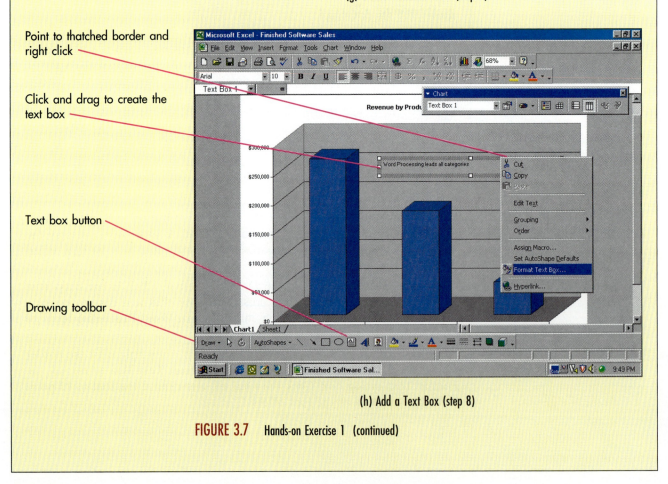

(h) Add a Text Box (step 8)

FIGURE 3.7   Hands-on Exercise 1 (continued)

➤ Click the **Colors and Lines tab** and select **white** as the fill color. Click **OK.** You should see red text on a white background. If necessary, size the text box so that the text fits on one line. Do not worry about the position of the text box at this time.

➤ Click the title of the chart. You will see sizing handles around the title to indicate it has been selected. Click the **drop-down arrow** in the Font Size box on the Formatting toolbar. Click **22** to increase the size of the title. Save the workbook.

> ### FLOATING TOOLBARS
>
> Any toolbar can be docked along the edge of the application window, or it can be displayed as a floating toolbar within the application window. To move a docked toolbar, drag the toolbar background or the move handles. To move a floating toolbar, drag its title bar. To size a floating toolbar, drag any border in the direction you want to go. Double click the background of any toolbar to toggle between a floating toolbar and a docked (fixed) toolbar.

STEP 9: Create a 3-D Shape

➤ Click on the **AutoShapes button** and, if necessary, click the double arrow to display additional commands. Click **Block Arrows** to display the various styles of arrows, then click the left arrow.

➤ Click in the chart (the mouse pointer changes to a thin crosshair), then click and drag to create an arrow. Release the mouse.

➤ Click the **3-D button** on the drawing toolbar and click **3-D Style 1** as shown in Figure 3.7i. Right click the arrow and click the **Format AutoShape** command to display the Format AutoShape dialog box. If necessary, click the **Colors and Lines tab.** Choose **Red** as the fill color. Click **OK,** then size the arrow as necessary.

➤ Select (click) the text box you created in the previous step, then click and drag the text box out of the way. Select (click) the 3-D arrow and position it next to the word processing column.

➤ Click and drag the text box into position on top of the arrow. If you do not see the text, right click the arrow, click the **Order command,** and click **Send to Back.** (This moves the arrow behind the text box.)

➤ Save the workbook, but do not print it at this time. Exit Excel if you do not want to continue with the next exercise at this time.

> ### FORMAT THE DATA SERIES
>
> Use the Format Data Series command to change the color, shape, or pattern of the columns within the chart. Right click any column to select the data series (be sure that all three columns are selected), then click Format Data Series to display the Format Data Series dialog box. Experiment with the various options, especially those on the Shapes and Patterns tabs within the dialog box. Click OK when you are satisfied with the changes. We warn you, it's addictive, so set a time limit in advance.

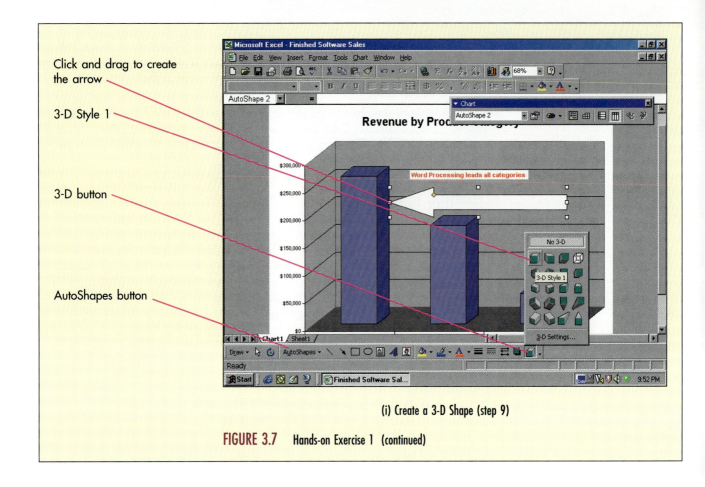

(i) Create a 3-D Shape (step 9)

FIGURE 3.7 Hands-on Exercise 1 (continued)

MULTIPLE DATA SERIES

The charts presented so far displayed only a single data series—for example, the total sales by location or the total sales by product category. Although such charts are useful, it is often necessary to view *multiple data series* on the same chart.

Figure 3.8a displays the sales in each location according to product category. We see how the products compare within each city, and further, that word processing is the leading application in three of the four cities. Figure 3.8b plots the identical data but in *stacked columns* rather than side-by-side.

The choice between the two types of charts depends on your message. If, for example, you want your audience to see the individual sales in each product category, the side-by-side columns are more appropriate. If, on the other hand, you want to emphasize the total sales for each city, the stacked columns are preferable. Note, too, the different scale on the Y axis in the two charts. The side-by-side columns in Figure 3.8a show the sales of each product category and so the Y axis goes only to $160,000. The stacked columns in Figure 3.8b, however, reflect the total sales for each city and thus the scale goes to $300,000.

The biggest difference is that the stacked column explicitly totals the sales for each city while the side-by-side column does not. The advantage of the stacked column is that the city totals are clearly shown and can be easily compared, and further the relative contributions of each product category within each city are apparent. The disadvantage is that the segments within each column do not start at the same point, making it difficult to determine the actual sales for the individual product categories or to compare the product categories among cities.

Realize, too, that for a stacked column chart to make sense, its numbers must be additive. This is true in Figure 3.8b, where the stacked columns consist of three

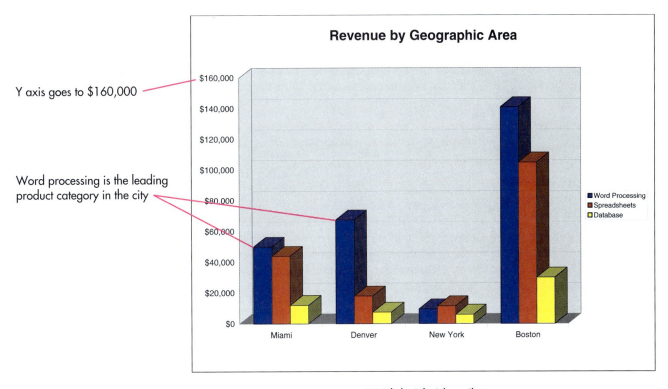

(a) Side-by-Side Column Chart

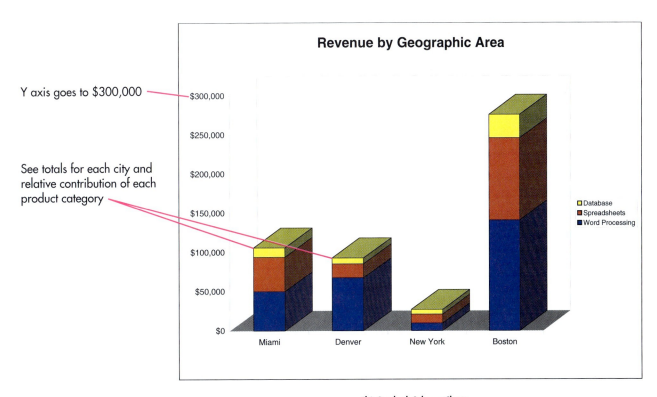

(b) Stacked Column Chart

FIGURE 3.8 Column Charts

CHAPTER 3: GRAPHS AND CHARTS

components, each of which is measured in dollars, and which can be logically added together to produce a total. You shouldn't, however, automatically convert a side-by-side column chart to its stacked column equivalent. It would not make sense, for example, to convert a column chart that plots unit sales and dollar sales side-by-side, into a stacked column chart that adds the two, because units and dollars represent different physical concepts and are not additive.

Rows versus Columns

Figure 3.9 illustrates a critical concept associated with multiple data series—whether the data series are in rows or columns. Figure 3.9a displays the worksheet with multiple data series selected. (Column A and Row 3 are included in the selection to provide the category labels and legend.) Figure 3.9b contains the chart when the data series are in rows (B4:E4, B5:E5, and B6:E6). Figure 3.9c displays the chart based on data series in columns (B4:B6, C4:C6, D4:D6, and E4:E6).

Both charts plot a total of twelve data points (three product categories for each of four locations), but they group the data differently. Figure 3.9b displays the data by city; that is, the sales of three product categories are shown for each of four cities. Figure 3.9c is the reverse and groups the data by product category; this time the sales in the four cities are shown for each of the three product categories. The choice between the two depends on your message and whether you want to emphasize revenue by city or by product category. The *legend,* an explanation of the data series, appears on the chart to distinguish the series from one another.

- If the data series are in rows (Figure 3.9b):
  - Use the first row (cells B3 through E3) in the selected range for the category labels on the X axis
  - Use the first column (cells A4 through A6) for the legend text
- If the data series are in columns (Figure 3.9c):
  - Use the first column (cells A4 through A6) in the selected range for the category labels on the X axis
  - Use the first row (cells B3 through E3) for the legend text

Stated another way, the data series in Figure 3.9b are in rows. Thus, there are three data series (B4:E4, B5:E5, and B6:E6), one for each product category. The first data series plots the word processing sales in Miami, Denver, New York, and Boston; the second series plots the spreadsheet sales for each city, and so on.

The data series in Figure 3.9c are in columns. This time there are four data series (B4:B6, C4:C6, D4:D6, and E4:E6), one for each city. The first series plots the Miami sales for word processing, spreadsheets, and database; the second series plots the Denver sales for each software category, and so on.

A3:E6 is selected

	A	B	C	D	E	F
1		Superior Software Sales				
2						
3		Miami	Denver	New York	Boston	Total
4	Word Processing	$50,000	$67,500	$9,500	$141,000	$268,000
5	Spreadsheets	$44,000	$18,000	$11,500	$105,000	$178,500
6	Database	$12,000	$7,500	$6,000	$30,000	$55,500
7	Total	$106,000	$93,000	$27,000	$276,000	$502,000

(a) The Worksheet

FIGURE 3.9 Multiple Data Series

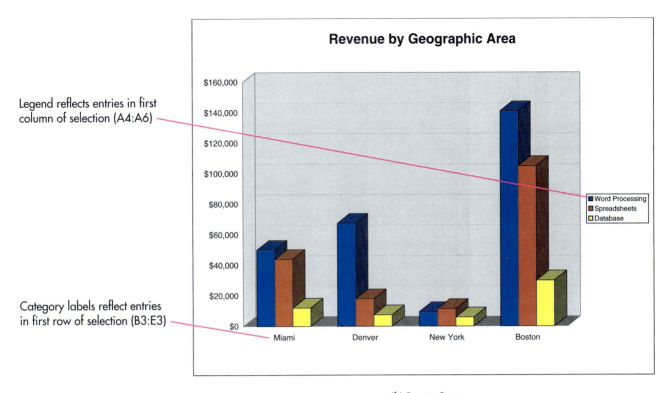

(b) Data in Rows

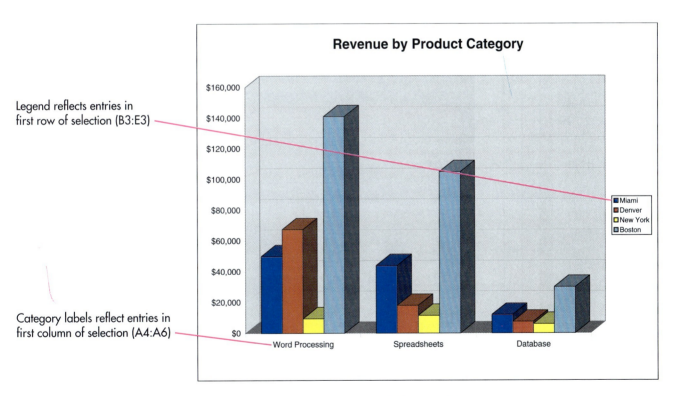

(c) Data in Columns

FIGURE 3.9 Multiple Data Series (continued)

CHAPTER 3: GRAPHS AND CHARTS

HANDS-ON EXERCISE 2

Multiple Data Series

Objective: To plot multiple data series in the same chart; to differentiate between data series in rows and columns; to create and save multiple charts associated with the same worksheet. Use Figure 3.10 as a guide in the exercise.

STEP 1: Rename the Worksheets

➤ Open the **Finished Software Sales** workbook from the previous exercise as shown in Figure 3.10a. The workbook contains an embedded chart and a separate chart sheet.

➤ Point to the workbook tab labeled **Sheet1,** click the **right mouse button** to display a shortcut menu, then click the **Rename** command. The name of the worksheet (Sheet1) is selected. Type **Sales Data** to change the name of the worksheet to the more descriptive name. Press the **enter key.**

➤ Point to the tab labeled **Chart1** (which contains the three-dimensional column chart created in the previous exercise). Click the **right mouse button** to display a shortcut menu, click **Rename,** then enter **Column Chart** as the name of the chart sheet. Press the **enter key.**

➤ Save the workbook.

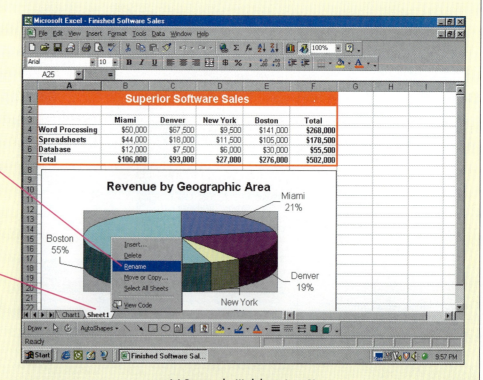

Click Rename

Point to Sheet1 tab and click right mouse button to display shortcut menu

(a) Rename the Worksheets (step 1)

FIGURE 3.10 Hands-on Exercise 2

STEP 2: The Office Assistant

➤ Click the **Sales Data tab,** then click and drag to select cells **A3 through E6.** Click the **Chart Wizard button** on the Standard toolbar to start the wizard and display the dialog box shown in Figure 3.10b.

➤ If necessary, click the **Office Assistant button** in the Chart Wizard dialog box to display the Office Assistant and the initial help screen. Click the option button for **Help with this feature.**

➤ The display for the Assistant changes to offer help about the various chart types available. (It's up to you whether you want to explore the advice at this time. You can close the Assistant, or leave it open and drag the title bar out of the way.)

➤ Select **Column** as the chart type and **Clustered column** with a 3-D visual effect as the subtype. Click **Next** to continue with the Chart Wizard.

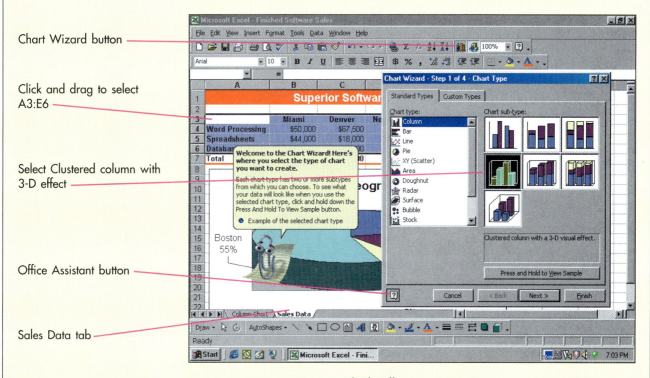

Chart Wizard button

Click and drag to select A3:E6

Select Clustered column with 3-D effect

Office Assistant button

Sales Data tab

(b) The Office Assistant (step 2)

FIGURE 3.10 Hands-on Exercise 2 (continued)

THE OFFICE ASSISTANT

The Office Assistant button is common to all Office applications and is an invaluable source of online help. You can activate the Assistant at any time by clicking its button on the Standard toolbar or from within a specialized dialog box. You can ask the Assistant a specific question and/or you can have the Assistant monitor your work and suggest tips as appropriate. You can tell that the Assistant has a suggestion when you see a lightbulb appear adjacent to the character.

STEP 3: View the Data Series

➤ You should see step 2 of the Chart Wizard as shown in Figure 3.10c. The help supplied by the Office Assistant changes automatically with the steps in the Chart Wizard.

➤ The data range should be specified as **Sales Data!$A$3:$E$6** as shown in Figure 3.10c. The option button for **Series in Rows** should be selected. To appreciate the concept of data series in rows (versus columns), click the **Series tab:**

- The series list box shows three data series (Word Processing, Spreadsheets, and Database) corresponding to the legends for the chart.
- The **Word Processing** series is selected by default. The legend in the sample chart shows that the data points in the series are plotted in blue. The values are taken from cells B4 through E4 in the Sales Data Worksheet.
- Click **Spreadsheets** in the series list box. The legend shows that the series is plotted in red. The values are taken from cells B5 through E5 in the Sales Data worksheet.
- Click **Database** in the series list box. The legend shows that the series is plotted in yellow. The values are taken from cells B6 through E6 in the Sales Data worksheet.

DEFAULT SELECTIONS

Excel makes a default determination as to whether the data is in rows or columns by assuming that you want fewer data series than categories. Thus, if the selected cells contain fewer rows than columns (or if the number of rows and columns are equal), it assumes the data series are in rows. If, on the other hand, there are fewer columns than rows, it will assume the data series are in columns.

STEP 4: Complete the Chart

➤ Click **Next** to continue creating the chart. You should see step 3 of the Chart Wizard. Click the **Titles tab.** Click the text box for Chart title. Type **Revenue by City.** Click **Next.**

➤ You should see step 4 of the Chart Wizard. Click the option button for **As new sheet.** Type **Revenue by City** in the associated text box to give the chart sheet a meaningful name. Click **Finish.**

➤ Excel creates the new chart in its own sheet named Revenue by City. Click **No** to tell the Assistant that you don't need further help. Right click the Assistant. Click **Hide.** Save the workbook.

THE F11 KEY

The F11 key is the fastest way to create a chart in its own sheet. Select the data, including the legends and category labels, then press the F11 key to create the chart according to the default format built into the Excel column chart. After the chart has been created, you can use the menu bar, Chart toolbar, or shortcut menus to choose a different chart type and/or customize the formatting.

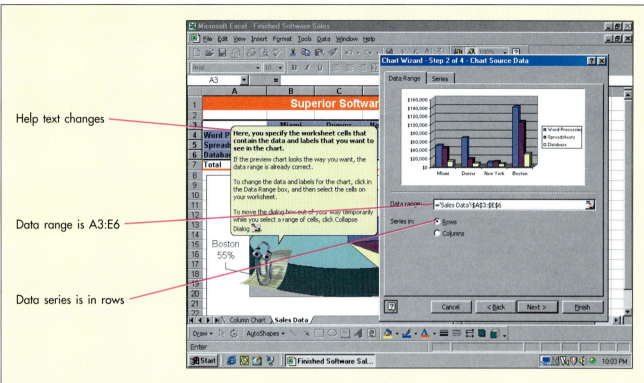

(c) View the Data Series (step 3)

FIGURE 3.10 Hands-on Exercise 2 (continued)

STEP 5: Copy the Chart

➤ Point to the tab named **Revenue by City.** Click the **right mouse button.** Click **Move or Copy** to display the dialog box in Figure 3.10d.

➤ Click **Sales Data** in the Before Sheet list box. Check the box to **Create a Copy.** Click **OK.**

➤ A duplicate worksheet called Revenue by City(2) is created and appears before (to the left of) the Sales Data worksheet.

➤ Rename the copied sheet **Revenue by Product.** Save the workbook.

MOVING AND COPYING A CHART SHEET

The fastest way to move or copy a chart sheet is to drag its tab. To move a sheet, point to its tab, then click and drag the tab to its new position. To copy a sheet, press and hold the Ctrl key as you drag the tab to the desired position for the second sheet. Rename the copied sheet (or any sheet for that matter) by double clicking its tab to select the existing name. Enter a new name for the worksheet, then press the enter key.

CHAPTER 3: GRAPHS AND CHARTS   113

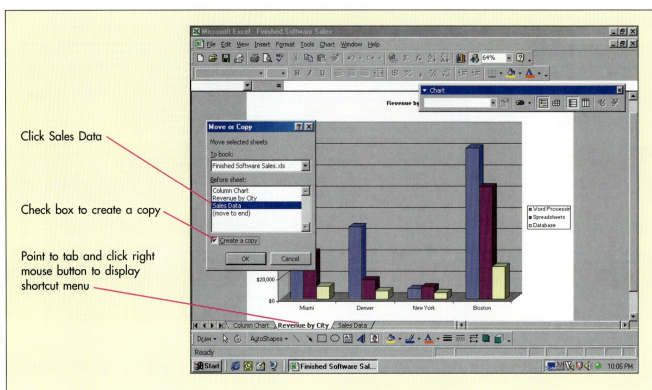

(d) Copy the Chart (step 5)

FIGURE 3.10 Hands-on Exercise 2 (continued)

STEP 6: Change the Source Data

➤ Click the **Revenue by Product tab** to make it the active sheet. Click anywhere in the title of the chart, drag the mouse over the word **City** to select the text, then type **Product Category** to replace the selected text. Click outside the title to deselect it.

➤ Pull down the **Chart menu.** If necessary, click the double arrow to see more commands, click **Source Data** (you will see the Sales Data worksheet), then click the **Columns option button** so that your screen matches Figure 3.10e. Click the **Series tab** and note the following:

- The current chart plots the data in rows. There are three data series (one series for each product).
- The new chart (shown in the dialog box) plots the data in columns. There are four data series (one for each city as indicated in the Series list box).

➤ Click **OK** to close the Source Data dialog box. Save the workbook.

THE HORIZONTAL SCROLL BAR

The horizontal scroll bar contains four scrolling buttons to scroll through the sheet tabs in a workbook. Click ◄ or ► to scroll one tab to the left or right. Click I◄ or ►I to scroll to the first or last tab in the workbook. Once the desired tab is visible, click the tab to select it.

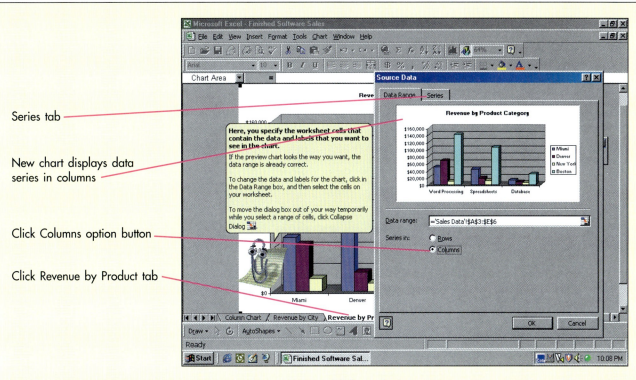

(e) Change the Source Data (step 6)

FIGURE 3.10 Hands-on Exercise 2 (continued)

STEP 7: Change the Chart Type

➤ Point to the chart area, click the **right mouse button** to display a shortcut menu, then click the **Chart Type** command to display the Chart Type dialog box.

➤ Select the **Stacked Column with a 3-D visual effect chart** (the middle entry in the second row). Click **OK.** The chart changes to a stacked column chart as shown in Figure 3.10f. Save the workbook.

➤ Pull down the File menu, click the **Print command,** then click the option button to print the **Entire Workbook.** Click **OK.**

➤ Submit the workbook to your instructor as proof that you completed the exercise. Close the workbook. Exit Excel if you do not want to continue with the next exercise at this time.

THE RIGHT MOUSE BUTTON

Point to a cell (or group of selected cells), a chart or worksheet tab, a toolbar, or chart (or a selected object on the chart), then click the right mouse button to display a shortcut menu. All shortcut menus are context-sensitive and display commands appropriate for the selected item. Right clicking a toolbar, for example, enables you to display (hide) additional toolbars. Right clicking a sheet tab enables you to rename, move, copy, or delete the sheet.

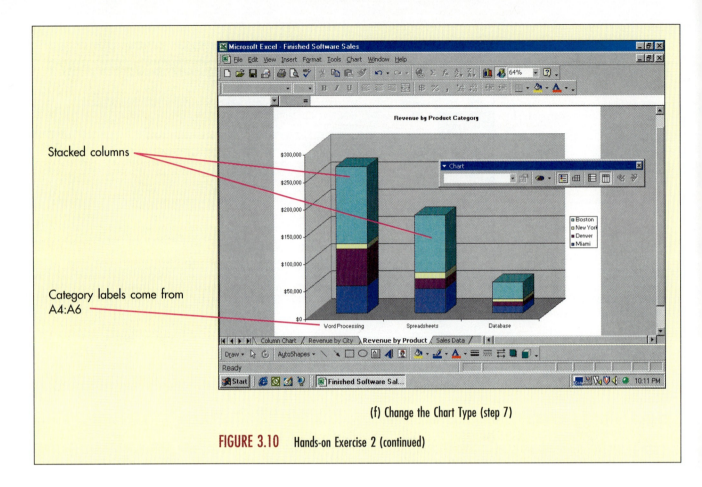

(f) Change the Chart Type (step 7)

FIGURE 3.10 Hands-on Exercise 2 (continued)

OBJECT LINKING AND EMBEDDING

One of the primary advantages of the Windows environment is the ability to create a *compound document* that contains data *(objects)* from multiple applications. The memo in Figure 3.11 is an example of a compound document. The memo was created in Microsoft Word, and it contains objects (a worksheet and a chart) that were developed in Microsoft Excel. *Object Linking and Embedding* (*OLE*, pronounced "oh-lay") is the means by which you create the compound document.

The essential difference between linking and embedding is whether the object is stored within the compound document *(embedding)* or in its own file *(linking)*. An *embedded object* is stored in the compound document, which in turn becomes the only client for that object. A *linked object* is stored in its own file, and the compound document is one of many potential clients for that object. The compound document does not contain the linked object per se, but only a representation of the object as well as a pointer (link) to the file containing the object. The advantage of linking is that any document that is linked to the object is updated automatically if the object is changed.

The choice between linking and embedding depends on how the object will be used. Linking is preferable if the object is likely to change and the compound document requires the latest version. Linking should also be used when the same object is in many documents, so that any change to the object has to be made in only one place. Embedding should be used if you need the actual object—for example, if you intend to edit the compound document on a different computer.

The following exercise uses linking to create a Word document containing an Excel worksheet and chart. As you do the exercise, both applications (Word and Excel) will be open, and it will be necessary to switch back and forth between the two. This in turn demonstrates the *multitasking* capability within Windows and the use of the Windows taskbar to switch between the open applications.

Superior Software
Miami, Florida

To: Mr. White
Chairman, Superior Software

From: Heather Bond
Vice President, Marketing

Subject: May Sales Data

The May sales data clearly indicate that Boston is outperforming our other geographic areas. It is my feeling that Ms. Brown, the office supervisor, is directly responsible for its success and that she should be rewarded accordingly. In addition, we may want to think about transferring her to New York, as they are in desperate need of new ideas and direction. I will be awaiting your response after you have time to digest the information presented.

Superior Software Sales					
	Miami	Denver	New York	Boston	Total
Word Processing	$50,000	$67,500	$9,500	$141,000	$268,000
Spreadsheets	$44,000	$18,000	$11,500	$105,000	$178,500
Database	$12,000	$7,500	$6,000	$30,000	$55,500
Total	$106,000	$93,000	$27,000	$276,000	$502,000

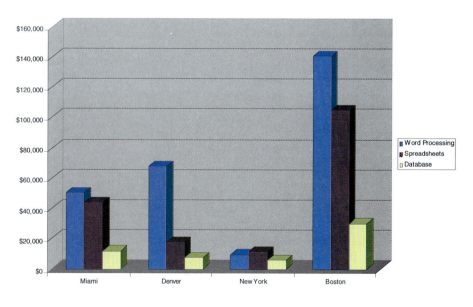

FIGURE 3.11 Object Linking and Embedding

HANDS-ON EXERCISE 3

Object Linking and Embedding

Objective: To create a compound document consisting of a memo, worksheet, and chart. Use Figure 3.12 as a guide in the exercise.

STEP 1: Open the Software Sales Document

➤ Click the **Start button** on the taskbar to display the Start menu. Click (or point to) the **Programs menu,** then click **Microsoft Word 2000** to start the program. Hide the Office Assistant if it appears.

➤ Word is now active, and the taskbar contains a button for Microsoft Word. It may (or may not) contain a button for Microsoft Excel, depending on whether or not you closed Excel at the end of the previous exercise.

➤ If necessary, click the **Maximize button** in the application window so that Word takes the entire desktop as shown in Figure 3.12a. (The Open dialog box is not yet visible.)

➤ Pull down the **File menu** and click **Open** (or click the **Open button** on the Standard toolbar).

- Click the **drop-down arrow** in the Look In list box. Click the appropriate drive, drive C or drive A, depending on the location of your data.
- Double click the **Exploring Excel folder** (we placed the Word memo in the Exploring Excel folder) to open the folder. Double click the **Software Memo** to open the document.
- Save the document as **Finished Software Memo.**

➤ Pull down the **View menu.** Click **Print Layout** to change to the Print Layout view. Pull down the **View menu.** Click **Zoom.** Click **Page Width.**

OBJECT LINKING AND EMBEDDING

Object Linking and Embedding (OLE) enables you to create a compound document containing objects (data) from multiple Windows applications. The two techniques, linking and embedding, can be implemented in different ways. Although OLE is one of the major benefits of working in the Windows environment, it would be impossible to illustrate all of the techniques in a single exercise. Accordingly, we have created the icon at the left to help you identify the many examples of object linking and embedding that appear throughout the *Exploring Windows* series.

STEP 2: Copy the Worksheet

➤ Open (or return to) the **Finished Software Sales workbook** from the previous exercise.

- If you did not close Microsoft Excel at the end of the previous exercise, you will see its button on the taskbar. Click the **Microsoft Excel button** to return to or open the Finished Software Sales workbook.
- If you closed Microsoft Excel, click the **Start button** to start Excel, then open the Finished Software Sales workbook.

➤ The taskbar should now contain a button for both Microsoft Word and Microsoft Excel. Click either button to move back and forth between the open applications. End by clicking the Microsoft Excel button so that you see the Finished Software Sales workbook.

➤ Click the tab for **Sales Data.** Click and drag to select **A1** through **F7** to select the entire worksheet as shown in Figure 3.12b.

➤ Point to the selected area and click the **right mouse button** to display the shortcut menu. Click **Copy.** A moving border appears around the entire worksheet, indicating that it has been copied to the clipboard.

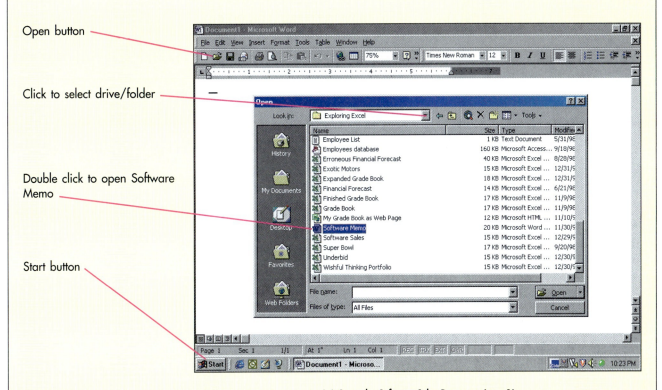

(a) Open the Software Sales Document (step 1)

FIGURE 3.12 Hands-on Exercise 3

THE WINDOWS TASKBAR

Multitasking, the ability to run multiple applications at the same time, is one of the primary advantages of the Windows environment. Each button on the taskbar appears automatically when its application or folder is opened, and disappears upon closing. (The buttons are resized automatically according to the number of open windows.) The taskbar can be moved to the left or right edge of the desktop, or to the top of the desktop, by dragging a blank area of the taskbar to the desired position.

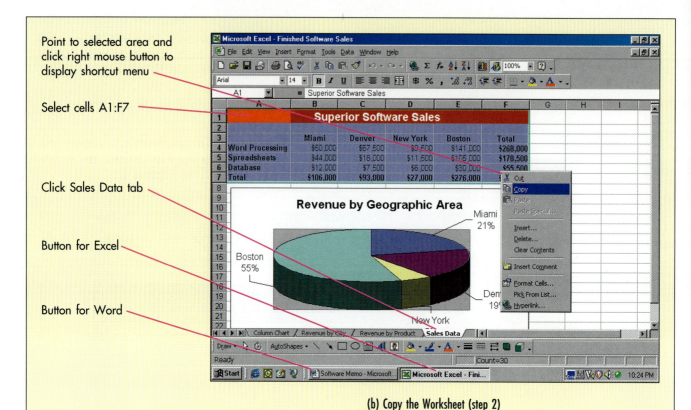

(b) Copy the Worksheet (step 2)

FIGURE 3.12 Hands-on Exercise 3 (continued)

STEP 3: Create the Link

➤ Click the **Microsoft Word button** on the taskbar to return to the memo as shown in Figure 3.12c. Press **Ctrl+End** to move to the end of the memo, which is where you will insert the Excel worksheet.

➤ Pull down the **Edit menu.** If necessary, click the double arrow to see more commands, then click **Paste Special** to display the dialog box in Figure 3.12c.

➤ Click **Microsoft Excel Worksheet Object** in the As list. Click the **Paste Link option button.** Click **OK** to insert the worksheet into the document.

➤ Click and drag the worksheet to center it between the margins. Save the memo.

THE COMMON USER INTERFACE

The common user interface provides a sense of familiarity from one Windows application to the next. Even if you have never used Microsoft Word, you will recognize many of the elements present in Excel. The applications share a common menu structure with consistent ways to execute commands from those menus. The Standard and Formatting toolbars are present in both applications. Many keyboard shortcuts are also common, such as Ctrl+Home and Ctrl+End to move to the beginning and end of a document.

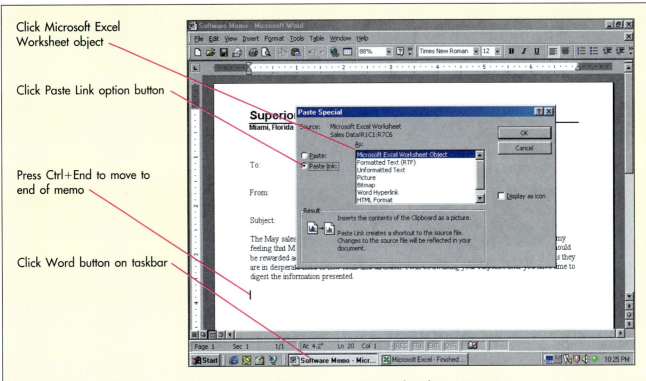

(c) Create the Link (step 3)

FIGURE 3.12 Hands-on Exercise 3 (continued)

STEP 4: Copy the Chart

➤ Click the **Microsoft Excel button** on the taskbar to return to the worksheet. Click outside the selected area (cells A1 through F7) to deselect the cells. Press **Esc** to remove the moving border.

➤ Click the **Revenue by City tab** to select the chart sheet. Point to the chart area, then click the left mouse button to select the chart. Be sure you have selected the entire chart and that you see the same sizing handles as in Figure 3.12d.

➤ Pull down the **Edit menu** and click **Copy** (or click the **Copy button** on the Standard toolbar). A moving border appears around the entire chart.

ALT+TAB STILL WORKS

Alt+Tab was a treasured shortcut in Windows 3.1 that enabled users to switch back and forth between open applications. The shortcut also works in Windows 95/98. Press and hold the Alt key while you press and release the Tab key repeatedly to cycle through the open applications, whose icons are displayed in a small rectangular window in the middle of the screen. Release the Alt key when you have selected the icon for the application you want.

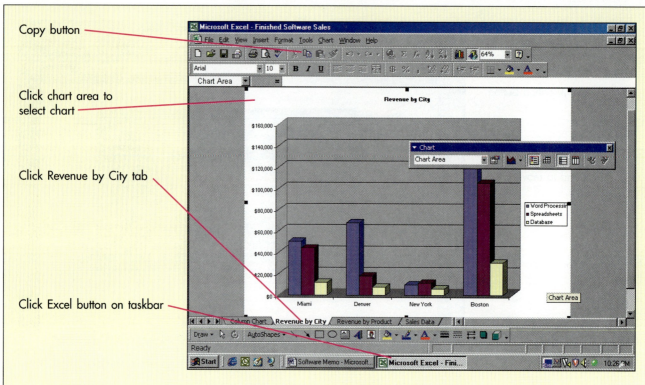

(d) Copy the Chart (step 4)

FIGURE 3.12 Hands-on Exercise 3 (continued)

STEP 5: Add the Chart

➤ Click the **Microsoft Word button** on the taskbar to return to the memo. If necessary, press **Ctrl+End** to move to the end of the Word document. Press the **enter key** to add a blank line.

➤ Pull down the **Edit menu.** Click **Paste Special.** Click the **Paste Link** option button. If necessary, click **Microsoft Excel Chart Object.** Click **OK** to insert the chart into the document.

➤ Zoom to **Whole Page** to facilitate moving and sizing the chart. You need to reduce its size so that it fits on the same page as the memo. Thus, scroll to the chart and click it to select it and display the sizing handles as shown in Figure 3.12e.

➤ Click and drag a corner sizing handle inward to make the chart smaller, then move it to the first page and center it on the page.

➤ Zoom to **Page Width.** Look carefully at the worksheet and chart in the document. The sales for Word Processing in New York are currently $9,500, and the chart reflects this amount. Save the memo.

➤ Point to the **Microsoft Excel button** on the taskbar and click the **right mouse button** to display a shortcut menu. Click **Close** to close Excel. Click **Yes** if prompted whether to save the changes to the Finished Software Sales workbook.

➤ Pull down the **File menu** and click the **Exit command.** The Microsoft Excel button disappears from the taskbar, indicating that Excel has been closed. Word is now the only open application.

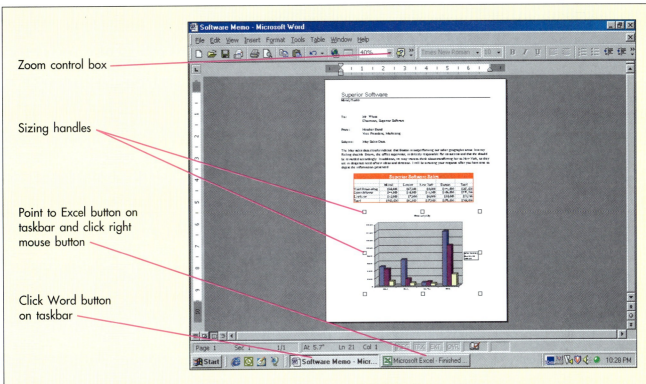

(e) Add the Chart (step 5)

FIGURE 3.12 Hands-on Exercise 3 (continued)

STEP 6: Modify the Worksheet

➤ Click anywhere in the worksheet to select the worksheet and display the sizing handles as shown in Figure 3.12f.

➤ The status bar indicates that you can double click to edit the worksheet. Double click anywhere within the worksheet to reopen Excel in order to change the data.

➤ The system pauses as it loads Excel and reopens the Finished Software Sales workbook. If necessary, click the **Maximize button** to maximize the Excel window. Hide the Office Assistant if it appears.

➤ If necessary, click the **Sales Data tab** within the workbook. Click in **cell D4.** Type **$200,000.** Press **enter.**

➤ Click the **I◄ button** to scroll to the first tab. Click the **Revenue by City tab** to select the chart sheet. The chart has been modified automatically and reflects the increased sales for New York.

LINKING VERSUS EMBEDDING

A linked object maintains its connection to the source file. An embedded object does not. Thus, a linked object can be placed in any number of destination files, each of which maintains a pointer (link) to the same source file. Any change to the object in the source file is reflected automatically in every destination file containing that object.

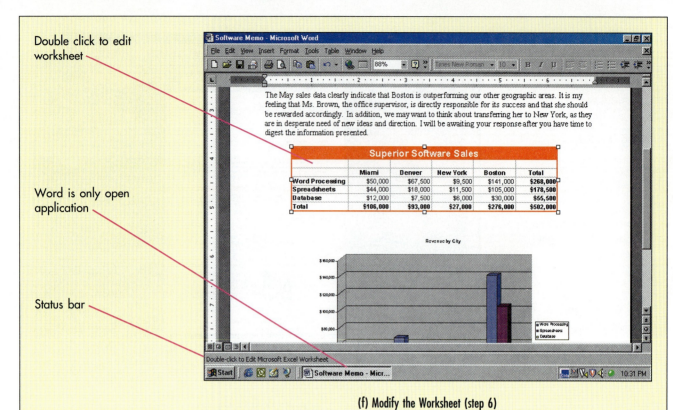

(f) Modify the Worksheet (step 6)

FIGURE 3.12 Hands-on Exercise 3 (continued)

STEP 7: Update the Links

➤ Click the **Microsoft Word button** on the taskbar to return to the Software memo. The links for the worksheet and chart should be updated automatically. If not:

- Pull down the **Edit menu.** Click **Links to** display the Links dialog box in Figure 3.12g.
- Select the link(s) to update. (You can press and hold the **Ctrl key** to select multiple links simultaneously.)
- Click the **Update Now button** to update the selected links.
- Close the Links dialog box.

➤ The worksheet and chart should both reflect $200,000 for word processing sales in New York. Save the Word document.

LINKING WORKSHEETS

A Word document can be linked to an Excel chart and/or worksheet; i.e., change the chart in Excel, and the Word document changes automatically. The chart itself is linked to the underlying worksheet; i.e, change the worksheet, and the chart changes. Worksheets can also be linked to one another; for example, a summary worksheet for the corporation as a whole can reflect data from detail worksheets for individual cities. See problem 4 at the end of the chapter.

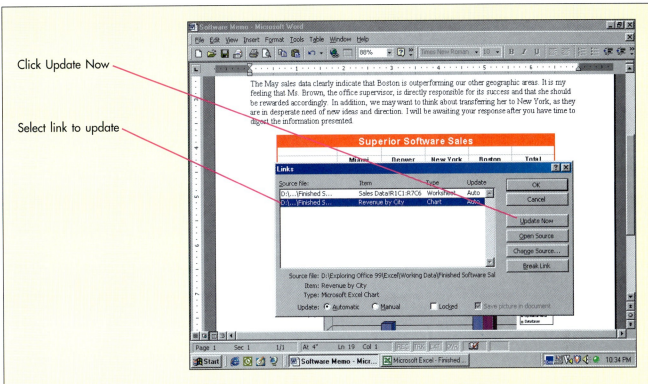

(g) Update the Links (step 7)

FIGURE 3.12 Hands-on Exercise 3 (continued)

STEP 8: The Finishing Touches

➤ Point to the chart, click the **right mouse button** to display a shortcut menu, then click the **Format Object command** to display the Format Object dialog box in Figure 3.12h.

➤ Click the **Colors and Lines Tab,** click the **drop-down arrow** in the Line Color box, then click **black** to display a line (border) around the worksheet. Click **OK.** Deselect the chart to see the border.

➤ Zoom to the **Whole Page** to view the completed document. Click and drag the worksheet and/or the chart within the memo to make any last minute changes. Save the memo a final time.

➤ Print the completed memo and submit it to your instructor. Exit Word. Exit Excel. Save the changes to the Finished Software Sales workbook.

➤ Congratulations on a job well done.

TO CLICK OR DOUBLE CLICK

Clicking an object selects the object after which you can move and/or size the object or change its properties. Double clicking an object starts the application that created the object and enables you to change underlying data. Any changes to the object in the source file (e.g., the worksheet) are automatically reflected in the object in the destination file (e.g., the Word document) provided the two are properly linked to one another.

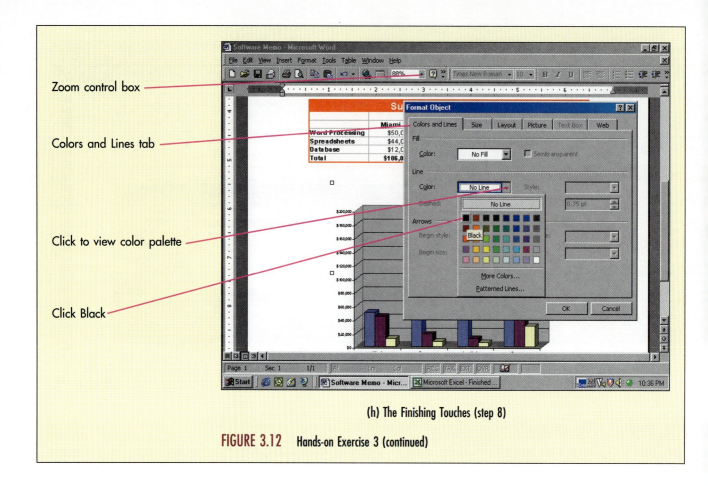

(h) The Finishing Touches (step 8)

FIGURE 3.12 Hands-on Exercise 3 (continued)

ADDITIONAL CHART TYPES

Excel offers a total of 14 standard *chart types,* each with several formats. The chart types are displayed in the Chart Wizard (see Figure 3.5b) and are listed here for convenience. The chart types are: Column, Bar, Line, Pie, XY (scatter), Area, Doughnut, Radar, Surface, Bubble, Stock, Cylinder, Cone, and Pyramid.

It is not possible to cover every type of chart, and so we concentrate on the most common. We have already presented the bar, column, and pie charts and continue with the line and combination charts. We use a different example, the worksheet in Figure 3.13a, which plots financial data for the National Widgets Corporation in Figures 3.13b and 3.13c. Both charts were created through the Chart Wizard, then modified as necessary using the techniques from the previous exercises.

	A	B	C	D	E	F
1		**National Widgets Financial Data**				
2						
3		*1992*	*1993*	*1994*	*1995*	*1996*
4	*Revenue*	$50,000,000	$60,000,000	$70,000,000	$80,000,000	$90,000,000
5	*Profit*	$10,000,000	$8,000,000	$6,000,000	$4,000,000	$2,000,000
6	*Stock Price*	$40	$35	$36	$31	$24

(a) The Worksheet

FIGURE 3.13 Additional Chart Types

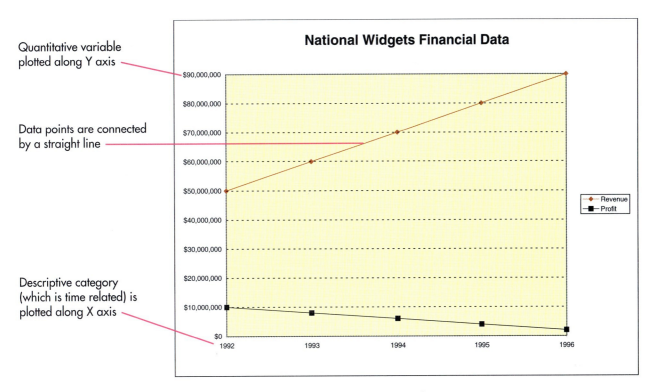

(b) Line Chart

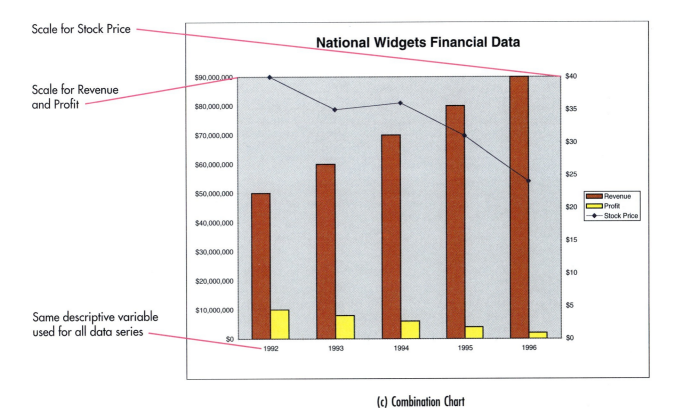

(c) Combination Chart

FIGURE 3.13 Additional Chart Types (continued)

CHAPTER 3: GRAPHS AND CHARTS

Line Chart

A *line chart* is best to display time-related information, such as the five-year trend of revenue and profit in Figure 3.13b. A line chart plots one or more data series (e.g., revenue and profit) against a descriptive category (e.g., year). As with a column chart, the quantitative values are plotted along the vertical scale (Y axis) and the descriptive category along the horizontal scale (X axis).

Combination Chart

A *combination chart* uses two or more chart types to display different kinds of information or when different scales are required for multiple data series. The chart in Figure 3.13c plots revenue, profit, and stock price over the five-year period. The same scale can be used for revenue and profit (both are in millions of dollars), but an entirely different scale is needed for the stock price. Investors in National Widgets can see at a glance the true status of their company.

USE AND ABUSE OF CHARTS

The hands-on exercises in the chapter demonstrate how easily numbers in a worksheet can be converted to their graphic equivalent. *The numbers can, however, just as easily be converted into erroneous or misleading charts, a fact that is often overlooked.* Indeed, some individuals are so delighted just to obtain the charts, that they accept the data without question. Accordingly, we present two examples of statistically accurate yet entirely misleading graphical data, drawn from charts submitted by our students in response to homework assignments.

> Lying graphics cheapen the graphical art everywhere ... When a chart on television lies, it lies millions of times over; when a *New York Times* chart lies, it lies 900,000 times over to a great many important and influential readers. The lies are told about the major issues of public policy—the government budget, medical care, prices, and fuel economy standards, for example. The lies are systematic and quite predictable, nearly always exaggerating the rate of recent change.
>
> **Edward Tufte**

Improper (Omitted) Labels

The difference between *unit sales* and *dollar sales* is a concept of great importance, yet one that is often missed. Consider, for example, the two pie charts in Figures 3.14a and 3.14b, both of which are intended to identify the leading salesperson, based on the underlying worksheet in Figure 3.14c. The charts yield two different answers, Jones and Smith, respectively, depending on which chart you use.

As you can see, the two charts reflect different percentages and would appear therefore to contradict each other. Both charts, however, are technically correct, as the percentages depend on whether they express unit sales or dollar sales. *Jones is the leader in terms of units, whereas Smith is the leader in terms of dollars.* The latter is generally more significant, and hence the measure that is probably most important to the reader. Neither chart, however, was properly labeled (there is no indication of whether units or dollars are plotted), which in turn may lead to erroneous conclusions on the part of the reader.

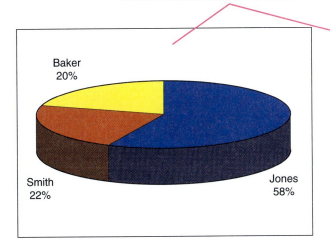
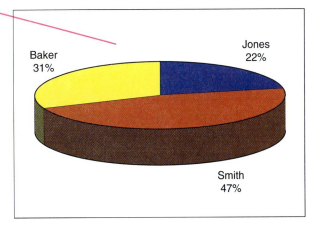

(a) Units (b) Dollars

Sales Data - First Quarter							
		Jones		Smith		Baker	
	Price	Units	Dollars	Units	Dollars	Units	Dollars
Product 1	$1	200	$200	20	$20	30	$30
Product 2	$5	50	$250	30	$150	30	$150
Product 3	$20	5	$100	50	$1,000	30	$600
	Totals	255	$550	100	$1,170	90	$780

(c) Underlying Spreadsheet

FIGURE 3.14 Omitted Labels

Good practice demands that every chart have a title and that as much information be included on the chart as possible to help the reader interpret the data. Use titles for the X axis and Y axis if necessary. Add text boxes for additional explanation.

Adding Dissimilar Quantities

The conversion of a side-by-side column chart to a stacked column chart is a simple matter, requiring only a few mouse clicks. Because the procedure is so easy, however, it can be done without thought, and in situations where the stacked column chart is inappropriate.

Figures 3.15a and 3.15b display a side-by-side and a stacked column chart, respectively. One chart is appropriate and one chart is not. The side-by-side columns in Figure 3.15a indicate increasing sales in conjunction with decreasing profits. This is a realistic portrayal of the company, which is becoming less efficient because profits are decreasing as sales are increasing.

The stacked column chart in Figure 3.15b plots the identical numbers. It is deceptive, however, as it implies an optimistic trend whose stacked columns reflect a nonsensical addition. The problem is that although sales and profits are both measured in dollars, they should not be added together because the sum does not represent a meaningful concept.

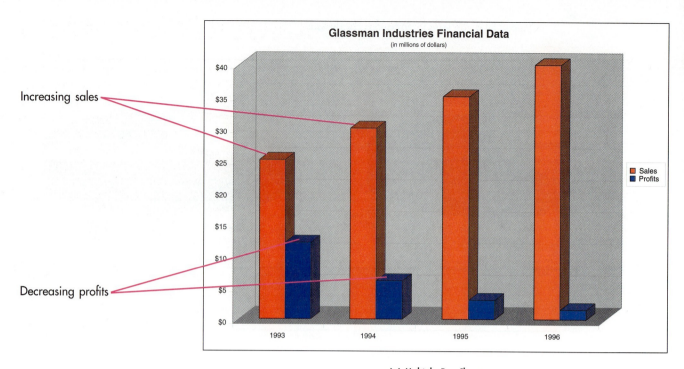

(a) Multiple Bar Chart

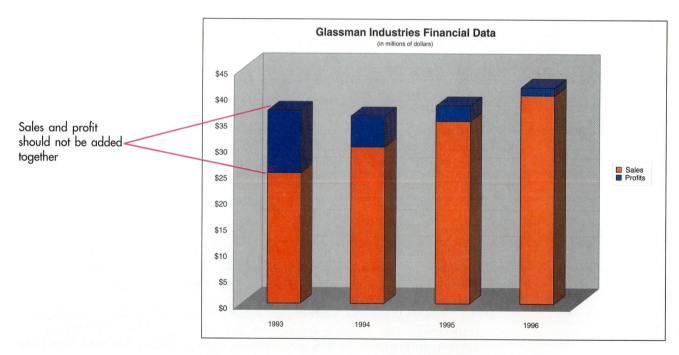

(b) Stacked Bar Chart

FIGURE 3.15 Adding Dissimilar Quantities

SUMMARY

A chart is a graphic representation of data in a worksheet. The type of chart chosen depends on the message to be conveyed. A pie chart is best for proportional relationships. A column or bar chart is used to show actual numbers rather than percentages. A line chart is preferable for time-related data. A combination chart uses two or more chart types when different scales are required for different data series.

The Chart Wizard is an easy way to create a chart. Once created, a chart can be enhanced with arrows and text boxes found on the Drawing toolbar.

A chart may be embedded in a worksheet or created in a separate chart sheet. An embedded chart may be moved within a worksheet by selecting it and dragging it to its new location. An embedded chart may be sized by selecting it and dragging any of the sizing handles in the desired direction.

Multiple data series may be specified in either rows or columns. If the data is in rows, the first row is assumed to contain the category labels, and the first column is assumed to contain the legend. Conversely, if the data is in columns, the first column is assumed to contain the category labels, and the first row the legend. The Chart Wizard makes it easy to switch from rows to columns and vice versa.

Object Linking and Embedding enables the creation of a compound document containing data (objects) from multiple applications. The essential difference between linking and embedding is whether the object is stored within the compound document (embedding) or in its own file (linking). An embedded object is stored in the compound document, which in turn becomes the only user (client) of that object. A linked object is stored in its own file, and the compound document is one of many potential clients of that object.

It is important that charts are created accurately and that they do not mislead the reader. The difference between dollar sales and unit sales is an important concept, which should be clearly indicated. Stacked column charts should not add dissimilar quantities.

KEY WORDS AND CONCEPTS

Bar chart
Category label
Chart
Chart sheet
Chart toolbar
Chart type
Chart Wizard
Column chart
Combination chart
Common user interface
Compound document
Data point
Data series
Default chart

Docked toolbar
Drawing toolbar
Embedded chart
Embedded object
Embedding
Exploded pie chart
Floating toolbar
Legend
Line chart
Linked object
Linking
Multiple data series
Multitasking
Object

Object Linking and
  Embedding (OLE)
Pie chart
Sizing handles
Stacked columns
Taskbar
Three-dimensional
  column chart
Three-dimensional pie
  chart
X axis
Y axis

MULTIPLE CHOICE

1. Which type of chart is best to portray proportion or market share?
   (a) Pie chart
   (b) Line
   (c) Column chart
   (d) Combination chart

2. Which of the following is a true statement about the Chart Wizard?
   (a) It is accessed via a button on the Standard toolbar
   (b) It enables you to choose the type of chart you want as well as specify the location for that chart
   (c) It enables you to retrace your steps via the Back command button
   (d) All of the above

3. Which of the following chart types is *not* suitable to display multiple data series?
   (a) Pie chart
   (b) Horizontal bar chart
   (c) Column chart
   (d) All of the above are equally suitable

4. Which of the following is best to display additive information from multiple data series?
   (a) A column chart with the data series stacked one on top of another
   (b) A column chart with the data series side by side
   (c) Both (a) and (b) are equally appropriate
   (d) Neither (a) nor (b) is appropriate

5. A workbook must contain:
   (a) A separate chart sheet for every worksheet
   (b) A separate worksheet for every chart sheet
   (c) Both (a) and (b)
   (d) Neither (a) nor (b)

6. Which of the following is true regarding an embedded chart?
   (a) It can be moved elsewhere within the worksheet
   (b) It can be made larger or smaller
   (c) Both (a) and (b)
   (d) Neither (a) nor (b)

7. Which of the following will produce a shortcut menu?
   (a) Pointing to a workbook tab and clicking the right mouse button
   (b) Pointing to an embedded chart and clicking the right mouse button
   (c) Pointing to a selected cell range and clicking the right mouse button
   (d) All of the above

8. Which of the following is done *prior* to invoking the Chart Wizard?
   (a) The data series are selected
   (b) The location of the embedded chart within the worksheet is specified
   (c) Both (a) and (b)
   (d) Neither (a) nor (b)

9. Which of the following will display sizing handles when selected?
   (a) An embedded chart
   (b) The title of a chart
   (c) A text box or arrow
   (d) All of the above

10. How do you switch between open applications?
    (a) Click the appropriate button on the taskbar
    (b) Use Alt+Tab to cycle through the applications
    (c) Both (a) and (b)
    (d) Neither (a) nor (b)

11. Which of the following is true regarding the compound document (the memo containing the worksheet and chart) that was created in the chapter?
    (a) The compound document contains more than one object
    (b) Excel is the server application and Word for Windows is the client application
    (c) Both (a) and (b)
    (d) Neither (a) nor (b)

12. In order to represent multiple data series on the same chart:
    (a) The data series must be in rows and the rows must be adjacent to one another on the worksheet
    (b) The data series must be in columns and the columns must be adjacent to one another on the worksheet
    (c) The data series may be in rows or columns so long as they are adjacent to one another
    (d) The data series may be in rows or columns with no requirement to be next to one another

13. If multiple data series are selected and rows are specified:
    (a) The first row will be used for the category (X axis) labels
    (b) The first column will be used for the legend
    (c) Both (a) and (b)
    (d) Neither (a) nor (b)

14. If multiple data series are selected and columns are specified:
    (a) The first column will be used for the category (X axis) labels
    (b) The first row will be used for the legend
    (c) Both (a) and (b)
    (d) Neither (a) nor (b)

15. Which of the following is true about the scale on the Y axis in a column chart that plots multiple data series side-by-side versus one that stacks the values one on top of another?
    (a) The scale for the stacked columns will contain larger values than if the columns are plotted side-by-side
    (b) The scale for the side-by-side columns will contain larger values than if the columns are stacked
    (c) The values on the scale will be the same regardless of whether the columns are stacked or side-by-side
    (d) The values on the scale will be different but it is not possible to tell which chart will contain the higher values

ANSWERS

1. a	6. c	11. c
2. d	7. d	12. d
3. a	8. a	13. c
4. a	9. d	14. c
5. d	10. c	15. a

PRACTICE WITH EXCEL 2000

1. **Michael Moldof Boutique:** A partially completed version of the worksheet in Figure 3.16 is available in the Exploring Excel folder as *Brief Chapter 3 Practice 1*. Open the workbook and save it as *Brief Chapter 3 Practice 1 Solution*. Follow the directions in steps (a) and (b) to compute the totals and format the worksheet, then create each of the charts listed below.

    a. Use the AutoSum command to enter the formulas to compute the totals for each store and each product.

    b. Select the whole worksheet. Use the AutoFormat command as the basis of a design for the worksheet. You do not have to accept the entire design and/or you can modify the design after it has been applied to the worksheet. For example, you may want to add currency formatting and change the column widths.

    c. A pie chart showing the percentage of total sales attributed to each store.

    d. A column chart showing the total sales for each store.

    e. A stacked column chart showing total sales for each store, broken down by clothing category.

    f. A stacked column chart showing total dollars for each clothing category, broken down by store.

    g. Create each chart in its own chart sheet. Rename the various chart sheets to reflect the charts they contain.

    h. Title each chart appropriately and enhance each chart as you see fit.

    i. Print the entire workbook (the worksheet and all four chart sheets).

    j. Add a title page with your name and date, then submit the completed assignment to your instructor.

	A	B	C	D	E	F
1			Michael Moldof Men's Boutique			
2			January Sales			
3						
4		Store 1	Store 2	Store 3	Store 4	Total
5	Slacks	$ 25,000	$ 28,750	$ 21,500	$ 9,400	$ 84,650
6	Shirts	$ 43,000	$ 49,450	$ 36,900	$ 46,000	$ 175,350
7	Underwear	$ 18,000	$ 20,700	$ 15,500	$ 21,000	$ 75,200
8	Accessories	$ 7,000	$ 8,050	$ 8,000	$ 4,000	$ 27,050
9						
10	Total	$ 93,000	$ 106,950	$ 81,900	$ 80,400	$ 362,250

FIGURE 3.16   Michael Moldof Boutique (Exercise 1)

2. **Unique Boutiques:** The worksheet in Figure 3.17 is to be used by the corporate marketing manager in a presentation in which she describes sales over the past four years. The worksheet is in the *Brief Chapter 3 Practice 2* workbook. Do the following:
   a. Format the worksheet attractively so that it can be used as part of the presentation. Include your name somewhere in the worksheet.
   b. Create any chart(s) you think appropriate to emphasize the successful performance enjoyed by the London office.
   c. Use the same data and chart type(s) as in part (a) but modify the title to emphasize the disappointing performance of the Paris office.
   d. Print the worksheet together with all charts and submit them to your instructor. Be sure to title all charts appropriately and to use the text and arrow tools to add the required emphasis.

	A	B	C	D	E	F
1	Unique Boutiques					
2	Sales for 1995-1998					
3						
4	Store	1995	1996	1997	1998	Totals
5	Miami	1500000	2750000	3000000	3250000	10500000
6	London	4300000	5500000	6700000	13000000	29500000
7	Paris	2200000	1800000	1400000	1000000	6400000
8	Rome	2000000	3000000	4000000	5000000	14000000
9	Totals	10000000	13050000	15100000	22250000	60400000

FIGURE 3.17 Unique Boutiques (Exercise 2)

3. **Hotel Capacities:** The worksheet in Figure 3.18 is to be used as the basis for several charts depicting information on hotel capacities. Each of the charts is to be created in its own chart sheet within the *Brief Chapter 3 Practice 3* workbook on the data disk. We describe the message we want to convey, but it is up to you to determine the appropriate chart and associated data range(s). Accordingly, you are to create a chart that:
   a. Compares the total capacity of the individual hotels to one another.
   b. Shows the percent of total capacity for each hotel.
   c. Compares the number of standard and deluxe rooms for all hotels, with the number of standard and deluxe rooms side-by-side for each hotel.
   d. Compares the standard and deluxe room rates for all hotels, with the two different rates side-by-side for each hotel.
   e. Add your name to the worksheet as the Hotel Manager, then print the complete workbook, which will consist of the original worksheet plus the four chart sheets you created.

	A	B	C	D	E	F
1		**Hotel Capacities and Room Rates**				
2						
3	Hotel	No. of Standard Rooms	Standard Rate	No. of Deluxe Rooms	Deluxe Rate	Total Number of Rooms
4	Holiday Inn	300	100	100	150	400
5	Hyatt	225	120	50	175	275
6	Ramada Inn	150	115	35	190	185
7	Sheraton	175	95	25	150	200
8	Marriott	325	100	100	175	425
9	Hilton	250	80	45	120	295
10	Best Western	150	75	25	125	175
11	Days Inn	100	50	15	100	115

FIGURE 3.18 Hotel Capacities (Exercise 3)

4. **Linking Worksheets:** This chapter described how a chart is linked to the data in an underlying worksheet. It is also possible to link the data from one worksheet to another as can be seen in Figure 3.19. The figure contains a table, which at first glance is very similar to the example that was used throughout the chapter. Look closely, however, and you will see that the workbook contains four worksheets, for the corporation as a whole, as well as for Phoenix, Minneapolis, and Los Angeles.

   The numbers in the corporate worksheet are linked to the numbers in the worksheets for the individual cities. The entry in cell B4 of the Corporate worksheet contains the formula =Phoenix!F2 to indicate that the entry comes from cell F2 in the Phoenix worksheet. Other cells in the table reference other cells in the Phoenix worksheet as well as cells in the other worksheets.

   a. Open the *Brief Chapter 3 Practice 4* workbook. Check that you are viewing the Corporate worksheet, then click in cell B4 of this worksheet. Type an = sign, click the Phoenix worksheet tab, click in cell F2 of this worksheet, and press the enter key. Click in cell C4, type an = sign, click the Minneapolis worksheet tab, click in cell F2 of that worksheet and press enter. Repeat this process to enter the sales for Los Angeles.

   b. Click and drag cells B4 through D4, then drag the fill handle to row 6 to copy the formulas for the other products. The operation works because the worksheet references are absolute, but the cell references are relative.

   c. Use the AutoSum button to compute the totals for the corporation as a whole as shown in the figure.

   d. Use the completed worksheet in Figure 3.19 as the basis of a side-by-side column chart with the data plotted in rows. Plot a second side-by-side chart with the data in columns. Put each chart in a separate chart sheet.

   e. Print the entire workbook for your instructor.

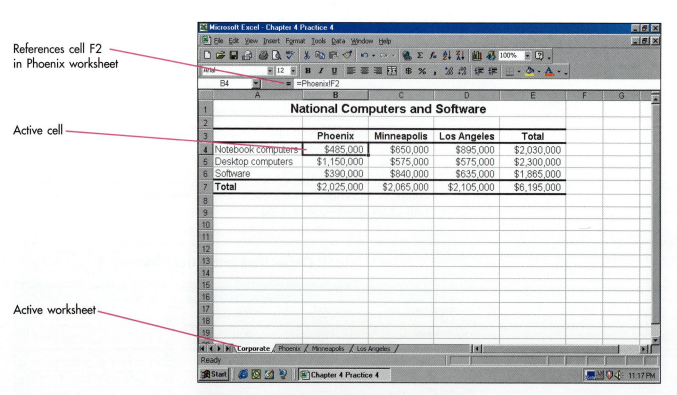

FIGURE 3.19 Linking Worksheets (Exercise 4)

5. Ralph Cordell Sporting Goods: A partially completed version of the worksheet in Figure 3.19 can be found on the data disk in the file *Brief Chapter 3 Practice 5*. Open the workbook and make all necessary entries so that your worksheet matches the one in Figure 3.20. Next, create a memo to your instructor containing the worksheet and a chart that plots the sales data in columns to emphasize the contribution of each salesperson. Use any wording you think is appropriate for the memo. Print the completed memo, add your name, and submit it to your instructor as proof you did this exercise.

	A	B	C	D	E	F
1		Ralph Cordell Sporting Goods				
2		Quarterly Sales Report				
3						
4	Salesperson	1st Qtr	2nd Qtr	3rd Qtr	4th Qtr	Total
5	Powell	$50,000	$55,000	$62,500	$85,400	$252,900
6	Blaney	$34,000	$48,500	$62,000	$62,000	$206,500
7	Rego	$49,000	$44,000	$42,500	$41,000	$176,500
8	Total	$133,000	$147,500	$167,000	$188,400	$635,900

FIGURE 3.20 Ralph Cordell Sporting Goods (Exercise 5)

6. **Object Linking and Embedding:** The compound document in Figure 3.21 contains a memo and combination chart. (The worksheet is contained in the *Brief Chapter 3 Practice 6* workbook. The text of the memo is in the *Brief Chapter 3 Practice 6 Memo,* which exists as a Word document in the Exploring Excel folder on the data disk.) You are to complete the compound document and submit it to your instructor by completing the following steps:
   a. Create a letterhead for the memo containing your name, address, phone number, and any other information you deem appropriate.
   b. Create the combination chart that appears in the memo. Select the data for the Chart Wizard in the usual fashion. You must specify the custom chart type (Line–Column on 2 Axis) as opposed to a standard line or column chart. (Click the Custom Types tab in step 1 of the Chart Wizard.)
   c. Link the chart to the memo.
   d. Print the compound document and submit it to your instructor.

7. **Object Linking and Embedding:** Create the document in Figure 3.22 based on the partially completed worksheet in *Brief Chapter 3 Practice 7*. You need to enter the text of the memo yourself, and in addition, create an interesting letterhead using Microsoft WordArt. You need not duplicate our letterhead exactly. This exercise gives you the opportunity to practice a variety of skills.

CASE STUDIES

University Enrollments

Your assistantship has placed you in the Provost's office, where you are to help create a presentation for the Board of Trustees. The Provost is expected to make recommendations to the Board regarding the expansion of some programs and the reduction of others. You are expected to help the Provost by developing a series of charts to illustrate enrollment trends. The Provost has created the *Student Enrollments workbook* on the data disk, which contains summary data.

Steven Stocks

100 Century Tower • New York, NY 10021 • (212) 333-3333

To: Carlos Rosell

From: Steven Stocks

Subject: Status Report on National Widgets

I have uncovered some information that I feel is important to the overall health of your investment portfolio. The graph below clearly shows that while revenues for National Widgets have steadily increased since 1996, profits have steadily decreased. In addition, the stock price is continuing to decline. Although at one time I felt that a turnaround was imminent, I am no longer so optimistic and am advising you to cut your losses and sell your National Widgets stock as soon as possible.

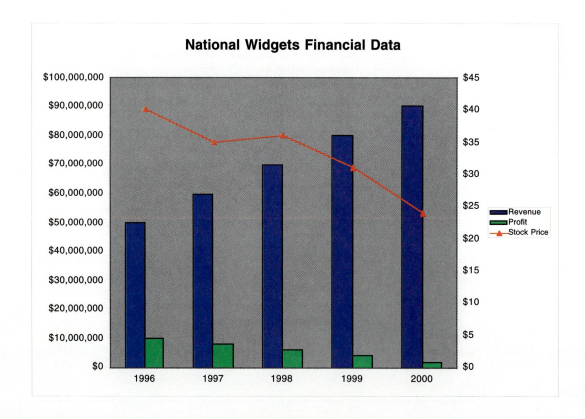

FIGURE 3.21   Compound Document for Practice (Exercise 6)

Office of Residential Living

University of Miami ∞ P.O. Box 248904 ∞ Coral Gables, FL 33124

January 10, 2000

Mr. Jeffrey Redmond, President
Dynamic Dining Services
4329 Palmetto Lane
Miami, FL 33157

Dear Jeff,

As per our conversation, occupancy is projected to be back up from last year. I have enclosed a spreadsheet and chart that show the total enrollment for the past four school years. Please realize, however, that the 1999-2000 figures are projections, as the Spring 2000 numbers are still incomplete. The final 1999-2000 numbers should be confirmed within the next two weeks. I hope that this helps with your planning. If you need further information, please contact me at the above address.

Dorm Occupancy				
	96-97	97-98	98-99	99-00
Beatty	330	285	270	250
Broward	620	580	620	565
Graham	450	397	352	420
Rawlings	435	470	295	372
Tolbert	550	554	524	635
Totals	2385	2286	2061	2242

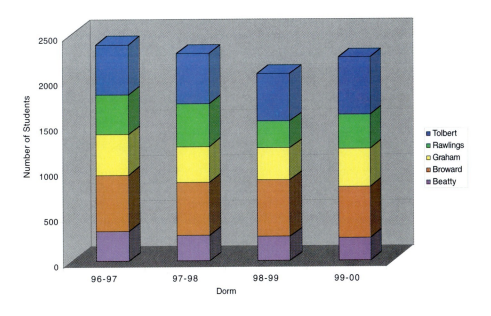

FIGURE 3.22 Compound Document for Practice (Exercise 7)

The Federal Budget

The National debt is staggering—in excess of $5 trillion, more than $1 trillion of which has been added under President Clinton. The per capita share is almost $20,000 for every man, woman, and child in the United States. The annual budget is approximately $1.5 trillion, with the deficit in the neighborhood of $150 billion. Medicare, defense, and interest on the debt itself are the largest expenditures and consume approximately 35%, 24%, and 14%, respectively. Personal income taxes and Social Security (including Medicare) taxes account for approximately 36% and 31% of the government's income.

Use the Internet to obtain exact figures for the current year, then create the appropriate charts to reflect the government's distribution of income and expenditures. Do some additional research and obtain data on the budget, the deficit, and the national debt for the years 1945, 1967, and 1980. The numbers may surprise you. For example, how does the interest expense for the current year compare to the total budget in 1967 (at the height of the Viet Nam War)? To the total budget in 1945 (at the end of World War II)?

The Annual Report

Corporate America spends a small fortune to produce its annual reports, which are readily available to the public at large. Choose any company and obtain a copy of its most recent annual report. Consolidate the information in the company's report to produce a two-page document of your own. Your report should include a description of the company's progress in the last year, a worksheet with any data you deem relevant, and at least two charts in support of the worksheet or written material. Use Microsoft Word in addition to the worksheet to present the information in an attractive manner.

Computer Mapping

Your boss has asked you to look into computer mapping in an effort to better analyze sales data for your organization. She suggested you use the online help facility to explore the Data Map feature within Excel, which enables you to create color-coded maps from columns of numerical data. You mentioned this assignment to a colleague who suggested that you open the *Mapstats workbook* that is installed with Excel to see the sample maps and demographic data included with Excel. You have two days to learn the potential for computer mapping. Your boss expects at least a three-page written report with real examples.

The Census Bureau

Use your favorite search engine to locate the home page of the United States Census Bureau, then download one or more series of population statistics of interest to you. Use the data to plot one or more charts that describe the population growth of the United States. There is an abundance of information available and you are free to choose any statistics you deem relevant.

chapter 1

INTRODUCTION TO MICROSOFT ACCESS: WHAT IS A DATABASE?

OBJECTIVES

After reading this chapter you will be able to:

1. Define the terms field, record, table, and database.
2. Start Microsoft Access; describe the Database window and the objects in an Access database.
3. Add, edit, and delete records within a table; use the Find command to locate a specific record.
4. Describe the record selector; explain when changes are saved to a table.
5. Explain the importance of data validation in table maintenance.
6. Apply a filter (by form or by selection) to a table; sort a table on one or more fields.
7. Describe a relational database; identify the one-to-many relationships that exist within a database.

OVERVIEW

All businesses and organizations maintain data of one kind or another. Companies store data about their employees. Schools and universities store data about their students and faculties. Magazines and newspapers store data about their subscribers. The list goes on and on, and while each of these examples refers to different types of data, they all operate under the same basic principles of database management.

The chapter introduces you to Microsoft Access, the application in the Microsoft Office suite that performs database management. We describe the objects in an Access database and show you how to add, edit, and delete records to a table. We explain how to obtain information from the database by running reports and queries that have been previously created. We discuss how to display selected records through a filter and how to display those records in different sequences. And finally, we provide a look ahead, by showing how the real power of Access is derived from a relational database that contains multiple tables.

The hands-on exercises in the chapter enable you to apply all of the material at the computer, and are indispensable to the learn-by-doing philosophy we follow throughout the text. As you do the exercises, you may recognize many commands from other Windows applications, all of which share a common user interface and consistent command structure.

CASE STUDY: THE COLLEGE BOOKSTORE

Imagine, if you will, that you are the manager of a college bookstore and that you maintain data for every book in the store. Accordingly, you have recorded the specifics of each book (the title, author, publisher, price, and so on) in a manila folder, and have stored the folders in one drawer of a file cabinet.

One of your major responsibilities is to order books at the beginning of each semester, which in turn requires you to contact the various publishers. You have found it convenient, therefore, to create a second set of folders with data about each publisher such as the publisher's phone number, address, discount policy, and so on. You also found it necessary to create a third set of folders with data about each order such as when the order was placed, the status of the order, which books were ordered, how many copies, and so on.

Normal business operations will require you to make repeated trips to the filing cabinet to maintain the accuracy of the data and keep it up to date. You will have to create a new folder whenever a new book is received, whenever you contract with a new publisher, or whenever you place a new order. Each of these folders must be placed in the proper drawer in the filing cabinet. In similar fashion, you will have to modify the data in an existing folder to reflect changes that occur, such as an increase in the price of a book, a change in a publisher's address, or an update in the status of an order. And, lastly, you will need to remove the folder of any book that is no longer carried by the bookstore, or of any publisher with whom you no longer have contact, or of any order that was canceled.

The preceding discussion describes the bookstore of 40 years ago—before the advent of computers and computerized databases. The bookstore manager of today needs the same information as his or her predecessor. Today's manager, however, has the information readily available, at the touch of a key or the click of a mouse, through the miracle of modern technology. The concepts are identical in both the manual and computerized systems.

Information systems have their own vocabulary. A *field* is a basic fact (or data element) such as the name of a book or the telephone number of a publisher. A *record* is a set of fields. A *table* is a set of records. Every record in a table contains the same fields in the same order. A *database* consists of one or more tables. In our example, each record in the Books table will contain the identical six fields—ISBN (a unique identifying number for the book), title, author, year of publication, price, and publisher. In similar fashion, every record in the Publishers table will have the same fields for each publisher just as every record in the Orders table has the same fields for each order. This terminology (field, record, file, and database) is extremely important and will be used throughout the text.

You can think of the file cabinet in the manual system as a database. Each set of folders in the file cabinet corresponds to a table within the database. Thus the bookstore database consists of three separate tables—for books, publishers, and orders. Each table, in turn, consists of multiple *records,* corresponding to the folders in the file cabinet. The Books table, for example, contains a record for every book title in the store. The Publishers table has a record for each publisher, just as the Orders table has a record for each order.

INTRODUCTION TO MICROSOFT ACCESS

Microsoft Access, the fourth major application in the Microsoft Office, is used to create and manage a database such as the one for the college bookstore. Consider now Figure 1.1, which shows how Microsoft Access appears on the desktop. Our discussion assumes a basic familiarity with the Windows operating system and the user interface that is common to all Windows applications. You should recognize, therefore, that the desktop in Figure 1.1 has two open windows—an application window for Microsoft Access and a document (database) window for the database that is currently open.

Each window has its own title bar and Minimize, Maximize (or Restore), and Close buttons. The title bar in the application window contains the name of the application (Microsoft Access). The title bar in the document (database) window contains the name of the database that is currently open (Bookstore). The application window for Access has been maximized to take up the entire desktop, and hence the Restore button is visible. The database window has not been maximized.

A menu bar appears immediately below the application title bar. A toolbar (similar to those in other Office applications) appears below the menu bar and offers alternative ways to execute common commands. The Windows taskbar appears at the bottom of the screen and shows the open applications.

The Database Window

The *Database window* displays the various objects in an Access database. There are seven types of objects—tables, queries, forms, reports, pages, macros, and modules. Every database must contain at least one table, and it may contain any

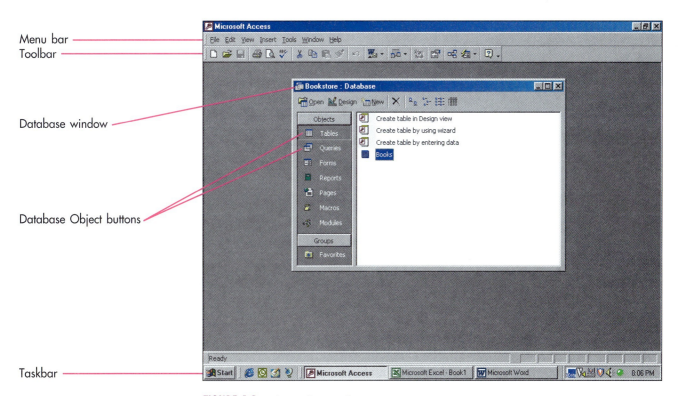

FIGURE 1.1 The Database Window

or all (or none) of the other objects. Each object type is accessed through the appropriate button within the Database window. In this chapter we concentrate on tables, but we briefly describe the other types of objects as a preview of what you will learn as you read our book.

- A *table* stores data about an entity (a person, place, or thing) and is the basic element in any database. A table is made up of records, which in turn are made up of fields. It is columnar in appearance, with each record in a separate row of the table and each field in a separate column.
- A *form* provides a more convenient and attractive way to enter, display, and/or print the data in a table.
- A *query* answers a question about the database. The most common type of query specifies a set of criteria, then searches the database to retrieve the records that satisfy the criteria.
- A *report* presents the data in a table or query in attractive fashion on the printed page.
- A *page* is an HTML document that can be posted to a Web server or Local Area Network, and which can be viewed by a Web browser.
- A *macro* is analogous to a computer program and consists of commands that are executed automatically one after the other. Macros are used to automate the performance of any repetitive task.
- A *module* provides a greater degree of automation through programming in Visual Basic for Applications (VBA).

ONE FILE HOLDS ALL

All of the objects in an Access database (tables, forms, queries, reports, pages, macros, and modules) are stored in a single file on disk. The database itself is opened through the Open command in the File menu or by clicking the Open button on the Database toolbar. The individual objects within a database are opened through the database window.

Tables

A table (or set of tables) is the heart of any database, as it contains the actual data. In Access a table is displayed in one of two views—the Design view or the Datasheet view. The ***Design view*** is used to define the table initially and to specify the fields it will contain. It is also used to modify the table definition if changes are subsequently necessary. The Design view is discussed in detail in Chapter 2. The ***Datasheet view***—the view you use to add, edit, or delete records—is the view on which we focus in this chapter.

Figure 1.2 shows the Datasheet view for the Books table in our bookstore. The first row in the table contains the ***field names.*** Each additional row contains a record (the data for a specific book). Each column represents a field (one fact about a book). Every record in the table contains the same fields in the same order: ISBN Number, Title, Author, Year, List Price, and Publisher.

The status bar at the bottom of Figure 1.2a indicates that there are five records in the table and that you are positioned on the first record. This is the record you are working on and is known as the ***current record.*** (You can work on only one record at a time.) There is a ***record selector symbol*** (a triangle, asterisk, or pencil) next to the current record to indicate its status.

Field names

Triangle indicates data has been saved to disk

Current record

Total number of records

ISBN Number	Title	Author	Year	List Price	Publisher
0-13-011108-2	Exploring Excel 2000	Grauer/Barber	1999	$28.95	Prentice Hall
0-13-011816-8	Exploring PowerPoint 2000	Grauer/Barber	1999	$28.95	Prentice Hall
0-13-020476-5	Exploring Access 2000	Grauer/Barber	1999	$28.95	Prentice Hall
0-13-020489-7	Exploring Word 2000	Grauer/Barber	1999	$28.95	Prentice Hall
0-13-754193-7	Exploring Windows 98	Grauer/Barber	1998	$28.95	Prentice Hall

Record: 1 of 5

(a) All Data Has Been Saved

Insertion point indicates where data is being entered

Pencil indicates data has not yet been saved to disk

Asterisk appears next to blank record

ISBN Number	Title	Author	Year	List Price	Publisher
0-13-011108-2	Exploring Excel 2000	Grauer/Barber	1999	$28.95	Prentice Hall
0-13-011816-8	Exploring PowerPoint 2000	Grauer/Barber	1999	$28.95	Prentice Hall
0-13-020476-5	Exploring Access 2000	Grauer/Barber	1999	$28.95	Prentice Hall
0-13-020489-7	Exploring Word 2000	Grauer/Barber	1999	$28.95	Prentice Hall
0-13-754193-7	Exploring Windows 98	Grauer/Barber	1998	$28.95	Prentice Hall
0-13-011190-0	Exploring Microsoft Office 2000 Volume I	Grauer/Barber	1999	$45.00	Prentice

Record: 6 of 6

(b) During Data Entry

FIGURE 1.2 Tables

A ***triangle*** indicates that the record has been saved to disk. A ***pencil*** indicates that you are working on the record and that the changes have not yet been saved. As soon as you move to the next record, however, the pencil changes to a triangle to indicate that the record on which you were working has been saved. (Access, unlike other Office applications, automatically saves changes made to a record without your having to execute the Save command.) An ***asterisk*** appears next to the blank record at the end of every table.

Figure 1.2a shows the table as it would appear immediately after you opened it. The first field in the first record is selected (highlighted), and anything you type at this point will replace the selected data. (This is the same convention as in any other Windows application.) The triangle next to the current record (record 1) indicates that changes have not yet been made. An asterisk appears as the record selector symbol next to the blank record at the end of the table. The blank record is used to add a record to the table and is not counted in determining the number of records in the table.

Figure 1.2b shows the table as you are in the process of entering data for a new record at the end of the table. The current record is now record 6. The ***insertion point*** (a flashing vertical bar) appears at the point where text is being entered. The record selector for the current record is a pencil, indicating that the record has not yet been saved. The asterisk has moved to the blank record at the end of the table, which now contains one more record than the table in Figure 1.2a.

Note, too, that each table in a database must have a field (or combination of fields) known as the ***primary key,*** which is unique for every record in the table. The ISBN (International Standard Book Number) is the primary key in our example, and it ensures that each record in the Books table is different from every other record. (Other fields may also have a unique value for every record, but only one field is designated as the primary key.)

HANDS-ON EXERCISE 1

Introduction to Microsoft Access

Objective: To open an existing database; to add a record to a table within the database. Use Figure 1.3 as a guide in the exercise.

STEP 1: Welcome to Windows

➤ Turn on the computer and all of its peripherals. The floppy drive should be empty prior to starting your machine. This ensures that the system starts by reading from the hard disk, which contains the Windows files, as opposed to a floppy disk, which does not.

➤ Your system will take a minute or so to get started, after which you should see the desktop in Figure 1.3a. Do not be concerned if the appearance of your desktop is different from ours. If necessary, click the **Close button** to close the Welcome window.

Start button

(a) Welcome to Windows (step 1)

FIGURE 1.3 Hands-on Exercise 1

TAKE THE WINDOWS TOUR

Windows 98 greets you with a Welcome window that describes the highlights in the operating system. Click Discover Windows 98 to take a guided tour or select one of the topics at the left of the window. If you do not see the Welcome window when you start your computer, click the Start button, click Run, type C:\Windows\Welcome in the text box, and press the enter key. Relax and enjoy the show.

STEP 2: Obtain the Practice Files:

➤ We have created a series of practice files for you to use throughout the text. Your instructor will make these files available to you in a variety of ways:
- You can download the files from our Web site if you have access to the Internet and World Wide Web (see boxed tip).
- The files may be on a network drive, in which case you use the Windows Explorer to copy the files from the network to a floppy disk.
- There may be an actual "data disk" that you are to check out from the lab in order to use the Copy Disk command to duplicate the disk.

➤ Check with your instructor for additional information.

DOWNLOAD THE PRACTICE FILES

Download the practice files for any book in the *Exploring Windows* series from the Exploring Windows home page. Go to www.prenhall.com/grauer, click the Office 2000 text, click the link to student resources, then click the link to download the student data disk. Our Web site has many other features such as the Companion Web Sites (online study guides) to enhance your learning experience. See problem 6 at the end of the chapter.

STEP 3: Start Microsoft Access

➤ Click the **Start button** to display the Start menu. Click (or point to) the **Programs menu,** then click **Microsoft Access** to start the program. Click and drag the Office Assistant out of the way if it appears. (The Office Assistant is described in the next hands-on exercise.)

➤ You should see the Microsoft Access dialog box with the option button to **Open an existing file** already selected. Click **More Files,** then click **OK** to display the Open dialog box in Figure 1.3b.

➤ Click the **down arrow** on the Views button, then click **Details** to change to the Details view. Click and drag the vertical border between columns to increase (or decrease) the size of a column.

➤ Click the **drop-down arrow** on the Look In list box. Click the appropriate drive (drive C is recommended rather than drive A), depending on the location of your data. Double click the **Exploring Access folder.**

➤ Click the **down scroll arrow** until you can click the **Bookstore database.** Click the **Open command button** to open the database.

WORK ON DRIVE C

Even in a lab setting it is preferable to work on the local hard drive, as opposed to a floppy disk. The hard drive is much faster, which becomes especially important when working with the large file sizes associated with Access. Use the Windows Explorer to copy the database from the network drive to the local hard drive prior to the exercise, then work on drive C throughout the exercise. Once you have completed the exercise, use the Explorer a second time to copy the modified database to a floppy disk that you can take with you.

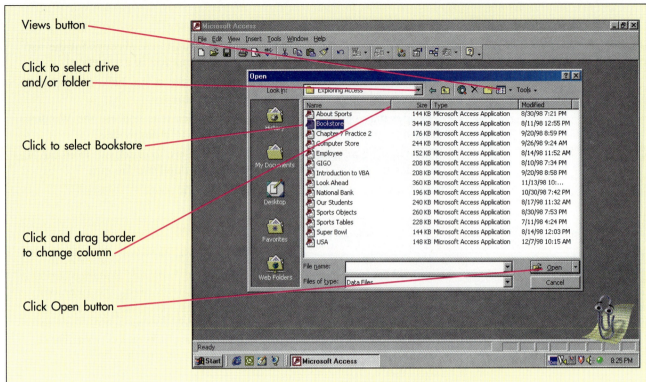

(b) Open an Existing Database (step 3)

FIGURE 1.3 Hands-on Exercise (continued)

STEP 4: Open the Books Table

➤ If necessary, click the **Maximize button** in the application window so that Access takes the entire desktop.

➤ You should see the Database window for the Bookstore database with the **Tables button** already selected. Double click the **Books table** to open the table as shown in Figure 1.3c.

➤ Click the **Maximize button** so that the Books table fills the Access window and reduces the clutter on the screen.

A SIMPLER DATABASE

The real power of Access is derived from a database with multiple tables that are related to one another. For the time being, however, we focus on a database with only one table so that you can learn the basics of Access. After you are comfortable working with a single table, we will show you how to work with multiple tables and how to relate them to one another.

STEP 5: Moving within a Table

➤ Click in any field in the first record. The status bar at the bottom of the Books Table indicates record 1 of 22.

➤ The triangle symbol in the record selector indicates that the record has not changed since it was last saved.

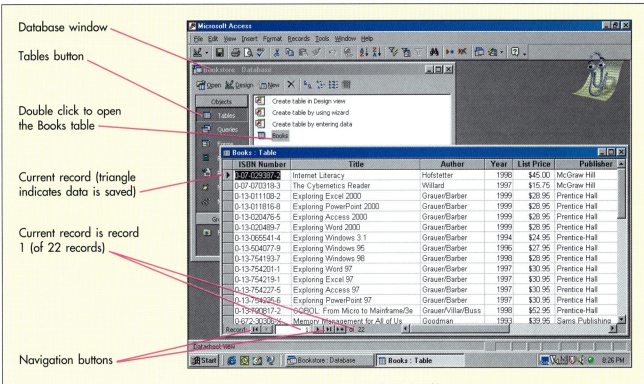

(c) Open the Books Table (step 4)

FIGURE 1.3   Hands-on Exercise 1 (continued)

➤ You can move from record to record (or field to field) using either the mouse or the arrow keys:
- Click in any field in the second record. The status bar indicates record 2 of 22.
- Press the **down arrow key** to move to the third record. The status bar indicates record 3 of 22.
- Press the **left and right arrow keys** to move from field to field within the third record.

➤ You can also use the navigation buttons above the status bar to move from one record to the next:
- Click |◄ to move to the first record in the table.
- Click ► to move forward in the table to the next record.
- Click ◄ to move back in the table to the previous record.

MOVING FROM FIELD TO FIELD

Press the Tab key, the right arrow key, or the enter key to move to the next field in the current record (or the first field in the next record if you are already in the last field of the current record). Press Shift+Tab or the left arrow key to return to the previous field in the current record (or the last field in the previous record if you are already in the first field of the current record).

- Click ▶| to move to the last record in the table.
- Click ▶* to move beyond the last record in order to insert a new record.

➤ Click |◀ to return to the first record in the table.

STEP 6: Add a New Record

➤ Pull down the **Insert menu** and click **New Record** (or click the **New Record button** on the Table Datasheet toolbar). The record selector moves to the last record (now record 23). The insertion point is positioned in the first field (ISBN Number).

➤ Enter data for the new record as shown in Figure 1.3d. The record selector changes to a pencil as soon as you enter the first character in the new record.

➤ Press the **enter key** when you have entered the last field for the record. The new record is saved, and the record selector changes to a triangle and moves automatically to the next record.

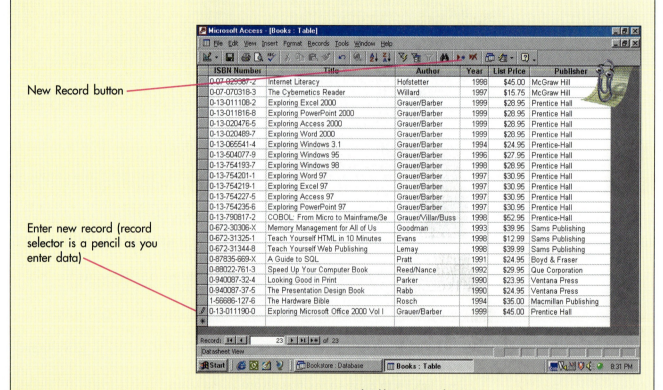

(d) Add a New Record (step 6)

FIGURE 1.3 Hands-on Exercise 1 (continued)

WHEN IS DATA SAVED?

There is one critical difference between Access and other Office applications such as Word for Windows or Microsoft Excel. *Access automatically saves any changes in the current record as soon as you move to the next record or when you close the table.* In other words, you do *not* have to execute the Save command explicitly to save the data in the table.

STEP 7: Add a Second Record

➤ The record selector is at the end of the table where you can add another record. Enter **0-07-054048-9** as the ISBN number for this record. Press the **Tab, enter,** or **right arrow key** to move to the Title field.

➤ Enter the title of this book as **Ace teh Technical Interview** (deliberately misspelling the word "the"). Try to look at the monitor as you type to see the AutoCorrect feature (common to all Office applications) in action. Access will correct the misspelling and change *teh* to *the*.

➤ If you did not see the correction being made, press the **backspace key** several times to erase the last several characters in the title, then re-enter the title.

➤ Complete the entry for this book. Enter **Rothstein** for the author. Enter **1998** for the year of publication. Enter **24.95** for the list price. Enter **McGraw Hill** for the publisher, then press **enter.**

CREATE YOUR OWN SHORTHAND

Use the AutoCorrect feature that is common to all Office applications to expand abbreviations such as "PH" for Prentice Hall. Pull down the Tools menu, click AutoCorrect, type the abbreviation in the Replace text box and the expanded entry in the With text box. Click the Add command button, then click OK to exit the dialog box and return to the document. The next time you type PH (in uppercase) as you enter a record, it will automatically be expanded to Prentice Hall.

STEP 8: Print the Table

➤ Pull down the **File menu.** Click **Page Setup** to display the Page Setup dialog box in Figure 1.3e.

➤ Click the **Page tab.** Click the **Landscape option button.** Click **OK** to accept the settings and close the dialog box.

➤ Click the **Print button** on the toolbar to print the table. Alternatively, you can pull down the **File menu,** click **Print** to display the Print dialog box, click the **All option button,** then click **OK.**

ABOUT MICROSOFT ACCESS

Pull down the Help menu and click About Microsoft Access to display the specific release number as well as other licensing information, including the Product ID. This help screen also contains two very useful command buttons, System Info and Tech Support. The first button displays information about the hardware installed on your system, including the amount of memory and available space on the hard drive. The Tech Support button provides telephone numbers for technical assistance.

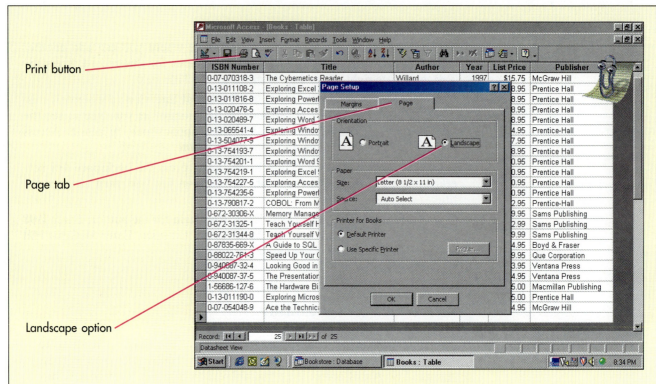

(e) Print the Table (step 8)

FIGURE 1.3 Hands-on Exercise 1 (continued)

STEP 9: Exit Access

➤ You need to close both the Books table and the Bookstore database:
- Pull down the **File menu** and click **Close** (or click the **Close button**) to close the Books table. Answer **Yes** if asked to save changes to the layout of the table.
- Pull down the **File menu** and click **Close** (or click the **Close button**) to close the Bookstore database.

➤ Pull down the **File menu** and click **Exit** to close Access if you do not want to continue with the next exercise at this time.

OUR FAVORITE BOOKSTORE

This exercise has taken you through our hypothetical bookstore database. It's more fun, however, to go to a real bookstore. Amazon Books (www.amazon.com), with a virtual inventory of more than three million titles, is one of our favorite sites on the Web. You can search by author, subject, or title, read reviews written by other Amazon visitors, or contribute your own review. It's not as cozy as your neighborhood bookstore, but you can order any title for mail-order delivery. And you never have to leave home.

MAINTAINING THE DATABASE

The exercise just completed showed you how to open an existing table and add records to that table. You will also need to edit and/or delete existing records in order to maintain the data as changes occur. These operations require you to find the specific record and then make the change. You can search the table manually, or more easily through the Find and Replace commands.

Find and Replace Commands

The Find and Replace commands are similar in function to the corresponding commands in all other Office applications. (The commands are executed from within the same dialog box by selecting the appropriate tab.) The **Find command** enables you to locate a specific record(s) by searching a table for a particular value. You could, for example, search the Books table for the title of a book, then move to the appropriate field to change its price. The **Replace command** incorporates the Find command and allows you to locate and optionally replace (one or more occurrences of) one value with another. The Replace command in Figure 1.4 searches for *PH* in order to substitute *Prentice Hall*.

Searches can be made more efficient by making use of the various options. A case-sensitive search, for example, matches not only the specific characters, but also the use of upper- and lowercase letters. Thus, *PH* is different from *ph,* and a case-sensitive search on one will not identify the other. A case-insensitive search (where Match Case is *not* selected) will find both *PH* and *ph.* Any search may specify a match on whole fields to identify *Davis,* but not *Davison.* And finally, a search can also be made more efficient by restricting it to the current field.

The replacement can be either selective or automatic. Selective replacement lets you examine each successful match in context and decide whether to replace it. Automatic replacement makes the substitution without asking for confirmation (and is generally not recommended). Selective replacement is implemented by clicking the Find Next command button, then clicking (or not clicking) the Replace button to make (or not make) the substitution. Automatic replacement (through the entire table) is implemented by clicking the Replace All button.

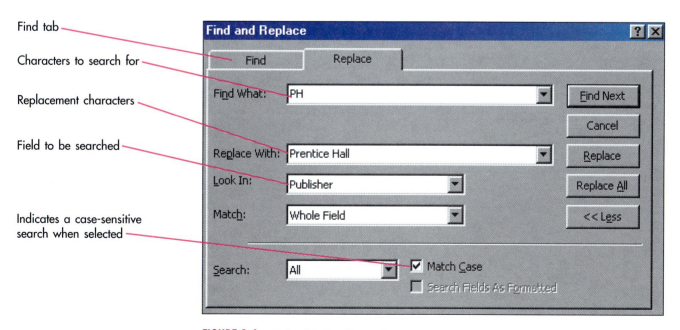

FIGURE 1.4 Find and Replace Commands

Data Validation

It is unwise to simply add (edit or delete) a record without adequate checks on the validity of the data. Ask yourself, for example, whether a search for all books by Prentice Hall (without a hyphen) will also return all books by *Prentice-Hall* (with a hyphen). The answer is *no* because the publisher's name is spelled differently and a search for one will not locate the other. *You* know the publisher is the same in both instances, but the computer does not.

Data validation is a crucial part of any system. Good systems are built to anticipate errors you might make and reject those errors prior to accepting data. Access automatically implements certain types of data validation. It will not, for example, let you enter letters where a numeric value is expected (such as the Year and List Price fields in our example). More sophisticated types of validation are implemented by the user when the table is created. You may decide, for example, to reject any record that omits the title or author. Data validation is described more completely in Chapter 2.

> **GARBAGE IN, GARBAGE OUT (GIGO)**
>
> A computer does exactly what you tell it to do, which is not necessarily what you want it to do. It is absolutely critical, therefore, that you validate the data that goes into a system, or else the associated information may not be correct. No system, no matter how sophisticated, can produce valid output from invalid input. In other words: garbage in, garbage out.

FORMS, QUERIES, AND REPORTS

As previously indicated, an Access database can contain as many as seven different types of objects. Thus far we have concentrated on tables. Now we extend the discussion to include other objects such as forms, queries, and reports as illustrated in Figure 1.5.

Figure 1.5a contains the Books table as it exists after the first hands-on exercise. There are 24 records in the table and six fields for each record. The status bar indicates that you are currently positioned in the first record. You can enter new records in the table as was done in the previous exercise. You can also edit or delete an existing record, as will be illustrated in the next exercise.

Figure 1.5b displays a form that is based on the table of Figure 1.5a. A form provides a friendlier interface than does a table and is easier to understand and use. Note, for example, the command buttons in the form to add a new record, or to find and/or delete an existing record. The status bar at the bottom of the form indicates that you are on the first of 24 records, and is identical to the status bar for the table in Figure 1.5a.

Figure 1.5c displays a query to list the books for a particular publisher (Prentice Hall in this example). A query consists of a question (e.g., enter the publisher name) and an answer (the records that satisfy the query). The results of the query are similar in appearance to that of a table, except that the query results contain selected records and/or selected fields for those records. The query may also list the records in a different sequence from that of the table.

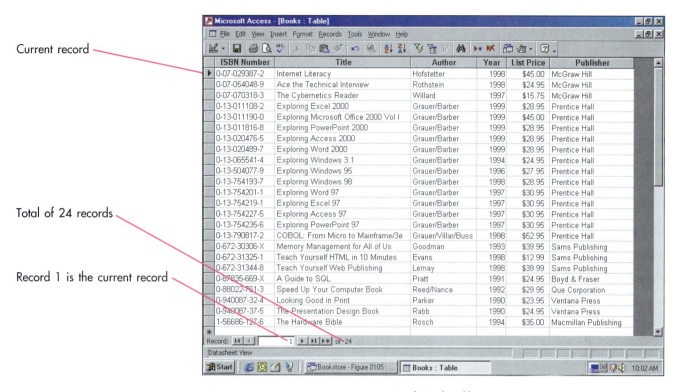

(a) The Books Table

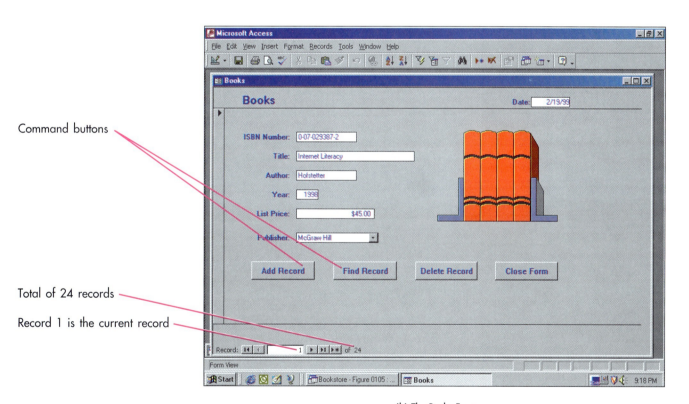

(b) The Books Form

FIGURE 1.5 The Objects in a Database

Records are sequenced by title within author

Query has total of 13 records

(c) The Publisher Query

Publisher's Report
13-Feb-99

Publisher	Author	Title	ISBN Number	Year	List Price
Prentice Hall	Grauer/Barber	Exploring Access 2000	0-13-020476-5	1999	$28.95
Prentice Hall	Grauer/Barber	Exploring Access 97	0-13-754227-5	1997	$30.95
Prentice Hall	Grauer/Barber	Exploring Excel 2000	0-13-011108-2	1999	$28.95
Prentice Hall	Grauer/Barber	Exploring Excel 97	0-13-754219-1	1997	$30.95
Prentice Hall	Grauer/Barber	Exploring Microsoft Office 2000 Vol I	0-13-011190-0	1999	$45.00
Prentice Hall	Grauer/Barber	Exploring PowerPoint 2000	0-13-011816-8	1999	$28.95
Prentice Hall	Grauer/Barber	Exploring Windows 3.1	0-13-065541-4	1994	$24.95
Prentice Hall	Grauer/Barber	Exploring PowerPoint 97	0-13-754235-6	1997	$30.95
Prentice Hall	Grauer/Barber	Exploring Windows 95	0-13-504077-9	1996	$27.95
Prentice Hall	Grauer/Barber	Exploring Windows 98	0-13-754193-7	1998	$28.95
Prentice Hall	Grauer/Barber	Exploring Word 2000	0-13-020489-7	1999	$28.95
Prentice Hall	Grauer/Barber	Exploring Word 97	0-13-754201-1	1997	$30.95
Prentice Hall	Grauer/Villar/Buss	COBOL:From Micro to Mainframe/3e	0-13-790817-2	1998	$52.95

(d) The Publisher's Report

FIGURE 1.5 The Objects in a Database (continued)

Figure 1.5d illustrates a report that includes only the books from Prentice Hall. A report provides presentation-quality output and is preferable to printing the datasheet view of a table or query. Note, too, that a report may be based on either a table or a query. You could, for example, base the report in Figure 1.5d on the Books table, in which case it would list every book in the table. Alternatively, the report could be based on a query, as in Figure 1.5d, and list only the books that satisfy the criteria within the query.

Later chapters discuss forms, queries, and reports in depth. The exercise that follows is intended only as a brief introduction to what can be accomplished in Access.

HANDS-ON EXERCISE 2

Maintaining the Database

Objective: To add, edit, and delete a record; to demonstrate data validation; to introduce forms, queries, and reports. Use Figure 1.6 as a guide.

STEP 1: Open the Bookstore Database

➤ Start Access. The Bookstore database should appear within the list of recently opened databases as shown in Figure 1.6a.

➤ Select the **Bookstore database** (its drive and folder may be different from that in Figure 1.6a). Click **OK** to open the database.

➤ Right click the Office Assistant if it appears and click the **Hide** command.

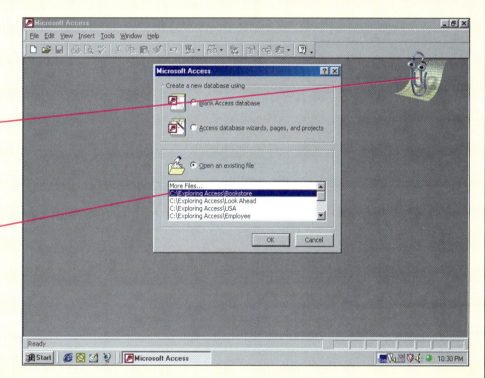

Right click the Office Assistant for shortcut menu

Click Bookstore to select it

(a) Open the Bookstore Database (step 1)

FIGURE 1.6 Hands-on Exercise 2

ABOUT THE ASSISTANT

The Assistant is very powerful and hence you want to experiment with various ways to use it. To ask a question, click the Assistant's icon to toggle its balloon on or off. If you find the Assistant distracting, click and drag the character out of the way or hide it altogether by pulling down the Help menu and clicking the Hide the Office Assistant command. Pull down the Help menu and click the Show the Office Assistant command to return the Assistant to the desktop.

CHAPTER 1: INTRODUCTION TO MICROSOFT ACCESS

STEP 2: The Find Command

➤ If necessary, click the **Tables button** in the Database window. Double click the icon for the **Books table** to open the table from the previous exercise.

➤ You should see the Books table in Figure 1.6b. (The Find dialog box is not yet displayed).

➤ If necessary, click the **Maximize button** to maximize the Books table within the Access window.

➤ *Exploring Microsoft Office 2000 Vol 1* and *Ace the Technical Interview,* the books you added in the previous exercise, appear in sequence according to the ISBN number because this field is the primary key for the Books table.

➤ Click in the **Title field** for the first record. Pull down the **Edit menu** and click **Find** (or click the **Find button** on the toolbar) to display the dialog box in Figure 1.6b. (You are still positioned in the first record.)

➤ Enter **Exploring Windows 95** in the Find What text box. Check that the other parameters for the Find command match the dialog box in Figure 1.6b. Be sure that the **Title field** is selected in the Look in list.

➤ Click the **Find Next command button.** Access moves to record 10, the record containing the designated character string, and selects the Title field for that record. Click **Cancel** to close the Find dialog box.

➤ Press the **tab key** three times to move from the Title field to the List Price field. The current price ($27.95) is already selected. Type **28.95,** then press the **enter key** to change the price to $28.95.

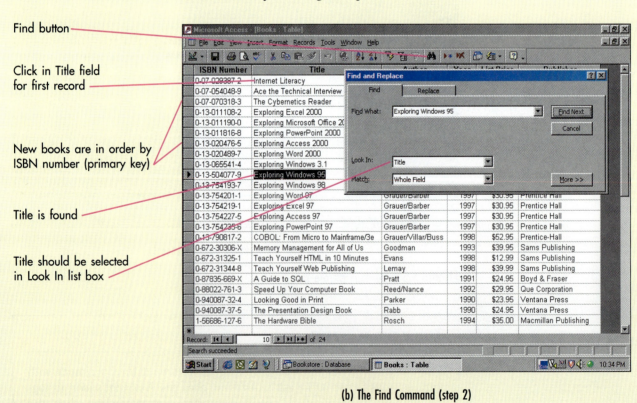

(b) The Find Command (step 2)

FIGURE 1.6   Hands-on Exercise 2 (continued)

EDITING A RECORD

The fastest way to replace the value in an existing field is to select the field, then type the new value. Access automatically selects the field for you when you use the keyboard (Tab, enter, or arrow keys) to move from one field to the next. Click the mouse within the field (to deselect the field) if you are replacing only one or two characters rather than the entire field.

STEP 3: The Undo Command
- Pull down the **Edit menu** and click **Undo Current Field/Record** (or click the **Undo button** on the toolbar). The price for Exploring Windows 95 returns to its previous value.
- Pull down the **Edit menu** a second time. The Undo command is dim (as is the Undo button on the toolbar), indicating that you can no longer undo any changes. Press **Esc.**
- Correct the List Price field a second time and move to the next record to save your change.

THE UNDO COMMAND

The Undo command is common to all Office applications, but is implemented differently from one application to the next. Microsoft Word, for example, enables you to undo multiple operations. Access, however, because it saves changes automatically as soon as you move to the next record, enables you to undo only the most recent command.

STEP 4: The Delete Command
- Click any field in the record for **A Guide to SQL.** (You can also use the **Find command** to search for the title and move directly to its record.)
- Pull down the **Edit menu.** Click **Select Record** to highlight the entire record.
- Press the **Del key** to delete the record. You will see a dialog box as shown in Figure 1.6c, indicating that you are about to delete a record and asking you to confirm the deletion. Click **Yes.**
- Pull down the **Edit menu.** The Undo command is dim, indicating that you cannot undelete a record. Press **Esc** to continue working.

THE RECORD SELECTOR

Click the record selector (the box immediately to the left of the first field in a record) to select the record without having to use a pull-down menu. Click and drag the mouse over the record selector for multiple rows to select several sequential records at the same time.

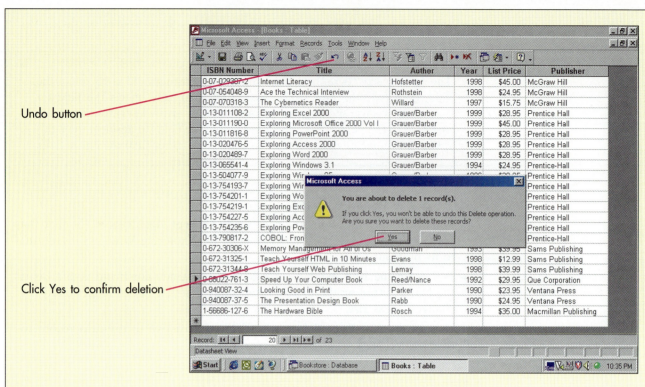

(c) The Delete Command (step 4)

FIGURE 1.6 Hands-on Exercise 2 (continued)

STEP 5: Data Validation

➤ Click the **New Record button** on the toolbar. The record selector moves to the last record (record 24).

➤ Add data as shown in Figure 1.6d, being sure to enter an invalid price **(XXX)** in the List Price field. Press the **Tab key** to move to the next field.

➤ Access displays the dialog box in Figure 1.6d, indicating that the value you entered (XXX) is inappropriate for the List Price field; in other words, you cannot enter letters when Access is expecting a numeric entry.

➤ Click the **OK command button** to close the dialog box and return to the table. Drag the mouse to select XXX, then enter the correct price of **$39.95.**

➤ Press the **Tab key** to move to the Publisher field. Type **McGraw Hill.** Press the **Tab key, right arrow key,** or **enter key** to complete the record.

➤ Click the **Close button** to close the Books table.

STEP 6: Open the Books Form

➤ Click the **Forms button** in the Database window. Double click the **Books form** to open the form as shown in Figure 1.6e, then (if necessary) maximize the form so that it takes the entire window.

➤ Click the **Add Record command button** to move to a new record. The status bar shows record 25 of 25.

➤ Click in the text box for **ISBN number,** then use the **Tab key** to move from field to field as you enter data for the book as shown in Figure 1.6e.

➤ Click the **drop-down arrow** on the Publisher's list box to display the available publishers and to select the appropriate one. The use of a list box ensures that you cannot misspell a publisher's name.

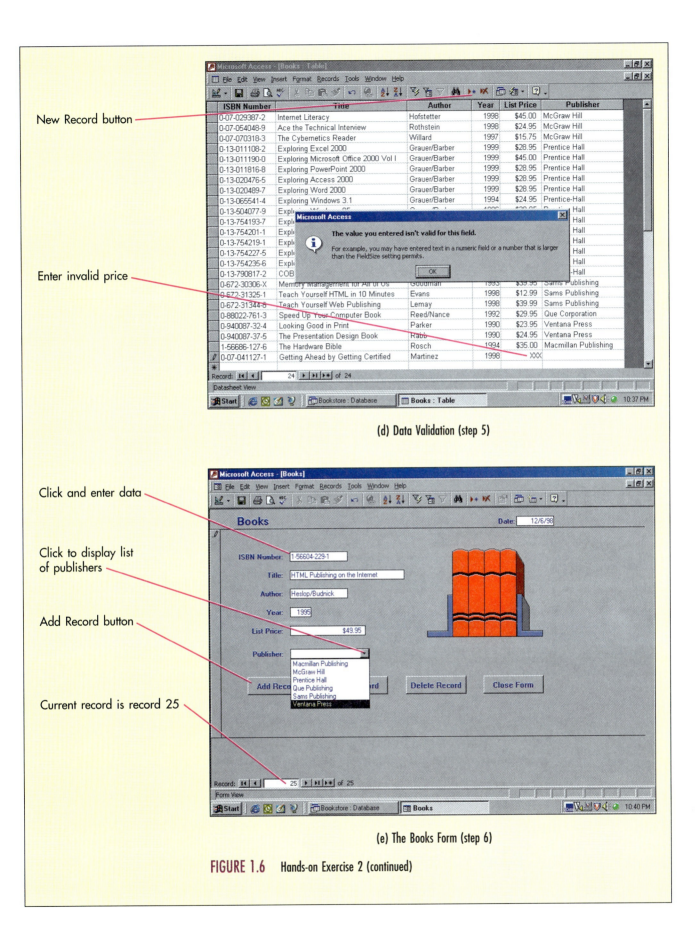

(d) Data Validation (step 5)

(e) The Books Form (step 6)

FIGURE 1.6 Hands-on Exercise 2 (continued)

STEP 7: The Replace Command

➤ Pull down the **View menu.** Click **Datasheet View** to switch from the Form view to the Datasheet view and display the table on which the form is based.

➤ Press **Ctrl+Home** to move to the first record in the Books table, then click in the **Publisher field** for that record. Pull down the **Edit menu.** Click **Replace.**

➤ Enter the parameters as they appear in Figure 1.6f, then click the **Find Next button** to move to the first occurrence of Prentice-Hall.

➤ Click **Replace** to make the substitution in this record and move to the next occurrence.

➤ Click **Replace** to make the second (and last) substitution, then close the dialog box when Access no longer finds the search string. Close the table.

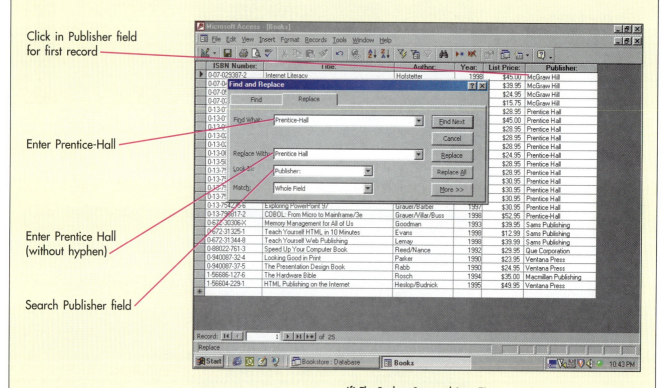

(f) The Replace Command (step 7)

FIGURE 1.6   Hands-on Exercise 2 (continued)

THE MENUS CHANGE

All applications in Office 2000 display a series of short menus that contain only basic commands. There is, however, a double arrow at the bottom of each menu that you can click to display the additional commands. In addition, each time you execute a command it is added to the menu, and conversely, commands are removed from a menu if they are not used after a period of time. You can, however, display the full menus through the Customize command in the Tools menu by clearing the check boxes in the Personalized Menus and Toolbars section.

STEP 8: Print a Report

➤ Click the **Reports button** in the Database window to display the available reports. Double click the icon for the **Publisher report.**

➤ Type **Prentice Hall** (or the name of any other publisher) in the Parameter dialog box. Press **enter** to create the report.

➤ If necessary, click the **Maximize button** in the Report Window so that the report takes the entire screen as shown in Figure 1.6g.

➤ Click the **drop-down arrow** on the Zoom box, then click **Fit** to display the whole page. Note that all of the books in the report are published by Prentice Hall, which is consistent with the parameter you entered earlier.

➤ Click the **Print button** on the Report toolbar to print the report.

➤ Click the **Close button** on the Print Review toolbar to close the Report window.

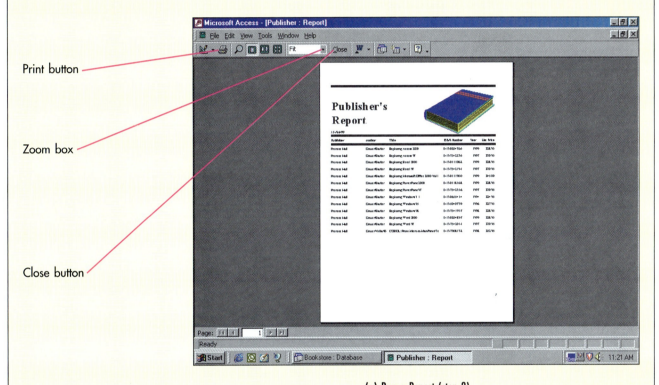

(g) Run a Report (step 8)

FIGURE 1.6   Hands-on Exercise 2 (continued)

TIP OF THE DAY

You can set the Office Assistant to greet you with a "tip of the day" each time you start Access. Click the Microsoft Access Help button (or press the F1 key) to display the Assistant, then click the Options button to display the Office Assistant dialog box. Click the Options tab, then check the Show the Tip of the Day at Startup box and click OK. The next time you start Access, you will be greeted by the Assistant, who will offer you the tip of the day.

STEP 9: The Office Assistant

- If necessary, pull down the **Help menu** and click the command to **Show the Office Assistant.** (You may see a different character.) Click the Assistant, then enter the question, **How do I get Help** in the balloon.
- Click the **Search button** in the Assistant's balloon to look for the answer. The size of the Assistant's balloon expands as the Assistant suggests several topics that may be appropriate.
- Select any topic (we selected **Ways to get assistance while you work**), which in turn displays a Help window with multiple links as shown in Figure 1.6h. Click any of the links in the Help window to read the information.
- Click the **Show button** in the Help window to display the Contents, Answer Wizard, and Index tabs. Click the **Contents tab,** then click the **plus sign** that appears next to the various book icons to expand the various help topics. Click the **icon** next to any topic to display the associated information.
- Continue to experiment, then close the Help window when you are finished.
- Exit Access if you do not want to continue with the next exercise at this time.

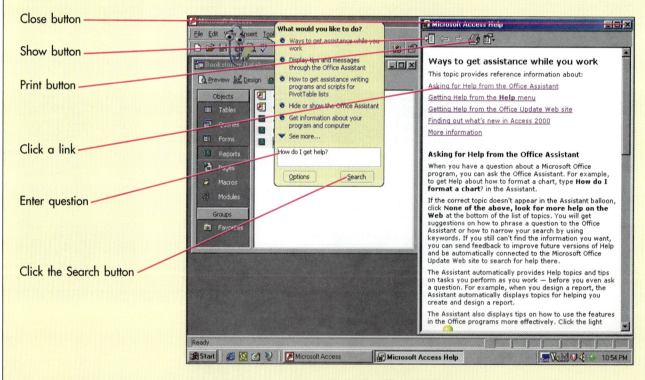

(h) The Office Assistant (step 9)

FIGURE 1.6 Hands-on Exercise 2 (continued)

CHOOSE YOUR OWN ASSISTANT

Choose your own personal assistant from one of several available candidates. Press the F1 key to display the Assistant, click the Assistant to display the balloon, click the Options button to display the Office Assistant dialog box, then click the Gallery tab where you choose your character. (The Office 2000 CD is required to select some characters.)

FILTERS AND SORTING

The exercise just completed described how to use an existing report to obtain information from the database. But what if you are in a hurry and don't have the time to create the report? There is a faster way. You can open the table in the Datasheet view, then apply a filter and/or a sort to the table to display selected records in any order. A *filter* displays a subset of records from the table according to specified criteria. A *sort* lists those records in a specific sequence such as alphabetically by last name or by social security number. We illustrate these concepts in conjunction with Figure 1.7.

Figure 1.7a displays an employee table with 14 records. Each record has 8 fields. The records in the table are displayed in sequence according to the social security number, which is also the primary key (the field or combination of fields that uniquely identifies a record). The status bar indicates that there are 14 records in the table.

Figure 1.7b displays a filtered view of the same table in which we see only the Account Reps. The status bar shows that this is a filtered list, and that there are 8 records that satisfy the criteria. (The employee table still contains the original 14 records, but only 8 records are visible with the filter in effect.) Note, too, that the selected employees are displayed in alphabetical order as opposed to social security order.

Two operations are necessary to go from Figure 1.7a to Figure 1.7b—filtering and sorting. The easiest way to implement a filter is to click in any cell that contains the value of the desired criterion (such as any cell that contains "Account Rep" in the Title field) then click the **Filter by Selection button** on the Database toolbar. To sort the table, click in the field on which you want to sequence the records (the LastName field in this example) then click the **Sort Ascending button** on the Database toolbar. The **Sort Descending button** is appropriate for numeric fields such as salary, if you want to display the records with the highest value listed first.

The operations can be done in any order; that is, you can filter a table to show only selected records, then you can sort the filtered table to display the records in a different order. Conversely, you can sort a table and then apply a filter. It does not matter which operation is performed first, and indeed, you can go back and forth between the two. You can also filter the table further, by applying a second (or third) criterion; e.g., click in a cell containing "Good," then click the Filter by Selection button a second time to display the Account Reps with good performance. You can also click the **Remove Filter button** at any time to display the complete table.

Figure 1.7c illustrates an alternate and more powerful way to apply a filter known as **Filter by Form,** in which you can select the criteria from a drop-down list, and/or apply multiple criteria simultaneously. However, the real advantage of the Filter by Form command extends beyond these conveniences to two additional capabilities. First, you can specify relationships within a criterion; for example, you can select employees with a salary greater than (or less than) $40,000. Filter by Selection, on the other hand, requires you to specify criteria equal to an existing value. Figure 1.7d displays the filtered table of Chicago employees earning more than $40,000.

A second advantage of the Filter by Form command is that you can specify alternative criterion (such as employees in Chicago *or* employees who are account reps) by clicking the Or tab. (The latter capability is not implemented in Figure 1.7.) Suffice it to say, however, that the availability of the various filter and sort commands enable you to obtain information from a database quickly and easily. And as you may have guessed, it's time for another hands-on exercise.

Records are in sequence by SSN (primary key)

Total of 14 records in table

SSN	LastName	FirstName	Location	Title	Salary	Gender	Performance
000-01-0000	Milgrom	Pamela	Boston	Manager	$57,500	F	Average
000-02-2222	Adams	Jennifer	Atlanta	Trainee	$19,500	F	Average
111-12-1111	Johnson	James	Chicago	Account Rep	$47,500	M	Good
123-45-6789	Coulter	Tracey	Atlanta	Manager	$100,000	F	Good
222-23-2222	Marlin	Billy	Miami	Manager	$125,000	M	Good
222-52-5555	Smith	Mary	Chicago	Account Rep	$42,500	F	Average
333-34-3333	Manin	Ann	Boston	Account Rep	$49,500	F	Average
333-43-4444	Smith	Frank	Atlanta	Account Rep	$65,000	M	Good
333-66-1234	Brown	Marietta	Atlanta	Trainee	$18,500	F	Poor
444-45-4444	Frank	Vernon	Miami	Account Rep	$75,000	M	Good
555-22-3333	Rubin	Patricia	Boston	Account Rep	$45,000	F	Average
555-56-5555	Charles	Kenneth	Boston	Account Rep	$40,000	M	Poor
776-67-6666	Adamson	David	Chicago	Manager	$52,000	M	Poor
777-78-7777	Marder	Kelly	Chicago	Account Rep	$38,500	F	Average

(a) The Employee Table (by Social Security Number)

Records are in alphabetical order by last name

Total of 8 records in filtered list

SSN	LastName	FirstName	Location	Title	Salary	Gender	Performance
555-56-5555	Charles	Kenneth	Boston	Account Rep	$40,000	M	Poor
444-45-4444	Frank	Vernon	Miami	Account Rep	$75,000	M	Good
111-12-1111	Johnson	James	Chicago	Account Rep	$47,500	M	Good
333-34-3333	Manin	Ann	Boston	Account Rep	$49,500	F	Average
777-78-7777	Marder	Kelly	Chicago	Account Rep	$38,500	F	Average
555-22-3333	Rubin	Patricia	Boston	Account Rep	$45,000	F	Average
333-43-4444	Smith	Frank	Atlanta	Account Rep	$65,000	M	Good
222-52-5555	Smith	Mary	Chicago	Account Rep	$42,500	F	Average

(b) A Filtered List (Account Reps by last name)

Select from a drop-down list to establish criteria

Or tab

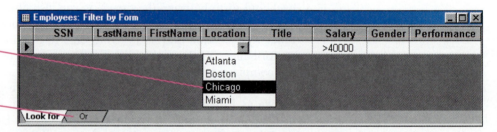

(c) Filter by Form

SSN	LastName	FirstName	Location	Title	Salary	Gender	Performance
776-67-6666	Adamson	David	Chicago	Manager	$52,000	M	Poor
111-12-1111	Johnson	James	Chicago	Account Rep	$47,500	M	Good
222-52-5555	Smith	Mary	Chicago	Account Rep	$42,500	F	Average

(d) Filtered List

FIGURE 1.7 Filters and Sorting

HANDS-ON EXERCISE 3

Filters and Sorting

Objective: To display selected records within a table by applying the Filter by Selection and Filter by Form criteria; to sort the records in a table. Use Figure 1.8 as a guide in the exercise.

STEP 1: Open the Employees Table

➤ Start Access as you did in the previous exercises, but this time you will open a different database. Click **More Files,** and click **OK** (if you see the Microsoft Access dialog box) or pull down the **File menu** and click the **Open command.** Either way, open the **Employees database** in the **Exploring Access folder.**

➤ If necessary, click the **Tables button** in the database window, then double click the **Employees table,** as shown in Figure 1.8a. Click the **maximize button** so that the Employees table fills the Access window. If necessary, click the **maximize button** in the application window so that Access takes the entire desktop.

➤ Pull down the **Insert menu** and click **New Record** (or click the **New Record button** on either the toolbar or the status bar). The record selector moves to the last record (now record 15).

➤ Add data for yourself, using your own social security number, and your first and last name. Assign yourself to **the Miami office** as an **Account Rep** with a salary of **$32,000** and a **Good performance.**

➤ Press **enter** after you have completed the last field.

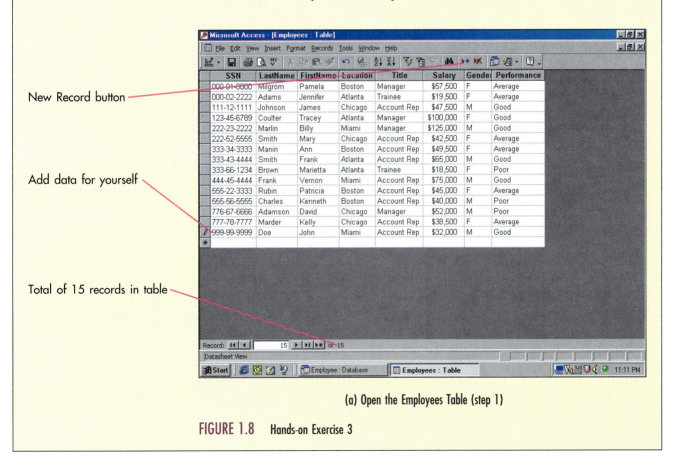

(a) Open the Employees Table (step 1)

FIGURE 1.8 Hands-on Exercise 3

STEP 2: Filter By Selection

➤ The Employees table should contain 15 records, including the record you added for yourself. Click in the Title field of any record that contains the title **Account Rep,** then click the **Filter by Selection button.**

➤ You should see 9 employees, all of whom are Account Reps, as shown in Figure 1.8b. The status bar indicates that there are 9 records (as opposed to 15) and that there is a filter condition in effect.

➤ Click in the performance field of any employee with a good performance (we clicked in the performance field of the first record, which should be yours), then click the **Filter by Selection button** a second time.

➤ This time you see 4 employees, each of whom is an Account Rep with a performance evaluation of good. The status bar indicates that 4 records satisfy this filter condition.

➤ Click the **Print button** to print the filtered table.

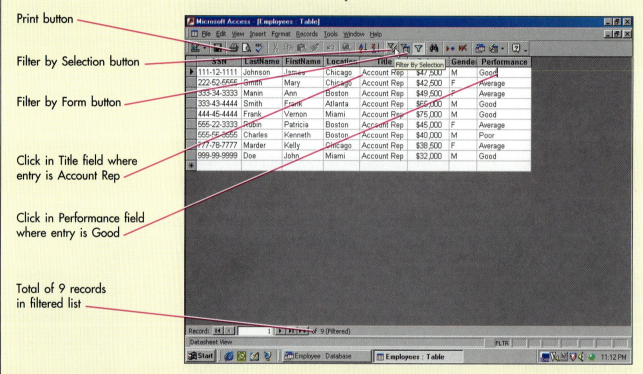

(b) Filter by Selection (step 2)

FIGURE 1.8 Hands-on Exercise 3 (continued)

FILTER EXCLUDING SELECTION

The Filter by Selection button on the Database toolbar selects all records that meet the designated criterion. The Filter Excluding Selection command does just the opposite and displays all records that do not satisfy the criterion. First, click the Remove Filter button to remove any filters that are in effect, then click in the appropriate field of any record that contains the value you want to exclude. Pull down the Records menu, click (or point to) the Filter command, then click the Filter Excluding Selection command to display the records that do not meet the criterion.

STEP 3: Filter by Form

➤ Click the **Filter by Form button** to display the form in Figure 1.8c where you can enter or remove criteria in any sequence. Each time you click in a field, a drop-down list appears that displays all of the values for the field that occur within the table.

➤ Click in the columns for Title and Performance to remove the criteria that were entered in the previous step. Select the existing entries and press the **Del key.**

➤ Click in the cell underneath the Salary field and type **>30000** (as opposed to selecting a specific value). Click in the cell underneath the Location Field and select **Chicago.**

➤ Click the **Apply Filter button** to display the records that satisfy these criteria. (You should see 4 records.) Click the **Print button.**

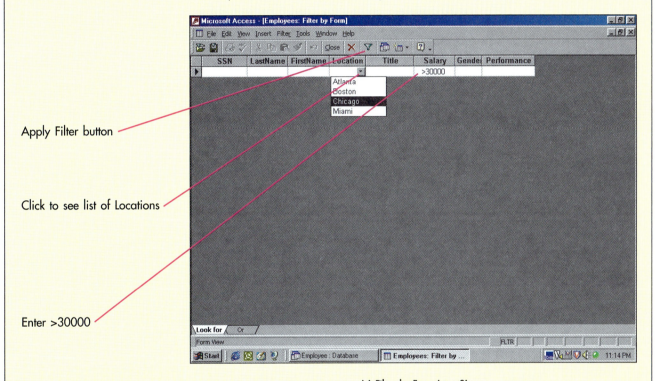

(c) Filter by Form (step 3)

FIGURE 1.8 Hands-on Exercise 3 (continued)

FILTER BY FORM VERSUS FILTER BY SELECTION

The Filter by Form command has all of the capabilities of the Filter by Selection command, and provides two additional capabilities. First, you can use relational operators such as >, >=, <, or <=, as opposed to searching for an exact value. Second, you can search for records that meet one of several conditions (the equivalent of an "Or" operation). Enter the first criteria as you normally would, then click the Or tab at the bottom of the window to display a second form in which you enter the alternate criteria. (To delete an alternate criterion, click the associated tab, then click the Delete button on the toolbar.)

STEP 4: Sort the Table

► Click the **Remove Filter button** to display the complete table of 15 employees. Click in the LastName field of any record, then click the **Sort Ascending button.** The records are displayed in alphabetical (ascending) order by last name.

► Click in the Salary field of any record, then click the **Sort Descending button.** The records are in descending order of salary; that is, the employee with the highest salary is listed first.

► Click in the Location field of any record, then click the **Sort Ascending button** to display the records by location, although the employees within a location are not in any specific order. You can sort on two fields at the same time provided the fields are next to each other, as described in the next step.

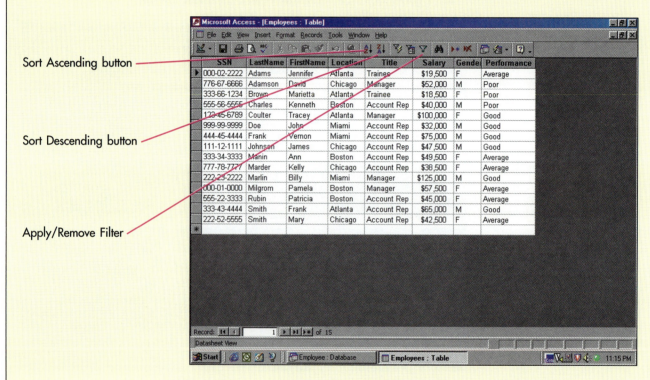

(d) Sort the Table (step 4)

FIGURE 1.8 Hands-on Exercise 3 (continued)

THE SORT OR FILTER—WHICH IS FIRST?

It doesn't matter whether you sort a table and then apply a filter, or filter first and then sort. The operations are cumulative. Thus, once a table has been sorted, any subsequent display of filtered records for that table will be in the specified sequence. Alternatively, you can apply a filter, then sort the filtered table by clicking in the desired field and clicking the appropriate sort button. Remember, too, that all filter commands are cumulative, and hence you must remove the filter to see the original table.

STEP 5: Sort on Two Fields

➤ Click the header for the Location field to select the entire column. Click and drag the Location header so that the Location field is moved to the left of the LastName field as shown in Figure 1.8e.

➤ Click anywhere to deselect the column, then click on the Location header and click and drag to select both the Location header and the LastName Header. Click the **Sort Ascending button.** The records are sorted by location and alphabetically within location.

➤ Click the **Print button** to print the table to prove to your instructor that you completed the exercise. Click the **close button** to close the Employees table.

➤ Click **Yes** when asked whether to save the changes to the Employees table. Saving the table automatically saves the filter and the associated sort.

➤ Exit Access if you do not want to continue with the next exercise at this time.

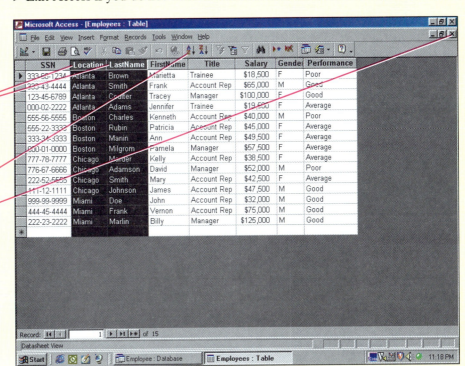

(e) Sort on Two Fields (step 5)

FIGURE 1.8   Hands-on Exercise 3 (continued)

REMOVING VERSUS DELETING A FILTER

Removing a filter displays all of the records in a table, but it does not delete the filter because the filter is stored permanently with the table. To delete the filter entirely is more complicated than simply removing it. Pull down the Record menu, click Filter, then click the Advanced Filter/Sort command to display a grid containing the criteria for the filter. Clear the Sort and Criteria rows by clicking in any cell containing an entry and deleting that entry, then click the Apply Filter button when all cells are clear to return to the Datasheet view. The Apply Filter button should be dim, indicating that the table does not contain a filter.

LOOKING AHEAD: A RELATIONAL DATABASE

The Bookstore and Employee databases are both examples of simple databases in that they each contained only a single table. The real power of Access, however, is derived from multiple tables and the relationships between those tables. This type of database is known as a *relational database* and is illustrated in Figure 1.9. This figure expands the original Employee database by adding two tables, for locations and titles, respectively.

The Employees table in Figure 1.9a is the same table we used at the beginning of the previous exercise, except for the substitution of a LocationID and TitleID for the location and title, respectively. The Locations table in turn has all

SSN	LastName	FirstName	LocationID	TitleID	Salary	Gender	Performance
000-01-0000	Milgrom	Pamela	L02	T02	$57,500	F	Average
000-02-2222	Adams	Jennifer	L01	T03	$19,500	F	Average
111-12-1111	Johnson	James	L03	T01	$47,500	M	Good
123-45-6789	Coulter	Tracey	L01	T02	$100,000	F	Good
222-23-2222	Marlin	Billy	L04	T02	$125,000	M	Good
222-52-5555	Smith	Mary	L03	T01	$42,500	F	Average
333-34-3333	Manin	Ann	L02	T01	$49,500	F	Average
333-43-4444	Smith	Frank	L01	T01	$65,000	M	Good
333-66-1234	Brown	Marietta	L01	T03	$18,500	F	Poor
444-45-4444	Frank	Vernon	L04	T01	$75,000	M	Good
555-22-3333	Rubin	Patricia	L02	T01	$45,000	F	Average
555-56-5555	Charles	Kenneth	L02	T01	$40,000	M	Poor
776-67-6666	Adamson	David	L03	T02	$52,000	M	Poor
777-78-7777	Marder	Kelly	L03	T01	$38,500	F	Average

(a) The Employees Table

LocationID	Location	Address	State	Zipcode	OfficePhone
L01	Atlanta	450 Peachtree Road	GA	30316	(404) 333-5555
L02	Boston	3 Commons Blvd	MA	02190	(617) 123-4444
L03	Chicago	500 Loop Highway	IL	60620	(312) 444-6666
L04	Miami	210 Biscayne Blvd	FL	33103	(305) 787-9999

(b) The Locations Table

TitleID	Title	Description	EducationRequired	MinimumSalary	MaximumSalary
T01	Account Rep	A marketing …	Four year degree	$25,000	$75,000
T02	Manager	A supervisory …	Four year degree	$50,000	$150,000
T03	Trainee	An entry-level …	Two year degree	$18,000	$25,000

(c) The Titles Table

FIGURE 1.9 A Relational Database

of the fields that pertain to each location: LocationID, Location, Address, State, Zipcode, and Office Phone. One field, the LocationID, appears in both Employees and Locations tables and links the two tables to one another. In similar fashion, the Titles table has the information for each title: the TitleID, Title, Description, Education Required, and Minimum and Maximum Salary. The TitleID appears in both the Employees and Titles tables to link those tables to one another.

It sounds complicated, but it is really quite simple and very elegant. More importantly, it enables you to obtain detailed information about any employee, location, or title. To show how it works, we will ask a series of questions that require you to look in one or more tables for the answer. Consider:

Query: At which location does Pamela Milgrom work? What is the phone number of her office?

Answer: Pamela works in the Boston office, at 3 Commons Blvd., Boston, MA, 02190. The phone number is (617) 123-4444.

Did you answer the question correctly? You had to search the Employees table for Pamela Milgrom to obtain the LocationID (L02 in this example) corresponding to her office. You then searched the Locations table for this LocationID to obtain the address and phone number for that location. The process required you to use both the Locations and Employees tables, which are linked to one another through a *one-to-many relationship.* One location can have many employees, but a specific employee can work at only one location. Let's try another question:

Query: Which employees are managers?

Answer: There are four managers: Pamela Milgrom, Tracey Coulter, Billy Marlin, and David Adamson

The answer to this question is based on the one-to-many relationship that exists between titles and employees. One title can have many employees, but a given employee has only one title. To answer the query, you search the Titles table for "manager" to determine its TitleID (T02). You then go to the Employees table and select those records that have this value in the TitleID field.

The design of a relational database enables us to extract information from multiple tables in a single query. Equally important, it simplifies the way data is changed in that modifications are made in only one place. Consider:

Query: Which employees work in the Boston office? What is their phone number? How many changes would be necessary if the Boston office were to get a new phone number?

Answer: There are four employees in Boston: Pamela Milgrom, Ann Manin, Patricia Rubin, and Kenneth Charles, each with the same number (617 123-4444). Only one change (in the Locations table) would be necessary if the phone number changed.

Once again, we draw on the one-to-many relationship between locations and employees. Thus, we begin in the Locations table where we search for "Boston" to determine its LocationID (L02) and phone number (617 123-4444). Then we go to the Employees table to select those records with this value in the LocationID field. Realize, however, that the phone number is stored in the Locations table. Thus, the new phone number is entered in the Boston record, where it is reflected automatically for each employee with a LocationID of L02 (corresponding to the Boston office).

HANDS-ON EXERCISE 4

A Look Ahead

Objective: To open a database with multiple tables; to identify the one-to-many relationships within the database and to produce reports based on those relationships. Use Figure 1.10 as a guide in the exercise.

STEP 1: Open the Relationships Window

➤ Start Access, click the **More Files option button,** and click **OK.** If Access is already open, pull down the **File menu** and click the **Open command.** Open the **Look Ahead database** in the **Exploring Access folder.**

➤ The Tables button should be selected as in Figure 1.10a. The database contains the Employees, Locations, and Titles tables.

➤ Pull down the **Tools menu** and click the **Relationships command** to open the Relationships window as shown in Figure 1.10a. (The tables are not yet visible in this window.)

➤ Pull down the **Relationships menu** and click the **Show Table command** to display the Show Table dialog box. Click (select) the **Locations table** (within the Show Table dialog box) then click the **Add button** to add this table to the Relationships window.

➤ Double click the **Titles** and **Employees tables** to add these tables to the Relationships window.

➤ Close the Show Table dialog box.

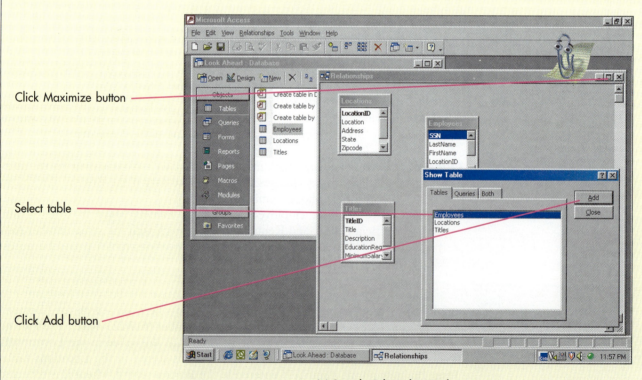

(a) Open the Relationships Window (step 1)

FIGURE 1.10 Hands-on Exercise 4

STEP 2: Create the Relationships

➤ Maximize the Relationships windows so that you have more room in which to work. Click and drag the title bar of each table so that the positions of the tables match those in Figure 1.10b. Click and drag the bottom (and/or right) border of each table so that you see all of the fields in each table.

➤ Click and drag the **LocationID field** in the Locations table field list to the **LocationID field** in the Employees field list. You will see the Edit Relationships dialog box. Check the box to **Enforce Referential Integrity.** Click the **Create button** to create the relationship.

➤ Click and drag the **TitleID field** in the Locations table field list to the **TitleID field** in the Employees field list. You will see the Edit Relationships dialog box. Check the box to **Enforce Referential Integrity** as shown in Figure 1.10b. Click the **Create button** to create the relationship.

➤ Click the **Save button** on the Relationship toolbar to save the Relationships window, then close the Relationships window.

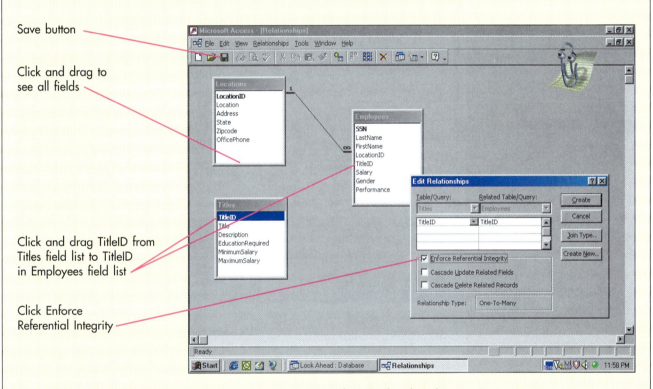

(b) Create the Relationships (step 2)

FIGURE 1.10 Hands-on Exercise 4 (continued)

THE RELATIONSHIPS ARE VISUAL

The tables in an Access database are created independently, then related to one another through the Relationships window. The number 1 and the infinity symbol (∞) appear at the ends of the line to indicate the nature of the relationship; e.g., a one-to-many relationship between the Locations and Employees tables.

STEP 3: Enter Your Own Record

➤ Double click the **Employees table** to open the table. Maximize the window. Pull down the **Insert** menu and click the **New Record** command (or click the **New Record button**) on the Table Datasheet toolbar.

➤ Enter data for yourself, using your own social security number, and your first and last name as shown in Figure 1.10c. Enter an invalid LocationID (e.g., **L44**) then complete the record as shown in the figure.

➤ Press the **enter key** when you have completed the data entry, then click **OK** when you see the error message. Access prevents you from entering a location that does not exist.

➤ Click in the **LocationID field** and enter **L04**, the LocationID for Miami. Press the **down arrow key** to move to the next record, which automatically saves the current record. Close the Employees table.

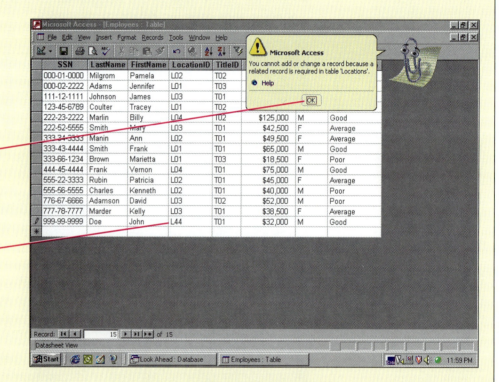

(c) Referential Integrity (step 3)

FIGURE 1.10 Hands-on Exercise 4 (continued)

REFERENTIAL INTEGRITY

The tables in a database must be consistent with one another, a concept known as referential integrity. Thus, Access automatically implements certain types of data validation to prevent such errors from occurring. You cannot, for example, enter a record in the Employees table that contains an invalid value for either the LocationID or the TitleID. Nor can you delete a record in the Locations or Titles table if it has related records in the Employees table.

STEP 4: Simplified Data Entry

➤ Click the **Forms button** in the Database window, then double click the **Employees Form** to open this form as shown in Figure 1.10d. Click the **Add Record button** then click in the text box for the Social Security Number.

➤ Enter the data for **Bob Grauer** one field at a time, pressing the **Tab key** to move from one field to the next. Click the **down arrow** when you come to the location field to display the available locations, then select (click) **Miami.**

➤ Press the **Tab key** to move to the Title field and choose **Account Rep.** Complete the data for Bob's record by entering **$150,000, M,** and **Excellent** in the Salary, Gender, and Performance fields, respectively.

➤ Click the **Close Form button** when you have finished entering the data.

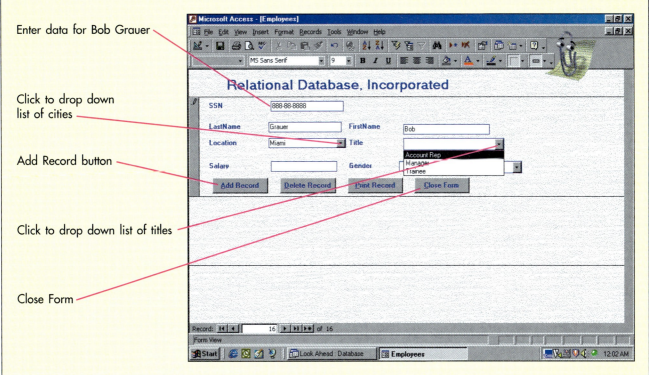

(d) Simplified Data Entry (step 4)

FIGURE 1.10 Hands-on Exercise 4 (continued)

SIMPLIFIED DATA ENTRY

The success of any system depends on the accuracy of its data as well as its ease of use. Both objectives are met through a well-designed form that guides the user through the process of data entry and simultaneously rejects invalid responses. The drop-down list boxes for the Location, Title, and Performance fields ensure that the user can enter only valid values in these fields. Data entry is also simplified in these fields in that you can enter just the first letter of a field, then press the Tab key to move to the next field.

STEP 5: View the Employee Master List

➤ Click the **Reports button** in the Database window. Double click the **Employee Master List** report to open the report as shown in figure 1.10e.

➤ This report lists selected fields for all employees in the database. Note that the two new employees, you and Bob Grauer, appear in alphabetical order. Both employees are in the Miami Office.

➤ Close the Report window.

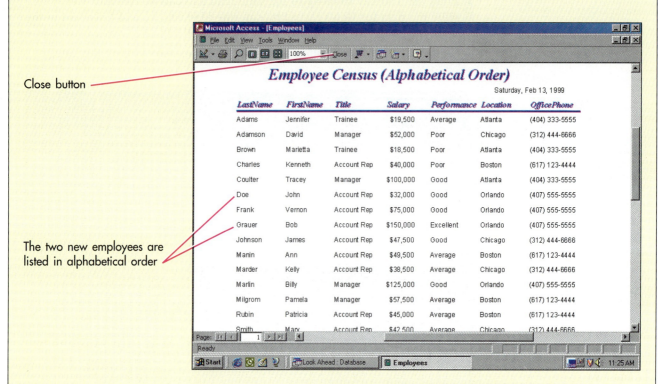

(e) View the Employee Master List (step 5)

FIGURE 1.10 Hands-on Exercise 4 (continued)

ADVICE FROM THE ASSISTANT

The Office Assistant monitors your work and displays a lightbulb when it has a suggestion to help you work more efficiently. Click the lightbulb to display the tip, then click OK or press the Esc key after you have read the information. The Assistant will not, however, repeat a tip from an earlier session unless it is reset at the start of a session. This is especially important in a laboratory situation where you are sharing a computer with many students. To reset the tips, click the Assistant to display its balloon, click the Options button in the balloon, then click the Options tab, then click the button to Reset My Tips.

STEP 6: Change the Locations Table

➤ Click the **Tables button** in the Database window, then double click the **Locations table** to open this table as shown in figure 1.10f. Maximize the window.

➤ Click the **plus sign** next to location L04 (Miami) to view the employees in this office. The plus sign changes to a minus sign as the employee records for this location are shown. Your name appears in this list as does Bob Grauer's. Click the **minus sign** and the list of related records disappears.

➤ Click and drag to select **Miami** (the current value in the Location field). Type **Orlando** and press the **Tab key.** Enter the corresponding values for the other field: **1000 Kirkman Road, FL, 32801** and **(407) 555-5555** for the address, state, zip code, and office phone, respectively.

➤ Close the **Locations table.** You have moved the Miami Office to Orlando.

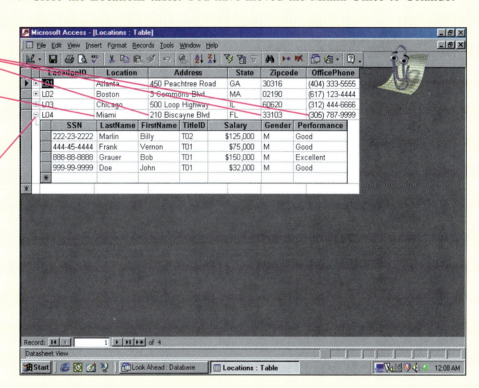

Change address and phone number

Change Miami to Orlando

Click + sign to display employees at Location LO4 (+ changes to a −)

(f) Change the Locations Table (step 6)

FIGURE 1.10 Hands-on Exercise 4 (continued)

ADD AND DELETE RELATED RECORDS

Take advantage of the one-to-many relationship between locations and employees (or titles and employees) to add and/or delete records in the Employees table. Open the Locations table, then click the plus sign next to the location where you want to add or delete an employee record. To add a new employee, click the New Record navigation button within the Employees table for that location, then add the new data. To delete a record, click the record, then click the Delete Record button on the Table Datasheet toolbar. Click the minus sign to close the employee list.

STEP 7: View the Employees by Title Report

➤ Click the **Reports button** in the Database window, then double click the **Employees by Title** report to open the report shown in Figure 1.10g.

➤ This report lists employees by title, rather than alphabetically. Note that you and Bob Grauer are both listed as Account Reps in the Orlando office; i.e., the location of the office was changed in the Locations table and that change is automatically reflected for all employees assigned to that office.

➤ Close the Report window. Close the Database window. Exit Access. Welcome to the world of relational databases.

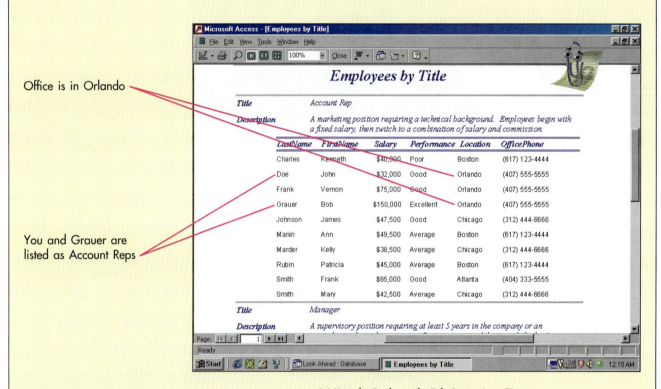

(g) View the Employees by Title Report (step 7)

FIGURE 1.10 Hands-on Exercise 4 (continued)

THE WHAT'S THIS COMMAND

Use the What's This command to obtain a detailed explanation for any toolbar button. Pull down the Help menu and click the What's This command (or press the Shift+F1 key) to change the mouse pointer to an arrow with a question mark. Now click any toolbar button for an explanation of that button. Press the Esc key to return the mouse pointer to normal and continue working.

SUMMARY

An Access database has seven types of objects—tables, forms, queries, reports, pages, macros, and modules. The database window displays these objects and enables you to open an existing object or create a new object.

Each table in the database is composed of records, and each record is in turn composed of fields. Every record in a given table has the same fields in the same order.

A table is displayed in one of two views—the Design view or the Datasheet view. The Design view is used to define the table initially and to specify the fields it will contain. The Datasheet view is the view you use to add, edit, or delete records.

A record selector symbol is displayed next to the current record and signifies the status of that record. A triangle indicates that the record has been saved. A pencil indicates that the record has not been saved and that you are in the process of entering (or changing) the data. An asterisk appears next to the blank record present at the end of every table, where you add a new record to the table.

Access automatically saves any changes in the current record as soon as you move to the next record or when you close the table. The Undo Current Record command cancels (undoes) the changes to the previously saved record.

No system, no matter how sophisticated, can produce valid output from invalid input. Data validation is thus a critical part of any system. Access automatically imposes certain types of data validation during data entry. Additional checks can be implemented by the user.

A filter is a set of criteria that is applied to a table in order to display a subset of the records in that table. Microsoft Access lets you filter by selection or filter by form. The application of a filter does not remove the records from the table, but simply suppresses them from view. The records in a table can be displayed in ascending or descending sequence by clicking the appropriate button on the Database toolbar.

A relational database contains multiple tables and enables you to extract information from those tables in a single query. The tables must be consistent with one another, a concept known as referential integrity. Thus, Access automatically implements certain types of data validation to prevent such errors from occurring.

KEY WORDS AND CONCEPTS

- Asterisk (record selector) symbol
- AutoCorrect
- Current record
- Data validation
- Database
- Database window
- Datasheet view
- Design view
- Field
- Field name
- Filter
- Filter by Form
- Filter by Selection
- Filter Excluding Selection
- Find command
- Form
- GIGO (garbage in, garbage out)
- Insertion point
- Macro
- Microsoft Access
- Module
- One-to-many relationship
- Page
- Pencil (record selector) symbol
- Primary key
- Query
- Record
- Record selector symbol
- Referential Integrity
- Relational database
- Remove filter
- Replace command
- Report
- Sort
- Sort Ascending
- Sort Descending
- Table
- Triangle (record selector) symbol
- Undo command

MULTIPLE CHOICE

1. Which sequence represents the hierarchy of terms, from smallest to largest?
   (a) Database, table, record, field
   (b) Field, record, table, database
   (c) Record, field, table, database
   (d) Field, record, database, table

2. Which of the following is true regarding movement within a record (assuming you are not in the first or last field of that record)?
   (a) Press Tab or the right arrow key to move to the next field
   (b) Press Shift+Tab or the left arrow key to return to the previous field
   (c) Both (a) and (b)
   (d) Neither (a) nor (b)

3. You're performing routine maintenance on a table within an Access database. When should you execute the Save command?
   (a) Immediately after you add, edit, or delete a record
   (b) Periodically during a session—for example, after every fifth change
   (c) Once at the end of a session
   (d) None of the above since Access automatically saves the changes as they are made

4. Which of the following objects are contained within an Access database?
   (a) Tables and forms
   (b) Queries and reports
   (c) Macros and modules
   (d) All of the above

5. Which of the following is true about the objects in an Access database?
   (a) Every database must contain at least one object of every type
   (b) A database may contain at most one object of each type
   (c) Both (a) and (b)
   (d) Neither (a) nor (b)

6. Which of the following is true of an Access database?
   (a) Every record in a table has the same fields as every other record in that table
   (b) Every table contains the same number of records as every other table
   (c) Both (a) and (b)
   (d) Neither (a) nor (b)

7. Which of the following is a *false* statement about the Open Database command?
   (a) It can be executed from the File menu
   (b) It can be executed by clicking the Open button on the Database toolbar
   (c) It loads a database from disk into memory
   (d) It opens the selected table from the Database window

8. Which of the following is true regarding the record selector symbol?
   (a) A pencil indicates that the current record has already been saved
   (b) A triangle indicates that the current record has not changed
   (c) An asterisk indicates the first record in the table
   (d) All of the above

9. Which view is used to add, edit, and delete records in a table?
   (a) The Design view
   (b) The Datasheet view
   (c) Either (a) or (b)
   (d) Neither (a) nor (b)

10. Which of the following is true with respect to a table within an Access database?
    (a) Ctrl+End moves to the last field in the last record of a table
    (b) Ctrl+Home moves to the first field in the first record of a table
    (c) Both (a) and (b)
    (d) Neither (a) nor (b)

11. What does GIGO stand for?
    (a) Gee, I Goofed, OK
    (b) Grand Illusions, Go On
    (c) Global Indexing, Global Order
    (d) Garbage In, Garbage Out

12. The find and replace values in a Replace command must be:
    (a) The same length
    (b) The same case
    (c) Both (a) and (b)
    (d) Neither (a) nor (b)

13. An Access table containing 10 records, and 10 fields per record, requires two pages for printing. What, if anything, can be done to print the table on one page?
    (a) Print in Landscape rather than Portrait mode
    (b) Decrease the left and right margins
    (c) Both (a) and (b)
    (d) Neither (a) nor (b)

14. Which of the following capabilities is available through Filter by Selection?
    (a) The imposition of a relational condition
    (b) The imposition of an alternate (OR) condition
    (c) Both (a) and (b)
    (d) Neither (a) nor (b)

15. Which of the following best describes the relationship between locations and employees as implemented in the Look Ahead database within the chapter?
    (a) One to one
    (b) One to many
    (c) Many to many
    (d) Impossible to determine

Answers

1. b	6. a	11. d
2. c	7. d	12. d
3. d	8. b	13. c
4. d	9. b	14. d
5. d	10. c	15. b

PRACTICE WITH ACCESS 2000

1. The Employee Database: Review and/or complete the third hands-on exercise that introduced the Employee database. Be sure to remove any filters that are in effect at the end of the exercise, then implement the following transactions:
   a. Delete the record for Kelly Marder.
   b. Change Pamela Milgrom's salary to $59,500.
   c. Use the Replace command to change all occurrences of "Manager" to "Supervisor."
   d. Print the Employee Census Report as shown in Figure 1.11 after making the changes in parts (a) through (c).
   e. Create a cover page (in Microsoft Word) and submit the assignment to your instructor.

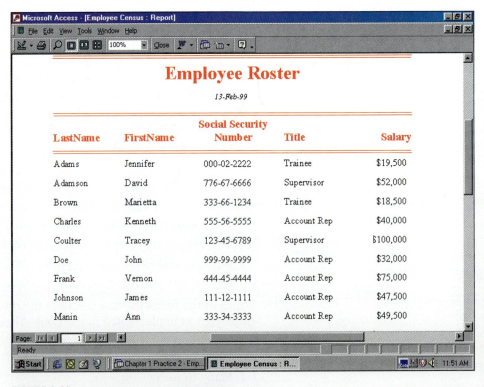

FIGURE 1.11   The Employee Database (Exercise 1)

2. Do the two hands-on exercises in the chapter, then modify the Bookstore database to accommodate the following:
   a. Add the book, *Exploring Microsoft Office 2000 Vol II* (ISBN: 013-011100-7) by Grauer/Barber, published in 1999 by Prentice Hall, selling for $45.00.
   b. Change the price of *Memory Management for All of Us* to $29.95.
   c. Delete *The Presentation Design Book*.
   d. Print the *All Books Report* after these changes have been made.

3. The United States: Figure 1.12 displays a table from the United States (USA) database that is one of our practice files. The database contains statistical data about all 50 states and enables you to produce various reports such as the 10 largest states in terms of population.
   a. Open the USA database, then open the USstates table. Click anywhere in the Population field, then click the Sort Descending button to list the states in descending order. Click and drag to select the first ten records so that you have selected the ten most populous states.
   b. Pull down the File menu, click the Print command, then click the option button to print the selected records. Be sure to print in Landscape mode so that all of the data fits on one page. (Use the Page Setup command in the File menu prior to printing.)
   c. Repeat the procedure in steps a and b, but this time print the ten states with the largest area.
   d. Repeat the procedure once again to print the first thirteen states admitted to the Union. (You have to sort in ascending rather than descending sequence.)
   e. Submit all three pages together with a title page (created in Microsoft Word) to your instructor.

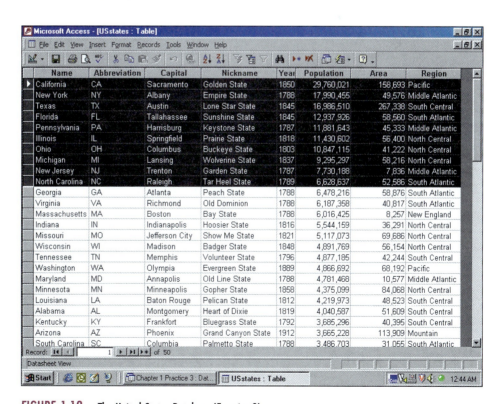

FIGURE 1.12 The United States Database (Exercise 3)

4. The Super Bowl: Open the Super Bowl database on the data disk and display the table in Figure 1.13. Our data stops with the 1999 Super Bowl and it may no longer be current. Thus, the first thing you will need to do is update our table.

   a. Pull down the View menu, click Toolbars, then toggle the Web toolbar on. Enter the address of the NFL home page (www.nfl.com) in the Address bar, then click the link to the Super Bowl. Follow the links that will allow you to determine the teams and score of any game(s) not included in our table.

   b. Click the New Record button and enter the additional data in the table. The additional data will be entered at the end of the table, and hence you need to sort the data after it is entered. Click anywhere in the Year field, then click the Descending Sort button to display the most recent Super Bowl first as shown in Figure 1.13c.

   c. Select the winner in any year that the AFC won. Click the Filter by Selection button to display only those records (i.e., the years in which the AFC won the game). Print these records.

   d. Click the Remove Filter button. Select any year in which the NFC won, then click the Filter by Selection button to display the years in which the NFC won. Print these records. Remove the filter.

   e. Create one additional filter (e.g., the years in which your team won the big game). Print these records as well.

   f. Create a cover sheet, then submit all three reports to your instructor.

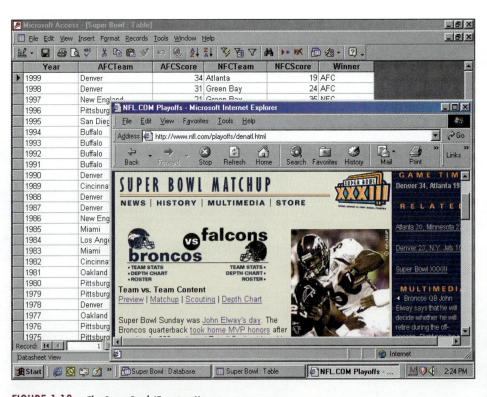

FIGURE 1.13 The Super Bowl (Exercise 4)

5. **A Look Ahead:** Review and/or complete the fourth hands-on exercise that pertained to the Look Ahead database. Enter the following additional transactions, then print the Employees by Location report shown in Figure 1.14.
   a. Add a new location to the Locations table. Use L05, New York, 1000 Broadway, NY, 10020, and (212) 666-6666 for the LocationID, Location, Address, State, ZipCode, and OfficePhone fields, respectively.
   b. Change the assigned location for Bob Grauer, Frank Smith, and yourself to the New York Office. Bob will be the manager of the New York office.
   c. Delete the record for Kenneth Charles.
   d. Change the title, "Account Rep" to "Account Exec."
   e. Print the Employees by Location report and submit it to your instructor as proof you did this exercise.

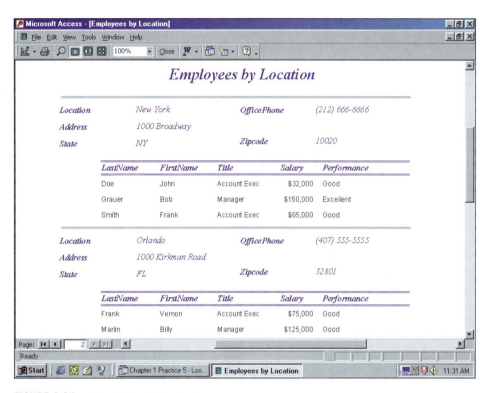

FIGURE 1.14 A Look Ahead (Exercise 5)

6. **A Companion Web site** (or online study guide) accompanies each book in the *Exploring Microsoft Office 2000* series. Go to the Exploring Windows home page at www.prenhall.com/grauer, click the book to Office 2000, and click the Companion Web site tab at the top of the screen. Choose the appropriate text (Exploring Access 2000) and the chapter within the text (e.g., Chapter 1).

   Each chapter contains a series of short-answer exercises (multiple-choice, true/false, and matching) to review the material in the chapter. You can take practice quizzes by yourself and/or e-mail the results to your instructor. You can try the essay questions for additional practice and engage in online chat sessions. We hope you will find the online guide to be a valuable resource.

CASE STUDIES

Planning for Disaster

This case has nothing to do with databases per se, but it is perhaps the most important case of all, as it deals with the question of backup. Do you have a backup strategy? Do you even know what a backup strategy is? Now is a good time to learn because sooner or later you will wish you had one. There will come a time when you will accidentally erase a file, be unable to read from a floppy disk, or worse yet, suffer a hardware failure in which you are unable to access the hard drive. The problem always seems to occur the night before an assignment is due. The ultimate disaster is the disappearance of your computer, by theft or natural disaster (e.g., Hurricane Andrew, the floods in the Midwest, or the Los Angeles earthquake). Describe in 250 or fewer words the backup strategy you plan to implement in conjunction with your work in this class.

The Common User Interface

One of the most significant benefits of the Windows environment is the common user interface, which provides a sense of familiarity when you go from one application to another—for example, when you go from Excel to Access. How many similarities can you find between these two applications? Which menus are common to both? Which keyboard shortcuts? Which formatting conventions? Which toolbar icons? Which shortcut menus?

Garbage In, Garbage Out

Your excellent work in this class has earned you an internship in the registrar's office. Your predecessor has created a student database that appears to work well, but in reality has several problems in that many of its reports do not produce the expected information. One problem came to light in conjunction with a report listing business majors: the report contained far fewer majors than were expected. Open the GIGO database on the data disk and see if you can find and correct the problem.

Changing Menus and Toolbars

Office 2000 implements one very significant change over previous versions of Office in that it displays a series of short menus that contain only basic commands. The additional commands are made visible by clicking the double arrow that appears at the bottom of the menu. New commands are added to the menu as they are used, and conversely, other commands are removed if they are not used. A similar strategy is followed for the Standard and Formatting toolbars which are displayed on a single row, and thus do not show all of the buttons at one time. The intent is to simplify Office 2000 for the new user by limiting the number of commands that are visible. The consequence, however, is that the individual is not exposed to new commands, and hence may not use Office to its full potential. Which set of menus do you prefer? How do you switch from one set to the other?

chapter 1

INTRODUCTION TO POWERPOINT: PRESENTATIONS MADE EASY

OBJECTIVES

After reading this chapter you will be able to:

1. Describe the common user interface; give several examples of how PowerPoint follows the same conventions as other Office applications.
2. Start PowerPoint; open, modify, and view an existing presentation.
3. Describe the different ways to print a presentation.
4. List the different views in PowerPoint; describe the unique features of each view.
5. Use the Outline view to create and edit a presentation; display and hide text within the Outline view.
6. Add a new slide to a presentation; explain how to change the layout of the objects on an existing slide.
7. Use the Microsoft Clip Gallery to add and/or change the clip art on a slide.
8. Apply a design template to a new presentation; change the template in an existing presentation.
9. Add transition effects to the slides in a presentation; apply build effects to the bullets and graphical objects in a specific slide.

OVERVIEW

This chapter introduces you to PowerPoint, one of the four major applications in the Professional version of Microsoft Office (Microsoft Word, Microsoft Excel, and Microsoft Access are the other three). PowerPoint enables you to create a professional presentation without relying on others, then it lets you deliver that presentation in a variety of ways. You can show the presentation on the computer, on the World Wide Web, or via 35-mm slides or overhead transparencies.

PowerPoint is easy to learn because it is a Windows application and follows the conventions associated with the common user interface. Thus, if you already know one Windows application, it is that much easier to learn PowerPoint because you can apply what you know. It's even easier if you use Word, Excel, or Access since there are over 100 commands that are common to Microsoft Office.

The chapter begins by showing you an existing PowerPoint presentation so that you can better appreciate what PowerPoint is all about. We discuss the various views within PowerPoint and the advantages of each. We describe how to modify an existing presentation and how to view a presentation on the computer. You are then ready to create your own presentation, a process that requires you to focus on the content and the message you want to deliver. We show you how to enter the text of the presentation, how to add and/or change the format of a slide, and how to apply a design template. We also explain how to animate the presentation to create additional interest.

As always, learning is best accomplished by doing, so we include three hands-on exercises that enable you to apply these concepts at the computer. One final point before we begin, is that while PowerPoint can help you create attractive presentations, the content and delivery are still up to you.

A POWERPOINT PRESENTATION

A PowerPoint presentation consists of a series of slides such as those in Figure 1.1. The various slides contain different elements (such as text, clip art, and WordArt), yet the presentation has a consistent look with respect to its overall design and color scheme. You might think that creating this type of presentation is difficult, but it isn't. It is remarkably easy, and that is the beauty of PowerPoint. In essence, PowerPoint allows you to concentrate on the content of a presentation without worrying about its appearance. You supply the text and supporting elements and leave the formatting to PowerPoint.

In addition to helping you create the presentation, PowerPoint provides a variety of ways to deliver it. You can show the presentation on a computer using animated transition effects as you move from one slide to the next. You can include sound and/or video in the presentation, provided your system has a sound card and speakers. You can also automate the presentation and distribute it on a disk for display at a convention booth or kiosk. If you cannot show the presentation on a computer, you can convert it to 35-mm slides or overhead transparencies.

PowerPoint also gives you the ability to print the presentation in various ways to distribute to your audience. You can print one slide per page, or you can print miniature versions of each slide and choose between two, three, four, six, or even nine slides per page. You can prepare speaker notes for yourself consisting of a picture of each slide together with notes about the slide. You can also print the text of the presentation in outline form. Giving the audience a copy of the presentation (in any format) enables them to follow it more closely, and to take it home when the session is over.

POLISH YOUR DELIVERY

The speaker is still the most important part of any presentation and a poor delivery will kill even the best presentation. Look at the audience as you speak to open communication and gain credibility. Don't read from a prepared script. Speak slowly and clearly and try to vary your delivery. Pause to emphasize key points and be sure the person in the last row can hear you.

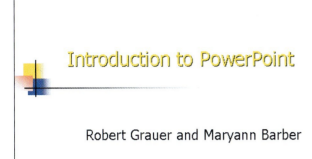
(a) Title Slide

The Essence of PowerPoint
- You focus on content
  - Enter your thoughts in an outline or directly on the individual slides
- PowerPoint takes care of the design
  - Professionally designed templates
  - Preformatted slide layouts

(b) Bullet Slide

Add Other Objects for Interest
- Clipart, WordArt, and organization charts
- Charts from Microsoft Excel
- Photographs from the Web
- Animation and sound

(c) Clip Art

Flexibility in Output
- Computer presentations
- Overhead transparencies
- Presentation on the Web
- 35mm slides
- Audience handouts
- Speaker notes

(d) Clip Art

PowerPoint is Easy To Learn
- It follows the same conventions as every Windows application
- It uses the same menus and command structure as other Office applications
- Keyboard shortcuts also apply, such as **Ctrl+B** for boldface
- Help is only a mouse click away

(e) Animated Text

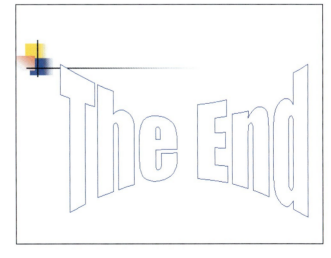

(f) Word Art

FIGURE 1.1   A PowerPoint Presentation

INTRODUCTION TO POWERPOINT

The desktop in Figure 1.2 should look somewhat familiar, even if you have never used PowerPoint, because PowerPoint shares the common user interface that is present in every Windows application. You should recognize, therefore, the two open windows in Figure 1.2—the application window for PowerPoint and the document window for the current presentation.

Each window has its own Minimize, Maximize (or Restore), and Close buttons. Both windows have been maximized and thus the title bars have been merged into a single title bar that appears at the top of the application window. The title bar indicates the application (Microsoft PowerPoint) as well as the name of the presentation on which you are working (Introduction to PowerPoint). The *menu bar* appears immediately below the title bar and it provides access to the pull-down menus within the application.

The Standard and Formatting toolbars are displayed below the menu bar and are similar to those in Word and Excel. Hence, you may recognize several buttons from those applications. The *Standard toolbar* contains buttons for the most basic commands in PowerPoint such as opening, saving, and printing a presentation. The *Formatting toolbar,* under the Standard toolbar, provides access to formatting operations such as boldface, italics, and underlining.

The vertical *scroll bar* is seen at the right of the document window and indicates that the presentation contains additional slides that are not visible. This is consistent with the *status bar* at the bottom of the window that indicates you are working on slide 1 of 6. The *Drawing toolbar* appears above the status bar and contains additional tools for working on the slide. The view buttons above the Drawing toolbar are used to switch between the different views of a presentation. PowerPoint views are discussed in the next section. The Windows 95/98 taskbar appears at the bottom of the screen and shows you the open applications.

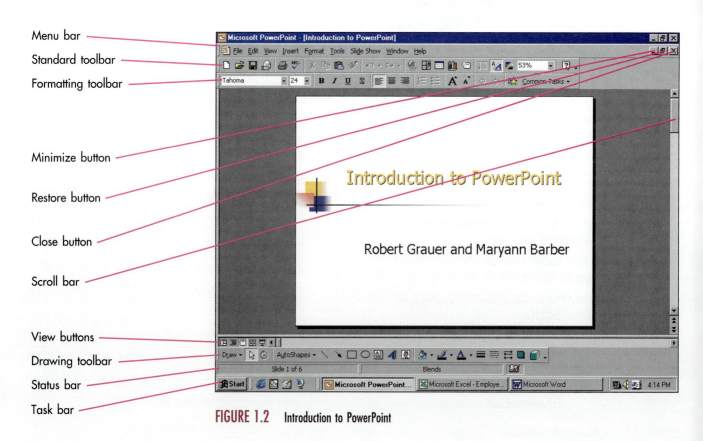

FIGURE 1.2 Introduction to PowerPoint

Six Different Views

PowerPoint offers six different views in which to create, modify, and/or show a presentation, as shown in Figure 1.3. Each view represents a different way of looking at the presentation, and each view has unique capabilities. Some views display only a single slide whereas others show multiple slides, making it easy to organize the presentation. You can switch back and forth between the views by clicking the appropriate view button at the bottom of the presentation window.

The *Slide view* in Figure 1.3a displays one slide at a time and enables all operations for that slide. You can enter, delete, or format text. You can also add other objects such as a graph, clip art, or organization chart, or even sound and video. The Drawing toolbar is displayed by default in this view.

The *Slide Sorter view* in Figure 1.3b displays multiple slides on the screen (each slide is in miniature) and lets you see the overall flow of the presentation. You can change the order of a presentation by clicking and dragging a slide from one position to another. You can delete a slide by clicking the slide and pressing the Del key. You can also set transition (animation) effects on each slide to add interest to the presentation. The Slide Sorter view has its own toolbar, which is discussed in conjunction with creating transition effects.

The *Outline view* in Figure 1.3c shows the presentation in outline form (in conjunction with a miniature slide and notes page). The Outline view is the fastest way to enter or edit text, in that you type directly into the outline. You can copy and/or move text from one slide to another. You can also rearrange the order of the slides within the presentation. You can also delete a slide by clicking its icon and pressing the Del key. The Outline view has its own toolbar that is displayed at the left of the slide.

The *Notes Page view* in Figure 1.3d lets you create speaker's notes for some or all of the slides in a presentation. These notes do not appear when you show the presentation, but can be printed for use during the presentation to help you remember the key points about each slide.

The *Normal view* in Figure 1.3e displays the Slide, Outline, and Notes Page views in a single window, with each view in its own pane. Anything that you do in one view is automatically reflected in the other views. If, for example, you add or format text in the Outline view, the changes are also made in the Slide view. Note, too, that the size of panes can be changed as necessary within the Normal view.

The *Slide Show view* in Figure 1.3f displays the slides one at a time as an electronic presentation on the computer. The show may be presented manually where you click the mouse to move from one slide to the next. The presentation can also be shown automatically, where each slide stays on the screen for a predetermined amount of time, after which the next slide appears automatically. Either way, the slide show may contain transition effects from one slide to the next, as you will see in the hands-on exercise that follows shortly.

THE MENUS CHANGE

PowerPoint 2000 displays abbreviated menus that contain only basic commands, so as to simplify the application for a new user. There is also a double arrow at the bottom of each menu that you can click to display the remaining commands. In addition, each time you execute a command it is added to the menu, and conversely, less frequently used commands are removed from the menu. You can choose, however, to display the full menus through the Customize command in the Tools menu.

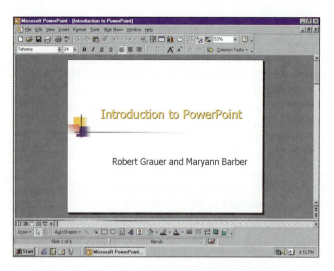
(a) Slide View

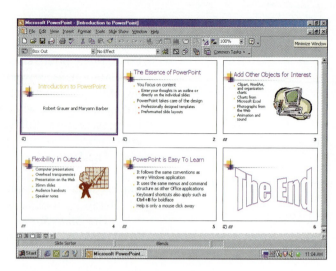
(b) Slide Sorter View

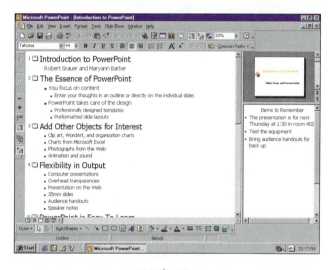
(c) Outline View

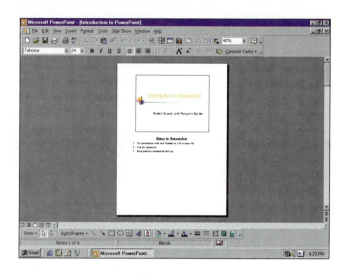
(d) Notes Page View

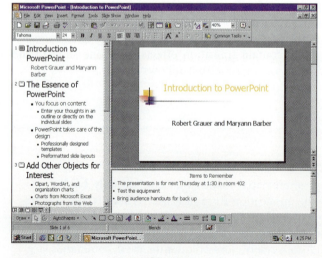
(e) Normal View

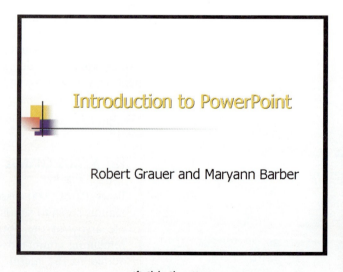
(f) Slide Show View

FIGURE 1.3 Six Different Views

The File Menu

The *File menu* is a critically important menu in virtually every Windows application. It contains the Save and Open commands to save a presentation on disk, then subsequently retrieve (open) that presentation at a later time. The File Menu also contains the **Print command** to print a presentation, the **Close command** to close the current presentation but continue working in the application, and the **Exit command** to quit the application altogether.

The **Save command** copies the presentation that you are working on (i.e., the presentation that is currently in memory) to disk. The command functions differently the first time it is executed for a new presentation, in that it displays the Save As dialog box as shown in Figure 1.4a. The dialog box requires you to specify the name of the presentation, the drive (and an optional folder) in which the presentation is to be stored, and its file type. All subsequent executions of the command save the presentation under the assigned name, replacing the previously saved version with the new version.

The *file name* (e.g., My First Presentation) can contain up to 255 characters including spaces, commas, and/or periods. (Periods are discouraged, however, since they are too easily confused with DOS extensions.) The Save In list box is used to select the drive (which is not visible in Figure 1.4a) and the folder (e.g., Exploring PowerPoint) in which the file will be saved. The **Places bar** provides shortcuts to frequently used folders without having to search through the Save In list box. Click the Desktop icon, for example, and the file is saved on the Windows desktop. The *file type* defaults to a PowerPoint 2000 presentation. You can, however, choose a different format, such as PowerPoint 95, to maintain compatibility with earlier versions of PowerPoint. You can also save any PowerPoint presentation as a Web page (or HTML document).

The **Open command** is the opposite of the Save command as it brings a copy of an existing presentation into memory, enabling you to work with that presentation. The Open command displays the Open dialog box in which you specify the file name, the drive (and optionally the folder) that contains the file, and the file type. PowerPoint will then list all files of that type on the designated drive (and folder), enabling you to open the file you want. The Save and Open commands work in conjunction with one another. The Save As dialog box in Figure 1.4a, for example, saves the file My First Presentation in the Exploring PowerPoint folder. The Open dialog box in Figure 1.4b loads that file into memory so that you can work with the file, after which you can save the revised file for use at a later time.

The toolbars in the Save As and Open dialog boxes have several buttons in common that facilitate the execution of either command. The Views button lets you display the files in one of four different views. The Details view (in Figure 1.4a) shows the file size as well as the date and time that the file was last modified. The Preview view (in Figure 1.4b) shows the first slide in a presentation, without having to open the presentation. The List view displays only the file names, and thus lets you see more files at one time. The Properties view shows information about the presentation including the date of creation and number of revisions.

SORT BY NAME, DATE, OR FILE SIZE

The files in the Save As and Open dialog boxes can be displayed in ascending or descending sequence by name, date modified, or size. Change to the Details view, then click the heading of the desired column; e.g., click the Modified column to list the files according to the date they were last changed. Click the column heading a second time to reverse the sequence; that is, to switch from ascending to descending, and vice versa.

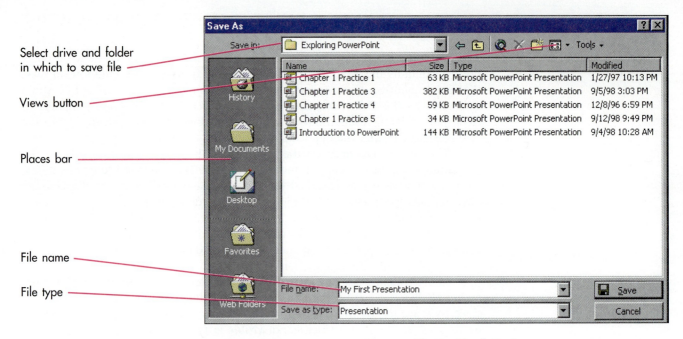

(a) Save as Dialog Box (Details View)

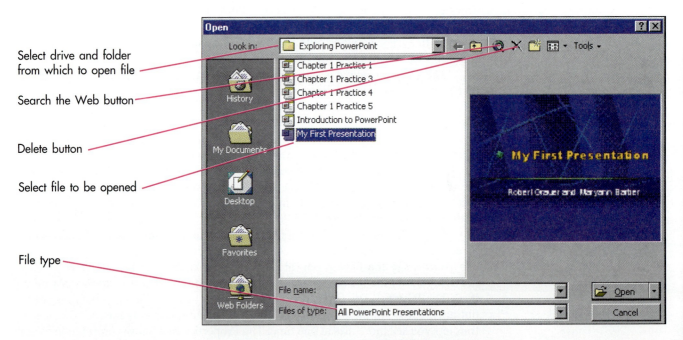

(b) Open Dialog Box (Preview View)

FIGURE 1.4   The Save and Open Commands

HANDS-ON EXERCISE 1

Introduction to PowerPoint

Objective: To start PowerPoint, open an existing presentation, and modify the text on an existing slide; to show an existing presentation and print handouts of its slides. Use Figure 1.5 as a guide in the exercise.

STEP 1: Welcome to Windows

➤ Turn on the computer and all of its peripherals. The floppy drive should be empty prior to starting your machine. This ensures that the system starts by reading from the hard disk, which contains the Windows files, as opposed to a floppy disk, which does not.

➤ Your system will take a minute or so to get started, after which you should see the desktop in Figure 1.5a. Do not be concerned if the appearance of your desktop is different from ours.

➤ You may see additional objects on the desktop in Windows 95 and/or the active desktop in Windows 98. It doesn't matter which operating system you are using because Office 2000 runs equally well under both Windows 95 and Windows 98, as well as Windows NT.

➤ You may also see a Welcome to Windows dialog box with commands to take a tour of the operating system. If so, click the appropriate button(s) or close the dialog box.

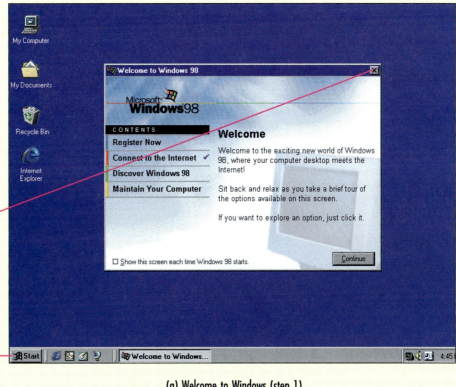

Click the close button to close the dialog box

Click the Start button

(a) Welcome to Windows (step 1)

FIGURE 1.5 Hands-on Exercise 1

STEP 2: Obtain the Practice Files

➤ We have created a series of practice files (also called a "data disk") for you to use throughout the text. Your instructor will make these files available to you in a variety of ways:
- The files may be on a network drive, in which case you use Windows Explorer to copy the files from the network to a floppy disk.
- There may be an actual "data disk" that you are to check out from the lab in order to use the Copy Disk command to duplicate the disk.

➤ You can also download the files from our Web site provided you have an Internet connection. Start Internet Explorer, then go to the Exploring Windows home page at **www.prenhall.com/grauer.**
- Click the book for **Office 2000,** which takes you to the Office 2000 home page. Click the **Student Resources tab** (at the top of the window) to go to the Student Resources page as shown in Figure 1.5b.
- Click the link to **Student Data Disk** (in the left frame), then scroll down the page until you can select PowerPoint 2000. Click the link to download the student data disk.
- You will see the File Download dialog box asking what you want to do. The option button to save this program to disk is selected. Click **OK.** The Save As dialog box appears.
- Click the down arrow in the Save In list box to enter the drive and folder where you want to save the file. It's best to save the file to the Windows desktop or to a temporary folder on drive C
- Double click the file after it has been downloaded to your PC, then follow the onscreen instructions.

➤ Check with your instructor for additional information.

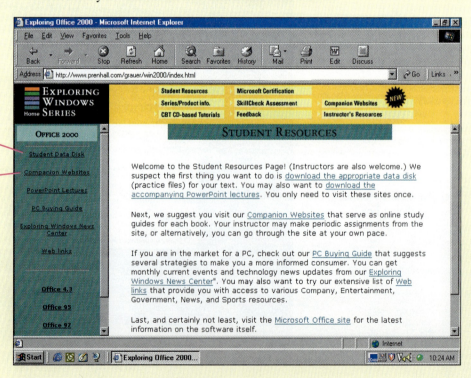

(b) Download the Data Disk (step 2)

FIGURE 1.5 Hands-on Exercise 1 (continued)

STEP 3: Start PowerPoint

➤ Click the **Start button** to display the Start menu. Slide the mouse pointer over the various menu options and notice that each time you point to a submenu, its items are displayed; i.e., you can point rather than click a submenu.

➤ Point to (or click) the **Programs menu,** then click **Microsoft PowerPoint 2000** to start the program and display the screen in Figure 1.5c. Right click the **Office Assistant** if it appears, then click the command to hide it. We return to the Assistant in step 7.

➤ Click the option button to **Open an Existing Presentation,** click **More Files** in the open list box, then click **OK.** (If you do *not* see the PowerPoint dialog box, pull down the **File menu** and click **Open** or click the **Open button** on the Standard toolbar.)

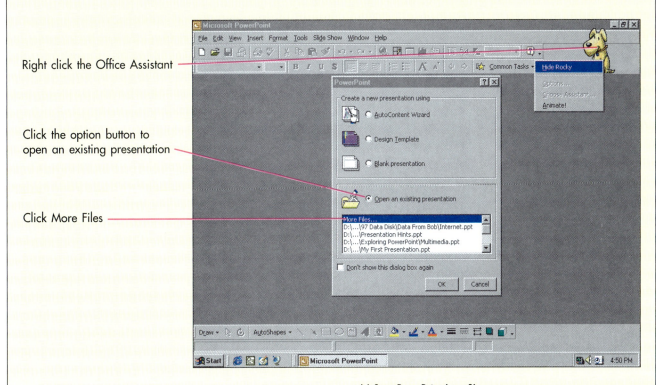

(c) Start PowerPoint (step 3)

FIGURE 1.5 Hands-on Exercise 1 (continued)

ABOUT THE ASSISTANT

The Assistant is very powerful and hence you want to experiment with various ways to use it. To ask a question, click the Assistant's icon to toggle its balloon on or off. To change the way in which the Assistant works, click the Options button within this balloon and experiment with the various check boxes to see their effects. If you find the Assistant distracting, click and drag the character out of the way or hide it altogether by pulling down the Help menu and clicking the Hide the Office Assistant command. Pull down the Help menu and click the Show the Office Assistant command to return to the Assistant.

STEP 4: Open a Presentation

➤ You should see an Open dialog box similar to the one in Figure 1.5d. Click the **drop-down arrow** on the Look In list box. Click the appropriate drive, drive C or drive A, depending on the location of your data.

➤ Double click the **Exploring PowerPoint folder** to make it the active folder. This is the folder from which you will retrieve and into which you will save the presentation.

➤ Click the **Views button** repeatedly to cycle through the different views. We selected the Preview view in Figure 1.5d.

➤ Double click **Introduction to PowerPoint** to open the presentation and begin the exercise.

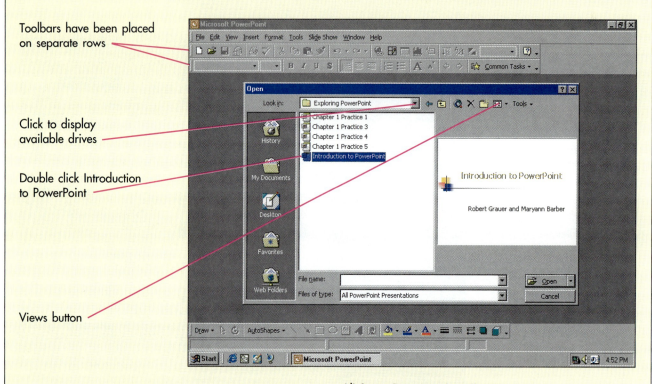

(d) Open a Presentation (step 4)

FIGURE 1.5 Hands-on Exercise 1 (continued)

SEPARATE THE TOOLBARS

Office 2000 displays the Standard and Formatting toolbars on the same row to save space within the application window. The result is that only a limited number of buttons are visible on each toolbar, and hence you may need to click the double arrow (More Buttons) tool at the end of the toolbar to view additional buttons. You can, however, separate the toolbars. Pull down the Tools menu, click the Customize command, click the Options tab, then clear the check box that has the Standard and Formatting toolbars share one row.

STEP 5: The Save As Command

➤ If necessary, click the maximize button in the application window so that PowerPoint takes the entire desktop. Click the maximize button in the document window (if necessary) so that the document window is as large as possible.

➤ Pull down the **File menu.** Click **Save As** to display the dialog box shown in Figure 1.5e. Enter **Finished Introduction** as the name of the new presentation. Click the **Save button.**

➤ There are now two identical copies of the file on disk, "Introduction to PowerPoint" which is the original presentation that we supplied, and "Finished Introduction" which you just created. The title bar shows the latter name, as it is the presentation currently in memory.

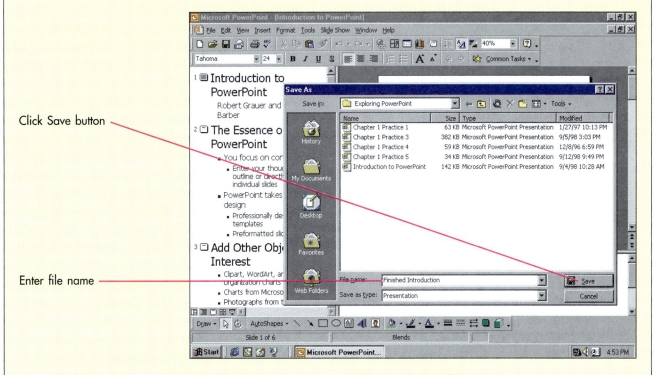

(e) The Save As Command (step 5)

FIGURE 1.5 Hands-on Exercise 1 (continued)

DIFFERENT FILE TYPES

The file format for PowerPoint 2000 is compatible with PowerPoint 97, but incompatible with earlier versions such as PowerPoint 95. The newer releases can open a presentation that was created using the older program (PowerPoint 95), but the reverse is not true; that is, you cannot open a presentation that was created in PowerPoint 2000 in PowerPoint 95 unless you change the file type. Pull down the File menu, click the Save As command, then specify the earlier (PowerPoint 6.0/PowerPoint 95) file type. You will be able to read the file in PowerPoint 95, but will lose any commands that are unique to the newer release.

STEP 6: Modify a Slide

➤ Press and hold the left mouse button as you drag the mouse over the presenters' names, **Robert Grauer and Maryann Barber.** You can select the text in either the outline or the slide pane.

➤ Release the mouse. The names should be highlighted (selected) as shown in Figure 1.5f. The selected text is the text that will be affected by the next command.

➤ Type your name, which automatically replaces the selected text in both the outline and the slide pane. Press **enter.**

➤ Type your class on the next line and note that the entry is made in both the slide and the outline pane.

➤ Pull down the **File menu** and click **Save** (or click the **Save button** on the Standard toolbar).

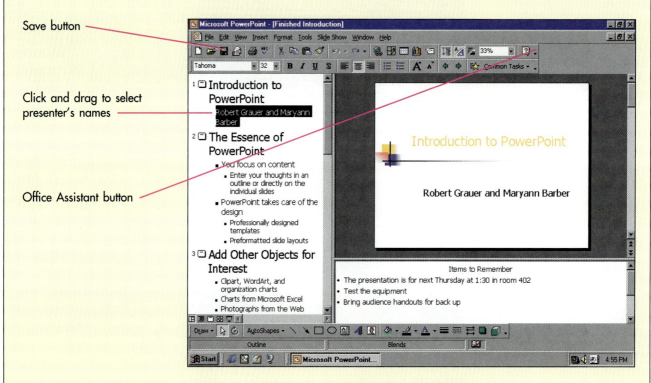

(f) Modify a Slide (step 6)

FIGURE 1.5 Hands-on Exercise 1 (continued)

THE AUTOMATIC SPELL CHECK

A red wavy line under a word indicates that the word is misspelled, or in the case of a proper name, that the word is spelled correctly, but that it is not in the dictionary. In either event, point to the underlined word and click the right mouse button to display a shortcut menu. Select the appropriate spelling from the list of suggestions or add the word to the supplementary dictionary. To enable (disable) the automatic spell check, pull down the Tools menu, click the Options command, click the Spelling and Style tab, then check (clear) the option to check spelling as you type.

STEP 7: The Office Assistant

➤ You can display the Assistant in one of three ways—press the **F1 key,** click the **Microsoft PowerPoint Help** button on the Standard toolbar, or pull down the **Help menu** and click the **Show the Office Assistant command.**

➤ If necessary, click the Assistant to display a balloon, then enter your question, for example, **How do I show a presentation?** Click the **Search button** within the balloon.

➤ The Assistant will return a list of topics that it considers potential answers to your question. Click the first topic, **Start a slide show,** to display the Help window in Figure 1.5g.

➤ Click the second topic in the Help window, **Start a slide show from within PowerPoint,** which displays steps that show the commands you need. You can print the contents by clicking the **Print button** in the Help window. Close the Help window.

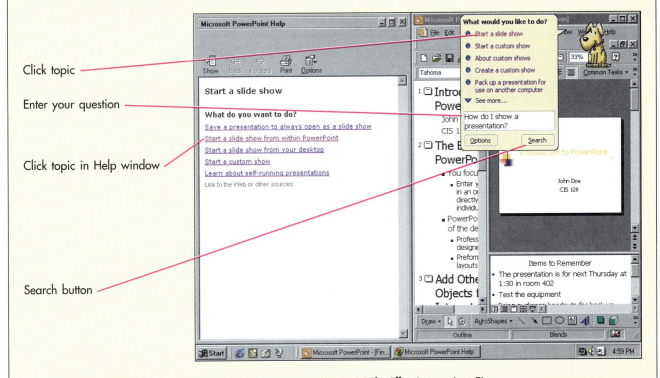

(g) The Office Assistant (step 7)

FIGURE 1.5 Hands-on Exercise 1 (continued)

CHOOSE YOUR OWN ASSISTANT

You can choose your own personal assistant from one of several available candidates. If necessary, press the F1 key to display the Assistant, click the Options button to display the Office Assistant dialog box, then click the Gallery tab where you choose your character. (The Office 2000 CD is required in order to select some of the other characters.) Some assistants are more animated (distracting) than others. The Office logo is the most passive, while Rocky is quite animated. Experiment with the various check boxes on the Options tab to see the effects on the Assistant.

STEP 8: Show the Presentation

➤ Click the **Slide Show button** above the status bar, or pull down the **View menu** and click **Slide Show.** The presentation will begin with the first slide as shown in Figure 1.5h. You should see your name on the slide because of the modification you made in the previous step.

➤ Click the mouse to move to the second slide, which comes into the presentation from the right side of your monitor. (This is one of several transition effects used to add interest to a presentation.)

➤ Click the mouse to the next (third) slide, which illustrates a build effect that requires you to click the mouse to display each succeeding bullet.

➤ Continue to view the show until you come to the end of the presentation. (You can press the **Esc key** at any time to cancel the show and return to the PowerPoint window.) Note the transition effects and the use of sound (provided you have speakers on your system) to enhance the presentation.

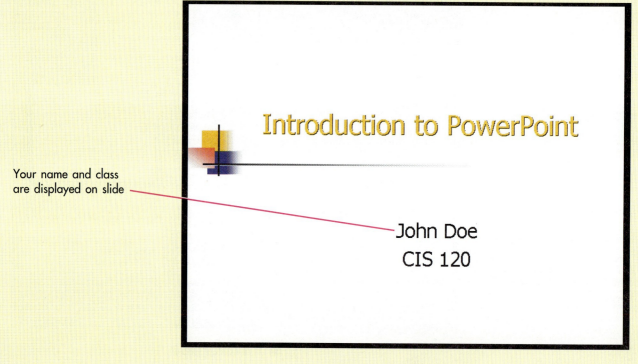

Your name and class are displayed on slide

(h) Show the Presentation (step 8)

TIP OF THE DAY

You can set the Office Assistant to greet you with a "tip of the day" each time you start PowerPoint. Click the Microsoft PowerPoint Help button (or press the F1 key) to display the Assistant, then click the Options button to display the Office Assistant dialog box. Click the Options tab, check the Show the Tip of the Day at Startup box, then click OK. The next time you start PowerPoint, you will be greeted by the Assistant, who will offer you the tip of the day.

STEP 9: Print the Presentation

➤ Pull down the **File menu.** Click **Print** to display the Print dialog box in Figure 1.5i. (Clicking the Print button on the Standard toolbar does not display the Print dialog box.)

➤ Click the **down arrow** in the **Print What** drop-down list box, click **Handouts,** and specify 6 slides per page as shown in Figure 1.5i.

➤ Check the box to **Frame Slides.** Check that the **All option button** is selected under Print range. Click the **OK command button** to print the handouts for the presentation.

➤ Pull down the **File menu.** Click **Close** to close the presentation but remain in PowerPoint. Click **Yes** when asked whether to save the changes.

➤ Pull down the **File menu.** Click **Exit** to exit PowerPoint if you do not want to continue with the next exercise at this time.

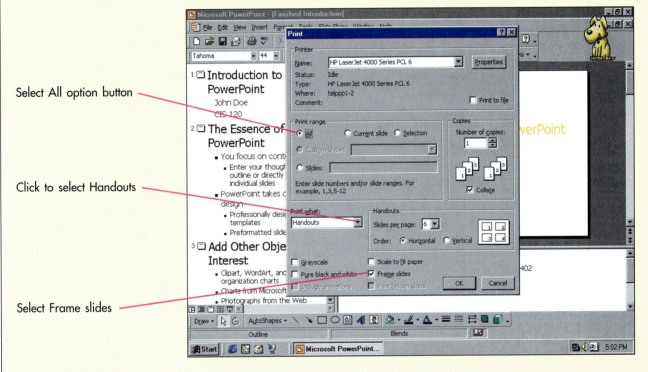

(i) Print the Presentation (step 9)

FIGURE 1.5 Hands-on Exercise 1 (continued)

SHOW THE KEYBOARD SHORTCUT IN A SCREENTIP

You can expand the ScreenTip associated with any toolbar button to include the equivalent keyboard shortcut. Pull down the View menu, click Toolbars, then click Customize to display the Customize dialog box. Click the Options tab and check the box to show the shortcut keys in the ScreenTips. Close the dialog box, then point to any toolbar button and you should see the name of the button as well as the equivalent keyboard shortcut.

CREATING A PRESENTATION

You are ready to create your own presentation, a process that requires you to develop its content and apply the formatting through the use of a template or design specification. You can do the steps in either order, but we suggest you start with the content. Both steps are iterative in nature and you are likely to go back and forth many times before you are finished.

You will also find yourself switching from one view to another as you develop the presentation. It doesn't matter which view you use, as long as you can accomplish what you set out to do. You can, for example, enter text one slide at a time in the Slide view. You can also use the Outline view as shown in Figure 1.6, to view the text of many slides at the same time and thus gain a better sense of the overall presentation.

Each slide in the outline contains a title, followed by bulleted items, which are indented one to five levels, corresponding to the importance of the item. The main points appear on level one. Subsidiary items are indented below the main point to which they apply. Any item can be promoted to a higher level or demoted to a lower level, either before or after the text is entered. Each slide in the outline is numbered and the numbers adjust automatically for the insertion or deletion of slides as you edit the presentation.

Consider, for example, slide 4 in Figure 1.6a. The title of the slide, *Develop the Content*, appears immediately after the slide number and icon. The first bullet, *Use the Outline view*, is indented one level under the title, and it in turn has two subsidiary bullets. The next main bullet, *Review the flow of ideas*, is moved back to level one, and it, too, has two subsidiary bullets.

The outline is (to us) the ideal way to create and edit the presentation. The **insertion point** marks the place where new text is entered and is established by clicking anywhere in the outline. (The insertion point is automatically placed at the title of the first slide in a new presentation.) Press enter after typing the title or after entering the text of a bulleted item, which starts a new slide or bullet, respectively. The new item may then be promoted or demoted as necessary.

Editing is accomplished through the same techniques used in other Windows applications. For example, you can use the Cut, Copy, and Paste commands in the Edit menu (or the corresponding buttons on the Standard toolbar) to move and copy selected text or you can simply drag and drop text from one place to another. You can also use the Find and Replace commands that are found in every Office application.

Note, too, that you can format text in the outline by using the **select-then-do** approach common to all Office applications; that is, you select the text, then you execute the appropriate command or click the appropriate button. The selected text remains highlighted and is affected by all subsequent commands until you click elsewhere in the outline.

Figure 1.6b displays a collapsed view of the outline, which displays only the title of each slide. The advantage to this view is that you see more slides on the screen at the same time, making it easier to move slides within the presentation. The slides are expanded or collapsed using tools on the Outlining toolbar.

CRYSTALLIZE YOUR MESSAGE

Every presentation exists to deliver a message, whether it's to sell a product, present an idea, or provide instruction. Decide on the message you want to deliver, then write the text for the presentation. Edit the text to be sure it is consistent with your objective. Then, and only then, should you think about formatting, but always keep the message foremost in your mind.

1. **A Guide to Successful Presentations**
    Robert Grauer and Maryann Barber
2. **Define the Audience**
    - Who is in the audience
        - Managers
        - Coworkers
        - Clients
    - What are their expectations
3. **Create the Presentation**
    - Develop the content
    - Format the presentation
    - Animate the slide show
4. **Develop the Content**
    - Use the Outline view
        - Demote items (Tab)
        - Promote items (Shift+Tab)
    - Review the flow of ideas
        - Cut, copy, and paste text
        - Drag and drop
5. **Format the Presentation**
    - Choose a design template
    - Customize the template
        - Change the color scheme
        - Change the background shading
    - Modify the slide masters
6. **Animate the Slide Show**
    - Transitions
    - Animations
    - Hidden slides
7. **Tips for Delivery**
    - Rehearse timings
    - Arrive early
    - Maintain eye contact
    - Know your audience

(a) The Expanded Outline

1. **A Guide to Successful Presentations**
2. **Define the Audience**
3. **Create the Presentation**
4. **Develop the Content**
5. **Format the Presentation**
6. **Animate the Slide Show**
7. **Tips for Delivery**

(b) The Collapsed Outline

FIGURE 1.6   The Outline View

Slide Layouts

All slides that are created in the Outline view are formatted as "bullet slides" that consist of a slide title and a single column of bullets. What if, however, you want to add clip art or another object, and/or display a double column of bullets? In other words you are satisfied with the text that is on the slide, but you want to add interest by including additional objects. You can add and/or arrange the objects manually in the Slide view, but it is often easier to change the slide layout and have PowerPoint do it for you.

PowerPoint provides a total of 24 predefined slide formats known as ***Slide Layouts*** that determine the position of the objects on a slide. To change the layout of a slide, click anywhere in the slide, pull down the Format menu, and click the Slide Layout command to display the Slide Layout dialog box. Select the type of slide you want and click the button to apply that layout. You can also insert a new slide in similar fashion. Pull down the Insert menu and click the New Slide command to display the slide layouts, then click OK. The slide will be added to the presentation immediately after the current slide. Either way, you are presented with a dialog box in which you choose the slide layout.

Figure 1.7 illustrates the creation of a bulleted slide with clip art after this slide layout was selected. The resulting slide has three *placeholders* that determine the position of each object. Just follow the directions on the slide by clicking the appropriate placeholder to add the title or text, or by double clicking to add the clip art. (The text that appears within a placeholder is there to guide the user and will not appear on the actual slide unless you click in the area and enter text as directed.) It's easy, as you will see in the exercise that follows shortly.

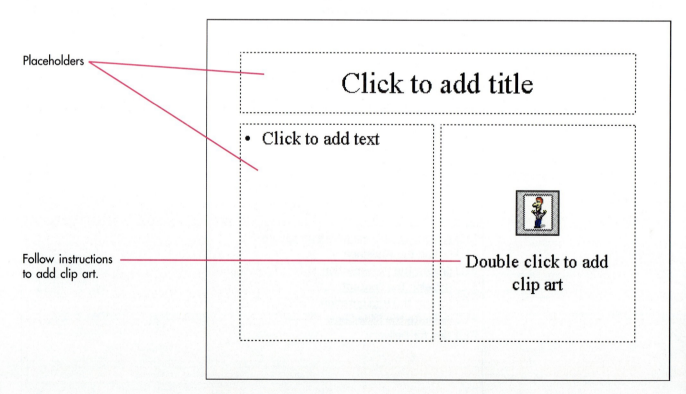

FIGURE 1.7 Slide Layouts

TEMPLATES

PowerPoint enables you to concentrate on the content of a presentation without concern for its appearance. You focus on what you are going to say, and trust in PowerPoint to format the presentation attractively. The formatting is implemented automatically by selecting one of the many templates that are supplied with PowerPoint.

A *template* is a design specification that controls every element in a presentation. It specifies the color scheme for the slides and the arrangement of the different elements (placeholders) on each slide. It determines the formatting of the text, the fonts that are used, and the size and placement of the bulleted text.

Figure 1.8 displays the title slide of a presentation in four different templates. Just choose the template you like, and PowerPoint formats the entire presentation according to that template. And don't be afraid to change your mind. You can use the Format menu at any time to select a different template and change the look of your presentation.

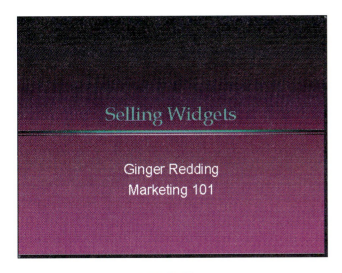

(a) Double Lines

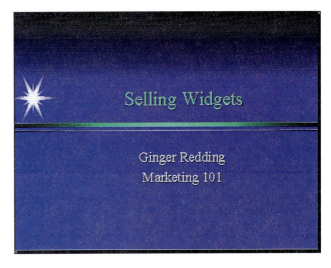

(b) Sparkle

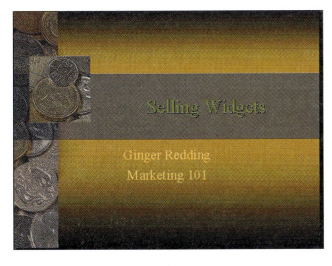

(c) Coins

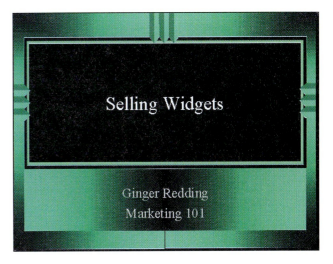

(d) Bevel

FIGURE 1.8 Templates

HANDS-ON EXERCISE 2

Creating a Presentation

Objective: To create a presentation by entering text in the Outline view; to apply a design template to a presentation. Use Figure 1.9 as a guide.

STEP 1: Create a New Presentation

➤ Start PowerPoint. Hide the Office Assistant if it appears. (You can unhide the Assistant at any time by clicking its button on the Standard toolbar.)

➤ Click the **option button** to create a new presentation using a **Blank Presentation.** Click **OK.**

➤ You should see the **New Slide** dialog box in Figure 1.9a with the AutoLayout for the title slide already selected. Click **OK** to create a title slide.

➤ If necessary, click the **Maximize buttons** in both the application and document windows so that PowerPoint takes the entire desktop.

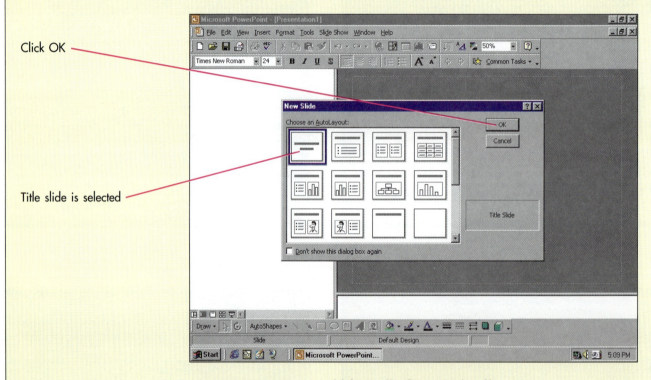

(a) Create a New Presentation (step 1)

FIGURE 1.9 Hands-on Exercise 2

CONTENT, CONTENT, AND CONTENT

It is much more important to focus on the content of the presentation than to worry about how it will look. Start with the AutoContent Wizard (described later in the chapter) or with a blank presentation in the Outline view. Save the formatting for last. Otherwise you will spend too much time changing templates and too little time developing the text.

---

22 MICROSOFT POWERPOINT 2000

STEP 2: Create the Title Slide

➤ Click anywhere in the box containing **Click to add title,** then type the title, **A Guide to Successful Presentations** as shown in Figure 1.9b. The title will automatically wrap to a second line.

➤ Click anywhere in the box containing **Click to add subtitle** and enter your name. Click outside the subtitle placeholder when you have entered your name.

➤ Click in the Notes pane and enter a speaker's note that pertains to the title slide; for example, the date and time that the presentation is scheduled.

➤ You may see a lightbulb indicating that the Office Assistant has a suggestion for you. The Assistant may suggest that you add clip art, apply a design template, or change the style (capitalization) on your slide.

➤ The suggestions are interesting, but we suggest you ignore them initially and focus on entering the content of your presentation.

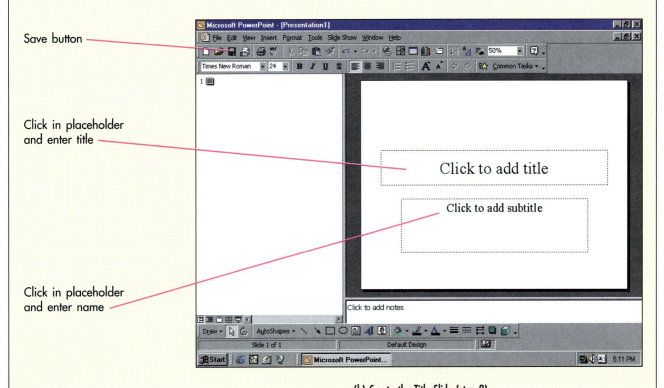

(b) Create the Title Slide (step 2)

FIGURE 1.9 Hands-on Exercise 2 (continued)

THE DEFAULT PRESENTATION

PowerPoint supplies a default presentation containing the specifications for color (a plain white background with black text), formatting, and AutoLayouts. The default presentation is selected automatically when you work on a blank presentation, and it remains in effect until you choose a different template.

STEP 3: Save the Presentation

➤ Pull down the **File menu** and click **Save** (or click the **Save button** on the Standard toolbar). You should see the Save dialog box in Figure 1.9c. If necessary, click the **down arrow** on the **Views button** and click **Details.**

➤ To save the file:
- Click the **drop-down arrow** on the Save In list box.
- Click the appropriate drive, drive C or drive A, depending on whether or not you installed the data disk on your hard drive.
- Double click the **Exploring PowerPoint folder** to make it the active folder (the folder in which you will save the document).
- Enter **My First Presentation** as the name of the presentation.
- Click **Save** or press the **enter key.** Click **Cancel** or press the **Esc key** if you see the Properties dialog box. The title bar changes to reflect the name of the presentation.

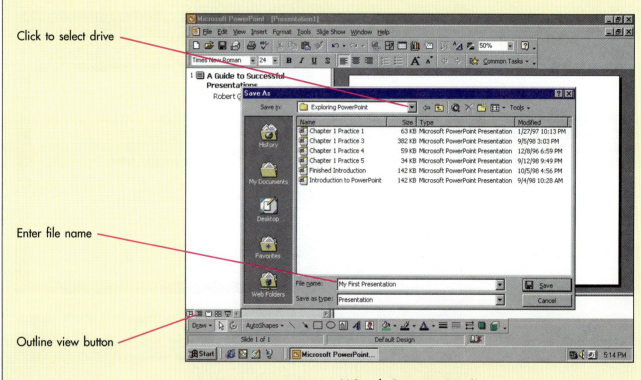

(c) Save the Presentation (step 3)

FIGURE 1.9 Hands-on Exercise 2 (continued)

STEP 4: Create the Presentation

➤ Click the **Outline View button** above the status bar so that the Outline pane is made larger within the Normal view.

➤ Click after your name in the Outline pane. Press **enter** to begin a new item, then press **Shift+Tab** to promote the item and create slide 2. Type **Define the Audience.** Press **enter.**

➤ Press the **Tab key** (or click the **Demote button** on the Outline toolbar) to enter the first bullet. Type **Who is in the audience** and press **enter.**

➤ Press the **Tab key** (or click the **Demote button** on the Outline toolbar) to enter the second-level bullets.
  • Type **Managers.** Press **enter.**
  • Type **Coworkers.** Press **enter.**
  • Type **Clients.** Press **enter.**
➤ Press **Shift+Tab** (or click the **Promote button** on the Outline toolbar) to return to the first-level bullets.
  • Type **What are their expectations.** Press **enter.**
➤ Press **Shift+Tab** to enter the title of the third slide. Type **Tips for Delivery.** Press **enter,** then press **Tab key** to create the first bullet.
➤ Add the remaining text for this slide and for slide 4 as shown in Figure 1.9d. Save the presentation.

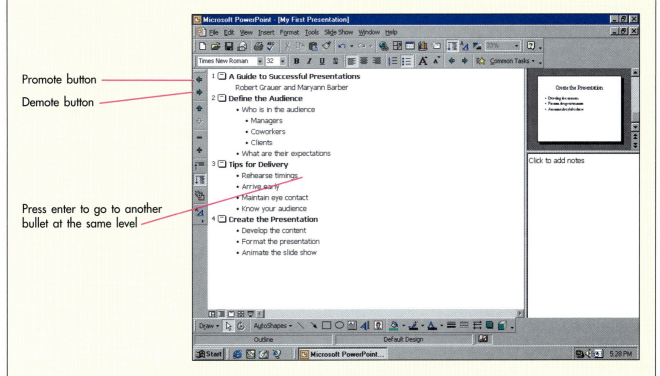

(d) Create the Presentation (step 4)

FIGURE 1.9   Hands-on Exercise 2 (continued)

JUST KEEP TYPING

The easiest way to enter the text for a presentation is to type continually in the Outline view. Just type an item, then press enter to move to the next item. You will be automatically positioned at the next item on the same level, where you can type the next entry. Continue to enter text in this manner. Press the Tab key as necessary to demote an item (move it to the next lower level). Press Shift+Tab to promote an item (move it to the next higher level).

STEP 5: The Spell Check

➤ Enter the text of the remaining slides as shown in Figure 1.9e. Do *not* press enter after entering the last bullet on the last slide or else you will add a blank bullet.

➤ Click the **Spelling button** on the Standard toolbar to check the presentation for spelling:

- The result of the Spell Check will depend on how accurately you entered the text of the presentation. We deliberately misspelled the word *Transitions* in the last slide.
- Continue to check the document for spelling errors. Click **OK** when PowerPoint indicates it has checked the entire presentation.

➤ Click the **Save button** on the Standard toolbar to save the presentation.

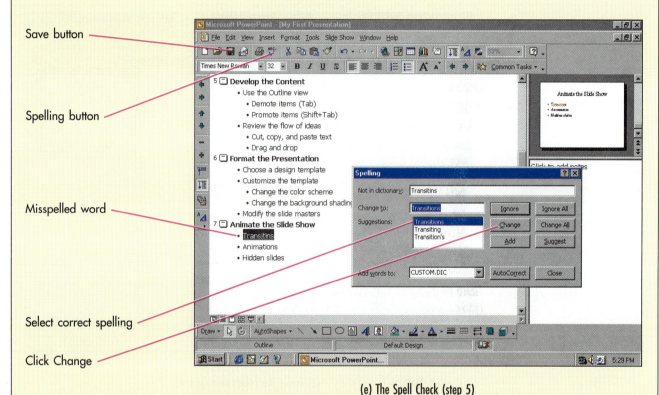

(e) The Spell Check (step 5)

FIGURE 1.9 Hands-on Exercise 2 (continued)

CREATE YOUR OWN SHORTHAND

Use the AutoCorrect feature, which is common to all Office applications, to expand abbreviations such as "usa" for United States of America. Pull down the Tools menu, click AutoCorrect, then type the abbreviation in the Replace text box and the expanded entry in the With text box. Click the Add command button, then click OK to exit the dialog box and return to the document. The next time you type usa in a presentation, it will automatically be expanded to United States of America.

STEP 6: Drag and Drop

➤ Press **Ctrl+Home** to move to the beginning of the presentation. If you don't see the Outlining toolbar, pull down the **View menu,** click the **Toolbars command,** and check **Outlining** to display the toolbar.

➤ Click the **Collapse All button** on the Outline toolbar to collapse the outline as shown in Figure 1.9f.

➤ Click the **icon** for **slide 3** (Tips for Delivery) to select the slide. Point to the **slide icon** (the mouse pointer changes to a four-headed arrow), then click and drag to move the slide to the end of the presentation.

➤ All of the slides have been renumbered. The slide titled Tips for Delivery has been moved to the end of the presentation and appears as slide 7. Click the **Expand All button** to display the contents of each slide. Click anywhere in the presentation to deselect the last slide.

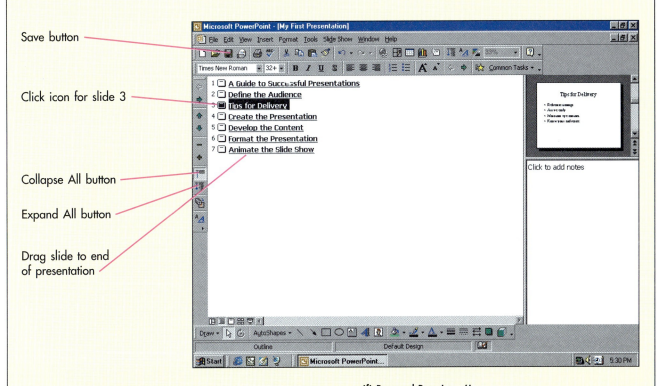

(f) Drag and Drop (step 6)

FIGURE 1.9 Hands-on Exercise 2 (continued)

SELECTING SLIDES IN THE OUTLINE VIEW

Click the slide icon or the slide number next to the slide title to select the slide. PowerPoint will select the entire slide (including its title, text, and any other objects that are not visible in the Outline view). Click the first slide, then press and hold the Shift key as you click the ending slide to select a group of sequential slides. Press Ctrl+A to select the entire outline. You can use these techniques to select multiple slides regardless of whether the outline is collapsed or expanded. The selected slides can be copied, moved, expanded, collapsed, or deleted as a unit.

STEP 7: Choose a Design Template

➤ Pull down the **Format menu** and click **Apply Design Template** to display the dialog box in Figure 1.9g:

➤ The **Presentation Designs folder** should appear automatically in the List box. If it doesn't, change to this folder which is contained within the Templates folder within the Microsoft Office Folder, which in turn is in the Program Files Folder on drive C.

➤ **Design Templates** should be selected in the Files of Type list box. If it isn't, click the **drop-down arrow** to change to this file type.

➤ The **Preview view** should be selected. If it isn't, click the **Views button** until you toggle to the Preview view where you can preview the selected template.

➤ Scroll through the available designs to select (click) the **Soaring template** as shown in Figure 1.9g. Click **Apply** to close the dialog box.

➤ The appearance of the slide changes in the Normal view. Save the presentation.

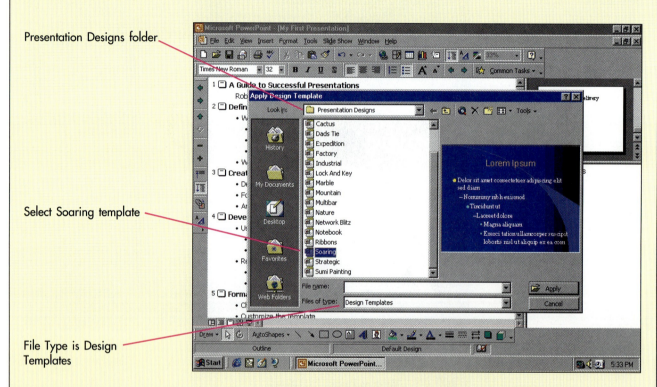

(g) Choose a Design Template (step 7)

FIGURE 1.9 Hands-on Exercise 2 (continued)

THE UNDO AND REDO COMMANDS

Click the drop-down arrow next to the Undo button to display a list of your previous actions, then click the action you want to undo which also undoes all of the preceding commands. Undoing the fifth command in the list, for example, will also undo the preceding four commands. The Redo command works in reverse and cancels the last Undo command.

STEP 8: View the Presentation

➤ Press **Ctrl+Home** to move to the beginning of the presentation. Click the **Slide Show button** on the status bar to view the presentation as shown in Figure 1.9h.

- To move to the next slide: Click the **left mouse button,** type the letter **N,** or press the **PgDn key.**
- To move to the previous slide: Type the letter **P,** or press the **PgUp key.**

➤ Continue to move from one slide to the next until you come to the end of the presentation and are returned to the Normal view.

➤ Save the presentation. Exit PowerPoint if you do not want to continue with the next exercise at this time.

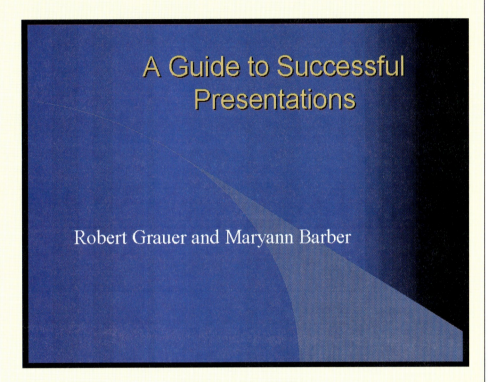

(h) View the Presentation (step 8)

FIGURE 1.9 Hands-on Exercise 2 (continued)

ADVICE FROM THE OFFICE ASSISTANT

The Office Assistant indicates it has a suggestion by displaying a lightbulb. Click the lightbulb to display the tip, then click the OK button to close the balloon and continue working. The Assistant will not, however, repeat a tip from an earlier session unless you reset it at the start of a new session. This is especially important in a laboratory situation where you are sharing a computer with many students. To reset the tips, click the Assistant to display the balloon, click the Options button in the balloon, click the Options tab, then click the Reset My Tips button.

CREATING A SLIDE SHOW

You develop the content of a presentation, then you format it attractively using a PowerPoint template. The most important step is yet to come—the delivery of the presentation to an audience, which is best accomplished through a computerized slide show (as opposed to using overhead transparencies or 35-mm slides). The computer becomes the equivalent of a slide projector, and the presentation is called a slide show.

PowerPoint can help you add interest to the slide show in two ways, transitions and animation effects. ***Transitions*** control the way in which one slide moves off the screen and the next slide appears. ***Animation effects*** vary the way in which objects on a slide appear during the presentation.

Transitions are created through the Slide Transition command in the Slide Show menu, which displays the dialog box in Figure 1.10a. The drop-down list box enables you to choose the transition effect. Slides may move on to the screen from the left or right, be uncovered by horizontal or vertical blinds, fade, dissolve, and so on. The dialog box also enables you to set the speed of the transition and/or to preview the effect.

Animation enables the bulleted items to appear one at a time with each successive mouse click. The effect is created through the Custom Animation command in the Slide Show menu, which displays the dialog box of Figure 1.10b. Each bullet can appear with its own transition effect. You can make the bullets appear one word or one letter at a time. You can specify that the bullets appear in reverse order (i.e., the bottom bullet first), and you can dim each bullet as the next one appears. You can even add sound and make the bullets appear in conjunction with a round of applause.

Transitions and animation effects can also be created from the Slide Sorter toolbar as shown in Figure 1.10c. As with the other toolbars, a ScreenTip is displayed when you point to a button on the toolbar.

Delivering the Presentation

PowerPoint can help you to create attractive presentations, but the content and delivery are still up to you. You have worked hard to gain the opportunity to present your ideas and you want to be well prepared for the session. Practice aloud several times, preferably under the same conditions as the actual presentation. Time your delivery to be sure that you do not exceed your allotted time. Everyone is nervous, but the more you practice the more confident you will be.

Arrive early. You need time to gather your thoughts as well as to set up the presentation. Start PowerPoint and open your presentation prior to addressing the audience. Be sure that your notes are with you and check that water is available for you during the presentation. Look at the audience to open communication and gain credibility. Speak clearly and vary your delivery. Try to relax. You'll be great!

QUESTIONS AND ANSWERS (Q & A)

Indicate at the beginning of your talk whether you will take questions during the presentation or collectively at the end. Announce the length of time that will be allocated to questions. Rephrase all questions so the audience can hear. If you do receive a hostile question, rephrase it in a neutral way and try to disarm the challenger by paying a compliment. If you don't know the answer, say so.

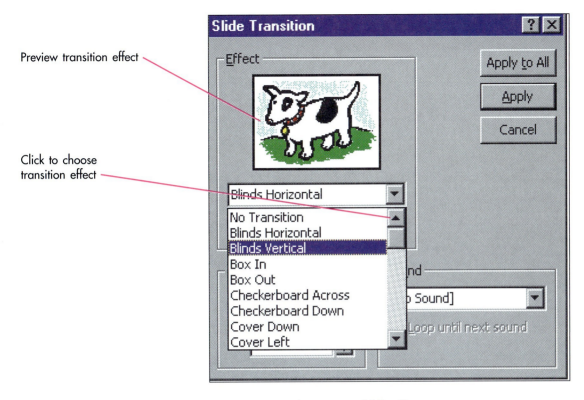

(a) Transitions

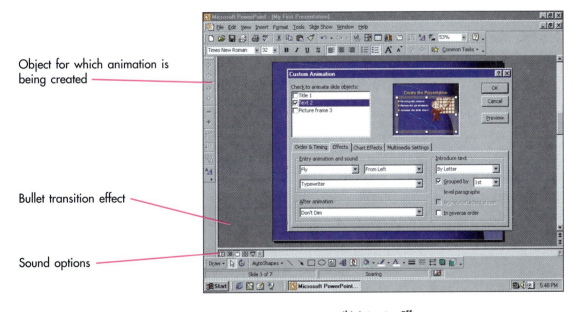

(b) Animation Effects

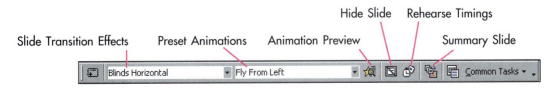

(c) Slide Sorter Toolbar

FIGURE 1.10 Transitions and Animation Effects

HANDS-ON EXERCISE 3

Animating the Presentation

Objective: To change the layout of an existing slide; to establish transition and animation effects. Use Figure 1.11 as a guide in the exercise.

STEP 1: Change the Slide Layout

➤ Start PowerPoint and open **My First Presentation** from the previous exercise. If necessary, switch to the **Slide view.** Press **Ctrl+End** to move to the last slide as shown in Figure 1.11a, which is currently a bulleted list.

➤ Pull down the **Format menu** and click **Slide Layout.**

➤ Choose the **Text and Clip Art layout** as shown in Figure 1.11a. Click the **Apply command button** to change the slide layout.

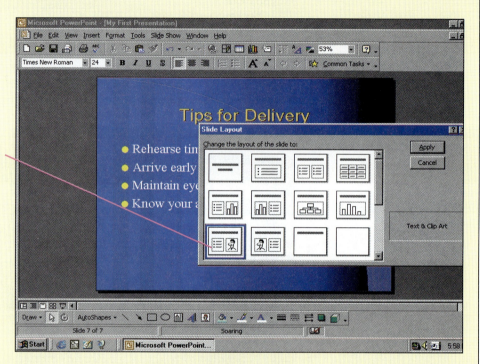

Select Text and Clip Art layout

(a) Change the AutoLayout (step 1)

FIGURE 1.11 Hands-on Exercise 3

THE MOST RECENTLY OPENED FILE LIST

The easiest way to open a recently used presentation is to select the presentation directly from the File menu. Pull down the File menu, but instead of clicking the Open command, check to see if the presentation appears on the list of the most recently opened presentations located at the bottom of the menu. If so, you can click the presentation name rather than having to make the appropriate selections through the Open dialog box.

STEP 2: Add the Clip Art

➤ Double click the **placeholder** on the slide to add the clip art. You will see the Microsoft Clip Gallery dialog box as shown in Figure 1.11b (although you may not see all of the categories listed in the figure).

➤ Select (click) the **Academic category,** choose any image, then click the **Insert Clip button** on the Shortcut menu. The clip art should appear on the slide within the placeholder.

➤ Click outside the clip art to deselect the picture so that you can continue working on the presentation.

➤ The clip art is sized automatically to fit the existing place holder. You can, however, move and size the clip art just like any other Windows object.

➤ Save the presentation.

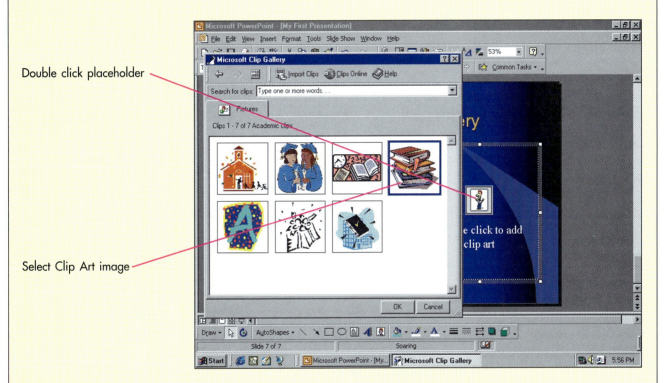

(b) Add the Clip Art (step 2)

FIGURE 1.11 Hands-on Exercise 3 (continued)

ROTATE AND FLIP AN OBJECT

Change the appearance of any clip art object by rotating it left or right, or flipping it horizontally or vertically. Right click the clip art to display a context sensitive menu, click the Grouping command, and click Ungroup. Click Yes if asked whether to convert the clip art to a PowerPoint object. Right click the ungrouped objects immediately (you must select all the objects), click the Grouping command, and click the group. Click the down arrow on the Draw menu, click the Rotate or Flip command, then experiment with the different options

STEP 3: Add Transition Effects

➤ Click the **Slide Sorter View button** to change to the Slide Sorter view as shown in Figure 1.11c. The number of slides you see at one time depends on the resolution of your monitor and the zoom percentage.

➤ Press **Ctrl+Home** to select the first slide. Pull down the **Slide Show menu,** then click **Slide Transition** to display the dialog box in Figure 1.11c. Click the **down arrow** on the Effect list box, then click the **Blinds Vertical** effect. You will see the effect displayed on the sample slide (dog) in the effect preview area. If you miss the effect, click the **dog** (or the **key**) to repeat the effect.

➤ Click **Apply** to accept the transition and close the dialog box. A slide icon appears under slide 1, indicating a transition effect.

➤ Point to slide 2, click the **right mouse button** to display a shortcut menu, then click the **Slide Transition command.** Choose **Checkerboard Across.** Click the **Slow option button.** Click **Apply** to close the dialog box.

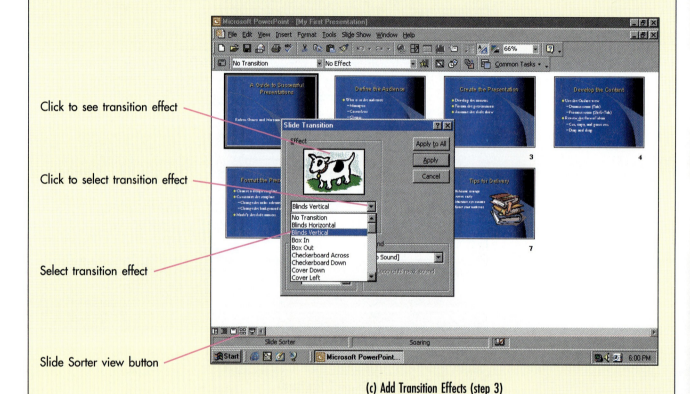

(c) Add Transition Effects (step 3)

FIGURE 1.11 Hands-on Exercise 3 (continued)

CHANGE THE MAGNIFICATION

Click the down arrow on the Zoom box to change the display magnification, which in turn controls the size of individual slides. The higher the magnification, the easier it is to read the text of an individual slide, but the fewer slides you see at one time. Conversely, changing to a smaller magnification decreases the size of the individual slides, but enables you to see more of the presentation.

STEP 4: Create a Summary Slide

➤ Pull down the **Edit menu** and press **Select All** to select every slide in the presentation. (Alternatively, you can also press and hold the **Shift key** as you click each slide in succession.)

➤ Click the **Summary Slide button** on the Slide Sorter toolbar to create a summary slide containing a bullet with the title of each selected slide. The new slide appears at the beginning of the presentation as shown in Figure 1.11d.

➤ Click and drag the **Summary Slide** to the end of the presentation. (As you drag the slide, the mouse pointer changes to include the outline of a miniature slide and a vertical line appears to indicate the new position of the slide.)

➤ Release the mouse. The Summary Slide has been moved to the end of the presentation and the slides are renumbered automatically.

➤ Save the presentation.

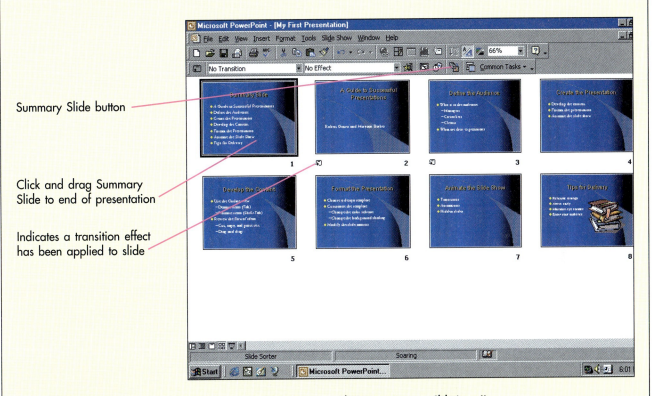

(d) Create a Summary Slide (step 4)

FIGURE 1.11 Hands-on Exercise 3 (continued)

SELECTING MULTIPLE SLIDES

You can apply the same transition or animation effect to multiple slides with a single command. Change to the Slide Sorter view, then select the slides by pressing and holding the Shift key as you click the slides. Use the Slide Show menu or the Slide Sorter toolbar to choose the desired transition or preset animation effect when all the slides have been selected. Click anywhere in the Slide Sorter view to deselect the slides and continue working.

STEP 5: Create Animation Effects

➤ Double click the Summary slide to select the slide and simultaneously change to the Slide view. Click anywhere within the title to select the title.

➤ Pull down the **Slide Show menu,** click **Preset Animation** to display a cascade menu, then click **Typewriter** to display the title with this effect during the slide show.

➤ Click anywhere within the bulleted text to select the bulleted text (and deselect the title). Pull down the **Slide Show menu** and select **Custom Animation** to display the dialog box in Figure 1.11e.

➤ Click the **Effects tab.** Click the first **drop-down arrow** under Entry animation and sound to display the entry transitions. Click **Fly.** Click the second drop-down arrow and select **From Left.**

➤ Click the **drop-down arrow** to show the Introduce Text effects and select **All at Once.** Click the **drop-down arrow** for sound effects, then scroll until you can select **Screeching Brakes.**

➤ Click the **Order & Timing tab.** Check that the title appears first within the animation order. If not, select the title, then click the **up arrow** to move it ahead of the text. Click **OK** to close the dialog box. Click outside the placeholder to deselect it.

➤ Pull down the **Slide Show menu** a second time. Click **Animation Preview** to display the slide miniature window to see (and hear) the animation effect. If you don't see the command, click the **double arrow** to see more commands.

➤ Close the miniature window. Save the presentation.

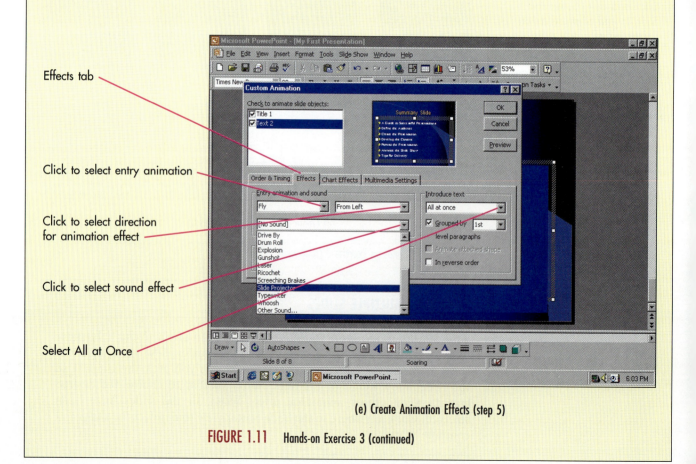

(e) Create Animation Effects (step 5)

FIGURE 1.11 Hands-on Exercise 3 (continued)

STEP 6: Show the Presentation

➤ Press **Ctrl+Home** to return to the first slide, then click the **Slide Show button** above the status bar to view the presentation. You should see the opening slide in Figure 1.11f.

➤ Click the **left mouse button** to move to the next slide (or to the next bullet on the current slide when animation is in effect).

➤ Click the **right mouse button** to display the Shortcut menu and return to the previous slide (or to the previous bullet on the current slide when a build is in effect).

➤ Continue to view the presentation until you come to the end. Click the **left mouse button** a final time to return to the regular PowerPoint window.

➤ Exit PowerPoint.

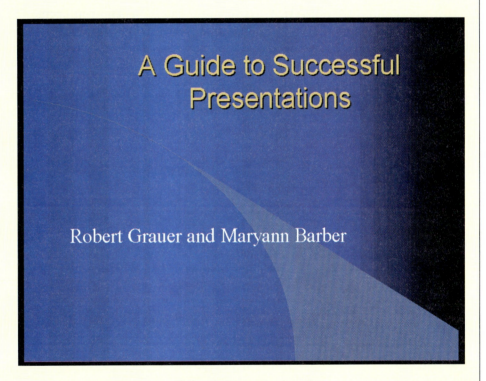

(f) Show the Presentation (step 6)

FIGURE 1.11   Hands-on Exercise 3 (continued)

ANNOTATE A SLIDE

You can annotate a slide just like the sports announcers on television. Click the Slide Show button to begin your presentation, press Ctrl+P to change the mouse pointer to a pen, then click and drag to draw on the slide. The effect is temporary and lasts only while the slide is on the screen. Use the PgDn and PgUp keys to move forward and back in the presentation when the drawing tool is in effect. Press Ctrl+A at any time to change the mouse pointer back to an arrow.

SUMMARY

Microsoft PowerPoint enables you to focus on the content of a presentation without worrying about its appearance. You supply the text and supporting elements and leave the formatting to PowerPoint. The resulting presentation consists of a series of slides with a consistent design and color scheme. You can deliver it in a variety of ways such as a computer slide show, the World Wide Web, or via overhead transparencies or 35-mm slides. You can also print the presentation in a variety of formats.

PowerPoint is easy to learn because it follows the conventions of every Windows application. The benefits of the common user interface are magnified further if you already know another application in Microsoft Office such as Word or Excel. PowerPoint is designed for a mouse but it provides keyboard equivalents for almost every command. Toolbars provide still another way to execute the most frequent operations.

PowerPoint has six different views, each with unique capabilities. The Slide view displays one slide at a time and enables all operations on that slide. The Slide Sorter view displays multiple slides on one screen (each slide is in miniature) and lets you see the overall flow of the presentation. The Outline view shows the presentation text in outline form and is the fastest way to enter or edit text. The Notes Page view enables you to create speaker's notes for use in giving the presentation. The Normal view displays the Slide, Outline, and Notes Page views in a single window, with each view in its own pane. The Slide Show view displays the slides one at a time with transition effects for added interest.

The easiest way to enter the text of a presentation is in the Outline view. You see the entire presentation and can change the order of the slides and/or move text from one slide to another as necessary. Text can be entered continually in the outline, then promoted or demoted so that it appears on the proper level in the slide.

Slides are added to a presentation using one of 24 predefined slide formats known as Slide Layouts. Each Slide Layout contains placeholders for the different objects on the slide. A slide may be deleted from a presentation in any view except the Slide Show view.

A template is a design specification that controls every aspect of a presentation. It specifies the formatting of the text, the fonts and colors that are used, and the design, size, and placement of the bullets.

Transitions and animations can be added to a presentation for additional interest. Transitions control the way in which one slide moves off the screen and the next slide appears. Animation effects are used to display the individual elements on a single slide.

KEY WORDS AND CONCEPTS

Animation effects	Formatting toolbar	Places bar
AutoCorrect	Insertion point	Print command
Clip art	Menu bar	Promote
Close command	Normal view	Redo command
Demote	Notes Page view	Save As command
Drawing toolbar	Open command	Save command
Exit command	Outline view	ScreenTip
File name	Outlining toolbar	Scroll bar
File type	Placeholders	Slide Layout

Slide Show view
Slide Sorter toolbar
Slide Sorter view
Slide view

Spell check
Standard toolbar
Status bar
Taskbar

Template
Transition effect
Undo command

MULTIPLE CHOICE

1. How do you save changes to a PowerPoint presentation?
   (a) Pull down the File menu and click the Save command
   (b) Click the Save button on the Standard toolbar
   (c) Both (a) and (b)
   (d) Neither (a) nor (b)

2. Which of the following can be printed in support of a PowerPoint presentation?
   (a) Audience handouts
   (b) Speaker's Notes
   (c) An outline
   (d) All of the above

3. Which menu contains the Undo command?
   (a) File menu
   (b) Edit menu
   (c) Tools menu
   (d) Format menu

4. Ctrl+Home and Ctrl+End are keyboard shortcuts that move to the beginning or end of the presentation in the:
   (a) Outline view
   (b) Slide Sorter view
   (c) Slide view
   (d) All of the above

5. The predefined slide formats in PowerPoint are known as:
   (a) View
   (b) Slide Layouts
   (c) Audience handouts
   (d) Speaker notes

6. Which menu contains the commands to save the current presentation, or to open a previously saved presentation?
   (a) The Tools menu
   (b) The File menu
   (c) The View menu
   (d) The Edit menu

7. The Open command:
   (a) Brings a presentation from disk into memory
   (b) Brings a presentation from disk into memory, then erases the presentation on disk
   (c) Stores the presentation in memory on disk
   (d) Stores the presentation in memory on disk, then erases the presentation from memory

8. The Save command:
   (a) Brings a presentation from disk into memory
   (b) Brings a presentation from disk into memory, then erases the presentation on disk
   (c) Stores the presentation in memory on disk
   (d) Stores the presentation in memory on disk, then erases the presentation from memory

9. Which view displays multiple slides while letting you change the text in a slide?
   (a) Outline view
   (b) Slide Sorter view
   (c) Both (a) and (b)
   (d) Neither (a) nor (b)

10. Where will the insertion point be after you complete the text for a bullet in the Outline view and press the enter key?
    (a) On the next bullet at the same level of indentation
    (b) On the next bullet at a higher level of indentation
    (c) On the next bullet at a lower level of indentation
    (d) It is impossible to determine

11. Which of the following is true?
    (a) Shift+Tab promotes an item to the next higher level
    (b) Tab demotes an item to the next lower level
    (c) Both (a) and (b)
    (d) Neither (a) nor (b)

12. What advantage, if any, is there to collapsing the Outline view so that only the slide titles are visible?
    (a) More slides are displayed at one time, making it easier to rearrange the slides in the presentation
    (b) Transition and build effects can be added
    (c) Graphic objects become visible
    (d) All of the above

13. Which of the following is true regarding transition and build effects?
    (a) Every slide must have the same transition effect
    (b) Every bullet must have the same build effect
    (c) Both (a) and (b)
    (d) Neither (a) nor (b)

14. Which of the following is true?
    (a) Slides can be added to a presentation after a template has been chosen
    (b) The template can be changed after all of the slides have been created
    (c) Both (a) and (b)
    (d) Neither (a) nor (b)

15. Which of the following can be changed after a slide has been created?
    (a) Its layout and transition effect
    (b) Its position within the presentation
    (c) Both (a) and (b)
    (d) Neither (a) nor (b)

ANSWERS

1. a	**4.** d	**7.** a	**10.** a	**13.** d
2. d	**5.** b	**8.** c	**11.** a	**14.** c
3. b	**6.** b	**9.** a	**12.** a	**15.** c

PRACTICE WITH POWERPOINT 2000

1. **Looking for a Job:** Figure 1.12 displays the Normal view of a presentation that was created by one of our students in a successful job search. Open the *Chapter 1 Practice 1* presentation, as it exists on the data disk (it is found in the Exploring PowerPoint folder), then modify the presentation to reflect your personal data. Print the revised Audience Handouts (six per page) and submit them to your instructor as proof you did this exercise.

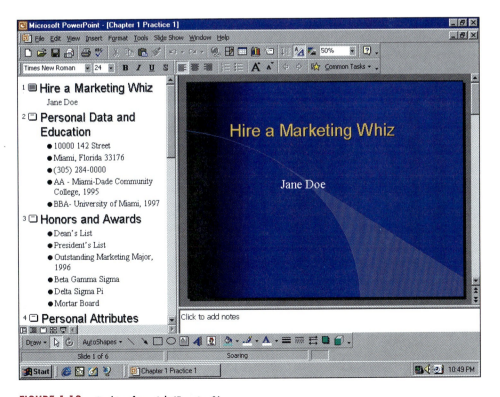

FIGURE 1.12   Looking for a Job (Exercise 1)

2. **Ready-Made Presentations:** The most difficult part of a presentation is getting started. PowerPoint anticipates the problem and provides general outlines on a variety of topics as shown in Figure 1.13.
   a. Pull down the File menu, click New, click the Presentations tab (if necessary), then click the Details button so that your screen matches Figure 1.13.
   b. Select Recommending a Strategy as shown in Figure 1.13. Click OK to open the presentation.
   c. Change to the Outline view so that you can see the text of the overall presentation, which is general in nature and intended for any type of strategy. Modify the presentation to develop a strategy for doing well in this class.
   d. Add your name to the title page. Print the presentation in miniature and submit it to your instructor.

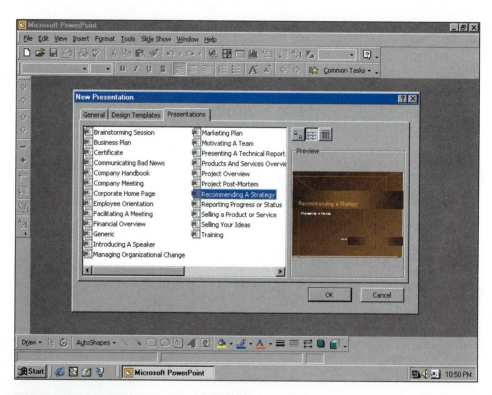

FIGURE 1.13 Ready-Made Presentations (Exercise 2)

3. **The Purchase of a PC:** Figure 1.14 displays the title slide of a presentation that can be found in the Exploring PowerPoint folder on the data disk. Much of the presentation has been created for you, but there are several finishing touches that need to be made:
   a. Open the existing presentation titled *Chapter 1 Practice 3*, then save it as *Chapter 1 Practice 3 Solution* so that you can return to the original presentation, if necessary.
   b. Replace our name with your name on the title slide.
   c. Move the slide on Modems after the one on Multimedia Requirements.
   d. Delete the slide on The PC, Then and Now.
   e. Add a slide at the end of the presentation on additional software that should be considered in addition to Windows and Microsoft Office.

f. Create a new slide that suggests several sources for a computer purchase. You can list computer magazines, vendor Web sites, and/or the campus bookstore.
g. Change the layout of slide 7 to a Two-column Text slide. Modify the text as necessary for the new layout.
h. Select a different design template.
i. Print the completed presentation in both outline and handout form. Submit both to your instructor.

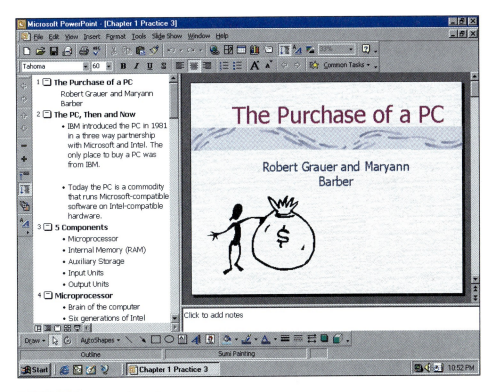

FIGURE 1.14 The Purchase of a PC (Exercise 3)

4. **The Internet and the World Wide Web:** A partially completed version of the presentation in Figure 1.15 can be found in the file *Chapter 1 Practice 4*. Open the presentation, then make the following changes:
   a. Add your name and e-mail address on the title page.
   b. Boldface and italicize the terms, *server, client,* and *browser* on slide 4. Boldface and italicize the acronyms, HTTP, HTTPS, HTML, and TCP/IP on slide 5.
   c. Use Internet Explorer to go to your favorite Web page. Press the Print Screen key to capture the screen image of that page and copy it to the clipboard, then use the Windows taskbar to switch to PowerPoint. Click the Paste button on the Standard toolbar to paste the screen into the PowerPoint presentation. Size the image as appropriate.
   d. Double click the WordArt image on the last slide to open the WordArt application. Change the words *Thank You* to *The End*. Change the style of the WordArt in any other way you see fit.
   e. Print the presentation in different ways. Print the outline of the entire presentation. Next, print the entire presentation to display six slides per page. Finally, select the first slide and print it as a slide to use as a cover page.
   f. Submit your output to your instructor as proof you did this exercise.

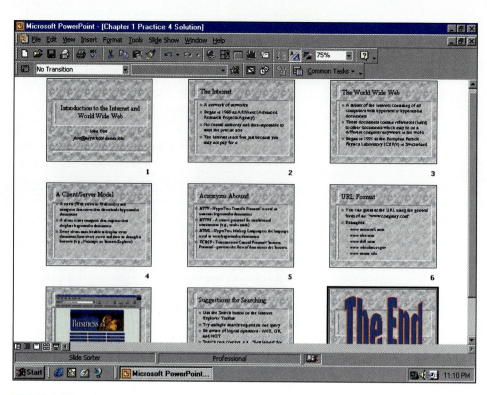

FIGURE 1.15 The Internet and the World Wide Web (Exercise 4)

5. **Visit the White House:** Create a presentation similar to the one in Figure 1.16. We have started the presentation for you and have saved it as *Chapter 1 Practice 5*. This presentation consists of three slides, a title slide, and two slides containing an object and text.

   a. Go to the White House Web site (www.whitehouse.gov). Click the link to White House History & Tours, then click the link to Presidents of the USA and select your favorite presidents. Point to the picture of the president, click the right mouse button to display a shortcut menu, then save the picture on your PC. Be sure you remember the location of the file when you save it on your local machine.

   b. You should still be at the White House Web site. Click the link to a familiar quotation from your president, then click and drag to select the text of that quotation. Pull down the Edit menu and click the Copy command to copy the selected text to the Windows clipboard (an area of memory that is available to every Windows application).

   c. Use the Windows taskbar to switch to PowerPoint. Select slide 2, the first slide containing bulleted text. Click in the text area, then click the Paste command on the Standard toolbar to paste the quotation into the slide. Click and drag the sizing handles that surround the text to make the box narrower in order to allow room for the president's picture. Click and drag a border of the text area to the right of the slide, again to make room for the president's picture.

   d. Click in the title area of the slide and add the president's name and years in office. Save the presentation.

   e. Click outside the text area. Pull down the Insert menu, click the Picture command, then click From File to display the Insert Picture dialog box. Enter the folder where you saved the file in step (a), then click the Insert button to insert the picture onto the slide. Move and size the picture as appropriate. Save the presentation.

f. Repeat these steps for a second president.

g. Create a title slide for the presentation with your name somewhere on the slide. Print all three slides and submit them to your instructor as proof you did this exercise.

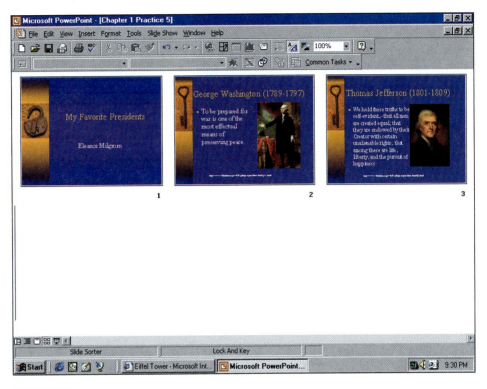

FIGURE 1.16   Visit the White House (Exercise 5)

6. **The Travel Agent:** Search the Web to select three different landmarks, download the picture of each, then create a short presentation consisting of a title slide plus three additional slides similar to the one in Figure 1.17. Be sure to include a reference to the Web page where you obtained each picture. Print the completed presentation for your instructor as proof you did this exercise.

7. **Your Favorite Performer:** The subject of a PowerPoint presentation is limited only by your imagination. Use any Internet search engine to locate information about your favorite singer or recording group, then download information about that person or group to create a presentation such as the one in Figure 1.18.

8. **Companion Web Sites:** Each book in the *Exploring Microsoft Office 2000* series is accompanied by an online study guide or Companion Web site. Start Internet Explorer and go to the Exploring Windows home page at www.prenhall.com/grauer. Click the book for Office 2000, click the link to student resources, click the Companion Web site tab at the top of the screen, then choose the appropriate text *(Exploring PowerPoint 2000)* and the chapter within the text (e.g., Chapter 1).

Each study guide contains a series of short-answer exercises (multiple-choice, true/false, and matching) to review the material in the chapter. You can take practice quizzes by yourself and/or e-mail the results to your instructor. You can try the essay questions for additional practice and engage in online chat sessions. We hope you will find the online guide to be a valuable resource.

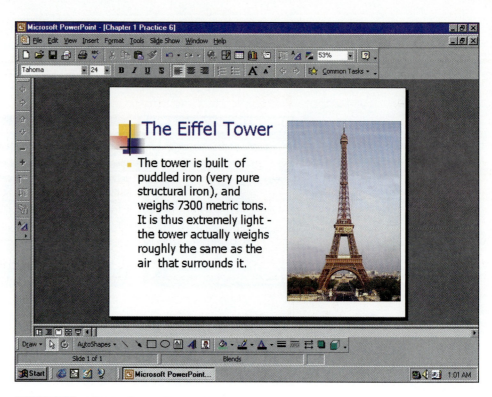

FIGURE 1.17 The Travel Agent (Exercise 6)

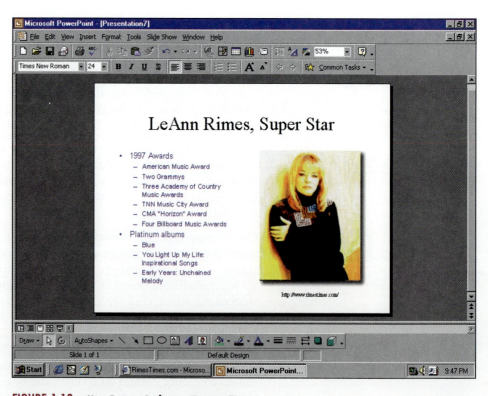

FIGURE 1.18 Your Favorite Performer (Exercise 7)

CASE STUDIES

Planning for Disaster

This case has nothing to do with presentations per se, but it is perhaps the most important case of all, as it deals with the question of backup. Do you have a backup strategy? Do you even know what a backup strategy is? This is a good time to learn, because sooner or later you will need to recover a file. The problem always seems to occur the night before an assignment is due. You accidentally erased a file, are unable to read from a floppy disk, or worse yet suffer a hardware failure in which you are unable to access the hard drive. The ultimate disaster is the disappearance of your computer, by theft or natural disaster. Describe in 250 words or less the backup strategy you plan to implement in conjunction with your work in this class.

Changing Menus and Toolbars

Office 2000 implements one very significant change over previous versions of Office in that it displays a series of short menus that contain only basic commands. The additional commands are made visible by clicking the double arrow that appears at the bottom of the menu. New commands are added to the menu as they are used, and conversely, other commands are removed if they are not used. A similar strategy is followed for the Standard and Formatting toolbars which are displayed on a single row, and thus do not show all of the buttons at one time. The intent is to simplify Office 2000 for the new user by limiting the number of commands that are visible. The consequence, however, is that the individual is not exposed to new commands, and hence may not use Office to its full potential. Which set of menus do you prefer? How do you switch from one set to the other?

Microsoft Online

Help for Microsoft PowerPoint is available from two primary sources, the Office Assistant, and the Microsoft Web site at www.microsoft.com/powerpoint. The latter enables you to obtain more recent, and often more detailed information. You will find the answer to the most frequently asked questions and you can access the same knowledge base used by Microsoft support engineers. Experiment with both sources of help, then submit a summary of your findings to your instructor.

Be Creative

One interesting way of exploring the potential of presentation graphics is to imagine it might have been used by historical figures had it been available. Choose any historical figure or current personality and create at least a six-slide presentation. You could, for example, show how Columbus might have used PowerPoint to request funding from Queen Isabella, or how Elvis Presley might have pleaded for his first recording contract. The content of your presentation should be reasonable but you don't have to spend an inordinate amount of time on research. Just be creative and use your imagination. Use clip art as appropriate, but don't overdo it. Place your name on the title slide as technical adviser.

INDEX

A = Access
E = Excel
P = PowerPoint
W = Word

A

Absolute reference, E44
Accounting format, E55
Active cell, E7, E15
Agenda Wizard, W138–W139
Alignment, E56, W81, W92
Animation effects, P30–P31, P36
Annotating a slide, P37
Application window, W5
Arial, W67
Assumptions (isolation of), E52
Asterisk (as record selector symbol), A5
AutoComplete, E27
AutoCorrect, A11, P26, W27, W38, W112, W120
AutoFormat, W120
AutoFormat Command, E98, E134
Automatic formatting, E61
Automatic replacement, W55
AutoShapes button, E105, W114, W121
AutoShapes toolbar, W121
AutoSum Command, E97, E134
AutoText, W27–W28, W39
AutoText toolbar, W39
AVERAGE function, E5

B

Backspace key, W5
Backup (options for), W31–W32, W35
Backup copy (creation of), W60
Bar chart, E89–E90
Boldface, W76
Border tab, E58, E63
Borders and Shading command, W87, W92

C

Calendar Wizard, W136
Case-insensitive search, W55
Case-sensitive search, W55
Category label, E86, E92
Cell, E4
Cell formulas
    displaying of, E29
    printing of, E67
Cell range, E43
Cell reference, E4
Center across selection, E59
Chart border, E101
Chart sheet, E92
    moving and copying, E113
Chart toolbar, E96
Chart type, E86–E92 126–E128
    changing of, E101, E115
Chart Wizard, E94–E95, E98–E100
Charts, E85–E131
Clear command, E25
Clip art, P33, W110, W115
    formatting of, W117
    moving of, W116
    sizing of, W116
Clipboard (see Windows clipboard; Office clipboard)
Close command, A12, E9, P7, W8, W16
Collapsed outline, P19
Color, E64
Column chart, E89–E92
    with multiple series, E106–E109
Column headings, E22, E23
Column width, E54, E60
Columns command, W88, W96
Combination chart, E126–E128
Comments, E66
Common user interface, E120
Companion Web Site, E37
Compound document, E116, W110, W115–W122
Constant, E5
Context-sensitive menu, E28
Copy command, E43–E44, W53, W63
    shortcut for, E50
Copyright, W124
Courier New, W67
Crop (a picture), W112
Currency format, E55
Current record, A4
Custom dictionary, W25
Custom format, E56
Custom view, E31
Cut command, E46, W53, W63
    shortcut for, E50

D

Data disk (*see* Practice files)
Data point, E86
Data series, E86
  formatting of, E105
  multiple, E106–E116
  rows versus columns, E108–E109
  viewing of, E112
Data validation, A14, A20
Database, A2
Database window, A3–A4
Datasheet view, A4–A5
Date format, E55
Dates (versus fractions), E56
Default presentation, P23
Del key, W5
Delete command, A19, E19–E20, E25, E32
Deleting text, W5, W22
Demote button, P25
Design view (table), A4
Desktop, W10
Destination range, E43
Dialog box (shortcuts in), E30, W78
Docked toolbar, E105
Document properties, W24
Document window, W5
Drag and drop, W66
Drawing toolbar, E96, P4, W114

E

Editing (cell contents), E49
E-mail, W24
  sending a workbook, E8, E39
  in Word document, W57
Embedded chart, E92–E93, E99
Embedded object, E116
Endnote, W125
Exit command, A12, E9, E18, P7, W8, W16
Expanded outline, P19
Exploded pie chart, E87–E88

F

Fair use exclusion, W124
Fax Wizard, W140–W141
Field, A2
Field name, A4
File list (recently opened), P32
File menu, E9–E10, P7, W8–W9
File name (rules for), E9, P7, W8
File type, E9, E24, P7, P13, W8, W34
Filter, A25–A31

Filter by Form, A25, A29
Filter by Selection, A25, A28, A29
Filter Excluding Selection, A28
Find command, A13–A14, A18, W54–W55
First line indent, W81, W83
Floating toolbar, E105
Folder (creation of), E48, W122
Font, E56, W67
Footers, E22–E23
Footnote, W125
Form, A4, A14–A15, A20–A21
Format Cells command, E54–E59
Format Font command, W69, W71, W75
Format Painter, E62, W77
Format Paragraph command, W85–W86
Format Picture command, W112, W117
Formatting, E53–E59
Formatting toolbar, E7–E8, E64, P4, W5, W7
  separation of, E14, W13, W20
Formula, E5
Formula bar, E7, E15
Fraction format, E55
Function, E5

G

General format, E54
GIGO (garbage in, garbage out), A14
Go To command, W54–W55
Grammar check, W29–W30, W36–W37
Gridlines (printing of), E22, E23

H

Hanging indent, W81, W83
Hard page break, W73
Hard return, W2
  display of, W20
Headers, E22–E23
Help menu, E17
Hiding columns, E70, E73
Horizontal alignment, E56
Horizontal ruler, W6
Horizontal scroll bar, E114
HTML, W123
HTML document, E68
Hyperlink, E68, E71–E72, W123, W130
Hyphenation, W85

I

Incompatibilities (in file type), E24
Indents, W81, W83, W86, W91

Ins key, W4, W21
Insert command, E19–E20, E26–E28, E32
Insert Comment command, E66
Insert Footnote command, W125, W131
Insert Hyperlink command, E71, W130
Insert mode, W4
Insert New Record command, A27
Insert Object command, W111
Insert Picture command, W111, W115
Insert Symbol command, W112, W120
Insertion point, A5, P18, W2
Internet, E68, W123
Italics, W76

J

Justification (*see* Alignment)

K

Keyboard shortcuts (displaying of), P17

L

Landscape orientation, E21, W72, W73
Leader character, W84
Left indent, W81, W83
Legend, E108–E109
Line chart, E126–E128
Line spacing, W85, W86, W90
Linked object, E116
Linking worksheets, E124, E136

M

Macro, A4
Margins, E21, E23, W72, W78
  versus indents, W81
Menu bar, P4
Merge cells, E56, E57
Microsoft Access
  introduction to, A3–A4
  starting of, A7
  version of, A11
Microsoft Clip Gallery, W111, W115
  properties in, W117
  searching of, W116
Microsoft Excel
  starting of, E13
  version of, E17
Microsoft Word
  file types in, W34
  starting of, W12
  version of, W16

Microsoft WordArt, W113, W118–W119
Mixed reference, E44, E80–E81
Module, A4
Monospaced typeface, W68–W69
Move operation, E45–E46
Moving text, W53
Multiple data series, E106–E109
Multitasking, E72, E116, E119
  Alt+Tab shortcut, E121

N

Name box, E7, E15
New command, W137
Nonbreaking hyphen, W85
Noncontiguous range, E62
Nonprinting symbols, W17
Normal view, P5, W17–W18, W58
Notes Page view, P5
Now function, E65
Number format, E55

O

Object Linking and Embedding (OLE), E116–E126, W110, W142
Office Assistant, A17, A24, A38, E13, E17, P15, P29, W12, W15, W93
  with charts, E111
  hiding of, E47
  selection of, W23
Office clipboard, E44, W53, W64
One-to-many relationship, A33
Open command, A7, E9–E10, E14, P7–P8, P12, W8–W9, W19
  previewing files, W33
  recently opened files, E23
Outline view, P5, P18–P19, P27
Outlining toolbar, P27
Overtype mode, W4

P

Page Border command, W92
Page break, W73
  insertion of, W79
  prevention of, W85, W86
Page Setup command, E21–E23, E30, E66, W71–W72
Paragraph formatting, W80–W95
Paste command, E44, E46, W53, W63
  shortcut for, E50
Paste Link command, E120
Paste Special command, E120
Patterns tab, E58

Pencil (as record selector symbol), A5, A10
Percentage format, E55
Picture toolbar, W112, W129
Pie chart, E87–E89
Placeholders, P20
Places bar, E9, P7, W8
Point size, W69–W70
Portrait orientation, E21, W72, W73
Practice files (downloading of), A7, E12, P10, W11
Primary key, A5
Print command, E9, E18, P7, P17, W8, W16
   selected pages, W95
Print Layout view, W17–W18, W58
Print Preview command, E18, E31
Promote button, P25
Proportional typeface, W68, W69
Public domain, W124

Q

Query, A14–A15

R

Record, A2
   adding of, A10
Record selector, A4–A5, A19
Redo command, E16, P28, W22, W53, W65
Referential Integrity, A36
Relational database, A32–A40
Relationships window, A34–A35
Relative reference, E44
Remove Filter button, A25
Replace command, A13–A14, A22, W54–W55, W61–W62
   with formatting, W75
Report, A4, A16, A23
Résumé Wizard, W134–W135
Right indent, W81, W83
Right mouse button, E28, E51
Rotating text, E56, E57
Row headings, E22, E23
Row height, E54, E60
Ruler
   with columns, W96
   with indents, W91

S

Sans serif typeface, W67
Save As command, E24, P7–P8, P13, W31, W34

Save as Web Page command, E73, W123, W132
Save command, E9–E10, P7, P24, W8–W9, W14, W31
Scientific format, E55–E56
ScreenTip, E7, P17, W5
Scroll bar, P4
Scrolling, W55–W57
   with the keyboard, W62
   with a mouse, W61
Section, W71, W88
Section break, W97
Selection bar, W74
Selective replacement, W55
Select-then-do, E54, P18, W52
Serif typeface, W67
Shading, W87
Show/Hide ¶ button, W17, W20
Sizing handles, E92, E99, W112, W116
Slide Layout, P20, P32
Slide Show view, P5, P16, P37
Slide Sorter toolbar, P31
Slide Sorter view, P5
Slide view, P5
Social Security Number (formatting of), E65
Soft page break, W73
Soft return, W2
Sort, A25, A30
   on two fields, 31
Sort ascending button, A25, A30
Sort descending button, A25, A30
Source range, E43
Special format, E56
Special indent, W81, W83
Spell check, P14, P26, W25–W26, W35–W36
Spreadsheet (introduction to), E2–E5
Stacked columns, E106–E107
Standard toolbar, E7–E8, P4, W5, W7
   separation of, E14, W13, W20
Status bar, E7, P4, W6
Strikethrough, W69
Summary slide, P35
Symbols font, W112

T

Table, A2, A4–A5
   moving in, A8–A9
   opening of, A8
Tabs, W84
Taskbar, E119
Template, P21, P28, W134–W141
Text box, E96, E103–E105
Text format, E56
Thesaurus, W28–W29, W37–W38
Three-dimensional pie charts, E87–E88
Three-dimensional shapes, E105

Time format, E55
Times New Roman, W67
Tip of the day, A23, P16, W15
Title slide, P23
Today function, E65
Toggle switch, W3
Toolbar, E7–E8, W5, W7
    hiding or displaying, W17
    separation of, E14, P12, W13, W20
Tools menu, W20
Transition effect, P30–P31, P34
Triangle (as record selector symbol), A5
Troubleshooting, W17–W18, W20
Tufte, Edward, E128
Type size, W69, W70
Type style, W69
Typeface, W67–W69
Typography, W67–W71

U

Underlining, W76
Undo command, A19, E16, P28, W22, W53, W65

V

Vertical alignment, E56
Vertical ruler, W6
View, E31
    changing magnification, E32
View button, P12, W128
View menu, W20, 58–W59
Views, P5

W

Web Page Wizard, W124
Web page, E68, W123
    saving as, E73
Web toolbar, E68
Web-enabled document, W57
Whole word replacement, W55
Widows and orphans, W85–W86, W90
Wild card (in Find command), W55
Windows (starting of), E11
Windows 98 (tour of), A6
Windows clipboard, E44, W53, W63
Windows desktop, W10
Wingdings font, W112
Wizard, W134–W141
Word wrap, W2–W3
WordArt (*see* Microsoft WordArt)
Workbook, E6–E7
Worksheet, E6–E7
    deletion of, E19
    insertion of, E19
    linking of, E124, E136
    moving between, E15
    renaming of, E32, E110
World Wide Web, E68, W123
    resources from, W126–W133
    searching of, W126
Wrapping text, E56

Z

Zoom box, E32
Zoom command, W58–W59, W93